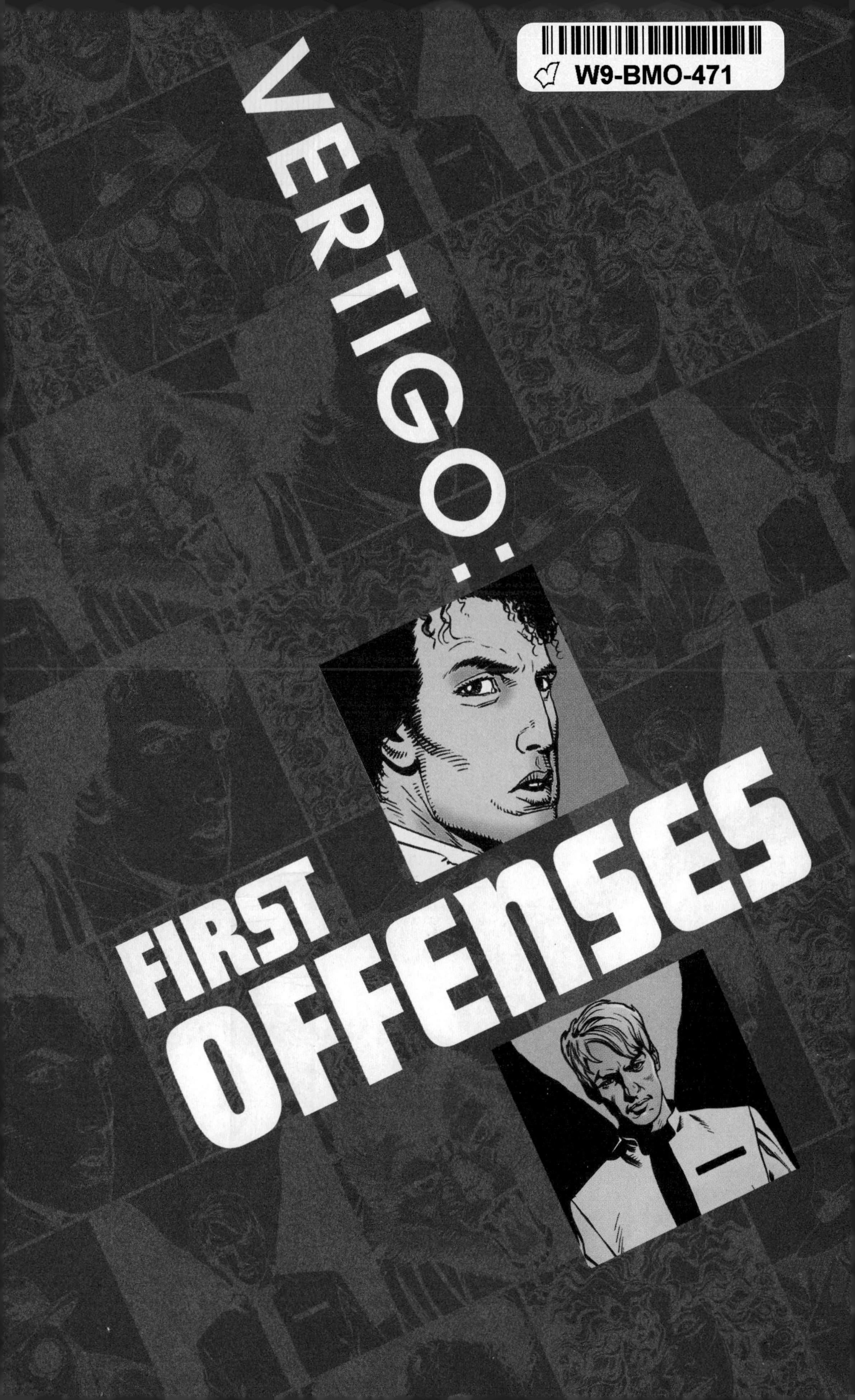
VERTIGO:
FIRST
OFFENSES

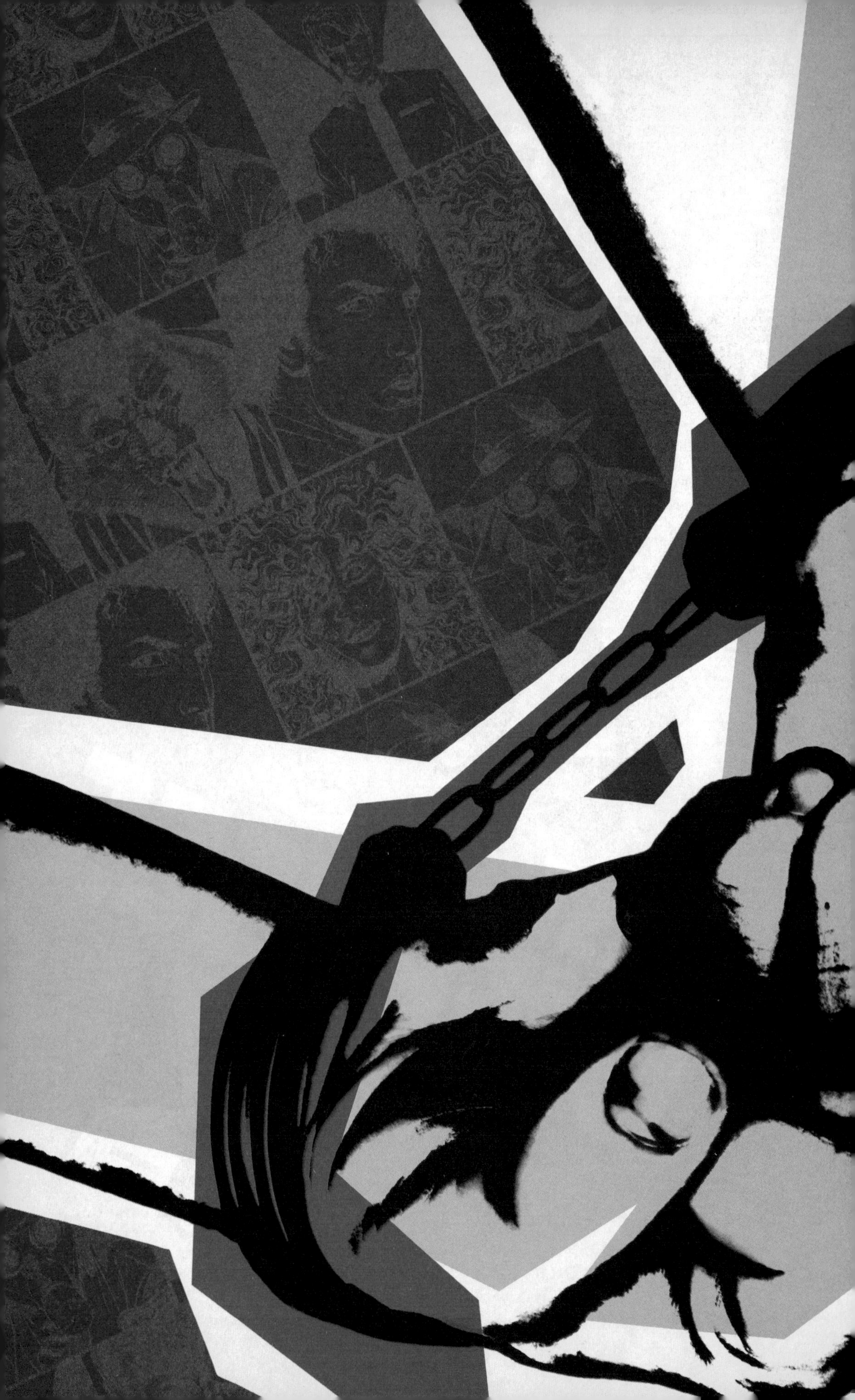

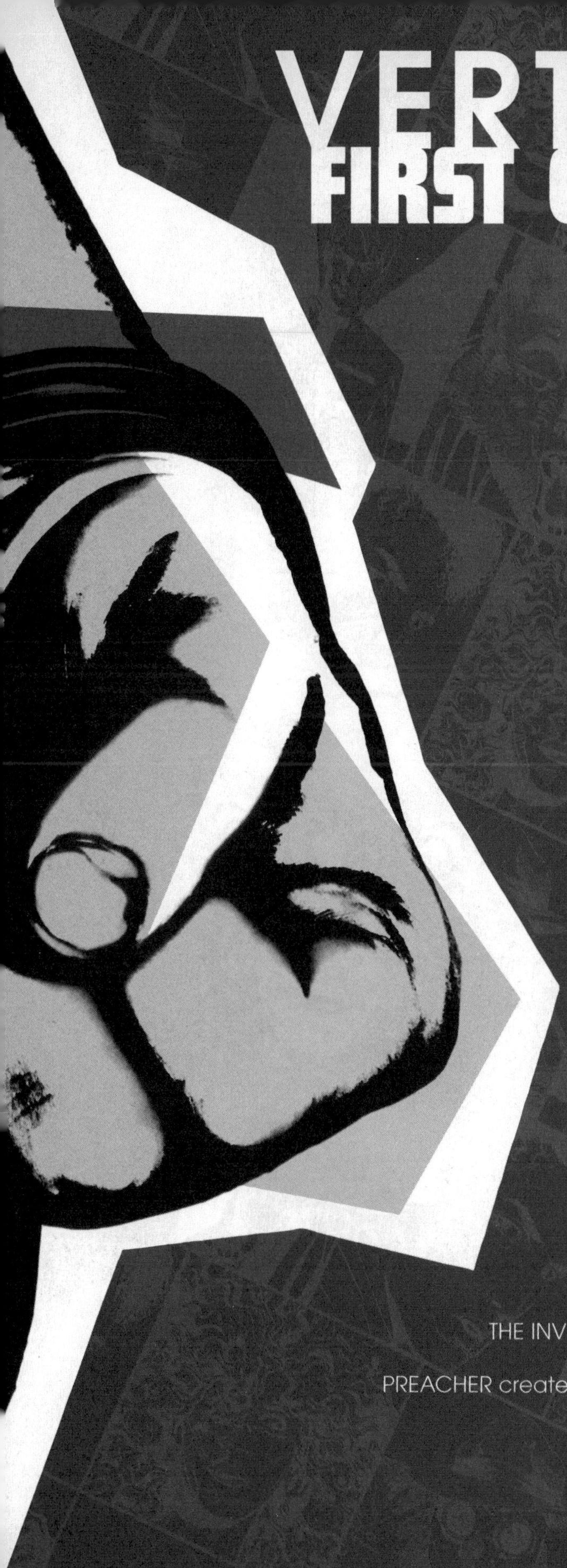

VERTIGO: FIRST OFFENSES

Grant Morrison
Bill Willingham
Garth Ennis
Matt Wagner
Mike Carey
Writers

Steve Yeowell
Lan Medina
Steve Leialoha
Steve Dillon
Guy Davis
Scott Hampton
Artists

Daniel Vozzo
Sherilyn van Valkenburgh
Matt Hollingsworth
David Hornung
Colorists

Clem Robins
Todd Klein
John Costanza
Letterers

Rian Hughes
James Jean
Glenn Fabry
Gavin Wilson
Richard Bruning
Duncan Fegredo
Original Series Covers

THE INVISIBLES created by **Grant Morrison**
FABLES created by **Bill Willingham**
PREACHER created by **Garth Ennis** and **Steve Dillon**

Karen Berger
VP-EXECUTIVE EDITOR

Karen Berger
Shelly Bond
Alisa Kwitney
Stuart Moore
EDITORS-ORIGINAL SERIES

Shelly Roeberg
ASSOCIATE EDITOR-ORIGINAL SERIES

Mariah Huehner
Jennifer Lee
ASSISTANT EDITORS-ORIGINAL SERIES

Scott Nybakken
EDITOR-COLLECTED EDITION

Robbin Brosterman
SENIOR ART DIRECTOR

Louis Prandi
ART DIRECTOR

Paul Levitz
PRESIDENT & PUBLISHER

Georg Brewer
VP-DESIGN & DC DIRECT CREATIVE

Richard Bruning
SENIOR VP-CREATIVE DIRECTOR

Patrick Caldon
SENIOR VP-FINANCE & OPERATIONS

Chris Caramalis
VP-FINANCE

Terri Cunningham
VP-MANAGING EDITOR

Stephanie Fierman
SENIOR VP-SALES & MARKETING

Alison Gill
VP-MANUFACTURING

Rich Johnson
VP-BOOK TRADE SALES

Hank Kanalz
VP-GENERAL MANAGER, WILDSTORM

Lillian Laserson
SENIOR VP & GENERAL COUNSEL

Jim Lee
EDITORIAL DIRECTOR-WILDSTORM

Paula Lowitt
SENIOR VP-BUSINESS & LEGAL AFFAIRS

David McKillips
VP-ADVERTISING & CUSTOM PUBLISHING

John Nee
VP-BUSINESS DEVELOPMENT

Gregory Noveck
SENIOR VP-CREATIVE AFFAIRS

Cheryl Rubin
SENIOR VP-BRAND MANAGEMENT

Jeff Trojan
VP-BUSINESS DEVELOPMENT, DC DIRECT

Bob Wayne
VP-SALES

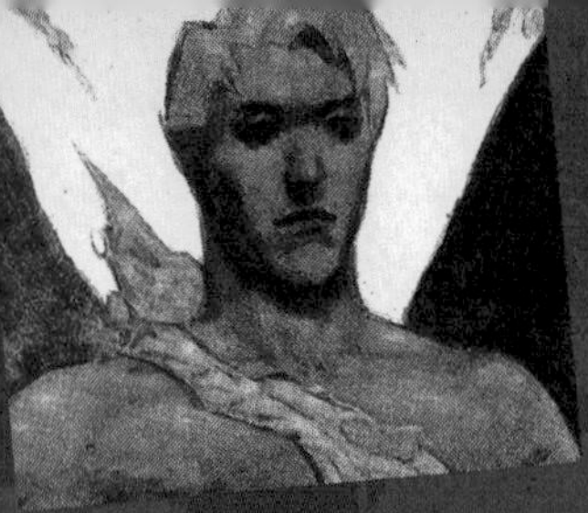

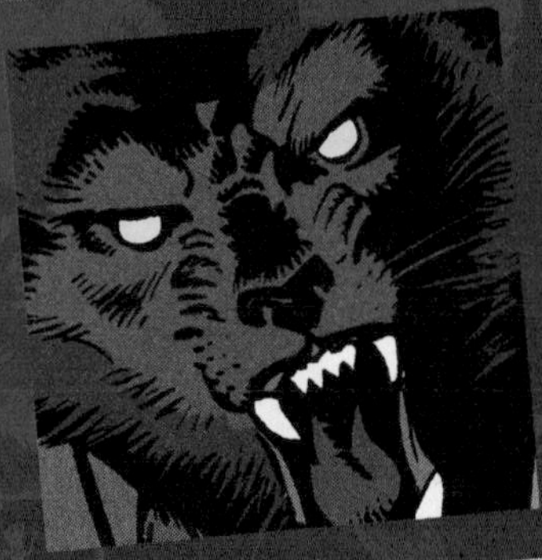

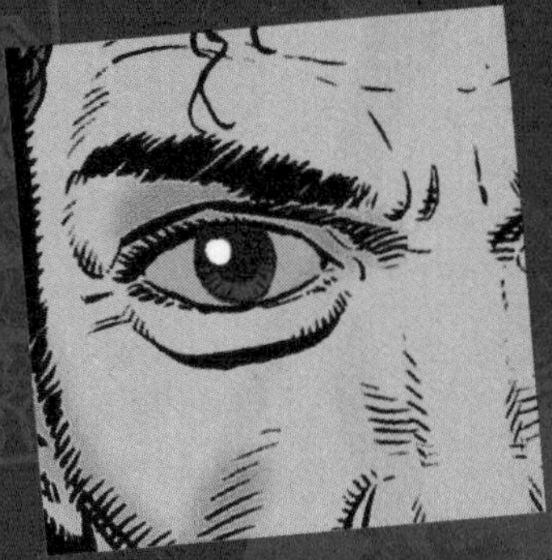

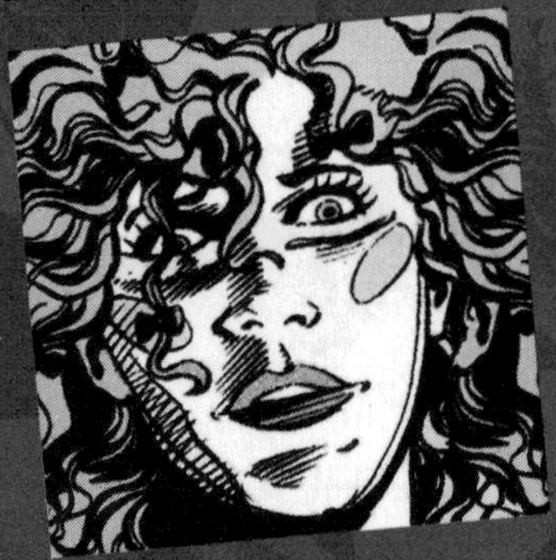

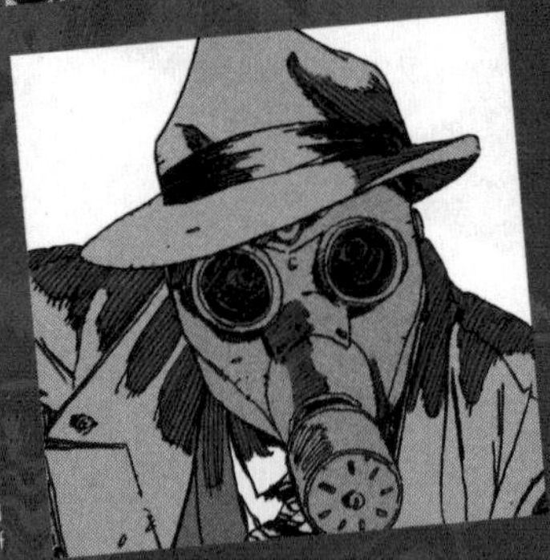

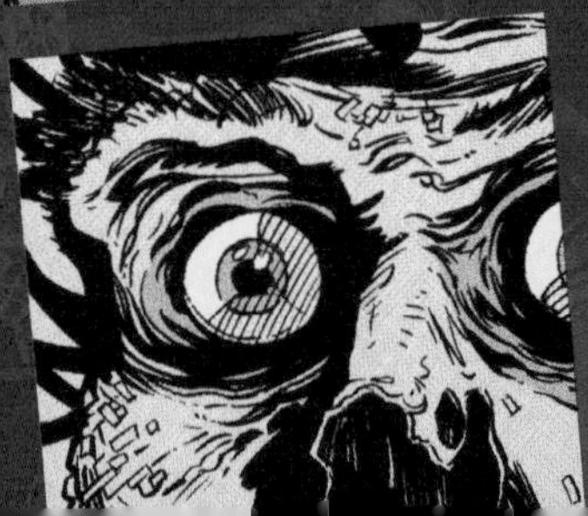

CONTENTS

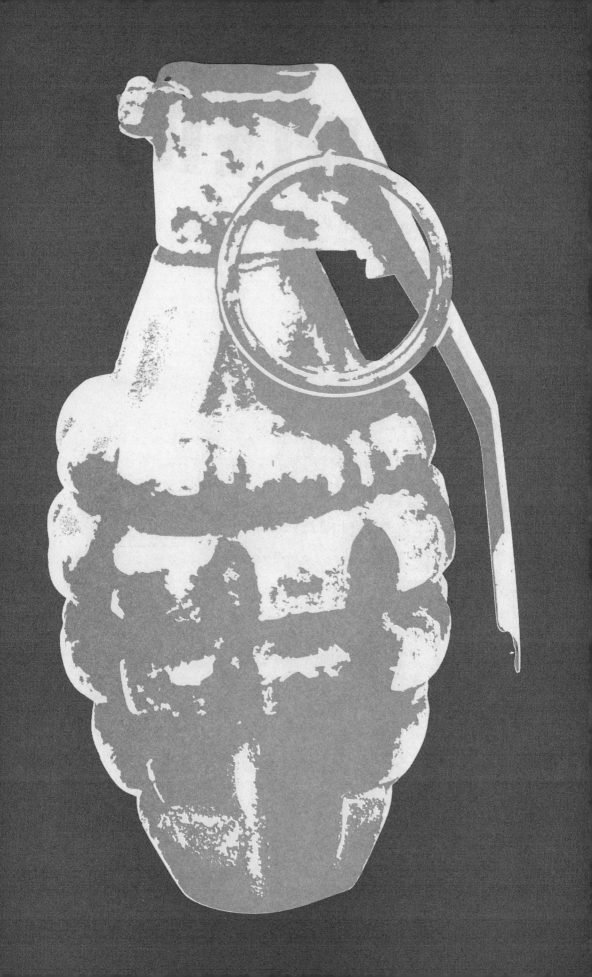

AND SO WE RETURN AND BEGIN AGAIN.

KHEPHRA, THE SACRED BEETLE, GOES DOWN INTO DARKNESS AND RISES AGAIN, BEARING THE SUN IN HIS MANDIBLES.

SOME SAY THAT WHEN WE LEAVE THIS PLANET, WE WILL LEAVE AS *INSECTS*. WHEN OUR BODIES ARE NO LONGER NEEDED, WE WILL SEND OUT OUR SPIRITS AS A SWARM OF GOLDEN BEETLES, CARRYING THE SUN OF PURE *UNDERSTANDING* OUT OF THE ABYSS TO OUR NEW HOME AMONG THE STARS.

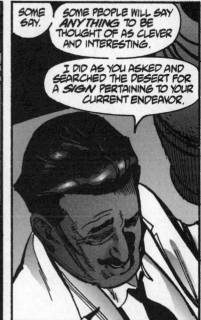

SOME SAY.

SOME PEOPLE WILL SAY *ANYTHING* TO BE THOUGHT OF AS CLEVER AND INTERESTING.

I DID AS YOU ASKED AND SEARCHED THE DESERT FOR A *SIGN* PERTAINING TO YOUR CURRENT ENDEAVOR.

NICE AND SMOOTH.

SO WHAT HAVE YOU GOT FOR ME, ELFAYED?

TRUTH SPEAKS BEST IN THE LANGUAGE OF POETRY AND SYMBOLISM, I THINK.

AND THOSE OLD EGYPTIANS WOULD WRAP UP ANYTHING. LOOK. A *SCARAB*, MUMMIFIED.

WHAT DO YOU SAY TO THAT, MY FRIEND, eh?

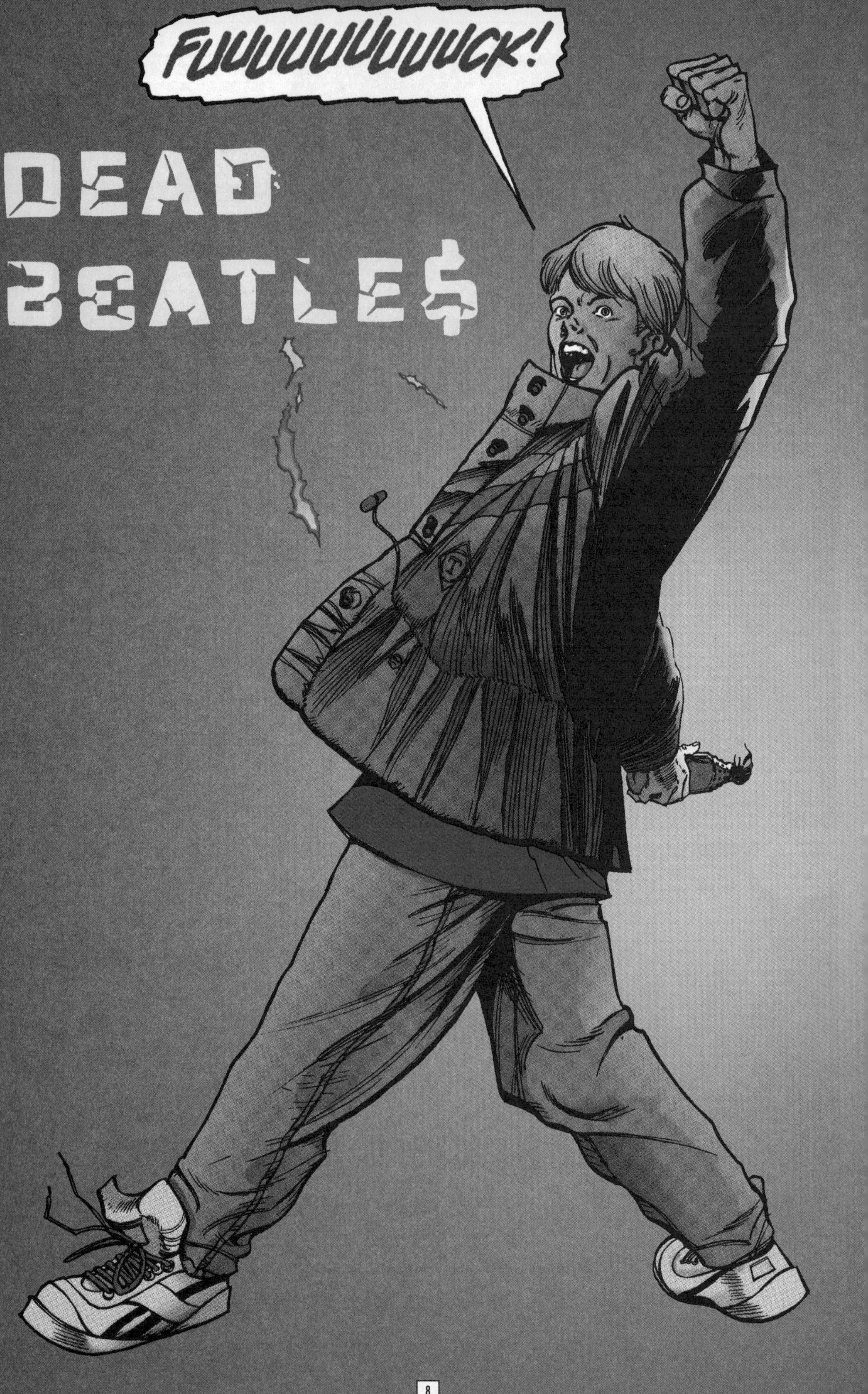
FUUUUUUUUUUUCK!
DEAD
BEATLE$

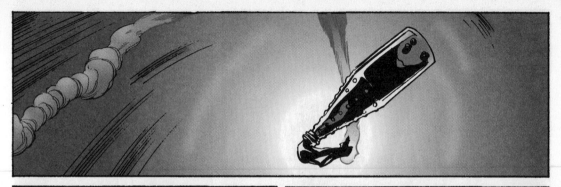

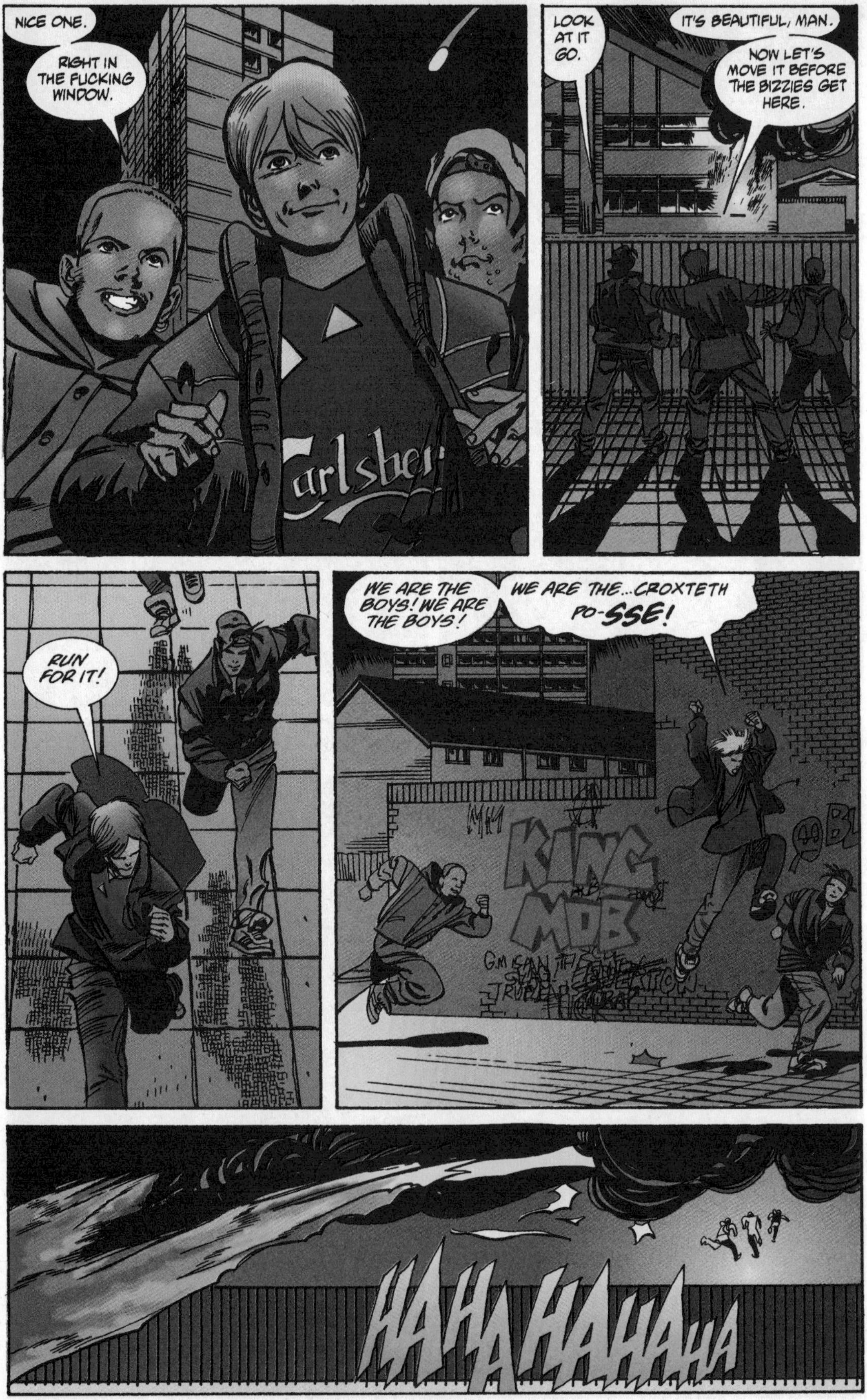
NICE ONE.
RIGHT IN THE FUCKING WINDOW.
Carlsber
LOOK AT IT GO.
IT'S BEAUTIFUL, MAN.
NOW LET'S MOVE IT BEFORE THE BIZZIES GET HERE.
RUN FOR IT!
WE ARE THE BOYS! WE ARE THE BOYS!
WE ARE THE...CROXTETH PO-SSE!
KING MOB
HAHAHAHAHAHA

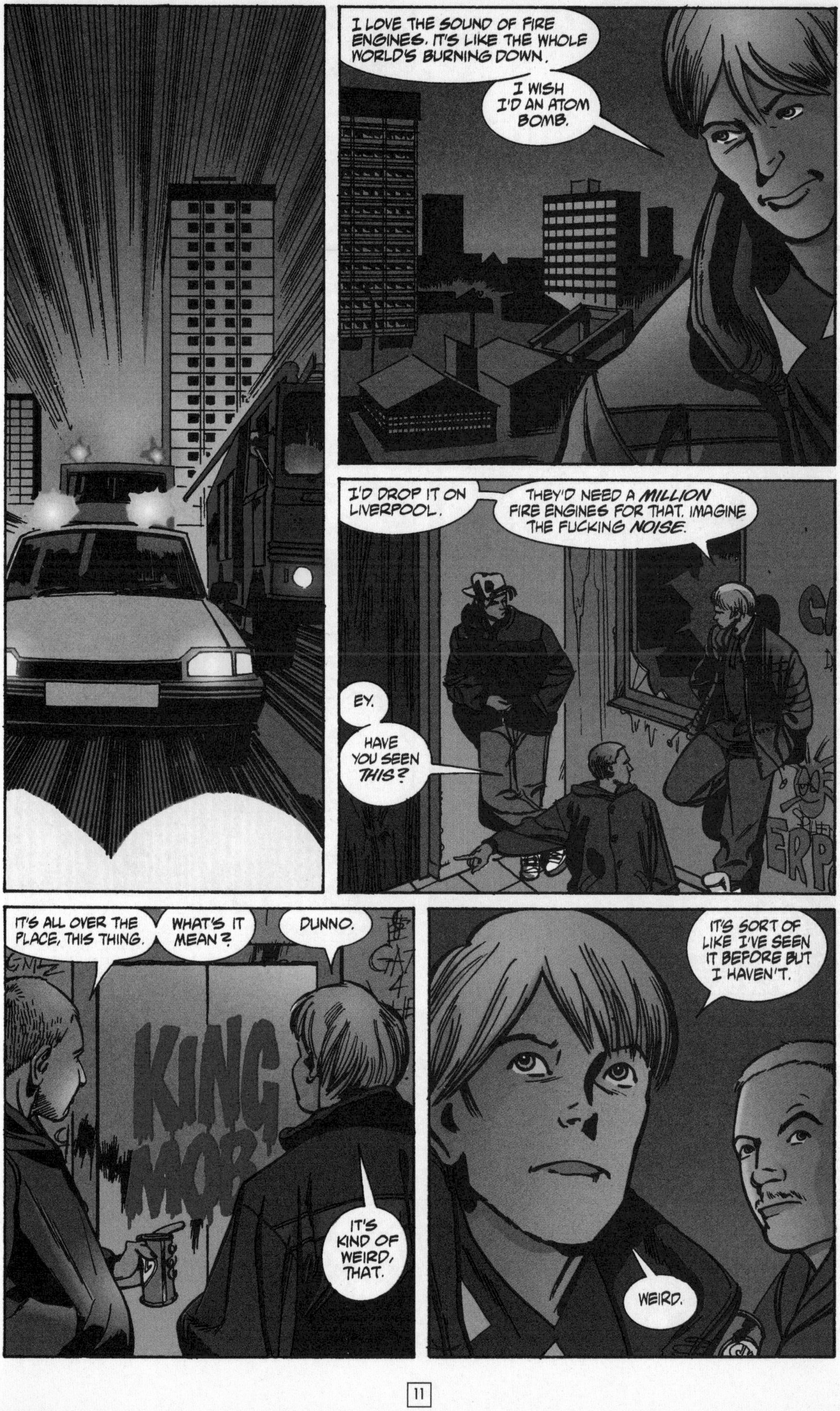
I LOVE THE SOUND OF FIRE ENGINES. IT'S LIKE THE WHOLE WORLD'S BURNING DOWN.
I WISH I'D AN ATOM BOMB.
I'D DROP IT ON LIVERPOOL.
THEY'D NEED A MILLION FIRE ENGINES FOR THAT. IMAGINE THE FUCKING NOISE.
EY.
HAVE YOU SEEN THIS?
IT'S ALL OVER THE PLACE, THIS THING.
WHAT'S IT MEAN?
DUNNO.
KING MOB
IT'S KIND OF WEIRD, THAT.
IT'S SORT OF LIKE I'VE SEEN IT BEFORE BUT I HAVEN'T.
WEIRD.

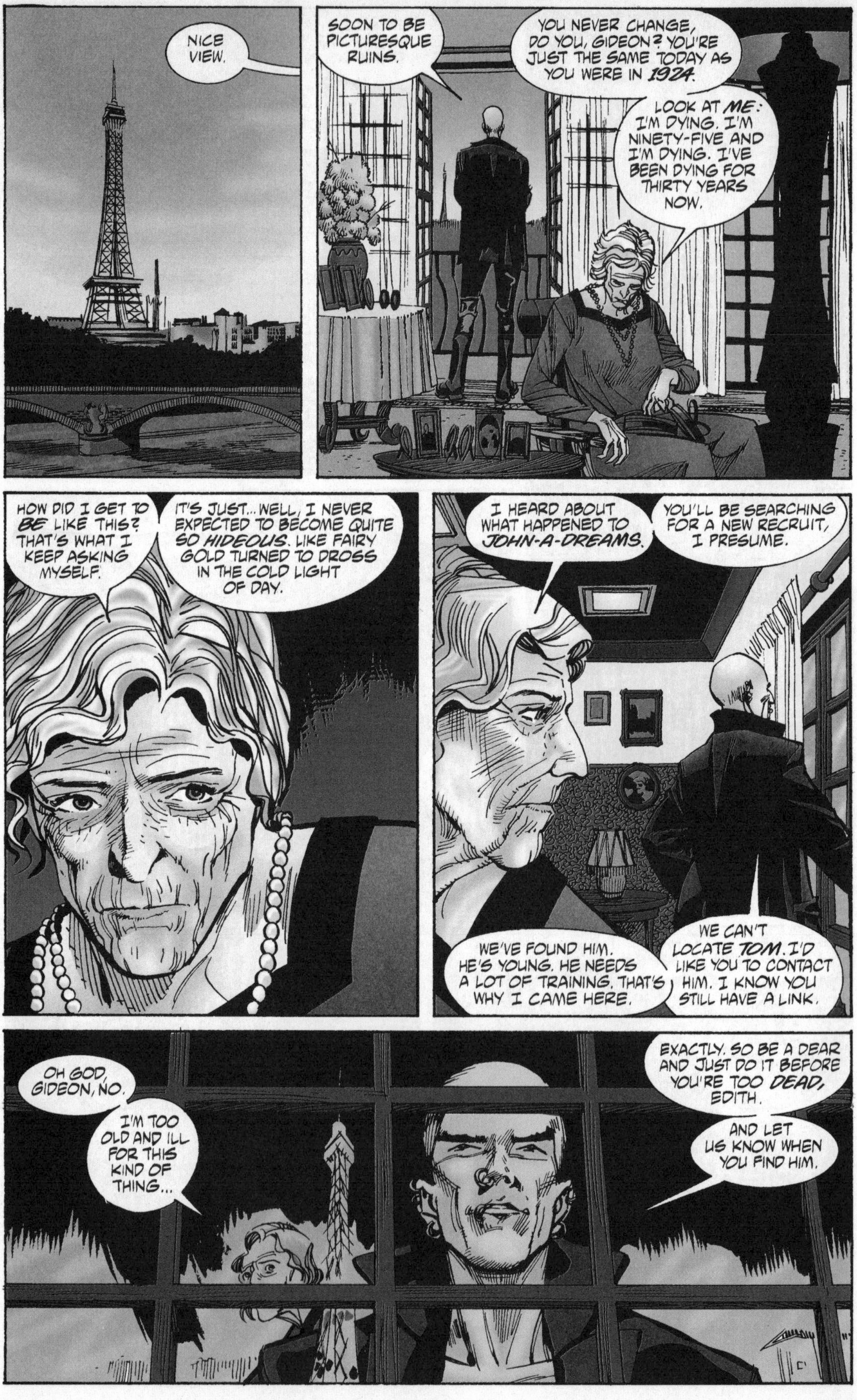
NICE VIEW.
SOON TO BE PICTURESQUE RUINS.
YOU NEVER CHANGE, DO YOU, GIDEON? YOU'RE JUST THE SAME TODAY AS YOU WERE IN 1924.
LOOK AT ME: I'M DYING. I'M NINETY-FIVE AND I'M DYING. I'VE BEEN DYING FOR THIRTY YEARS NOW.
HOW DID I GET TO BE LIKE THIS? THAT'S WHAT I KEEP ASKING MYSELF.
IT'S JUST... WELL, I NEVER EXPECTED TO BECOME QUITE SO HIDEOUS. LIKE FAIRY GOLD TURNED TO DROSS IN THE COLD LIGHT OF DAY.
I HEARD ABOUT WHAT HAPPENED TO JOHN-A-DREAMS.
YOU'LL BE SEARCHING FOR A NEW RECRUIT, I PRESUME.
WE'VE FOUND HIM. HE'S YOUNG. HE NEEDS A LOT OF TRAINING. THAT'S WHY I CAME HERE.
WE CAN'T LOCATE TOM. I'D LIKE YOU TO CONTACT HIM. I KNOW YOU STILL HAVE A LINK.
OH GOD, GIDEON, NO.
I'M TOO OLD AND ILL FOR THIS KIND OF THING...
EXACTLY. SO BE A DEAR AND JUST DO IT BEFORE YOU'RE TOO DEAD, EDITH.
AND LET US KNOW WHEN YOU FIND HIM.

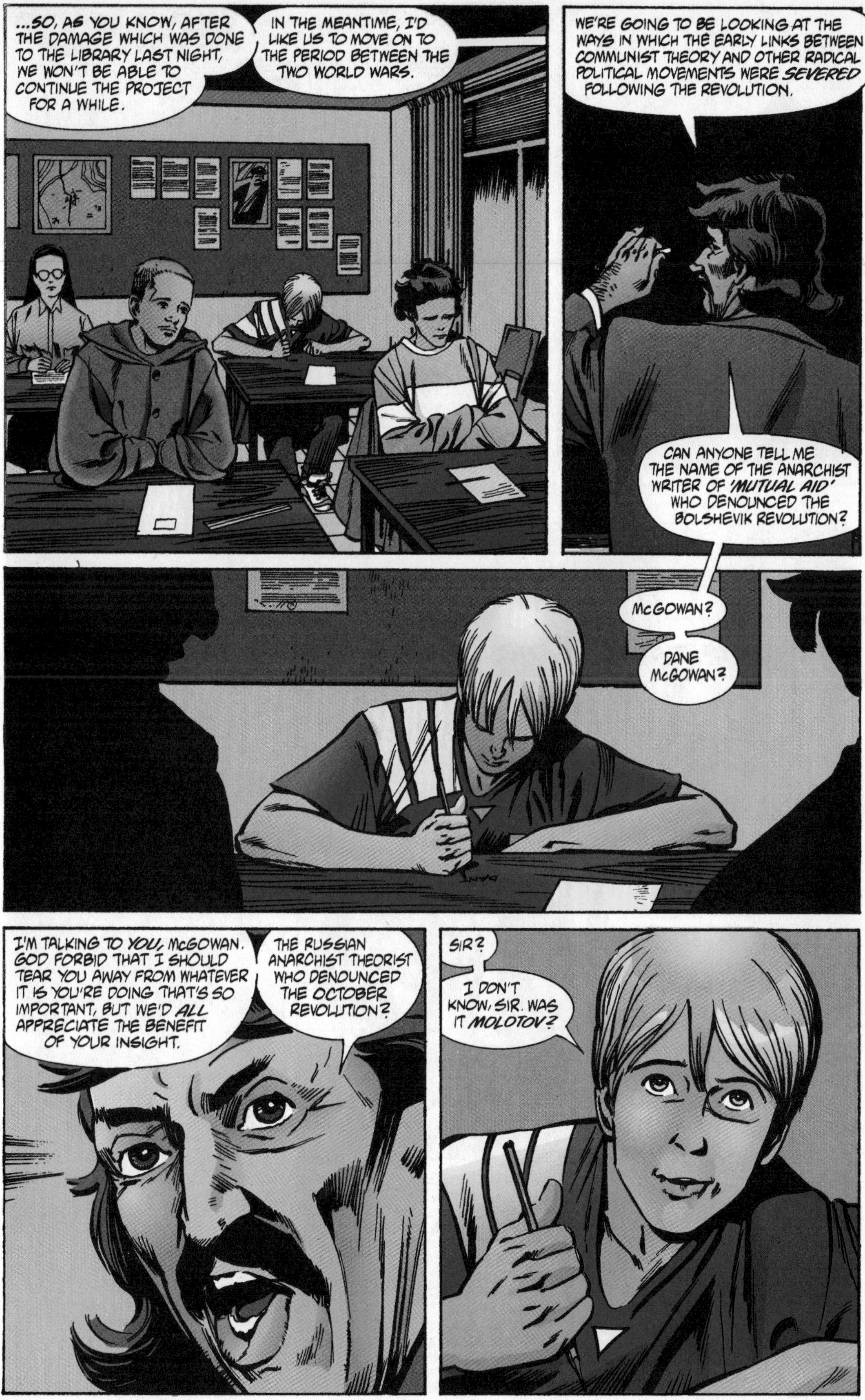
...SO, AS YOU KNOW, AFTER THE DAMAGE WHICH WAS DONE TO THE LIBRARY LAST NIGHT, WE WON'T BE ABLE TO CONTINUE THE PROJECT FOR A WHILE.
IN THE MEANTIME, I'D LIKE US TO MOVE ON TO THE PERIOD BETWEEN THE TWO WORLD WARS.
WE'RE GOING TO BE LOOKING AT THE WAYS IN WHICH THE EARLY LINKS BETWEEN COMMUNIST THEORY AND OTHER RADICAL POLITICAL MOVEMENTS WERE SEVERED FOLLOWING THE REVOLUTION.
CAN ANYONE TELL ME THE NAME OF THE ANARCHIST WRITER OF 'MUTUAL AID' WHO DENOUNCED THE BOLSHEVIK REVOLUTION?
McGOWAN?
DANE McGOWAN?
I'M TALKING TO YOU, McGOWAN. GOD FORBID THAT I SHOULD TEAR YOU AWAY FROM WHATEVER IT IS YOU'RE DOING THAT'S SO IMPORTANT, BUT WE'D ALL APPRECIATE THE BENEFIT OF YOUR INSIGHT.
THE RUSSIAN ANARCHIST THEORIST WHO DENOUNCED THE OCTOBER REVOLUTION?
SIR?
I DON'T KNOW, SIR. WAS IT MOLOTOV?

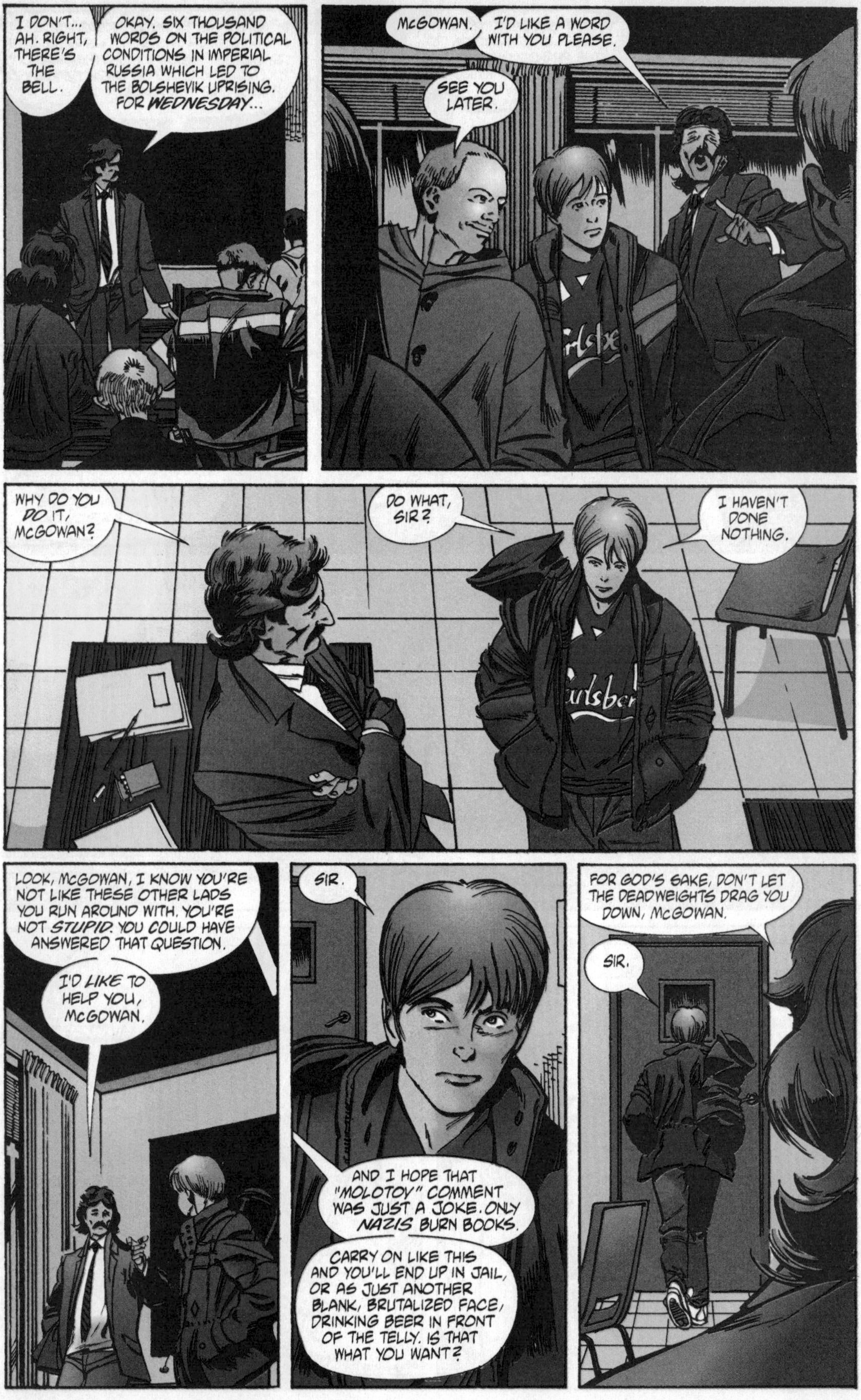
I DON'T... AH. RIGHT, THERE'S THE BELL.
OKAY. SIX THOUSAND WORDS ON THE POLITICAL CONDITIONS IN IMPERIAL RUSSIA WHICH LED TO THE BOLSHEVIK UPRISING. FOR WEDNESDAY...
McGOWAN.
I'D LIKE A WORD WITH YOU PLEASE.
SEE YOU LATER.
WHY DO YOU DO IT, McGOWAN?
DO WHAT, SIR?
I HAVEN'T DONE NOTHING.
LOOK, McGOWAN, I KNOW YOU'RE NOT LIKE THESE OTHER LADS YOU RUN AROUND WITH. YOU'RE NOT STUPID. YOU COULD HAVE ANSWERED THAT QUESTION.
I'D LIKE TO HELP YOU, McGOWAN.
SIR.
AND I HOPE THAT "MOLOTOV" COMMENT WAS JUST A JOKE. ONLY NAZIS BURN BOOKS.
CARRY ON LIKE THIS AND YOU'LL END UP IN JAIL, OR AS JUST ANOTHER BLANK, BRUTALIZED FACE, DRINKING BEER IN FRONT OF THE TELLY. IS THAT WHAT YOU WANT?
FOR GOD'S SAKE, DON'T LET THE DEADWEIGHTS DRAG YOU DOWN, McGOWAN.
SIR.

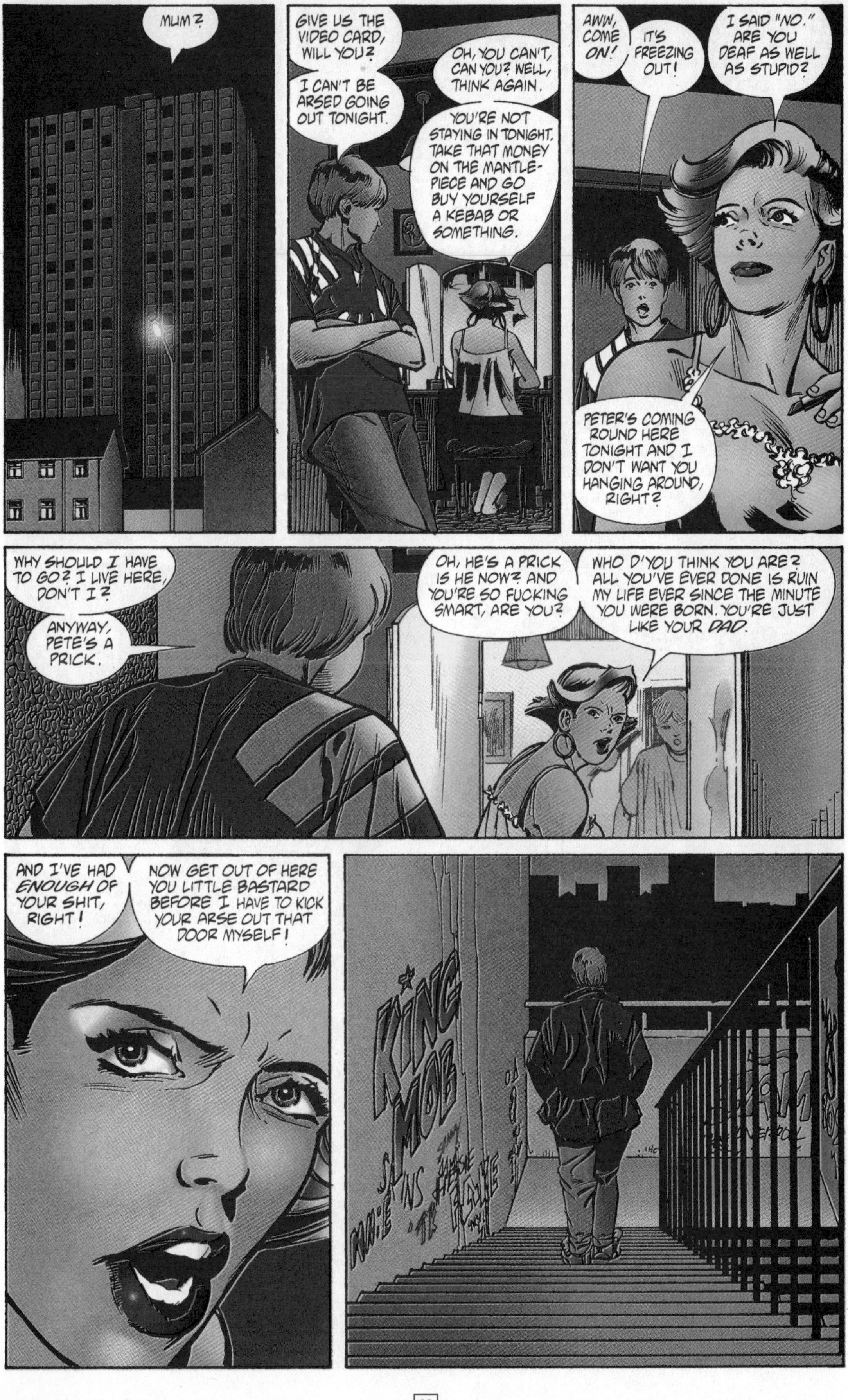
MUM?
GIVE US THE VIDEO CARD, WILL YOU?
I CAN'T BE ARSED GOING OUT TONIGHT.
OH, YOU CAN'T, CAN YOU? WELL, THINK AGAIN.
YOU'RE NOT STAYING IN TONIGHT. TAKE THAT MONEY ON THE MANTLE-PIECE AND GO BUY YOURSELF A KEBAB OR SOMETHING.
AWW, COME *ON*!
IT'S FREEZING OUT!
I SAID "*NO*." ARE YOU DEAF AS WELL AS STUPID?
PETER'S COMING ROUND HERE TONIGHT AND I DON'T WANT YOU HANGING AROUND, RIGHT?
WHY SHOULD *I* HAVE TO GO? I LIVE HERE, DON'T I?
ANYWAY, PETE'S A PRICK.
OH, HE'S A PRICK IS HE NOW? AND YOU'RE SO FUCKING SMART, ARE YOU?
WHO D'YOU THINK YOU ARE? ALL YOU'VE EVER DONE IS RUIN MY LIFE EVER SINCE THE MINUTE YOU WERE BORN. YOU'RE JUST LIKE YOUR *DAD*.
AND I'VE HAD *ENOUGH* OF YOUR SHIT, RIGHT!
NOW GET OUT OF HERE YOU LITTLE BASTARD BEFORE I HAVE TO KICK YOUR ARSE OUT THAT DOOR MYSELF!
KING MOB

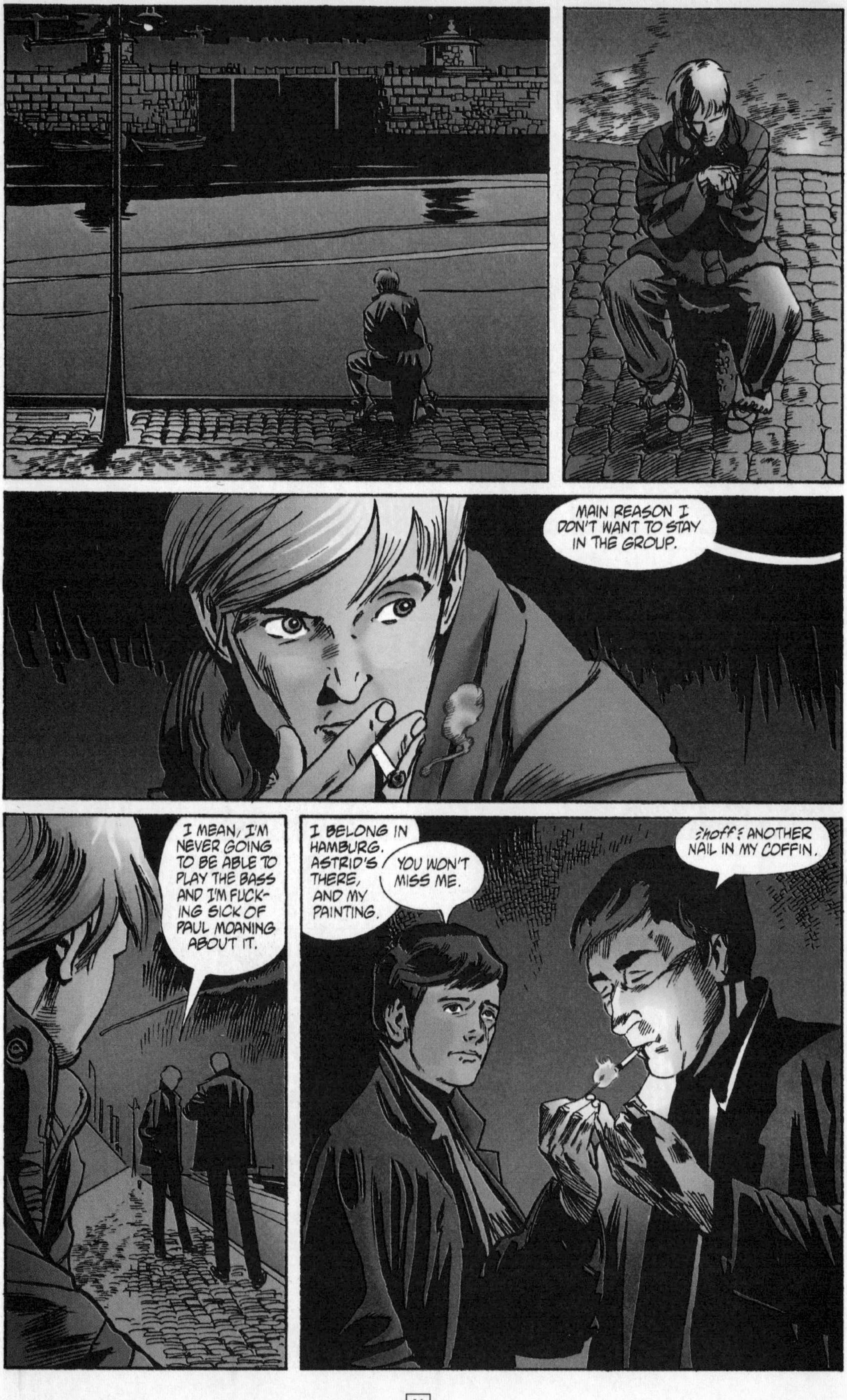
MAIN REASON I DON'T WANT TO STAY IN THE GROUP.
I MEAN, I'M NEVER GOING TO BE ABLE TO PLAY THE BASS AND I'M FUCKING SICK OF PAUL MOANING ABOUT IT.
I BELONG IN HAMBURG. ASTRID'S THERE, AND MY PAINTING.
YOU WON'T MISS ME.
≈hoff≈ ANOTHER NAIL IN MY COFFIN.

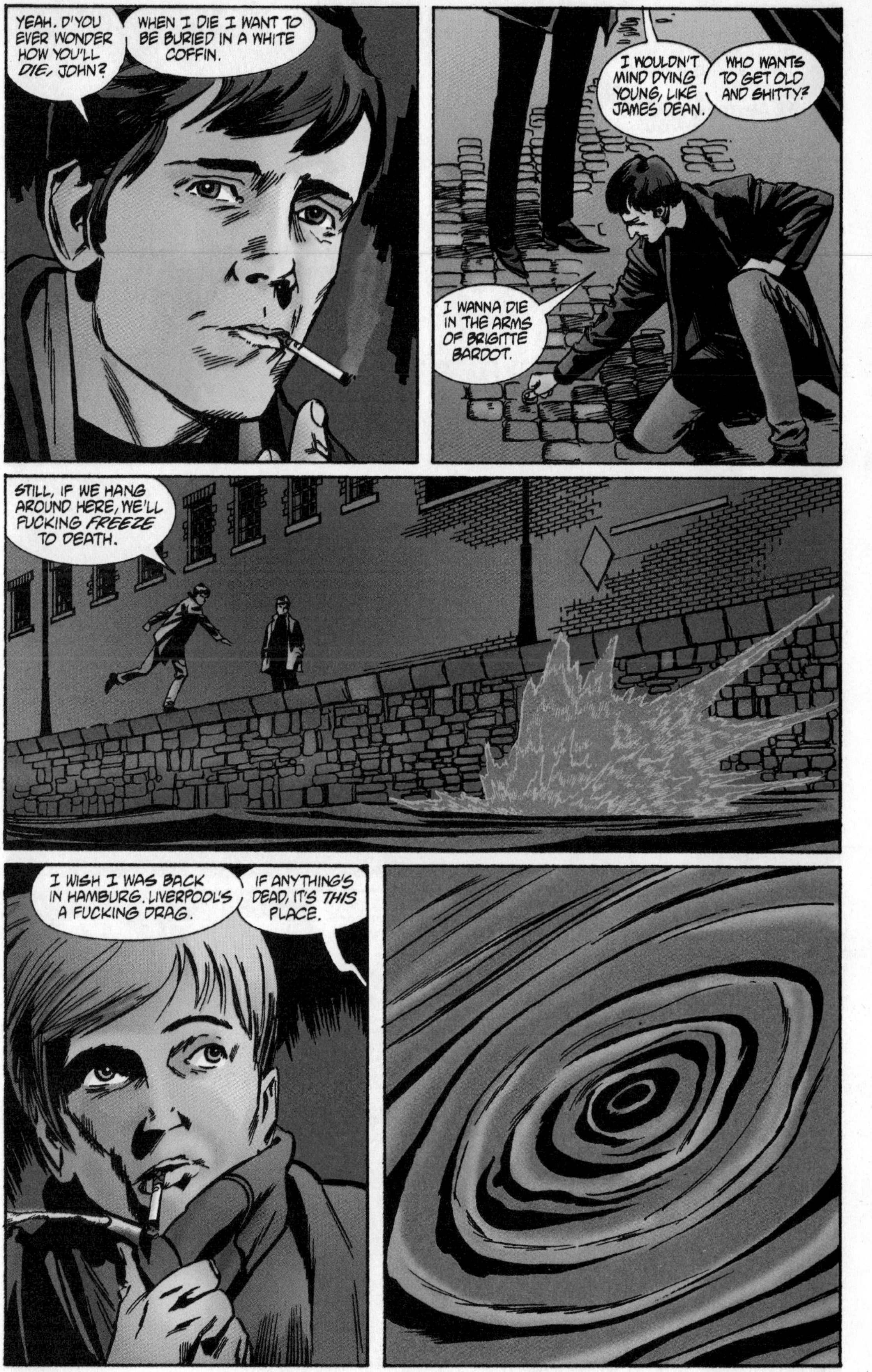
YEAH. D'YOU EVER WONDER HOW YOU'LL *DIE*, JOHN?
WHEN I DIE I WANT TO BE BURIED IN A WHITE COFFIN.
I WOULDN'T MIND DYING YOUNG, LIKE JAMES DEAN.
WHO WANTS TO GET OLD AND SHITTY?
I WANNA DIE IN THE ARMS OF BRIGITTE BARDOT.
STILL, IF WE HANG AROUND HERE, WE'LL FUCKING *FREEZE* TO DEATH.
I WISH I WAS BACK IN HAMBURG. LIVERPOOL'S A FUCKING DRAG.
IF ANYTHING'S DEAD, IT'S *THIS* PLACE.

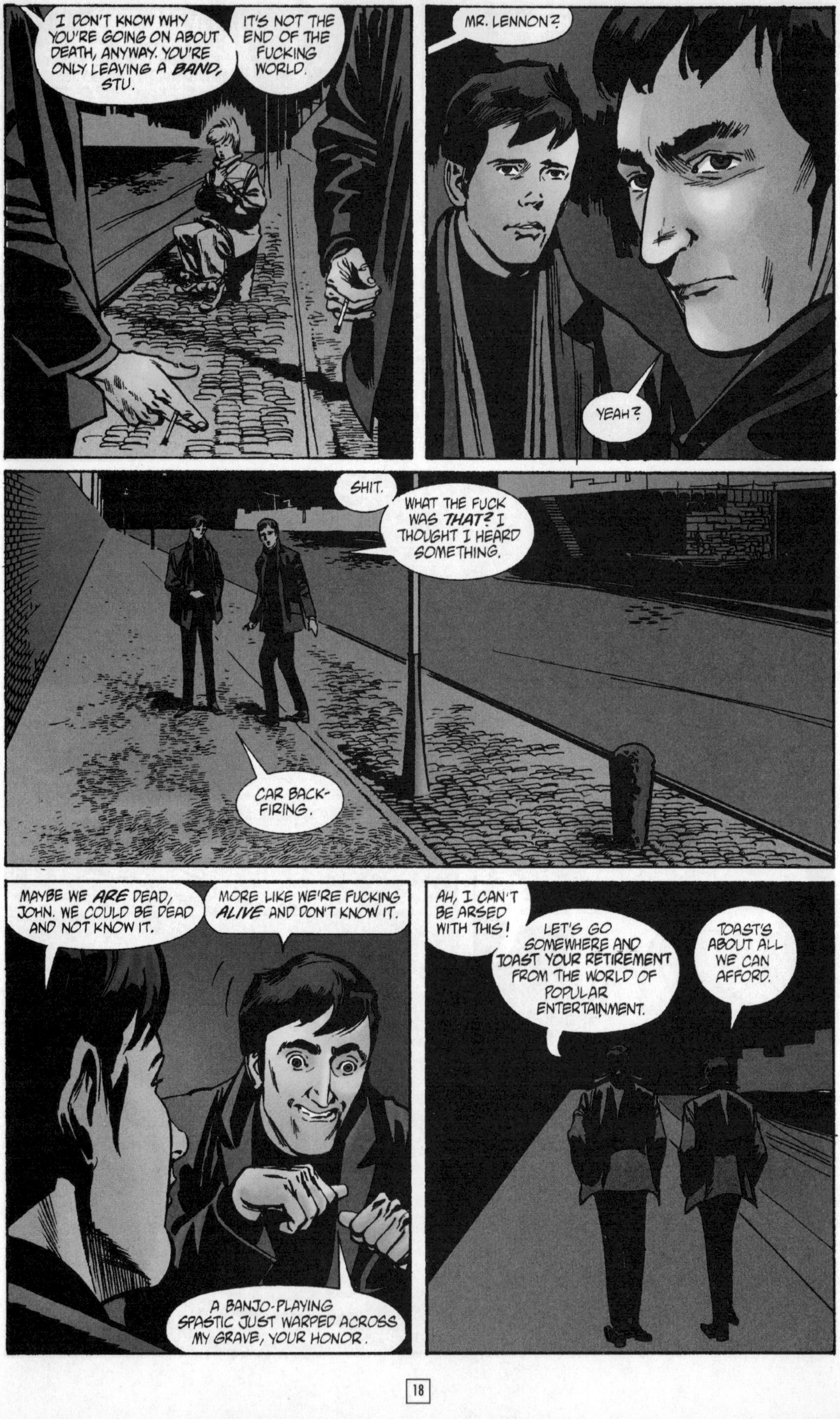

I DON'T KNOW WHY YOU'RE GOING ON ABOUT DEATH, ANYWAY. YOU'RE ONLY LEAVING A BAND, STU.
IT'S NOT THE END OF THE FUCKING WORLD.
MR. LENNON?
YEAH?
SHIT.
WHAT THE FUCK WAS THAT? I THOUGHT I HEARD SOMETHING.
CAR BACK-FIRING.
MAYBE WE ARE DEAD, JOHN. WE COULD BE DEAD AND NOT KNOW IT.
MORE LIKE WE'RE FUCKING ALIVE AND DON'T KNOW IT.
A BANJO-PLAYING SPASTIC JUST WARPED ACROSS MY GRAVE, YOUR HONOR.
AH, I CAN'T BE ARSED WITH THIS!
LET'S GO SOMEWHERE AND TOAST YOUR RETIREMENT FROM THE WORLD OF POPULAR ENTERTAINMENT.
TOAST'S ABOUT ALL WE CAN AFFORD.

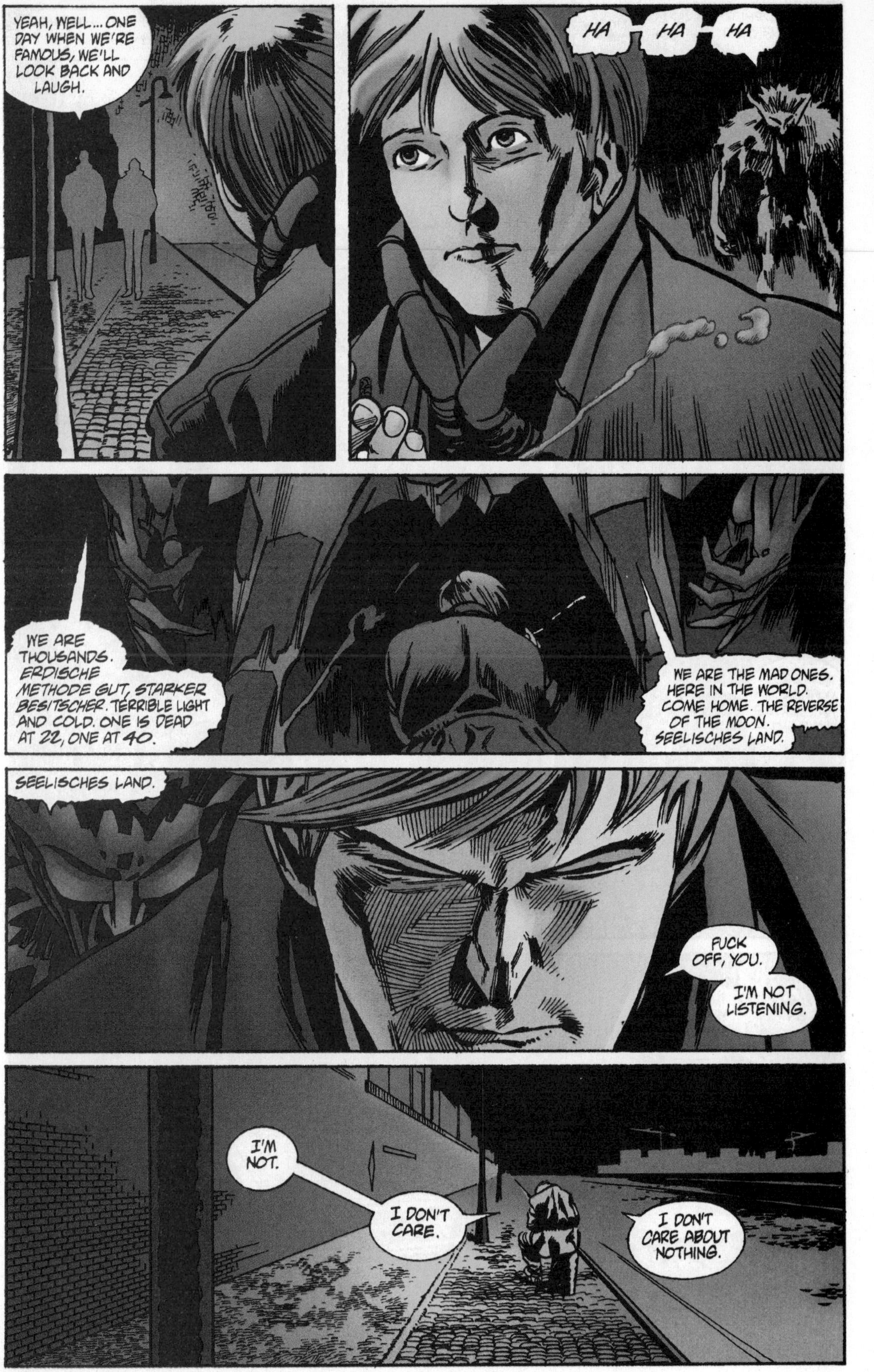
YEAH, WELL... ONE DAY WHEN WE'RE FAMOUS, WE'LL LOOK BACK AND LAUGH.
HA HA HA
WE ARE THOUSANDS. ERDISCHE METHODE GUT, STARKER BESITSCHER. TERRIBLE LIGHT AND COLD. ONE IS DEAD AT 22, ONE AT 40.
WE ARE THE MAD ONES. HERE IN THE WORLD. COME HOME. THE REVERSE OF THE MOON. SEELISCHES LAND.
SEELISCHES LAND.
FUCK OFF, YOU.
I'M NOT LISTENING.
I'M NOT.
I DON'T CARE.
I DON'T CARE ABOUT NOTHING.

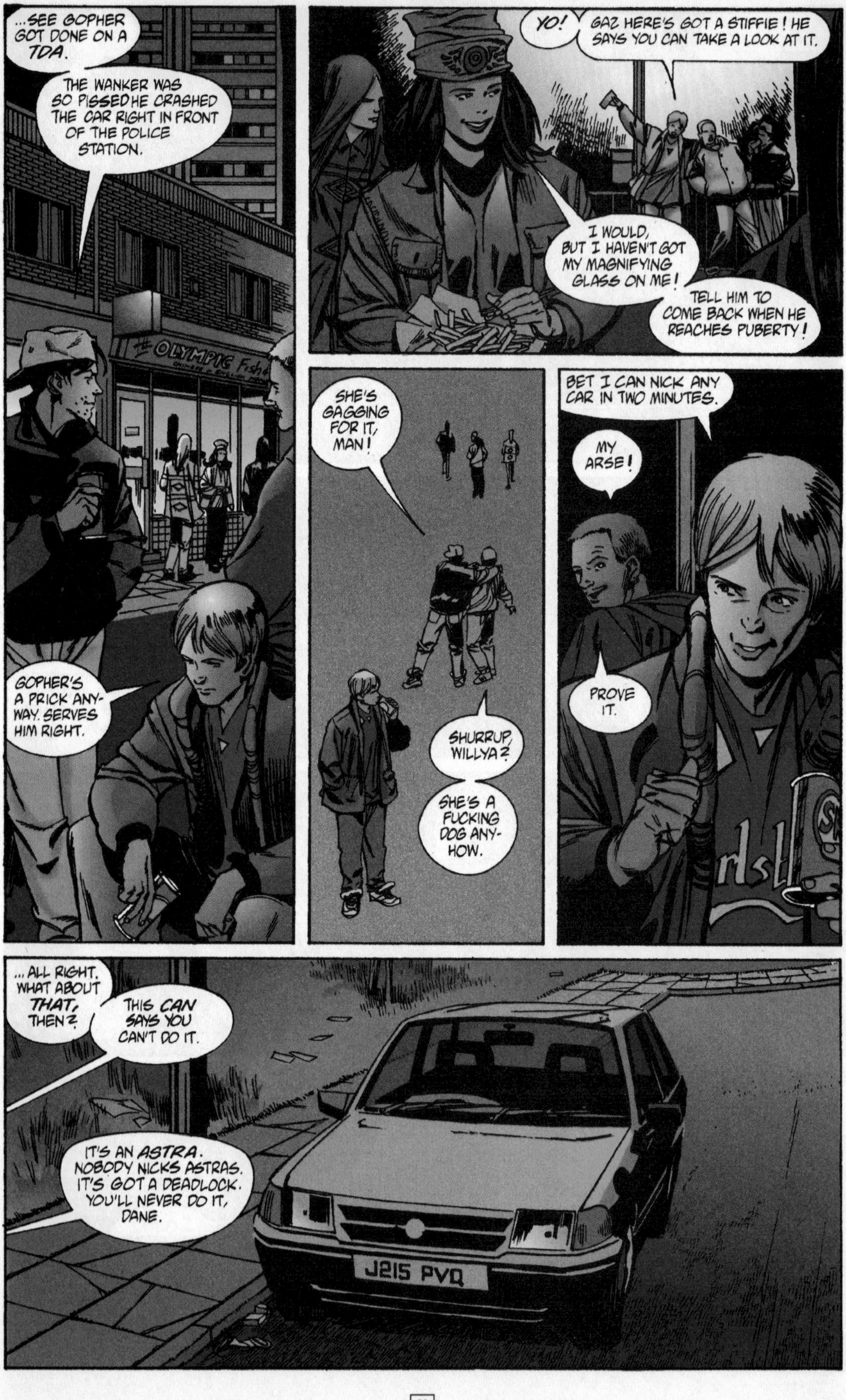
...SEE GOPHER GOT DONE ON A TDA.
THE WANKER WAS SO PISSED HE CRASHED THE CAR RIGHT IN FRONT OF THE POLICE STATION.
OLYMPIC Fish
GOPHER'S A PRICK ANYWAY. SERVES HIM RIGHT.
YO!
GAZ HERE'S GOT A STIFFIE! HE SAYS YOU CAN TAKE A LOOK AT IT.
I WOULD, BUT I HAVEN'T GOT MY MAGNIFYING GLASS ON ME!
TELL HIM TO COME BACK WHEN HE REACHES PUBERTY!
SHE'S GAGGING FOR IT, MAN!
SHURRUP, WILLYA?
SHE'S A FUCKING DOG ANYHOW.
BET I CAN NICK ANY CAR IN TWO MINUTES.
MY ARSE!
PROVE IT.
...ALL RIGHT. WHAT ABOUT THAT, THEN?
THIS CAN SAYS YOU CAN'T DO IT.
IT'S AN ASTRA. NOBODY NICKS ASTRAS. IT'S GOT A DEADLOCK. YOU'LL NEVER DO IT, DANE.
J215 PVQ

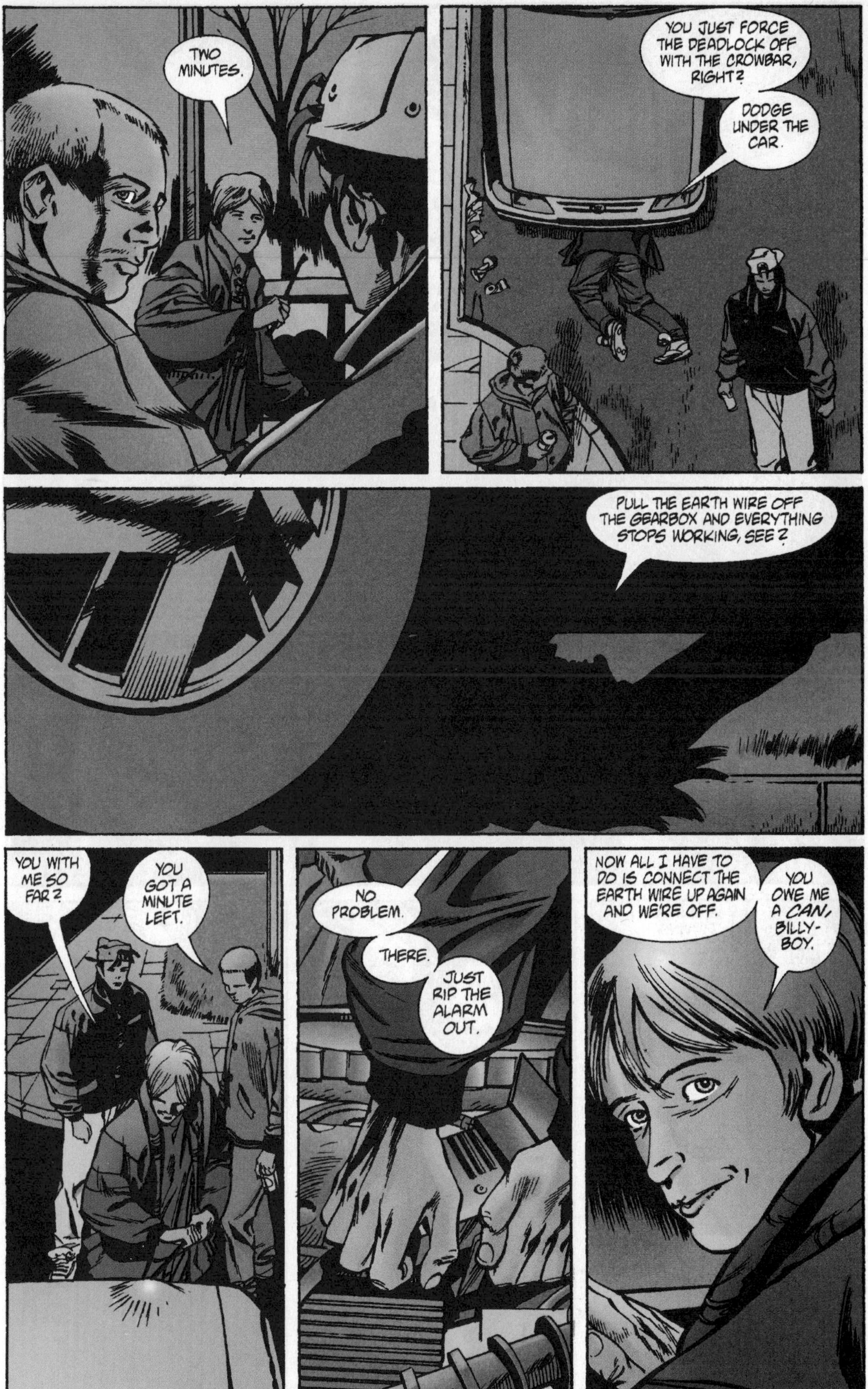

TWO MINUTES.
YOU JUST FORCE THE DEADLOCK OFF WITH THE CROWBAR, RIGHT?
DODGE UNDER THE CAR.
PULL THE EARTH WIRE OFF THE GEARBOX AND EVERYTHING STOPS WORKING, SEE?
YOU WITH ME SO FAR?
YOU GOT A MINUTE LEFT.
NO PROBLEM.
THERE.
JUST RIP THE ALARM OUT.
NOW ALL I HAVE TO DO IS CONNECT THE EARTH WIRE UP AGAIN AND WE'RE OFF.
YOU OWE ME A *CAN*, BILLY-BOY.

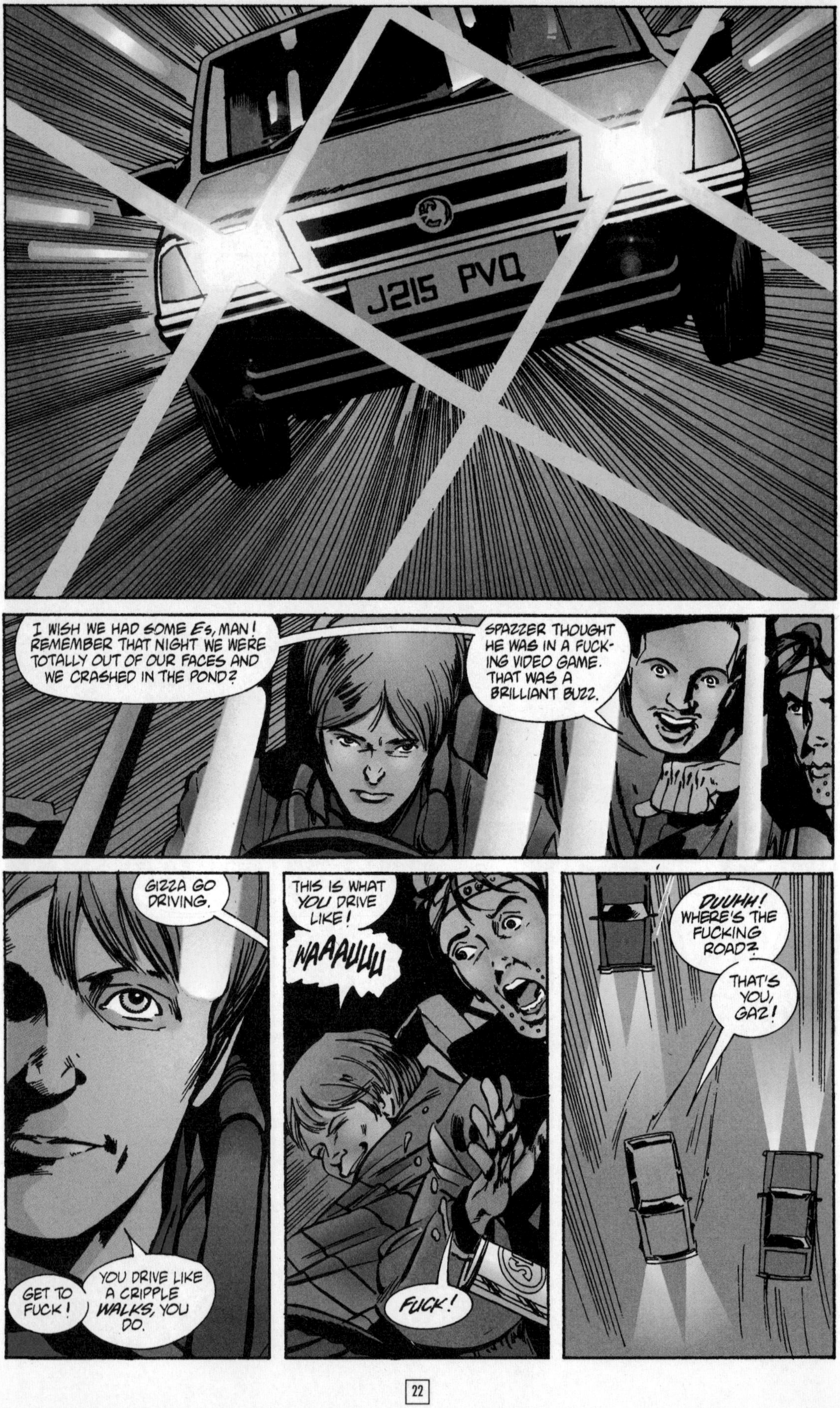
J215 PVQ
I WISH WE HAD SOME Es, MAN! REMEMBER THAT NIGHT WE WERE TOTALLY OUT OF OUR FACES AND WE CRASHED IN THE POND?
SPAZZER THOUGHT HE WAS IN A FUCKING VIDEO GAME. THAT WAS A BRILLIANT BUZZ.
GIZZA GO DRIVING.
GET TO FUCK!
YOU DRIVE LIKE A CRIPPLE WALKS, YOU DO.
THIS IS WHAT YOU DRIVE LIKE!
WAAAUUU
FUCK!
DUUHH! WHERE'S THE FUCKING ROAD?
THAT'S YOU, GAZ!

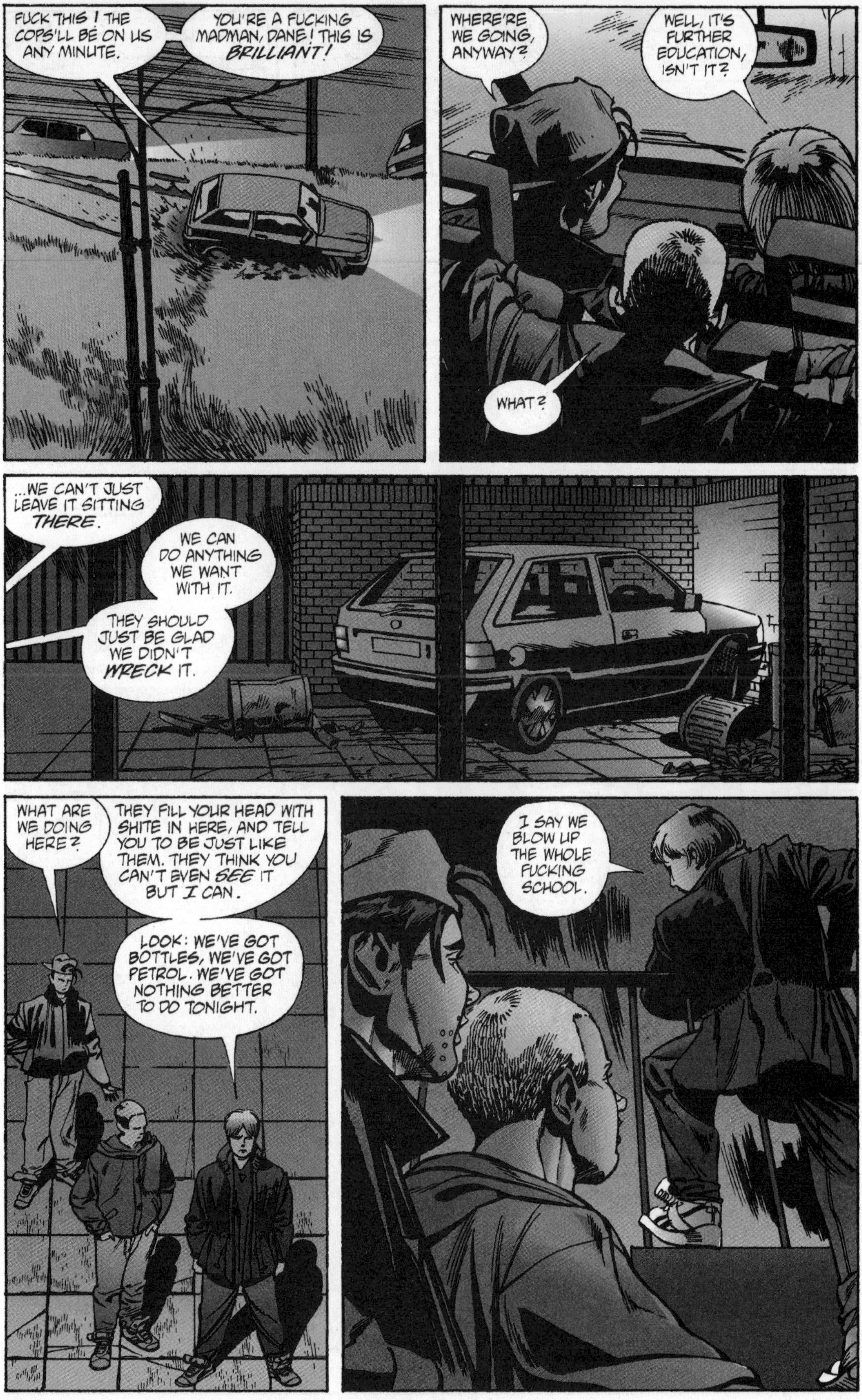
FUCK THIS ! THE COPS'LL BE ON US ANY MINUTE.
YOU'RE A FUCKING MADMAN, DANE! THIS IS BRILLIANT!
WHERE'RE WE GOING, ANYWAY?
WELL, IT'S FURTHER EDUCATION, ISN'T IT?
WHAT?
...WE CAN'T JUST LEAVE IT SITTING THERE.
WE CAN DO ANYTHING WE WANT WITH IT.
THEY SHOULD JUST BE GLAD WE DIDN'T WRECK IT.
WHAT ARE WE DOING HERE?
THEY FILL YOUR HEAD WITH SHITE IN HERE, AND TELL YOU TO BE JUST LIKE THEM. THEY THINK YOU CAN'T EVEN SEE IT BUT I CAN.
LOOK: WE'VE GOT BOTTLES, WE'VE GOT PETROL. WE'VE GOT NOTHING BETTER TO DO TONIGHT.
I SAY WE BLOW UP THE WHOLE FUCKING SCHOOL.

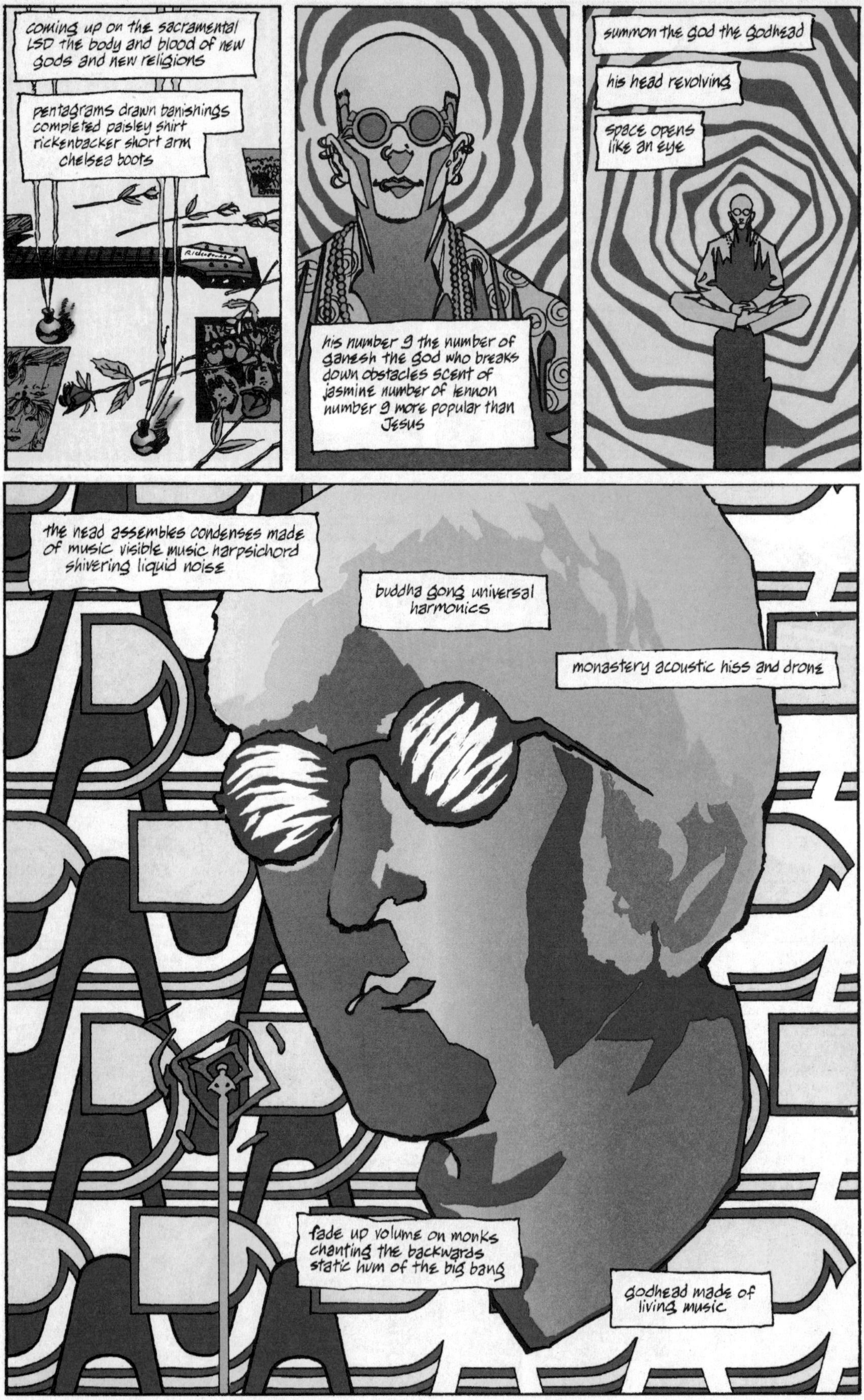
coming up on the sacramental LSD the body and blood of new gods and new religions
pentagrams drawn banishings completed paisley shirt rickenbacker short arm chelsea boots
his number 9 the number of ganesh the god who breaks down obstacles scent of jasmine number of lennon number 9 more popular than Jesus
summon the god the godhead
his head revolving
space opens like an eye
the head assembles condenses made of music visible music harpsichord shivering liquid noise
buddha gong universal harmonics
monastery acoustic hiss and drone
fade up volume on monks chanting the backwards static hum of the big bang
godhead made of living music

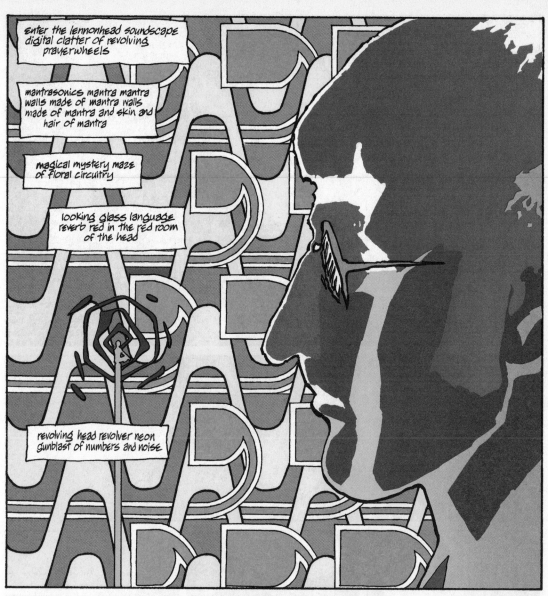

enter the lennonhead soundscape digital clatter of revolving prayerwheels

mantrasonics mantra mantra walls made of mantra walls made of mantra and skin and hair of mantra

magical mystery maze of floral circuitry

looking glass language reverb red in the red room of the head

revolving head revolver neon gunblast of numbers and noise

fizzing sherbetstorms of light particles

bumper tilt eggman hologram blizzard

the head the oracle head speaks in rhyming sounds hammerchime fuzztone piano

let me take you down down

say the word

it is not dying

be reborn be light go and come again

rise from the grave of himself

bonny jock lennon is did and goon

it is not dying

the boy born again beautiful boy beautiful boy

it is not dying

25

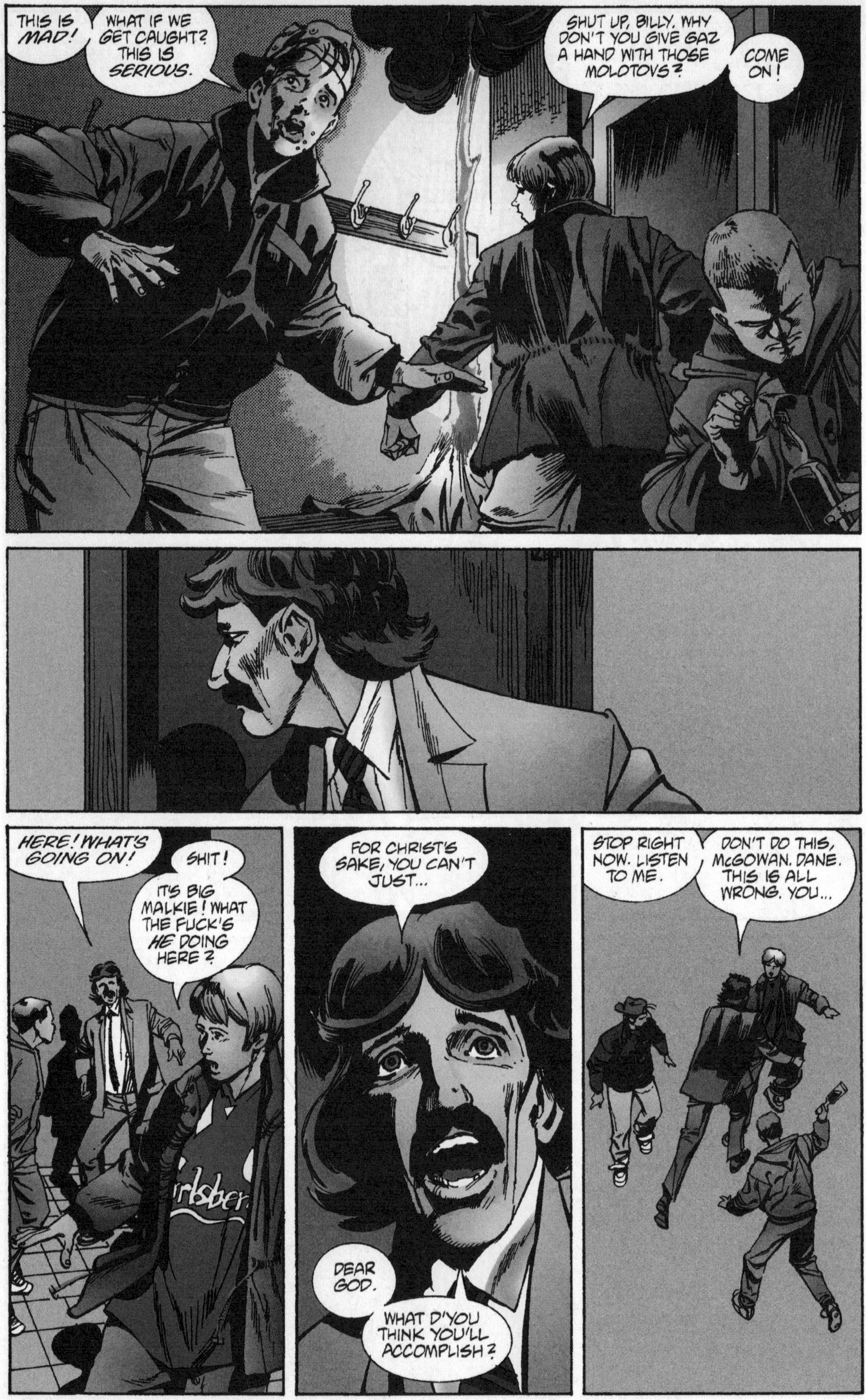
THIS IS *MAD*!
WHAT IF WE GET CAUGHT? THIS IS *SERIOUS*.
SHUT UP, BILLY. WHY DON'T YOU GIVE GAZ A HAND WITH THOSE MOLOTOVS?
COME ON!
HERE! WHAT'S GOING ON!
SHIT!
IT'S BIG MALKIE! WHAT THE FUCK'S *HE* DOING HERE?
FOR CHRIST'S SAKE, YOU CAN'T JUST...
DEAR GOD.
WHAT D'YOU THINK YOU'LL ACCOMPLISH?
STOP RIGHT NOW. LISTEN TO ME.
DON'T DO THIS, McGOWAN. DANE. THIS IS ALL WRONG. YOU...

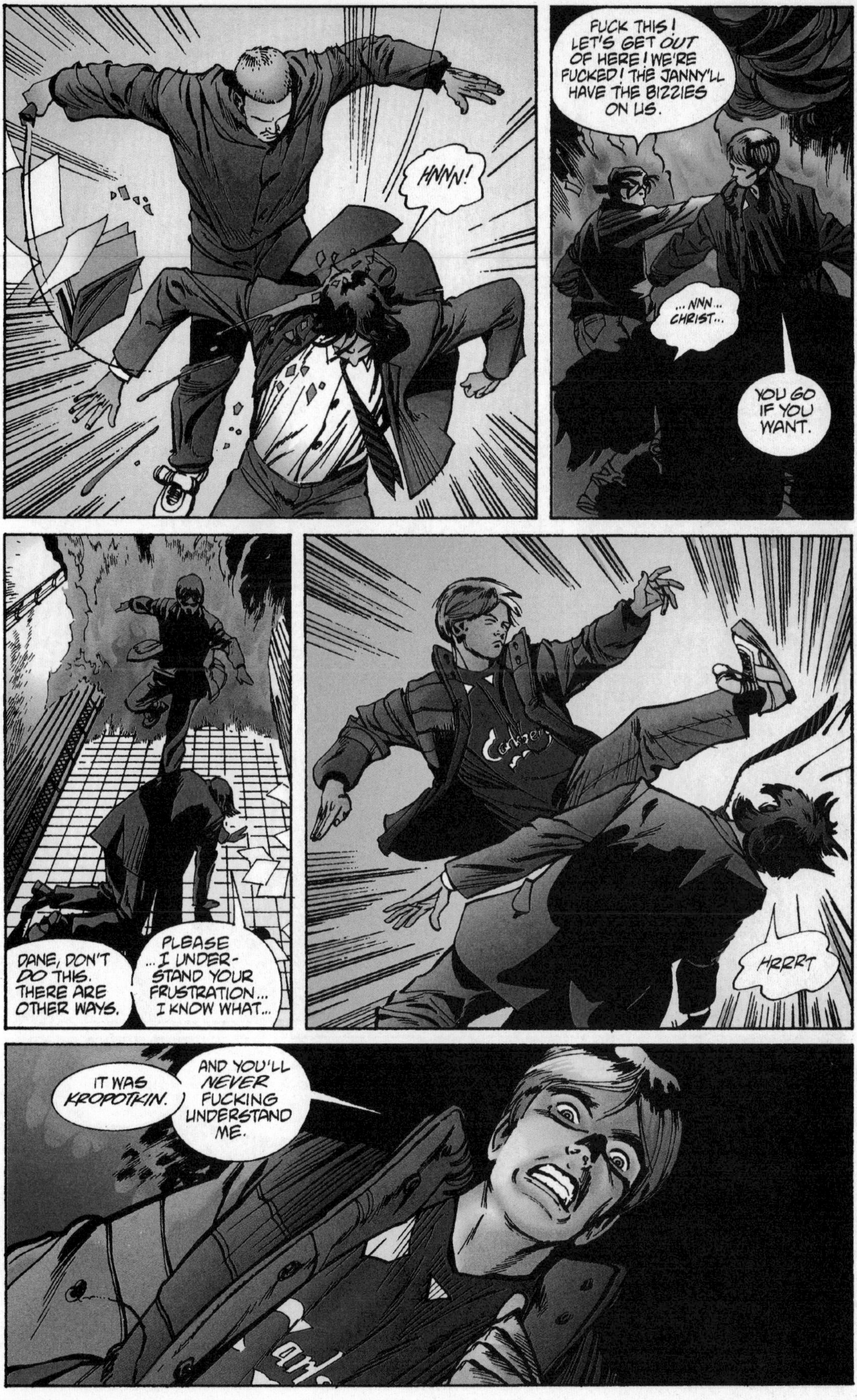
HNNN!
FUCK THIS! LET'S GET OUT OF HERE! WE'RE FUCKED! THE JANNY'LL HAVE THE BIZZIES ON US.
...NNN... CHRIST...
YOU GO IF YOU WANT.
DANE, DON'T DO THIS. THERE ARE OTHER WAYS.
PLEASE ...I UNDERSTAND YOUR FRUSTRATION... I KNOW WHAT...
HRRRT
IT WAS KROPOTKIN.
AND YOU'LL NEVER FUCKING UNDERSTAND ME.

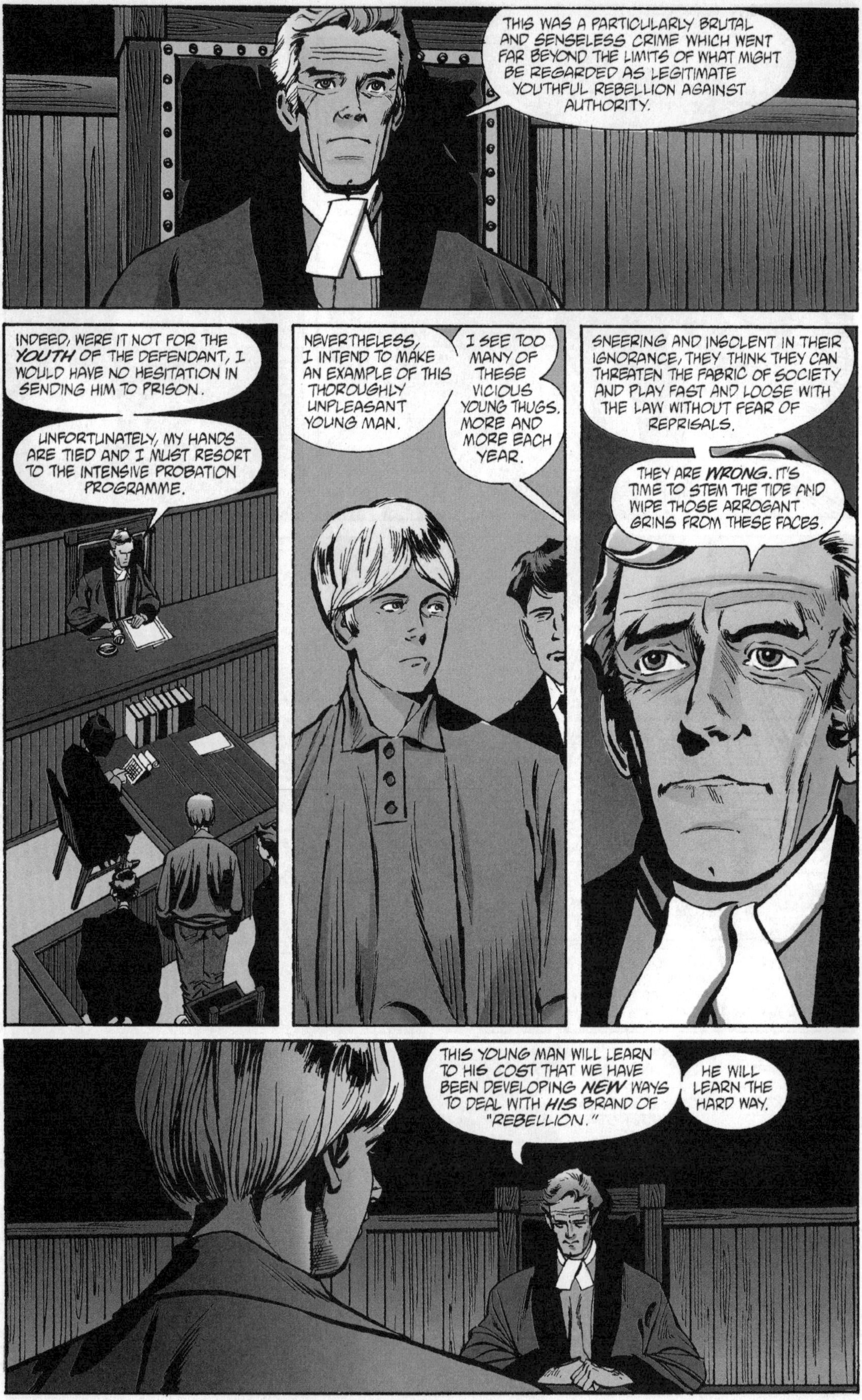
THIS WAS A PARTICULARLY BRUTAL AND SENSELESS CRIME WHICH WENT FAR BEYOND THE LIMITS OF WHAT MIGHT BE REGARDED AS LEGITIMATE YOUTHFUL REBELLION AGAINST AUTHORITY.
INDEED, WERE IT NOT FOR THE YOUTH OF THE DEFENDANT, I WOULD HAVE NO HESITATION IN SENDING HIM TO PRISON.
UNFORTUNATELY, MY HANDS ARE TIED AND I MUST RESORT TO THE INTENSIVE PROBATION PROGRAMME.
NEVERTHELESS, I INTEND TO MAKE AN EXAMPLE OF THIS THOROUGHLY UNPLEASANT YOUNG MAN.
I SEE TOO MANY OF THESE VICIOUS YOUNG THUGS. MORE AND MORE EACH YEAR.
SNEERING AND INSOLENT IN THEIR IGNORANCE, THEY THINK THEY CAN THREATEN THE FABRIC OF SOCIETY AND PLAY FAST AND LOOSE WITH THE LAW WITHOUT FEAR OF REPRISALS.
THEY ARE WRONG. IT'S TIME TO STEM THE TIDE AND WIPE THOSE ARROGANT GRINS FROM THESE FACES.
THIS YOUNG MAN WILL LEARN TO HIS COST THAT WE HAVE BEEN DEVELOPING NEW WAYS TO DEAL WITH HIS BRAND OF "REBELLION."
HE WILL LEARN THE HARD WAY.

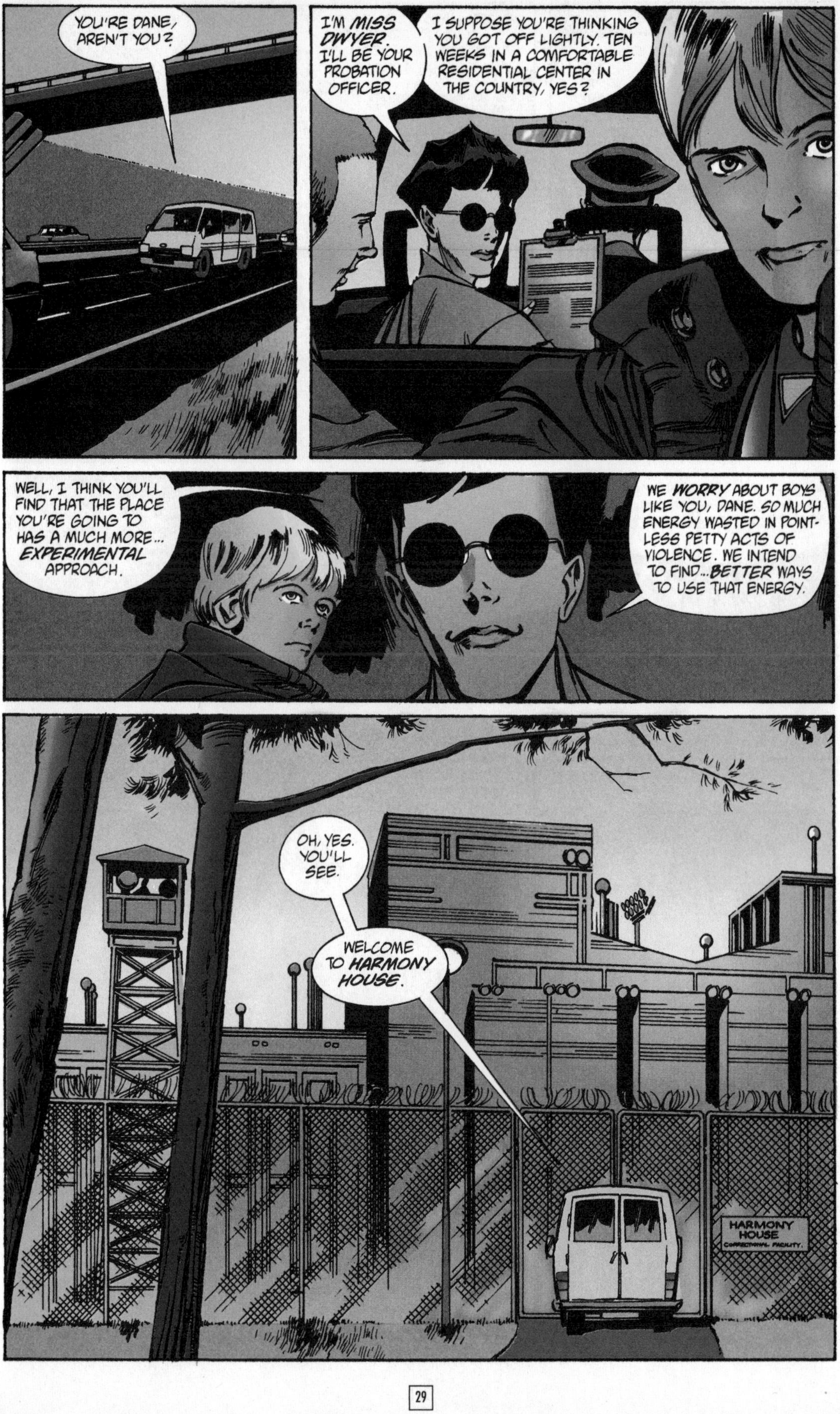
YOU'RE DANE, AREN'T YOU?
I'M MISS DWYER. I'LL BE YOUR PROBATION OFFICER.
I SUPPOSE YOU'RE THINKING YOU GOT OFF LIGHTLY. TEN WEEKS IN A COMFORTABLE RESIDENTIAL CENTER IN THE COUNTRY, YES?
WELL, I THINK YOU'LL FIND THAT THE PLACE YOU'RE GOING TO HAS A MUCH MORE... EXPERIMENTAL APPROACH.
WE WORRY ABOUT BOYS LIKE YOU, DANE. SO MUCH ENERGY WASTED IN POINTLESS PETTY ACTS OF VIOLENCE. WE INTEND TO FIND... BETTER WAYS TO USE THAT ENERGY.
OH, YES. YOU'LL SEE.
WELCOME TO HARMONY HOUSE.
HARMONY HOUSE
CORRECTIONAL FACILITY

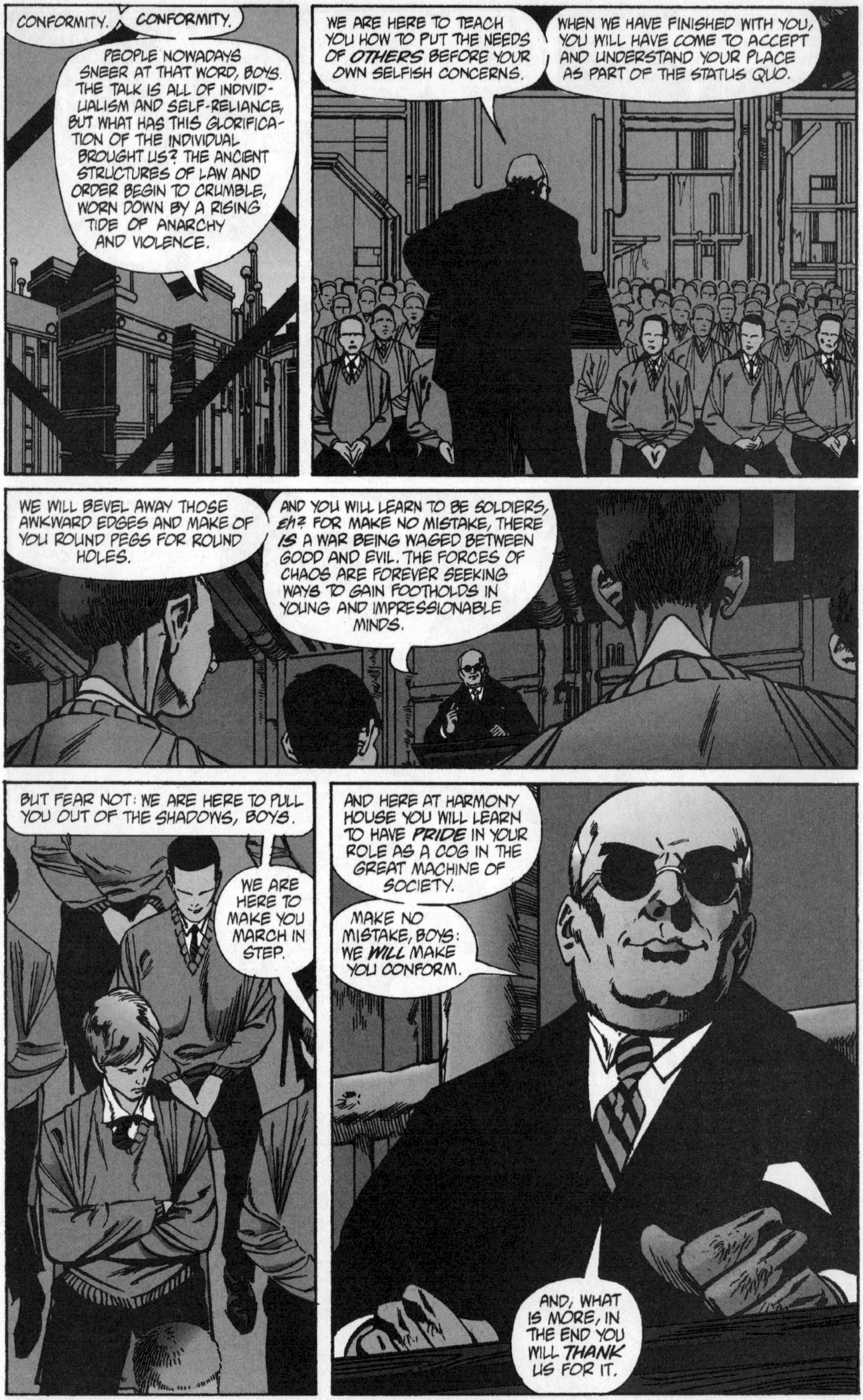
CONFORMITY.
CONFORMITY.
PEOPLE NOWADAYS SNEER AT THAT WORD, BOYS. THE TALK IS ALL OF INDIVIDUALISM AND SELF-RELIANCE, BUT WHAT HAS THIS GLORIFICATION OF THE INDIVIDUAL BROUGHT US? THE ANCIENT STRUCTURES OF LAW AND ORDER BEGIN TO CRUMBLE, WORN DOWN BY A RISING TIDE OF ANARCHY AND VIOLENCE.
WE ARE HERE TO TEACH YOU HOW TO PUT THE NEEDS OF OTHERS BEFORE YOUR OWN SELFISH CONCERNS.
WHEN WE HAVE FINISHED WITH YOU, YOU WILL HAVE COME TO ACCEPT AND UNDERSTAND YOUR PLACE AS PART OF THE STATUS QUO.
WE WILL BEVEL AWAY THOSE AWKWARD EDGES AND MAKE OF YOU ROUND PEGS FOR ROUND HOLES.
AND YOU WILL LEARN TO BE SOLDIERS, EH? FOR MAKE NO MISTAKE, THERE IS A WAR BEING WAGED BETWEEN GOOD AND EVIL. THE FORCES OF CHAOS ARE FOREVER SEEKING WAYS TO GAIN FOOTHOLDS IN YOUNG AND IMPRESSIONABLE MINDS.
BUT FEAR NOT: WE ARE HERE TO PULL YOU OUT OF THE SHADOWS, BOYS.
WE ARE HERE TO MAKE YOU MARCH IN STEP.
AND HERE AT HARMONY HOUSE YOU WILL LEARN TO HAVE PRIDE IN YOUR ROLE AS A COG IN THE GREAT MACHINE OF SOCIETY.
MAKE NO MISTAKE, BOYS: WE WILL MAKE YOU CONFORM.
AND, WHAT IS MORE, IN THE END YOU WILL THANK US FOR IT.

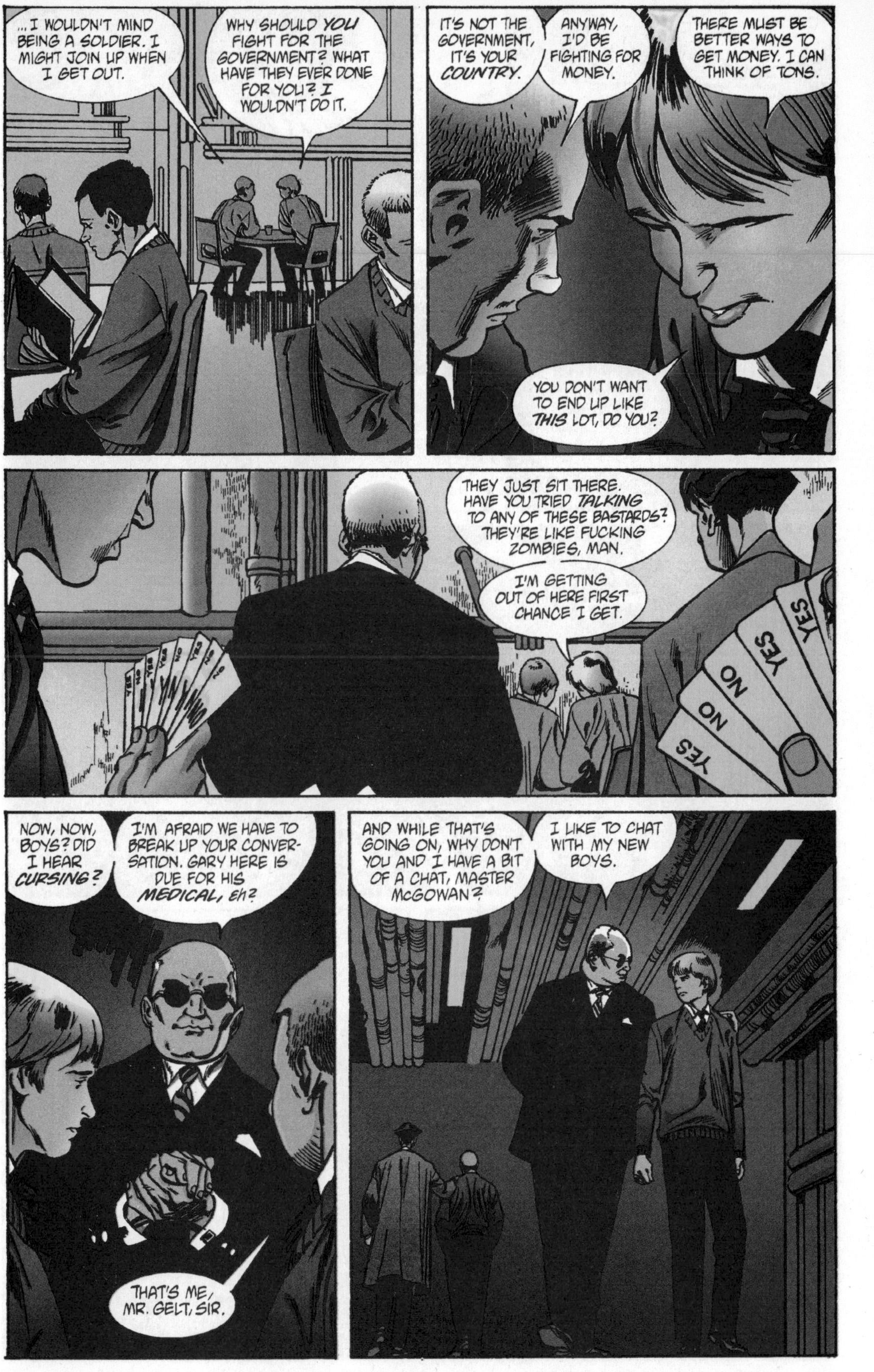
...I WOULDN'T MIND BEING A SOLDIER. I MIGHT JOIN UP WHEN I GET OUT.
WHY SHOULD *YOU* FIGHT FOR THE GOVERNMENT? WHAT HAVE THEY EVER DONE FOR YOU? *I* WOULDN'T DO IT.
IT'S NOT THE GOVERNMENT, IT'S YOUR *COUNTRY*.
ANYWAY, I'D BE FIGHTING FOR MONEY.
THERE MUST BE BETTER WAYS TO GET MONEY. I CAN THINK OF TONS.
YOU DON'T WANT TO END UP LIKE *THIS* LOT, DO YOU?
THEY JUST SIT THERE. HAVE YOU TRIED *TALKING* TO ANY OF THESE BASTARDS? THEY'RE LIKE FUCKING ZOMBIES, MAN.
I'M GETTING OUT OF HERE FIRST CHANCE I GET.
YES
NO
NO
YES
YES
NOW, NOW, BOYS? DID I HEAR *CURSING*?
I'M AFRAID WE HAVE TO BREAK UP YOUR CONVERSATION. GARY HERE IS DUE FOR HIS *MEDICAL*, EH?
THAT'S ME, MR. GELT, SIR.
AND WHILE THAT'S GOING ON, WHY DON'T YOU AND I HAVE A BIT OF A CHAT, MASTER McGOWAN?
I LIKE TO CHAT WITH MY NEW BOYS.

IT'S THE MOON AGAIN.

DARKNESS CLEARING AWAY

THE MOON
ISXIS – THE OCCULT POWERS
Hidden Enemies

18

7

THE DARKNESS THAT GIVES BIRTH TO LIGHT, BLAH, BLAH, BLAH.

YOU KNOW THIS STUFF ANYWAY. I DON'T KNOW WHY YOU ASKED *ME* TO READ THE TAROT. I THINK IT'S BULLSHIT.

YES, MISS.

THAT'S *EXACTLY* WHY I ASKED YOU TO READ IT. THESE BEETLE SYNCHRONICITIES HAVE BEEN TURNING UP FOR THE PAST MONTH. IT'S ALL TOO PERSISTENT TO IGNORE.

THE BEETLE'S SUPPOSED TO STAND FOR DEATH AND RESURRECTION, ISN'T IT?

TRIALS. INITIATIONS.

IS THAT WHY YOU INVOKED *JOHN LENNON*?

YEAH. I FIGURED HE'S GOT ALL THE ATTRIBUTES OF A GOD NOW, SO I USED TRADITIONAL CEREMONIAL MAGIC METHODS AND SUMMONED HIM FOR ADVICE.

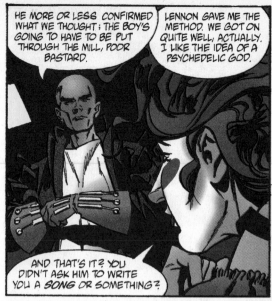

HE MORE OR LESS CONFIRMED WHAT WE THOUGHT; THE BOY'S GOING TO HAVE TO BE PUT THROUGH THE MILL, POOR BASTARD.

LENNON GAVE ME THE METHOD. WE GOT ON QUITE WELL, ACTUALLY. I LIKE THE IDEA OF A PSYCHEDELIC GOD.

AND THAT'S IT? YOU DIDN'T ASK HIM TO WRITE YOU A *SONG* OR SOMETHING?

HE JUST SUGGESTED I GIVE YOU *THIS*.

AN APPLE FOR THE TEACHER.

EVE MAY HAVE FALLEN FOR THAT ONE. *RAGGED ROBIN'S* NOT SO DUMB.

I GUESS YOU WANT ME TO CONTACT THE *OTHERS* NOW? *BOY'S* STILL IN NEW YORK. *FANNY'S* AT THE ACADEMY.

I'M GOING TO NEED *ALL* OF YOU. WE HAVE TO SET THIS ONE UP REALLY CAREFULLY. WE CAN'T AFFORD TO LOSE THIS KID.

THAT'S IF WE HAVEN'T ALREADY LOST HIM.

I'VE BEEN LOOKING FORWARD TO VISITING HARMONY HOUSE.

YOU KNOW, WHEN I WAS A KID, I WANTED TO GROW UP AND FIND MYSELF LIVING IN A '60s *SPY* SERIES.

FUNNY HOW THINGS TURN OUT, ISN'T IT?

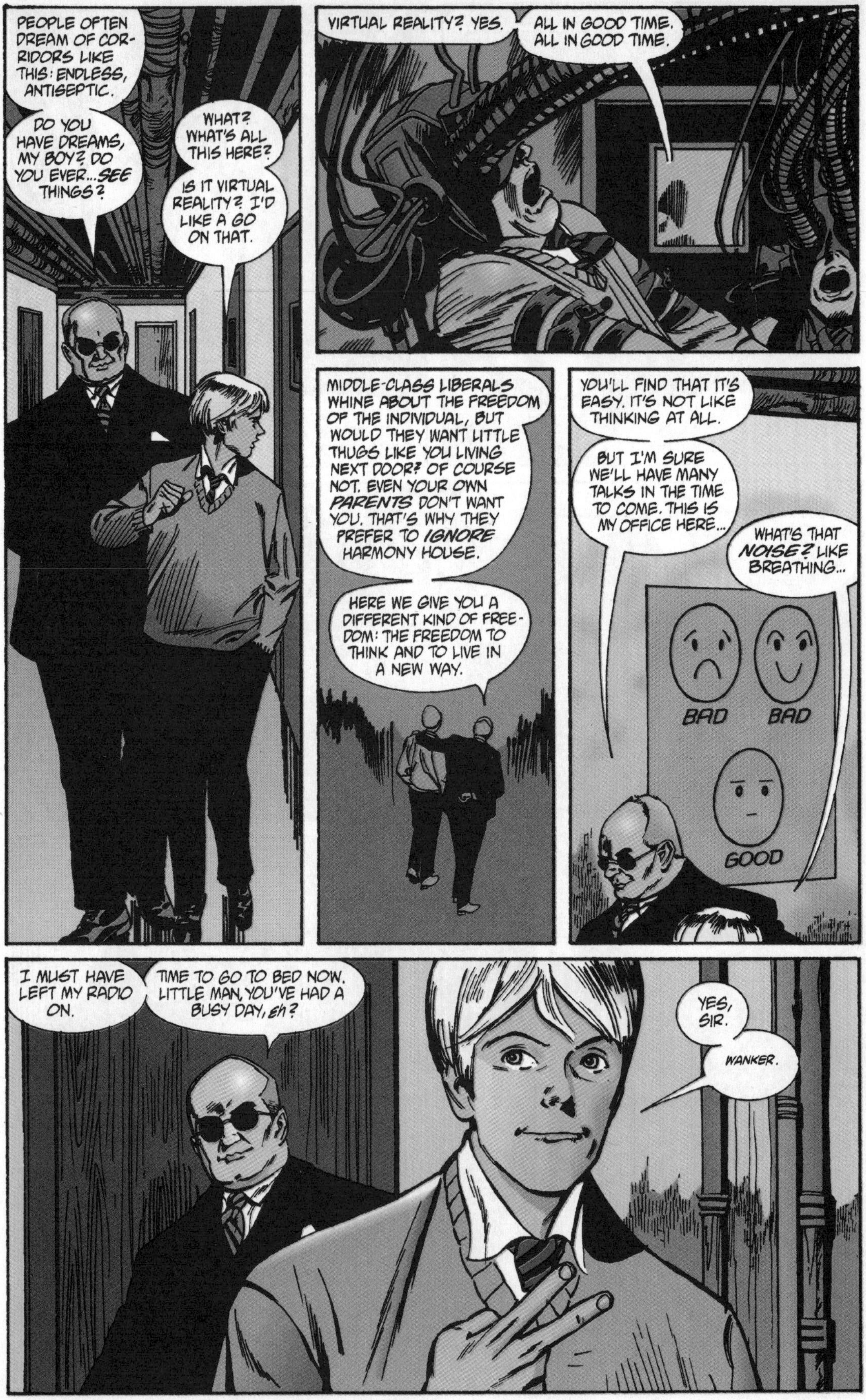
PEOPLE OFTEN DREAM OF CORRIDORS LIKE THIS: ENDLESS, ANTISEPTIC.
DO YOU HAVE DREAMS, MY BOY? DO YOU EVER...SEE THINGS?
WHAT? WHAT'S ALL THIS HERE?
IS IT VIRTUAL REALITY? I'D LIKE A GO ON THAT.
VIRTUAL REALITY? YES.
ALL IN GOOD TIME. ALL IN GOOD TIME.
MIDDLE-CLASS LIBERALS WHINE ABOUT THE FREEDOM OF THE INDIVIDUAL, BUT WOULD THEY WANT LITTLE THUGS LIKE YOU LIVING NEXT DOOR? OF COURSE NOT. EVEN YOUR OWN PARENTS DON'T WANT YOU. THAT'S WHY THEY PREFER TO IGNORE HARMONY HOUSE.
HERE WE GIVE YOU A DIFFERENT KIND OF FREEDOM: THE FREEDOM TO THINK AND TO LIVE IN A NEW WAY.
YOU'LL FIND THAT IT'S EASY. IT'S NOT LIKE THINKING AT ALL.
BUT I'M SURE WE'LL HAVE MANY TALKS IN THE TIME TO COME. THIS IS MY OFFICE HERE...
WHAT'S THAT NOISE? LIKE BREATHING...
BAD
BAD
GOOD
I MUST HAVE LEFT MY RADIO ON.
TIME TO GO TO BED NOW. LITTLE MAN, YOU'VE HAD A BUSY DAY, Eh?
YES, SIR.
WANKER.

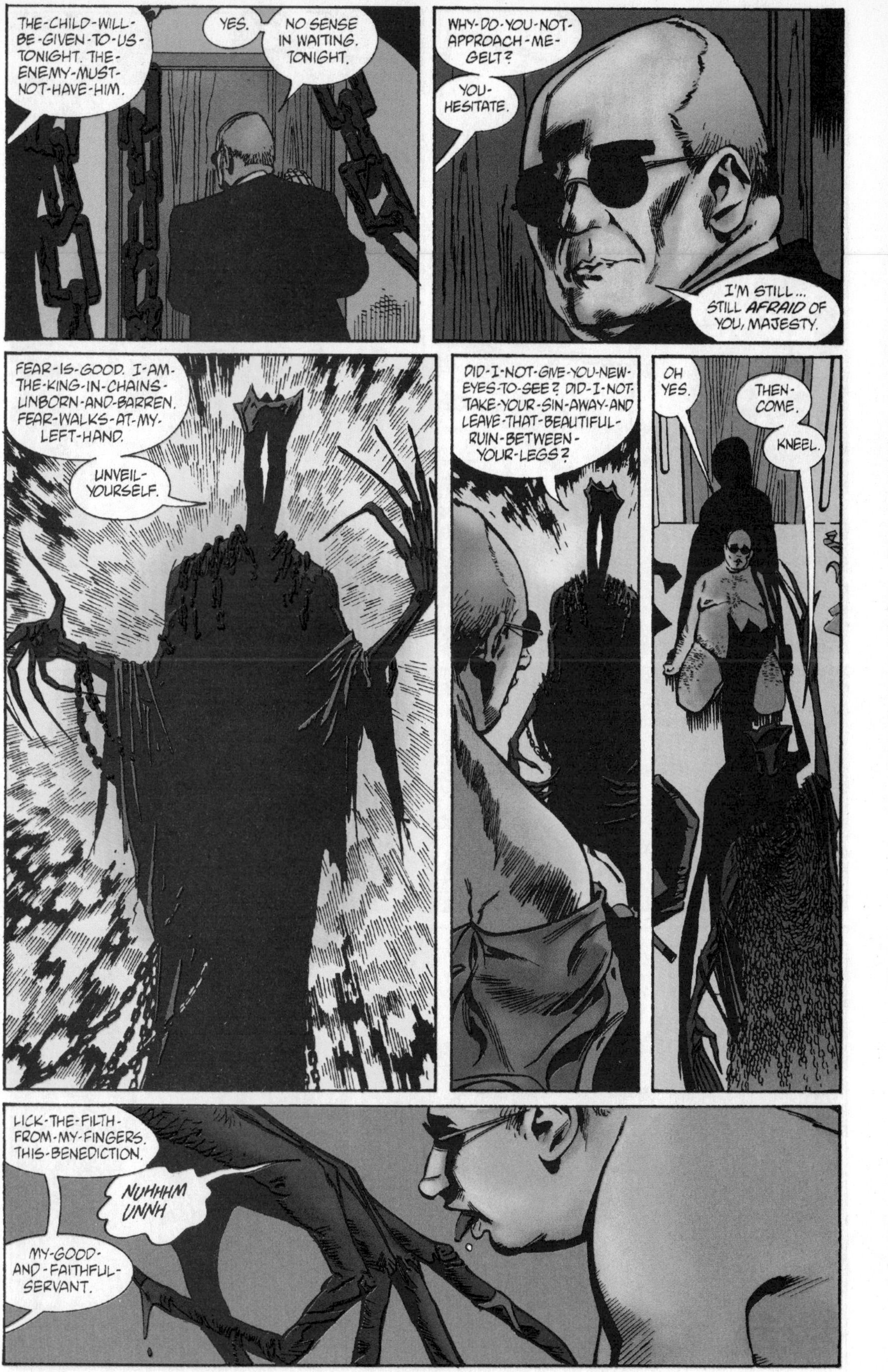
THE-CHILD-WILL-BE-GIVEN-TO-US-TONIGHT. THE-ENEMY-MUST-NOT-HAVE-HIM.
YES.
NO SENSE IN WAITING. TONIGHT.
WHY-DO-YOU-NOT-APPROACH-ME-GELT?
YOU-HESITATE.
I'M STILL... STILL *AFRAID* OF YOU, MAJESTY.
FEAR-IS-GOOD. I-AM-THE-KING-IN-CHAINS-UNBORN-AND-BARREN. FEAR-WALKS-AT-MY-LEFT-HAND.
UNVEIL-YOURSELF.
DID-I-NOT-GIVE-YOU-NEW-EYES-TO-SEE? DID-I-NOT-TAKE-YOUR-SIN-AWAY-AND LEAVE-THAT-BEAUTIFUL-RUIN-BETWEEN-YOUR-LEGS?
OH YES.
THEN-COME.
KNEEL.
LICK-THE-FILTH-FROM-MY-FINGERS. THIS-BENEDICTION.
NUHHHM UNNH
MY-GOOD-AND-FAITHFUL-SERVANT.

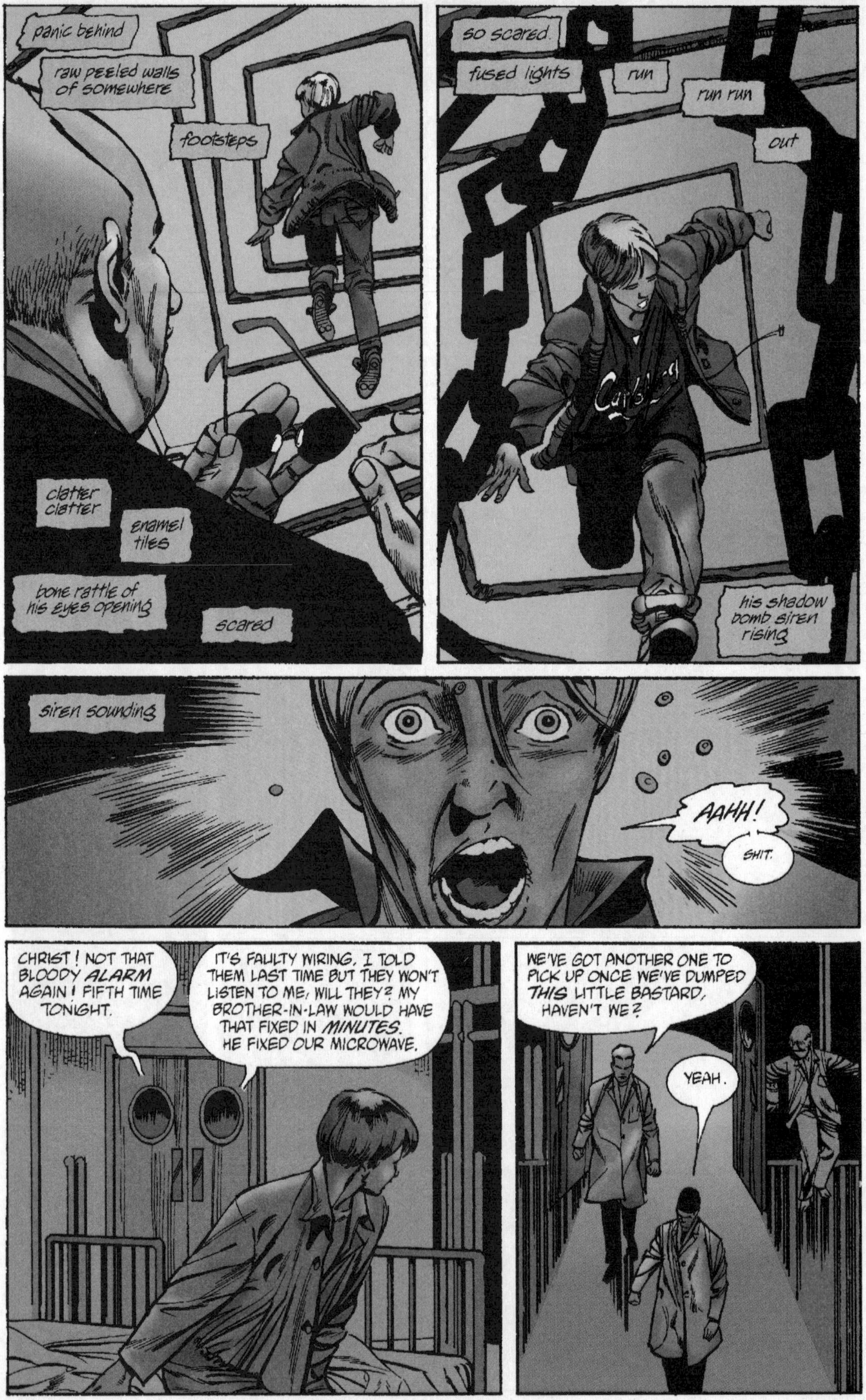
panic behind
raw peeled walls of somewhere
footsteps
clatter clatter
enamel tiles
bone rattle of his eyes opening
scared
so scared.
fused lights
run
run run
out
his shadow bomb siren rising
siren sounding
AAHH!
SHIT.
CHRIST! NOT THAT BLOODY ALARM AGAIN! FIFTH TIME TONIGHT.
IT'S FAULTY WIRING, I TOLD THEM LAST TIME BUT THEY WON'T LISTEN TO ME, WILL THEY? MY BROTHER-IN-LAW WOULD HAVE THAT FIXED IN MINUTES. HE FIXED OUR MICROWAVE.
WE'VE GOT ANOTHER ONE TO PICK UP ONCE WE'VE DUMPED THIS LITTLE BASTARD, HAVEN'T WE?
YEAH.

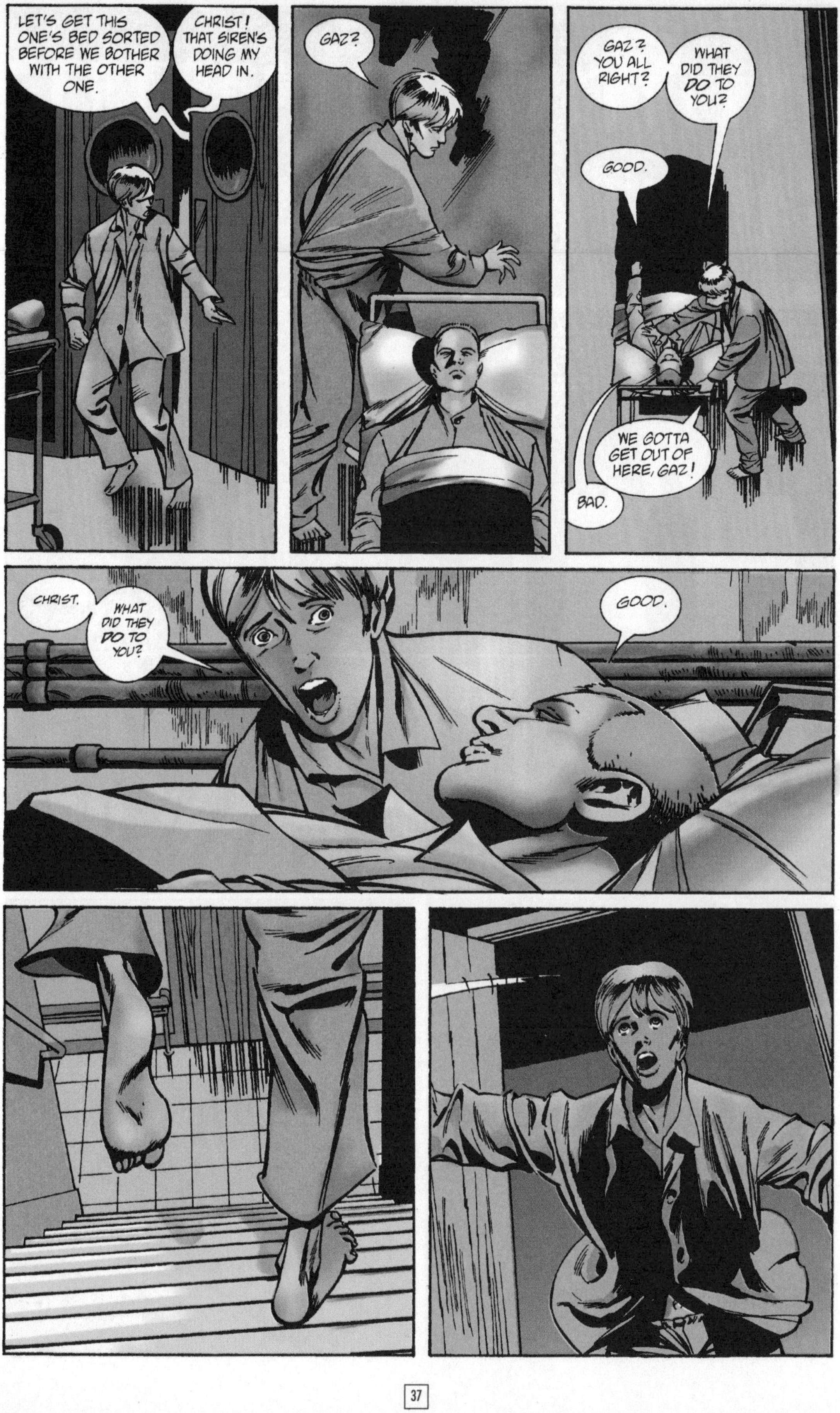
LET'S GET THIS ONE'S BED SORTED BEFORE WE BOTHER WITH THE OTHER ONE.
CHRIST! THAT SIREN'S DOING MY HEAD IN.
GAZ?
GAZ? YOU ALL RIGHT?
WHAT DID THEY DO TO YOU?
GOOD.
WE GOTTA GET OUT OF HERE, GAZ!
BAD.
CHRIST.
WHAT DID THEY DO TO YOU?
GOOD.

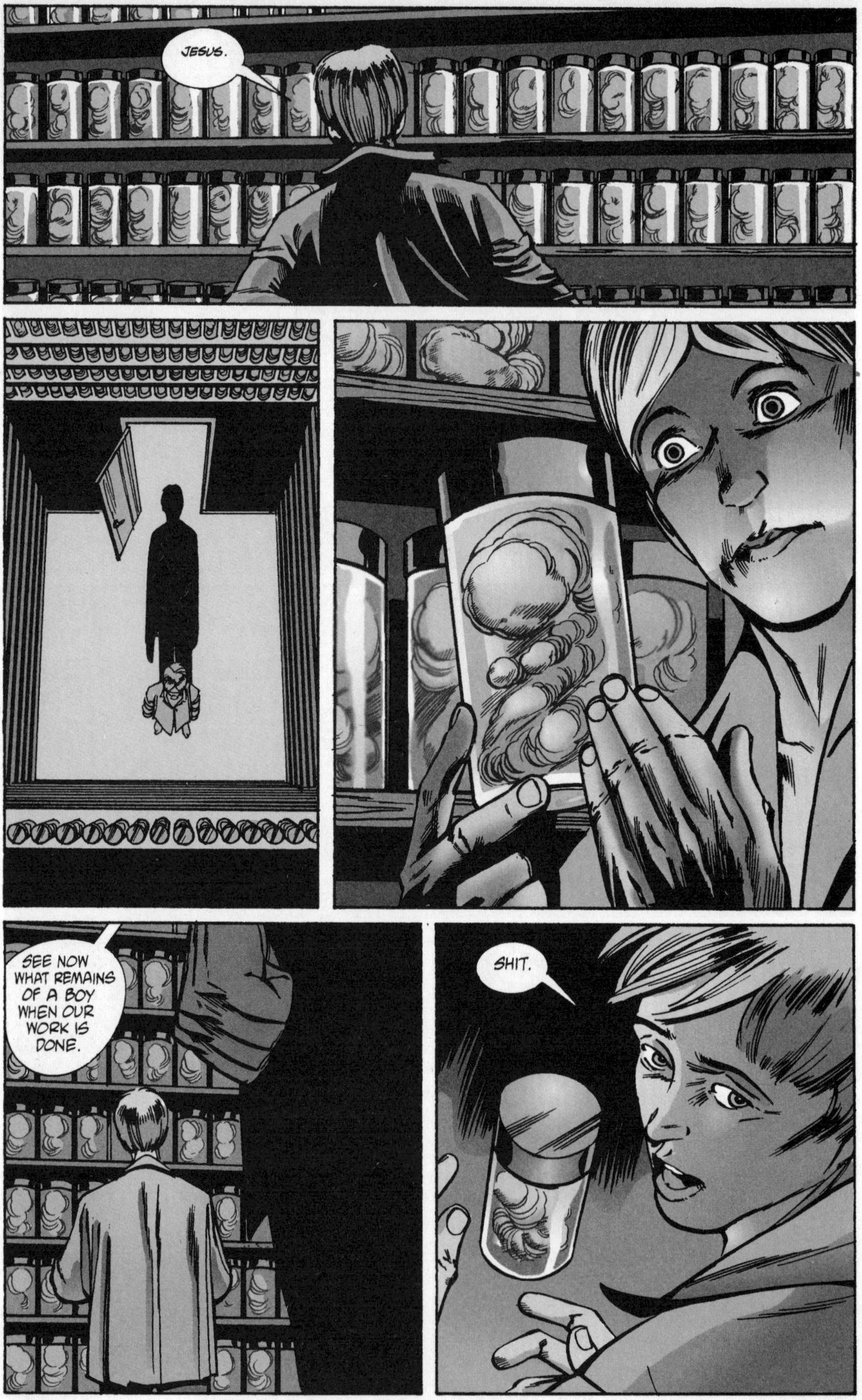
JESUS.
SEE NOW WHAT REMAINS OF A BOY WHEN OUR WORK IS DONE.
SHIT.

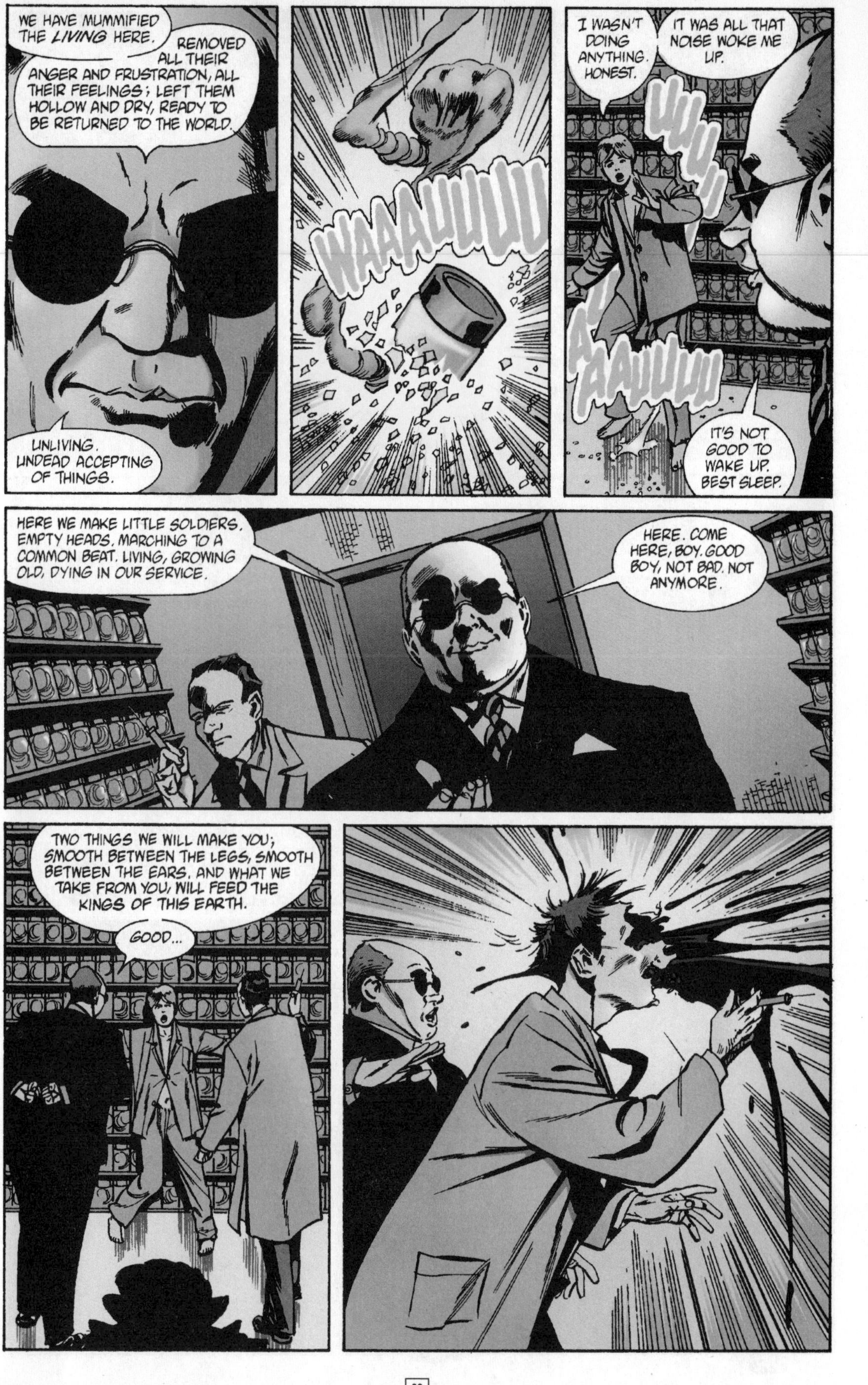

WE HAVE MUMMIFIED THE LIVING HERE.
REMOVED ALL THEIR ANGER AND FRUSTRATION, ALL THEIR FEELINGS; LEFT THEM HOLLOW AND DRY, READY TO BE RETURNED TO THE WORLD.
UNLIVING. UNDEAD ACCEPTING OF THINGS.
WAAAUUUUU
I WASN'T DOING ANYTHING. HONEST.
IT WAS ALL THAT NOISE WOKE ME UP.
UUUU
AU AAUUUU
IT'S NOT GOOD TO WAKE UP. BEST SLEEP.
HERE WE MAKE LITTLE SOLDIERS. EMPTY HEADS, MARCHING TO A COMMON BEAT. LIVING, GROWING OLD, DYING IN OUR SERVICE.
HERE. COME HERE, BOY. GOOD BOY, NOT BAD. NOT ANYMORE.
TWO THINGS WE WILL MAKE YOU; SMOOTH BETWEEN THE LEGS, SMOOTH BETWEEN THE EARS. AND WHAT WE TAKE FROM YOU, WILL FEED THE KINGS OF THIS EARTH.
GOOD...

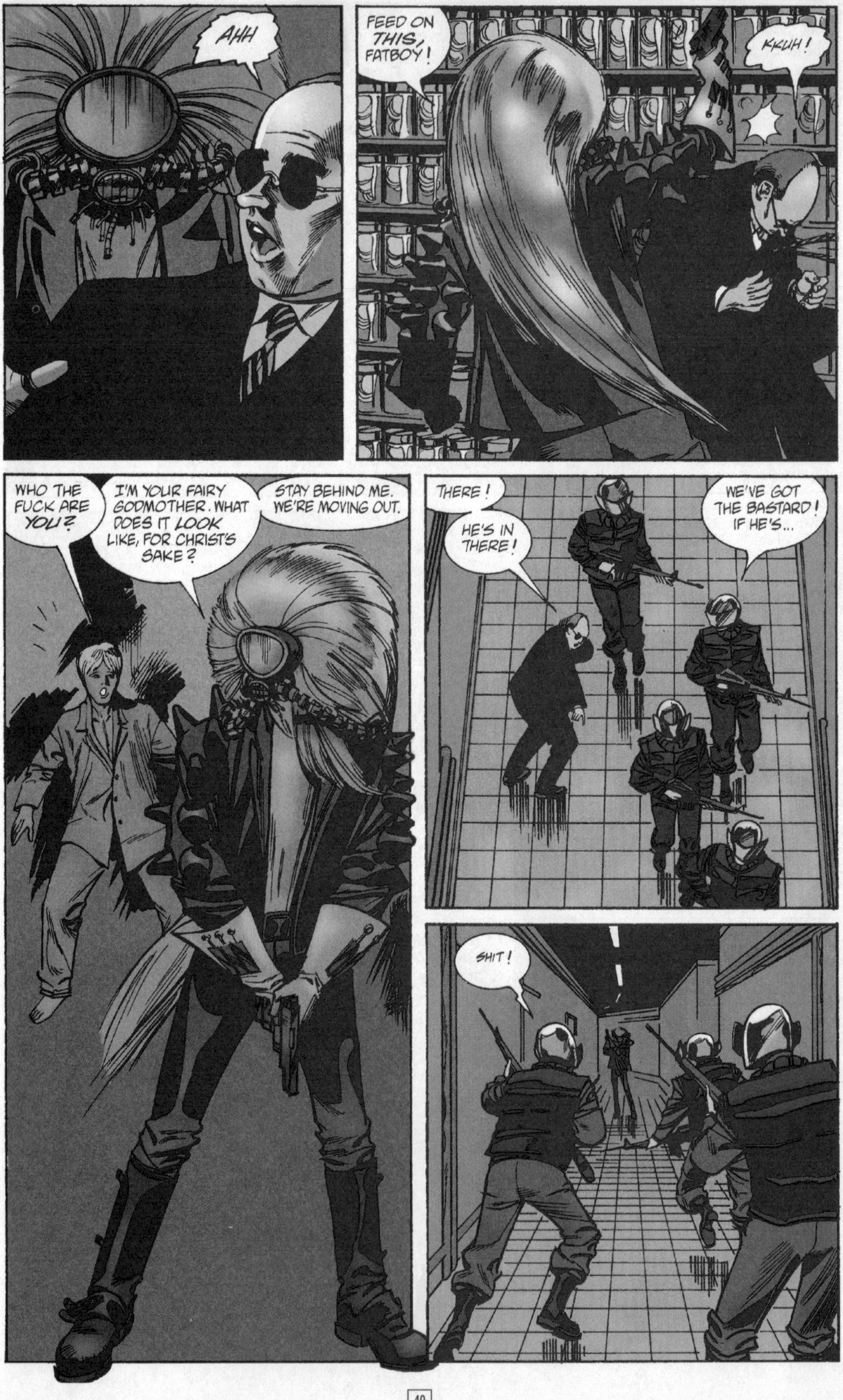
AHH
FEED ON THIS, FATBOY!
KKUH!
WHO THE FUCK ARE YOU?
I'M YOUR FAIRY GODMOTHER. WHAT DOES IT LOOK LIKE, FOR CHRIST'S SAKE?
STAY BEHIND ME. WE'RE MOVING OUT.
THERE!
HE'S IN THERE!
WE'VE GOT THE BASTARD! IF HE'S...
SHIT!

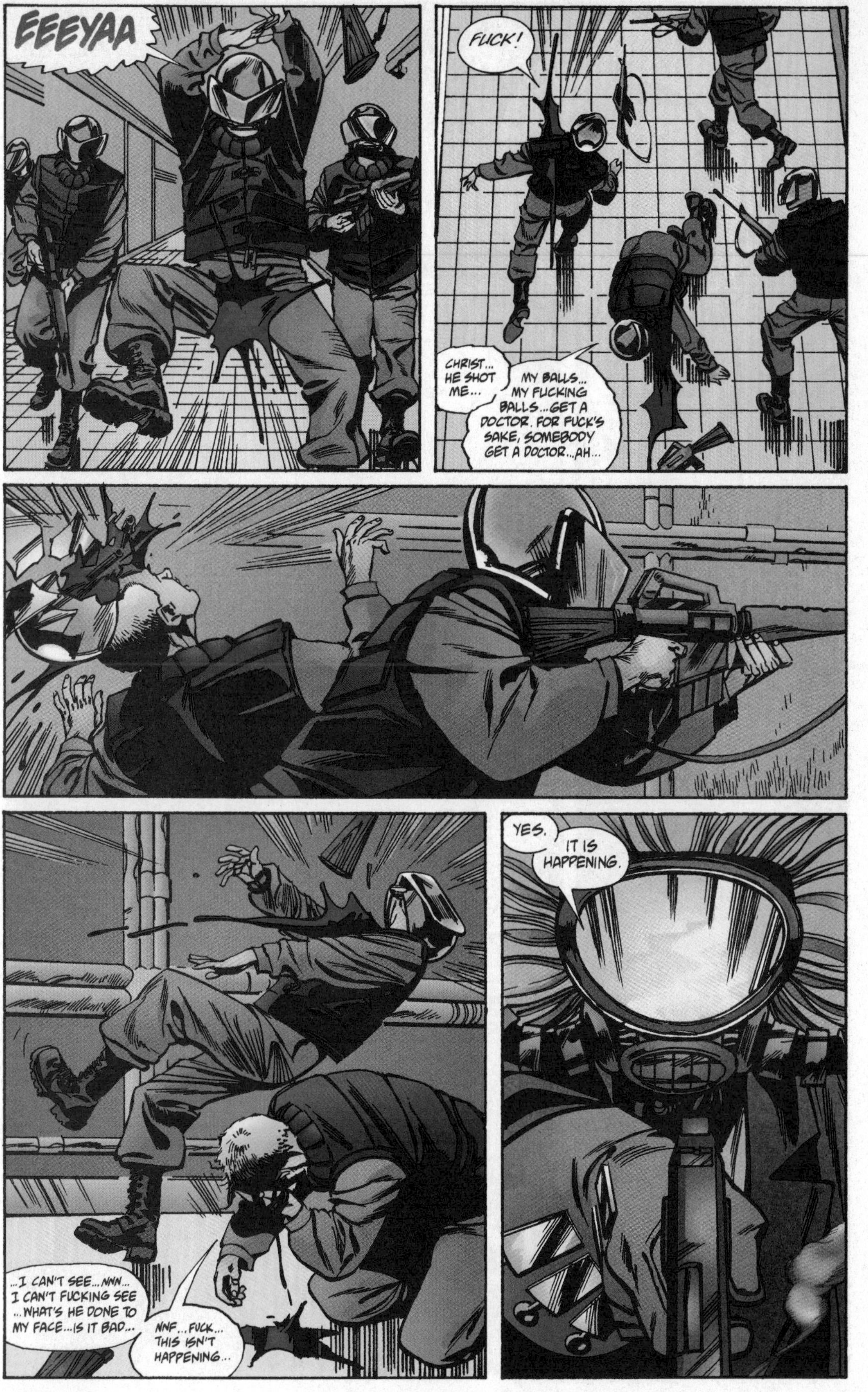
EEEYAA
FUCK!
CHRIST... HE SHOT ME...
MY BALLS... MY FUCKING BALLS...GET A DOCTOR. FOR FUCK'S SAKE, SOMEBODY GET A DOCTOR...AH...
...I CAN'T SEE...NNN... I CAN'T FUCKING SEE ...WHAT'S HE DONE TO MY FACE...IS IT BAD...
NNF...FUCK... THIS ISN'T HAPPENING...
YES.
IT IS HAPPENING.

GELT!

YOU WANTED TO SEE ME, HEADMASTER?

AH, YES, THE USUAL PATHETIC SHOW OF BRAVADO. DON'T YOU KNOW THIS FACILITY IS ONLY ONE OF DOZENS?

"INVISIBLES"! SOON YOU WILL *BEG* US TO TEACH YOU THE MYSTERIES OF SUBMISSION.

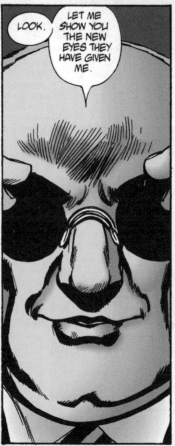

LOOK.

LET ME SHOW YOU THE NEW EYES THEY HAVE GIVEN ME.

YOU FIND THEM, I'LL LOOK AT THEM.

GOODBYE, MR. CHIPS.

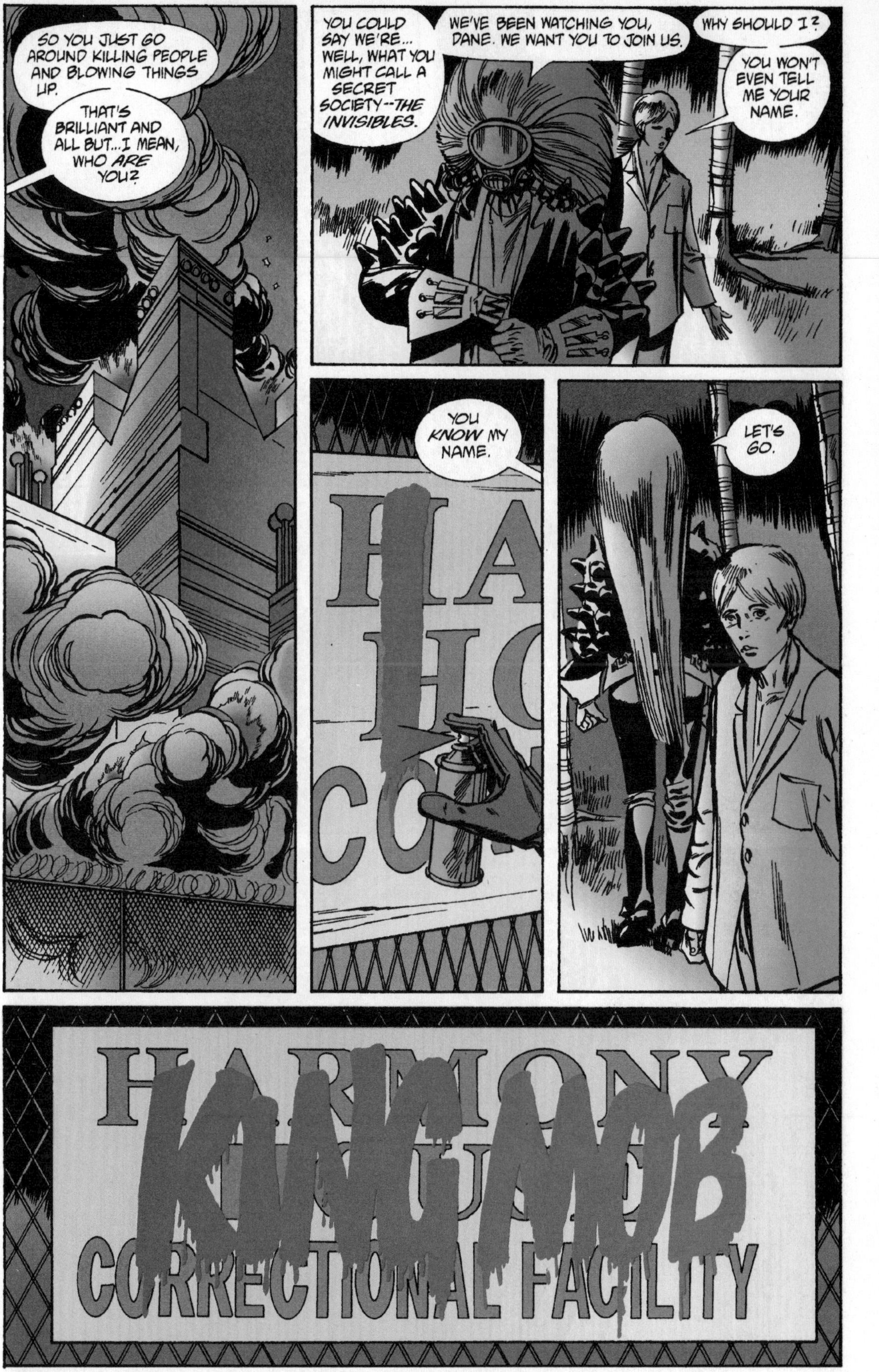
SO YOU JUST GO AROUND KILLING PEOPLE AND BLOWING THINGS UP.
THAT'S BRILLIANT AND ALL BUT...I MEAN, WHO *ARE* YOU?
YOU COULD SAY WE'RE... WELL, WHAT YOU MIGHT CALL A SECRET SOCIETY--*THE INVISIBLES.*
WE'VE BEEN WATCHING YOU, DANE. WE WANT YOU TO JOIN US.
WHY SHOULD I?
YOU WON'T EVEN TELL ME YOUR NAME.
YOU *KNOW* MY NAME.
LET'S GO.
HARMONY
CORRECTIONAL FACILITY
KING MOB

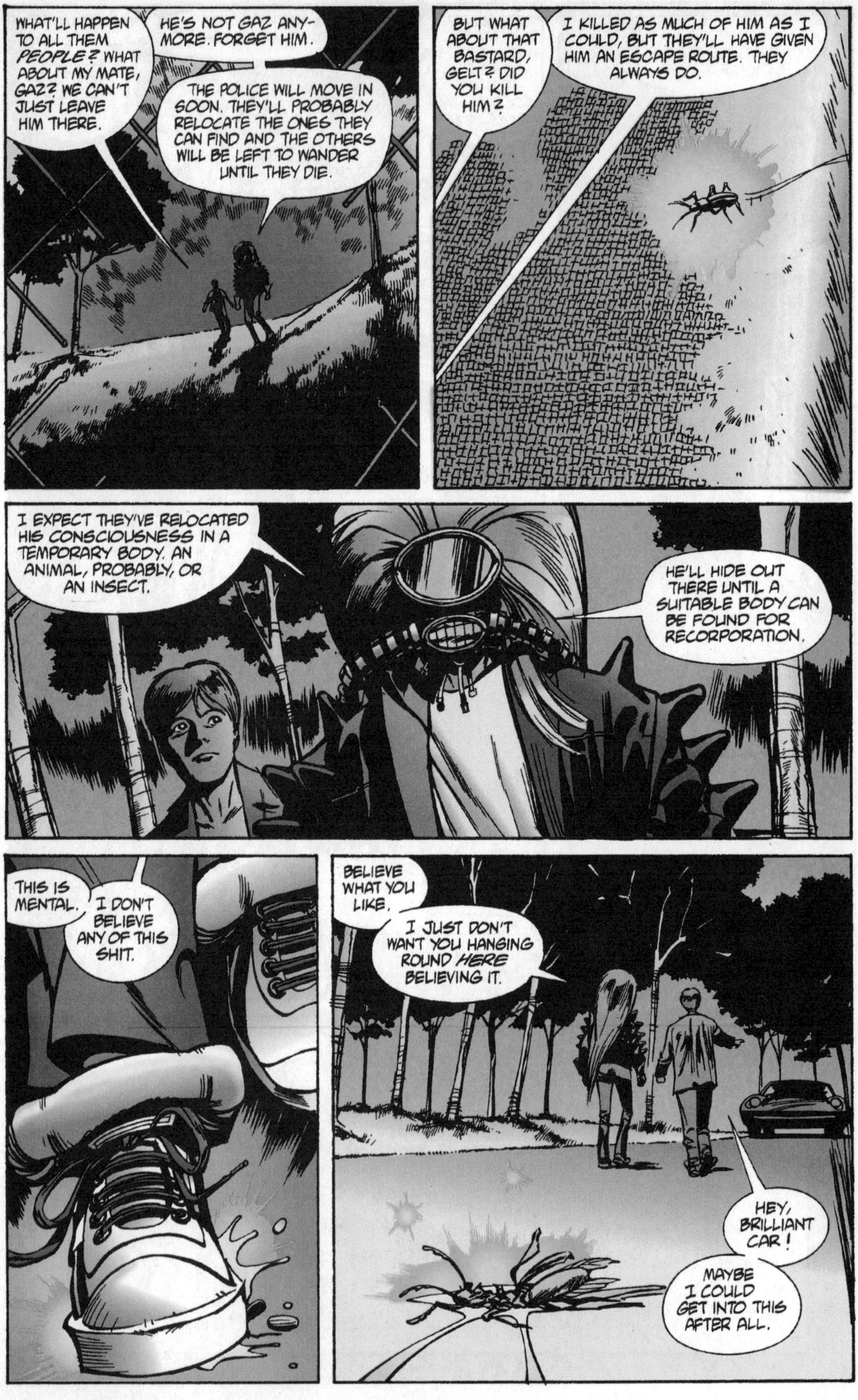
WHAT'LL HAPPEN TO ALL THEM PEOPLE? WHAT ABOUT MY MATE, GAZ? WE CAN'T JUST LEAVE HIM THERE.
HE'S NOT GAZ ANY-MORE. FORGET HIM.
THE POLICE WILL MOVE IN SOON. THEY'LL PROBABLY RELOCATE THE ONES THEY CAN FIND AND THE OTHERS WILL BE LEFT TO WANDER UNTIL THEY DIE.
BUT WHAT ABOUT THAT BASTARD, GELT? DID YOU KILL HIM?
I KILLED AS MUCH OF HIM AS I COULD, BUT THEY'LL HAVE GIVEN HIM AN ESCAPE ROUTE. THEY ALWAYS DO.
I EXPECT THEY'VE RELOCATED HIS CONSCIOUSNESS IN A TEMPORARY BODY. AN ANIMAL, PROBABLY, OR AN INSECT.
HE'LL HIDE OUT THERE UNTIL A SUITABLE BODY CAN BE FOUND FOR RECORPORATION.
THIS IS MENTAL.
I DON'T BELIEVE ANY OF THIS SHIT.
BELIEVE WHAT YOU LIKE.
I JUST DON'T WANT YOU HANGING ROUND HERE BELIEVING IT.
HEY, BRILLIANT CAR!
MAYBE I COULD GET INTO THIS AFTER ALL.

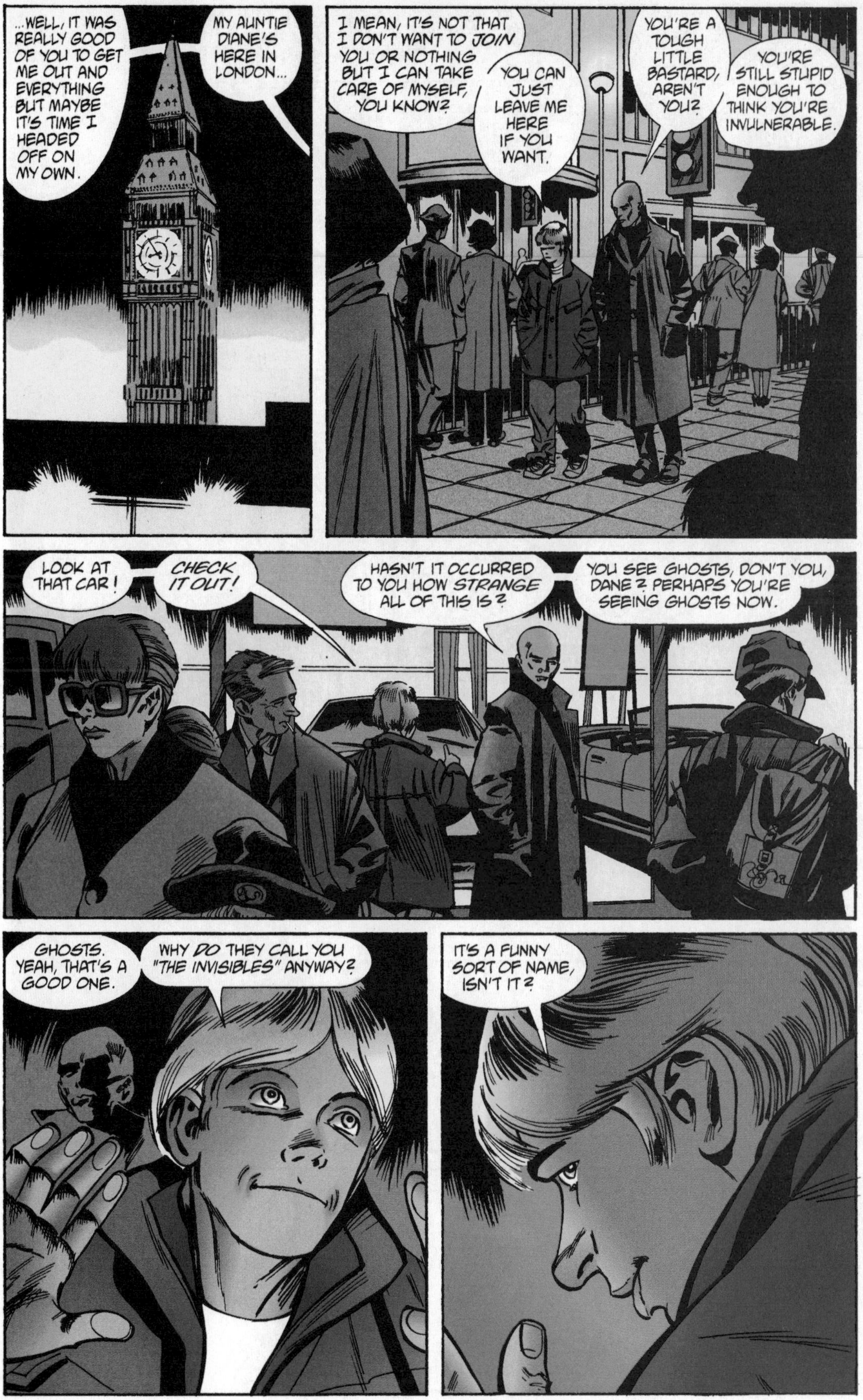
...WELL, IT WAS REALLY GOOD OF YOU TO GET ME OUT AND EVERYTHING BUT MAYBE IT'S TIME I HEADED OFF ON MY OWN.
MY AUNTIE DIANE'S HERE IN LONDON...
I MEAN, IT'S NOT THAT I DON'T WANT TO JOIN YOU OR NOTHING BUT I CAN TAKE CARE OF MYSELF, YOU KNOW?
YOU CAN JUST LEAVE ME HERE IF YOU WANT.
YOU'RE A TOUGH LITTLE BASTARD, AREN'T YOU?
YOU'RE STILL STUPID ENOUGH TO THINK YOU'RE INVULNERABLE.
LOOK AT THAT CAR!
CHECK IT OUT!
HASN'T IT OCCURRED TO YOU HOW STRANGE ALL OF THIS IS?
YOU SEE GHOSTS, DON'T YOU, DANE? PERHAPS YOU'RE SEEING GHOSTS NOW.
GHOSTS. YEAH, THAT'S A GOOD ONE.
WHY DO THEY CALL YOU "THE INVISIBLES" ANYWAY?
IT'S A FUNNY SORT OF NAME, ISN'T IT?

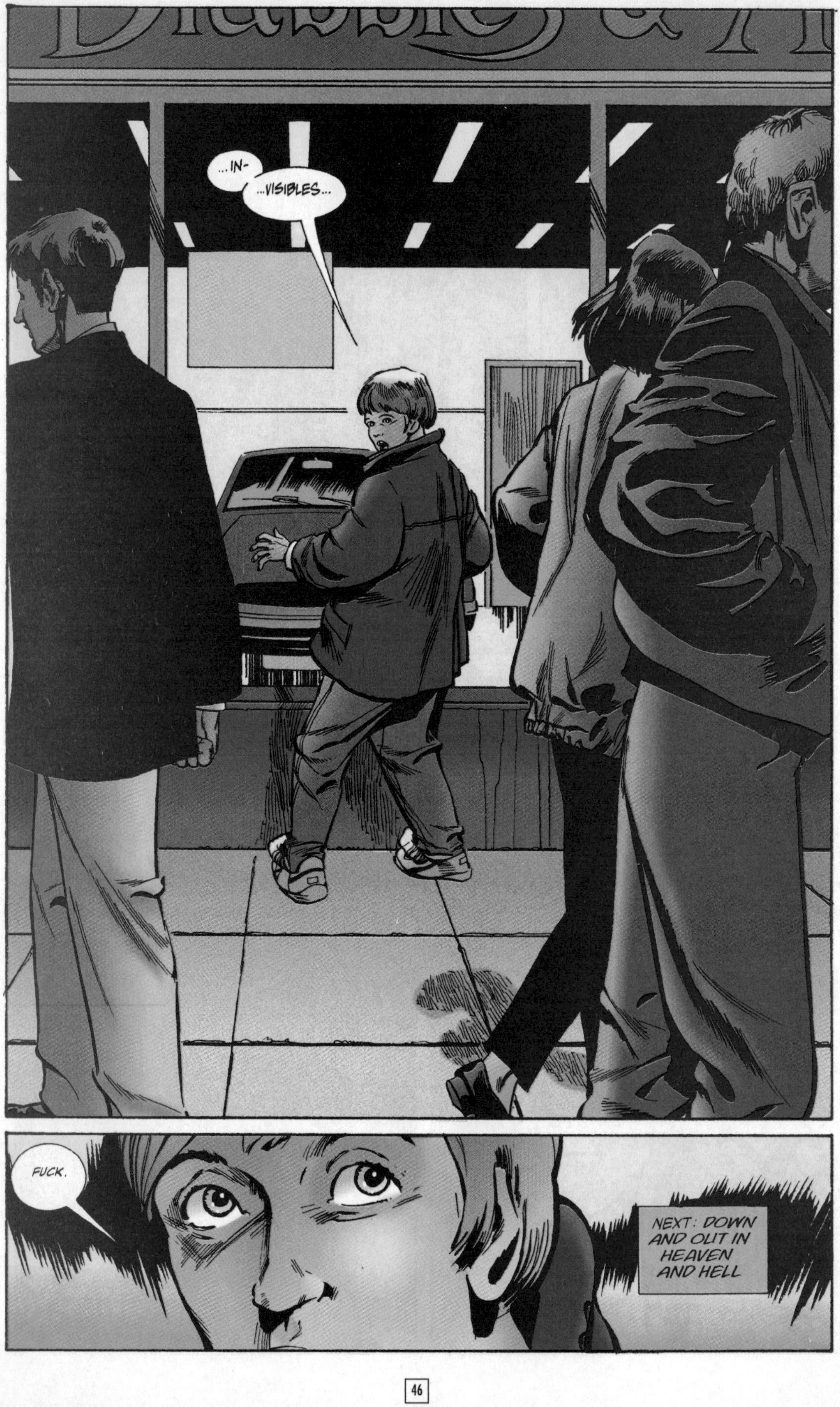
...IN-
...VISIBLES...
FUCK.
NEXT: DOWN AND OUT IN HEAVEN AND HELL

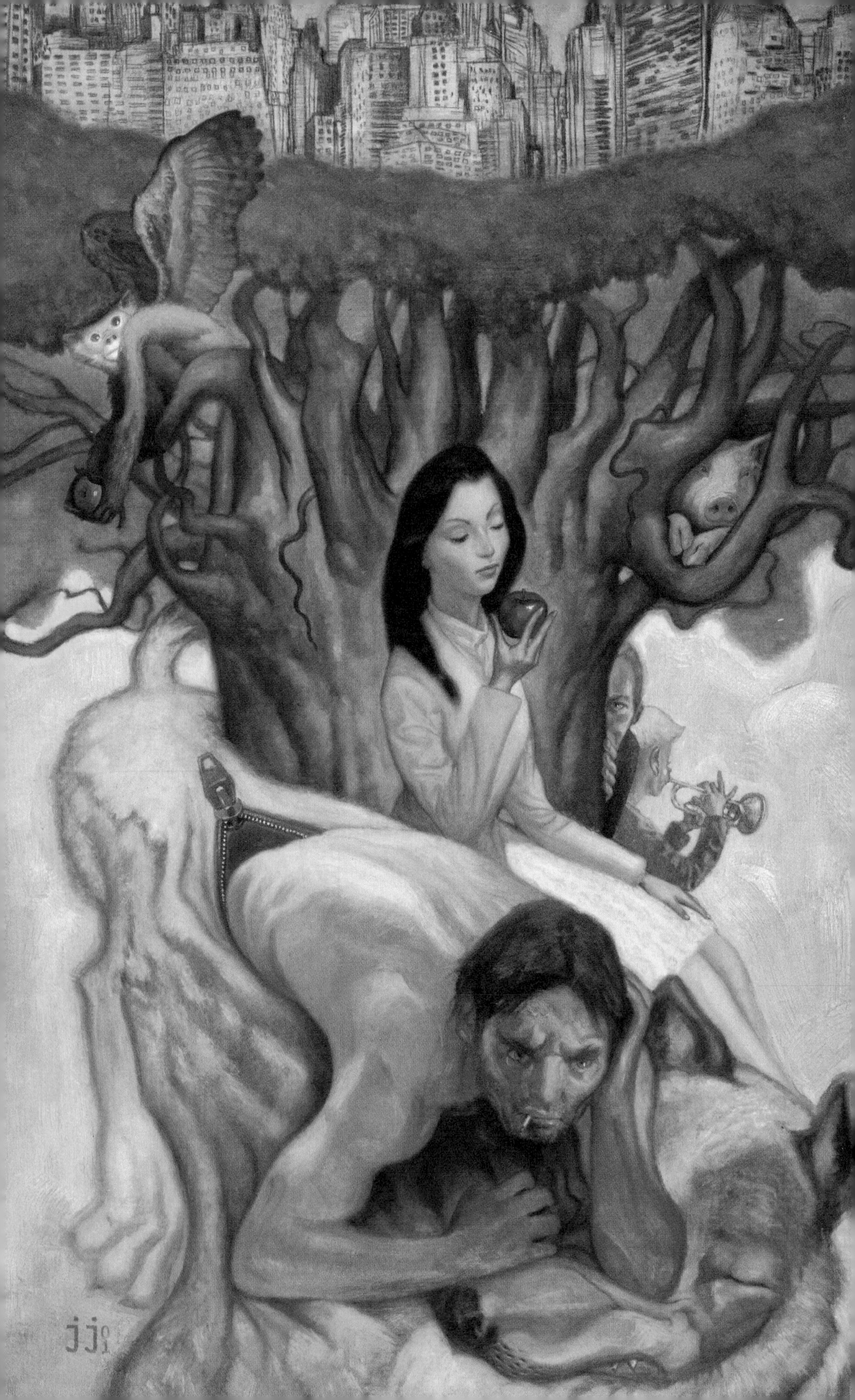

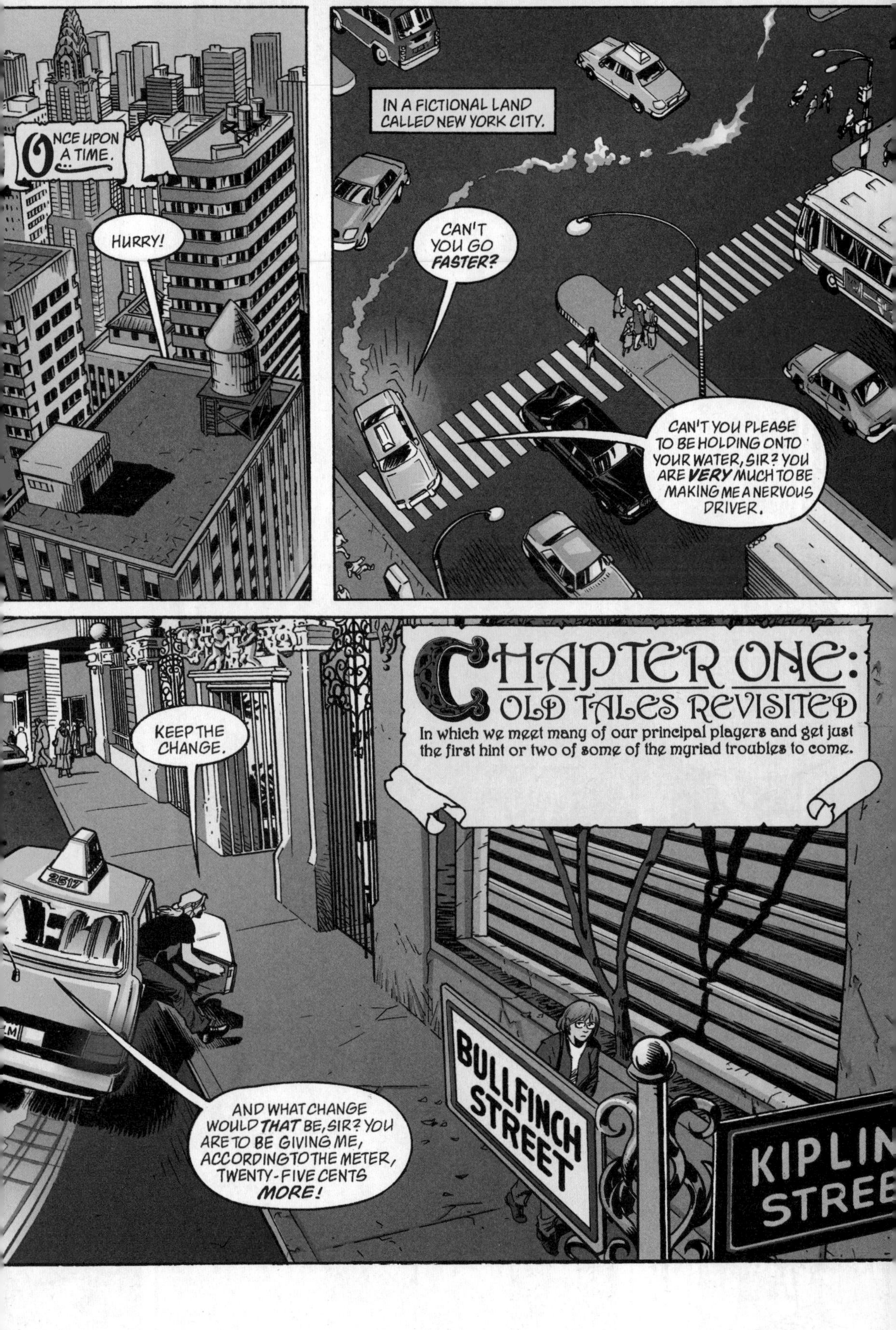
ONCE UPON A TIME.
HURRY!
IN A FICTIONAL LAND CALLED NEW YORK CITY.
CAN'T YOU GO FASTER?
CAN'T YOU PLEASE TO BE HOLDING ONTO YOUR WATER, SIR? YOU ARE VERY MUCH TO BE MAKING ME A NERVOUS DRIVER.
CHAPTER ONE: OLD TALES REVISITED
In which we meet many of our principal players and get just the first hint or two of some of the myriad troubles to come.
KEEP THE CHANGE.
2517
AND WHAT CHANGE WOULD THAT BE, SIR? YOU ARE TO BE GIVING ME, ACCORDING TO THE METER, TWENTY-FIVE CENTS MORE!
BULLFINCH STREET
KIPLIN
STREE

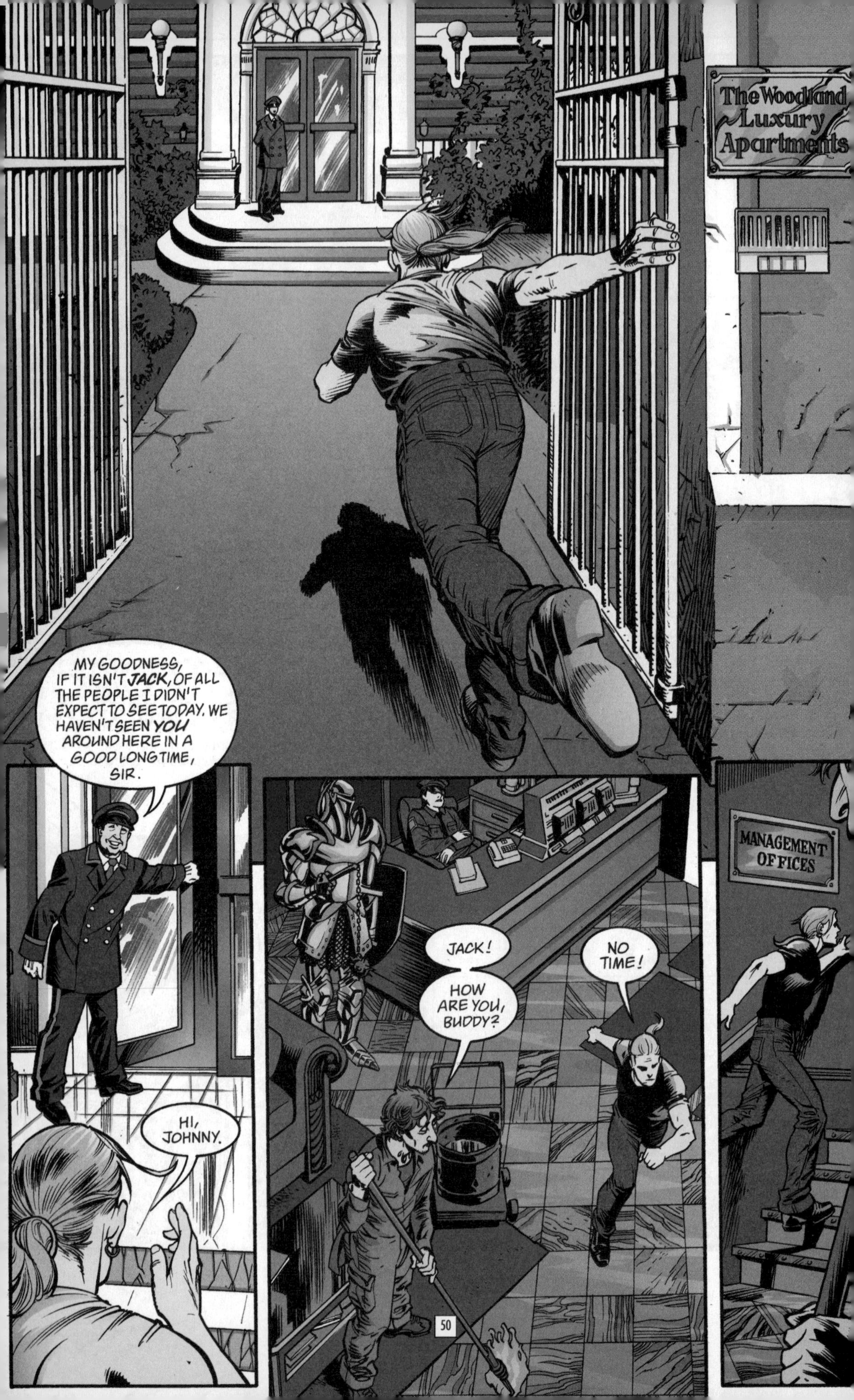
The Woodland Luxury Apartments
MY GOODNESS, IF IT ISN'T JACK, OF ALL THE PEOPLE I DIDN'T EXPECT TO SEE TODAY. WE HAVEN'T SEEN YOU AROUND HERE IN A GOOD LONG TIME, SIR.
HI, JOHNNY.
JACK!
HOW ARE YOU, BUDDY?
NO TIME!
MANAGEMENT OFFICES

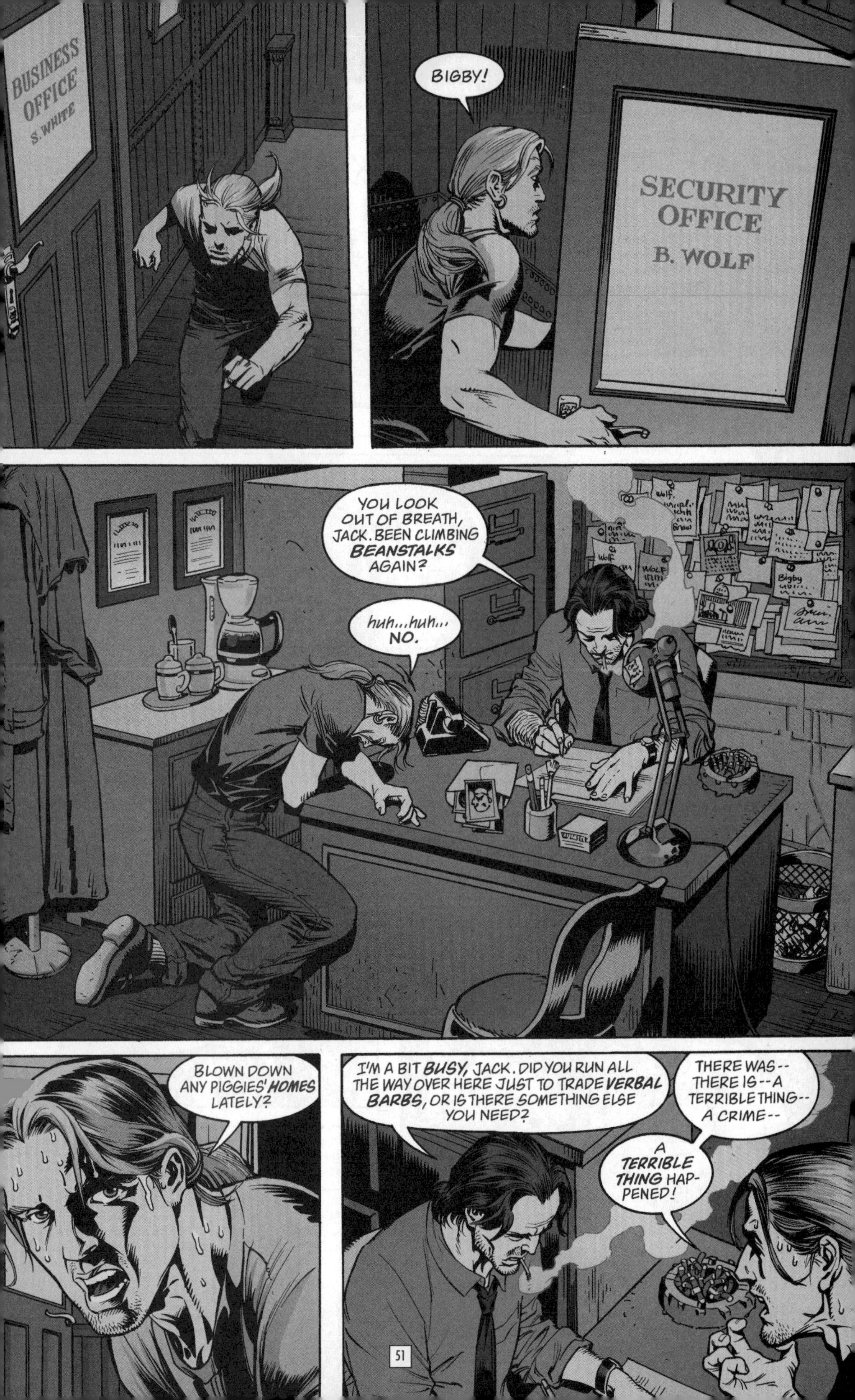
BUSINESS OFFICE S. WHITE
BIGBY!
SECURITY OFFICE B. WOLF
YOU LOOK OUT OF BREATH, JACK. BEEN CLIMBING BEANSTALKS AGAIN?
huh...huh... NO.
BLOWN DOWN ANY PIGGIES' HOMES LATELY?
I'M A BIT BUSY, JACK. DID YOU RUN ALL THE WAY OVER HERE JUST TO TRADE VERBAL BARBS, OR IS THERE SOMETHING ELSE YOU NEED?
THERE WAS-- THERE IS--A TERRIBLE THING--A CRIME--
A TERRIBLE THING HAPPENED!

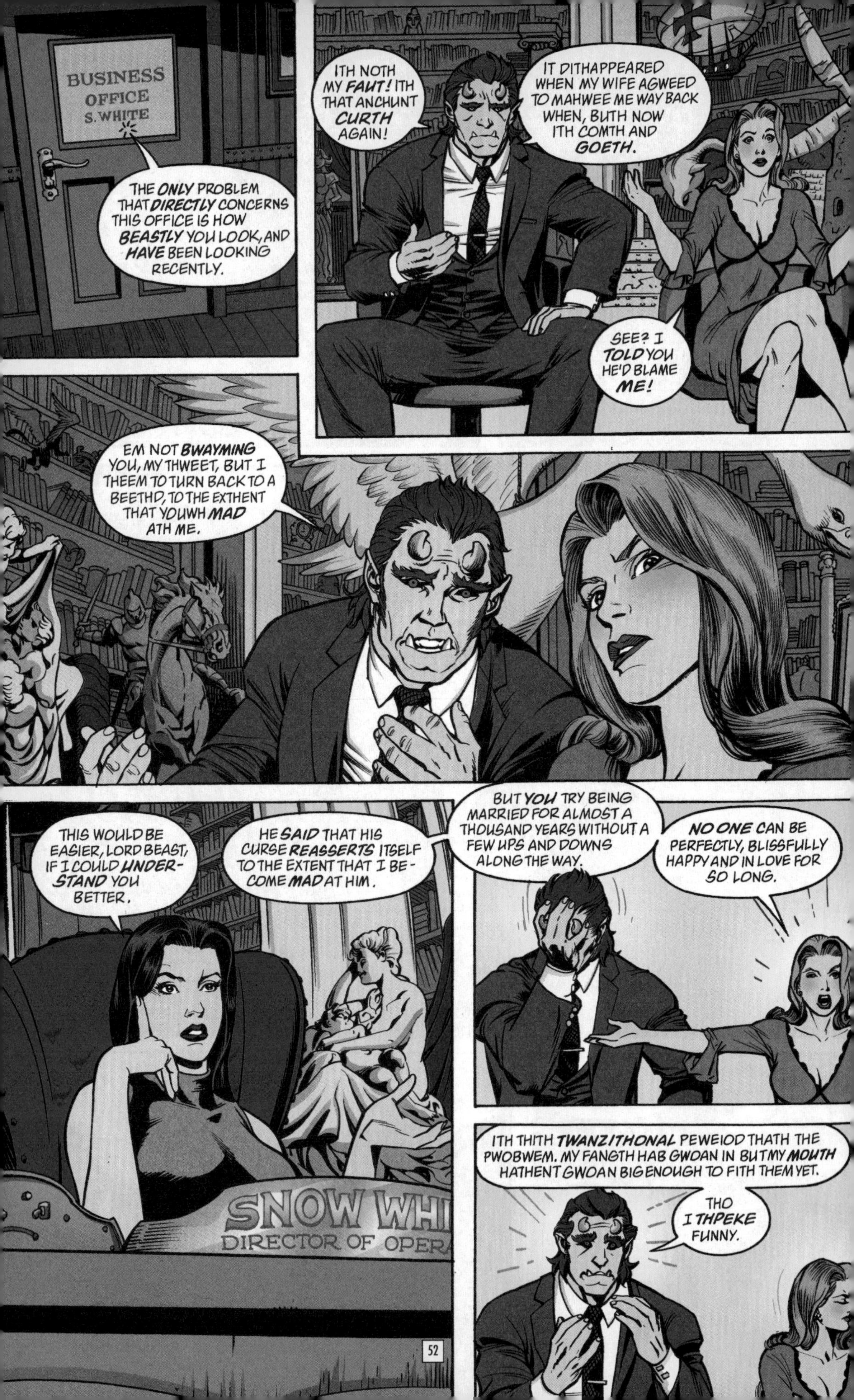
BUSINESS OFFICE S. WHITE
THE ONLY PROBLEM THAT DIRECTLY CONCERNS THIS OFFICE IS HOW BEASTLY YOU LOOK, AND HAVE BEEN LOOKING RECENTLY.
ITH NOTH MY FAUT! ITH THAT ANCHUNT CURTH AGAIN!
IT DITHAPPEARED WHEN MY WIFE AGWEED TO MAHWEE ME WAY BACK WHEN, BUTH NOW ITH COMTH AND GOETH.
SEE? I TOLD YOU HE'D BLAME ME!
EM NOT BWAYMING YOU, MY THWEET, BUT I THEEM TO TURN BACK TO A BEETHD, TO THE EXTHENT THAT YOUWH MAD ATH ME.
THIS WOULD BE EASIER, LORD BEAST, IF I COULD UNDER-STAND YOU BETTER.
HE SAID THAT HIS CURSE REASSERTS ITSELF TO THE EXTENT THAT I BE-COME MAD AT HIM.
SNOW WHI
DIRECTOR OF OPERA
BUT YOU TRY BEING MARRIED FOR ALMOST A THOUSAND YEARS WITHOUT A FEW UPS AND DOWNS ALONG THE WAY.
NO ONE CAN BE PERFECTLY, BLISSFULLY HAPPY AND IN LOVE FOR SO LONG.
ITH THITH TWANZITHONAL PEWEIOD THATH THE PWOBWEM. MY FANGTH HAB GWOAN IN BUT MY MOUTH HATHENT GWOAN BIG ENOUGH TO FITH THEM YET.
THO I THPEKE FUNNY.

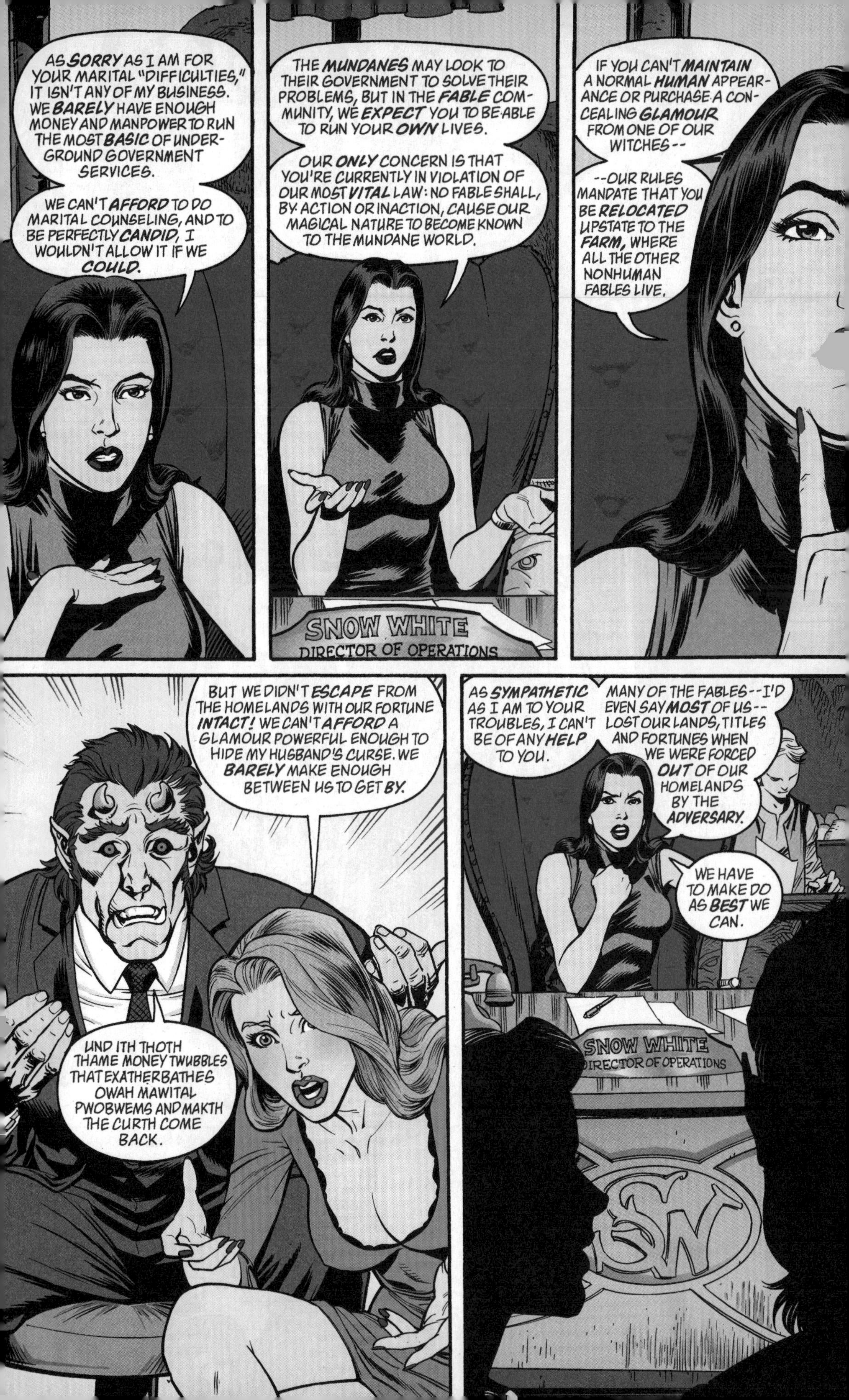
AS SORRY AS I AM FOR YOUR MARITAL "DIFFICULTIES," IT ISN'T ANY OF MY BUSINESS. WE BARELY HAVE ENOUGH MONEY AND MANPOWER TO RUN THE MOST BASIC OF UNDERGROUND GOVERNMENT SERVICES.
WE CAN'T AFFORD TO DO MARITAL COUNSELING, AND TO BE PERFECTLY CANDID, I WOULDN'T ALLOW IT IF WE COULD.
THE MUNDANES MAY LOOK TO THEIR GOVERNMENT TO SOLVE THEIR PROBLEMS, BUT IN THE FABLE COMMUNITY, WE EXPECT YOU TO BE ABLE TO RUN YOUR OWN LIVES.
OUR ONLY CONCERN IS THAT YOU'RE CURRENTLY IN VIOLATION OF OUR MOST VITAL LAW: NO FABLE SHALL, BY ACTION OR INACTION, CAUSE OUR MAGICAL NATURE TO BECOME KNOWN TO THE MUNDANE WORLD.
SNOW WHITE
DIRECTOR OF OPERATIONS
IF YOU CAN'T MAINTAIN A NORMAL HUMAN APPEARANCE OR PURCHASE A CONCEALING GLAMOUR FROM ONE OF OUR WITCHES --
--OUR RULES MANDATE THAT YOU BE RELOCATED UPSTATE TO THE FARM, WHERE ALL THE OTHER NONHUMAN FABLES LIVE.
BUT WE DIDN'T ESCAPE FROM THE HOMELANDS WITH OUR FORTUNE INTACT! WE CAN'T AFFORD A GLAMOUR POWERFUL ENOUGH TO HIDE MY HUSBAND'S CURSE. WE BARELY MAKE ENOUGH BETWEEN US TO GET BY.
UND ITH THOTH THAME MONEY TWUBBLES THAT EXATHERBATHES OWAH MAWITAL PWOBWEMS AND MAKTH THE CURTH COME BACK.
AS SYMPATHETIC AS I AM TO YOUR TROUBLES, I CAN'T BE OF ANY HELP TO YOU.
MANY OF THE FABLES--I'D EVEN SAY MOST OF US--LOST OUR LANDS, TITLES AND FORTUNES WHEN WE WERE FORCED OUT OF OUR HOMELANDS BY THE ADVERSARY.
WE HAVE TO MAKE DO AS BEST WE CAN.
SNOW WHITE
DIRECTOR OF OPERATIONS

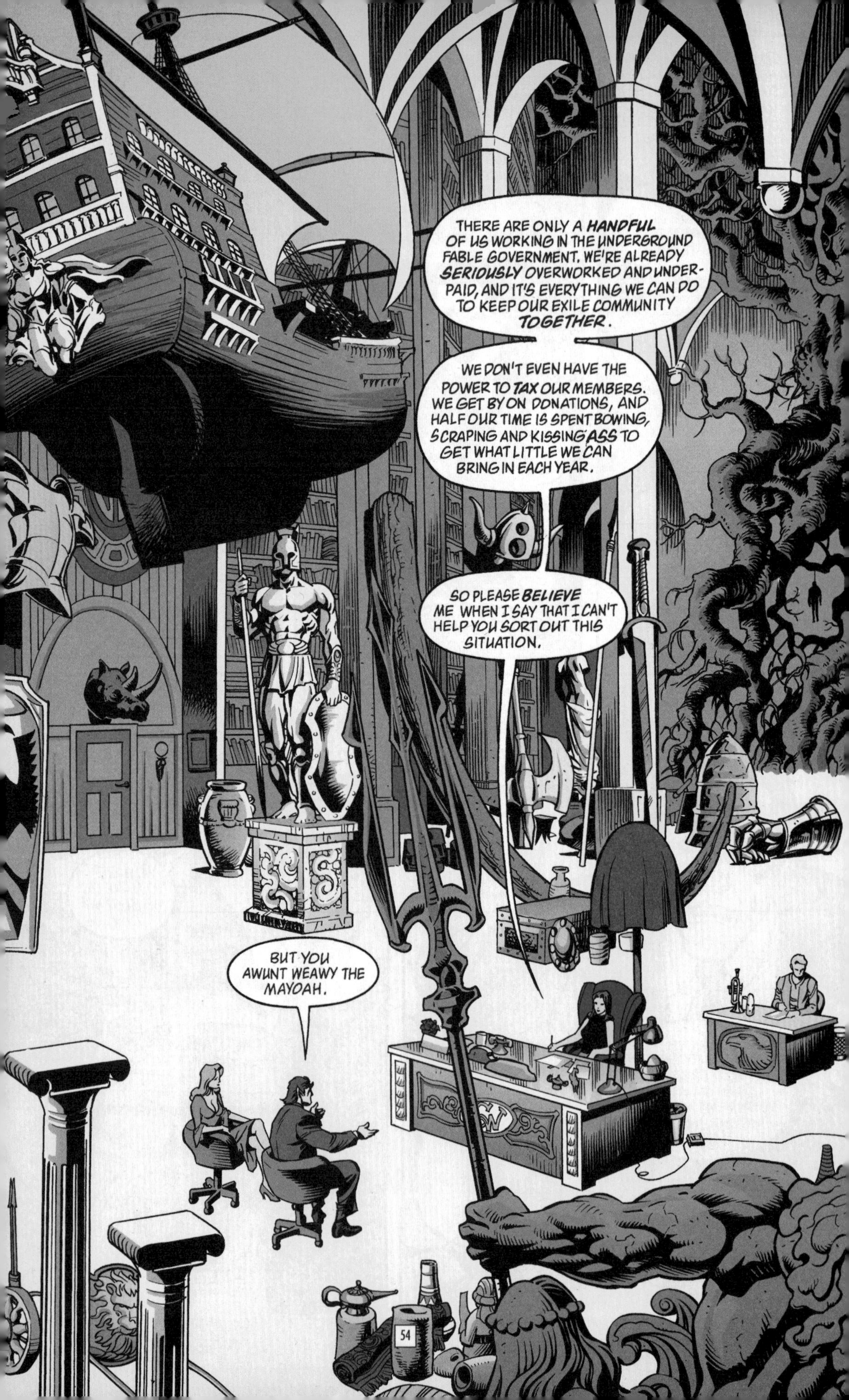
THERE ARE ONLY A HANDFUL OF US WORKING IN THE UNDERGROUND FABLE GOVERNMENT. WE'RE ALREADY SERIOUSLY OVERWORKED AND UNDER-PAID, AND IT'S EVERYTHING WE CAN DO TO KEEP OUR EXILE COMMUNITY TOGETHER.
WE DON'T EVEN HAVE THE POWER TO TAX OUR MEMBERS. WE GET BY ON DONATIONS, AND HALF OUR TIME IS SPENT BOWING, SCRAPING AND KISSING ASS TO GET WHAT LITTLE WE CAN BRING IN EACH YEAR.
SO PLEASE BELIEVE ME WHEN I SAY THAT I CAN'T HELP YOU SORT OUT THIS SITUATION.
BUT YOU AWUNT WEAWY THE MAYOAH.
54

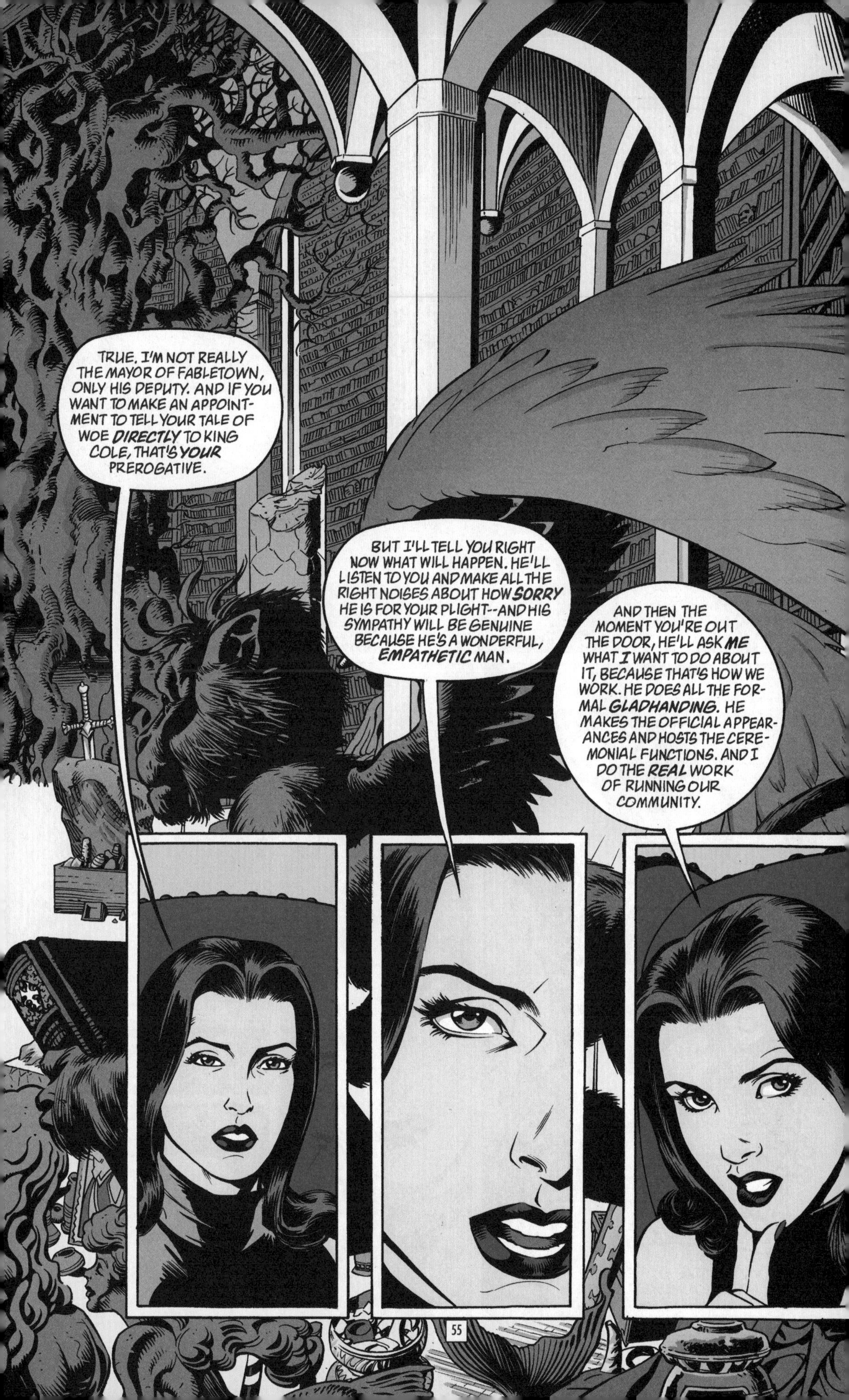
TRUE. I'M NOT REALLY THE MAYOR OF FABLETOWN, ONLY HIS DEPUTY. AND IF YOU WANT TO MAKE AN APPOINTMENT TO TELL YOUR TALE OF WOE DIRECTLY TO KING COLE, THAT'S YOUR PREROGATIVE.
BUT I'LL TELL YOU RIGHT NOW WHAT WILL HAPPEN. HE'LL LISTEN TO YOU AND MAKE ALL THE RIGHT NOISES ABOUT HOW SORRY HE IS FOR YOUR PLIGHT--AND HIS SYMPATHY WILL BE GENUINE BECAUSE HE'S A WONDERFUL, EMPATHETIC MAN.
AND THEN THE MOMENT YOU'RE OUT THE DOOR, HE'LL ASK ME WHAT I WANT TO DO ABOUT IT, BECAUSE THAT'S HOW WE WORK. HE DOES ALL THE FORMAL GLADHANDING. HE MAKES THE OFFICIAL APPEARANCES AND HOSTS THE CEREMONIAL FUNCTIONS. AND I DO THE REAL WORK OF RUNNING OUR COMMUNITY.

FOR BETTER OR **WORSE**, YOU'VE JUST HAD YOUR **APPEAL** TO CITY HALL.

YOU DIVORCED **YOUR** PRINCE **CENTURIES** AGO. YOU HAVE **NO IDEA** HOW HARD IT IS TO KEEP A MARRIAGE GOING SO LONG.

NOWAH, DEAH. THEWES NO WEASON TO GET **PERSONOAH**.

SNOW WHITE
DIRECTOR OF ~~OPE~~RATIONS

DON'T GET **PERSONAL**? AFTER SHE OPENLY **CRITICIZED** OUR MARRIED LIFE?

I DID **NO SUCH THING**.

AND JUST WHO IS **SHE** TO CRITICIZE **ANYONE'S** PERSONAL LIFE, AFTER WHAT **I** HEARD ABOUT HER TAWDRY LITTLE ADVENTURE WITH THOSE SEVEN DWARVES?

OKAY, FOLKS, BUSINESS IS PILING **UP** AND WE NEED TO MOVE THINGS ALONG TO MISS WHITE'S **NEXT** APPOINTMENT.

SNOW WHITE
DIRECTOR OF ~~OPERATIONS~~

BUT--?

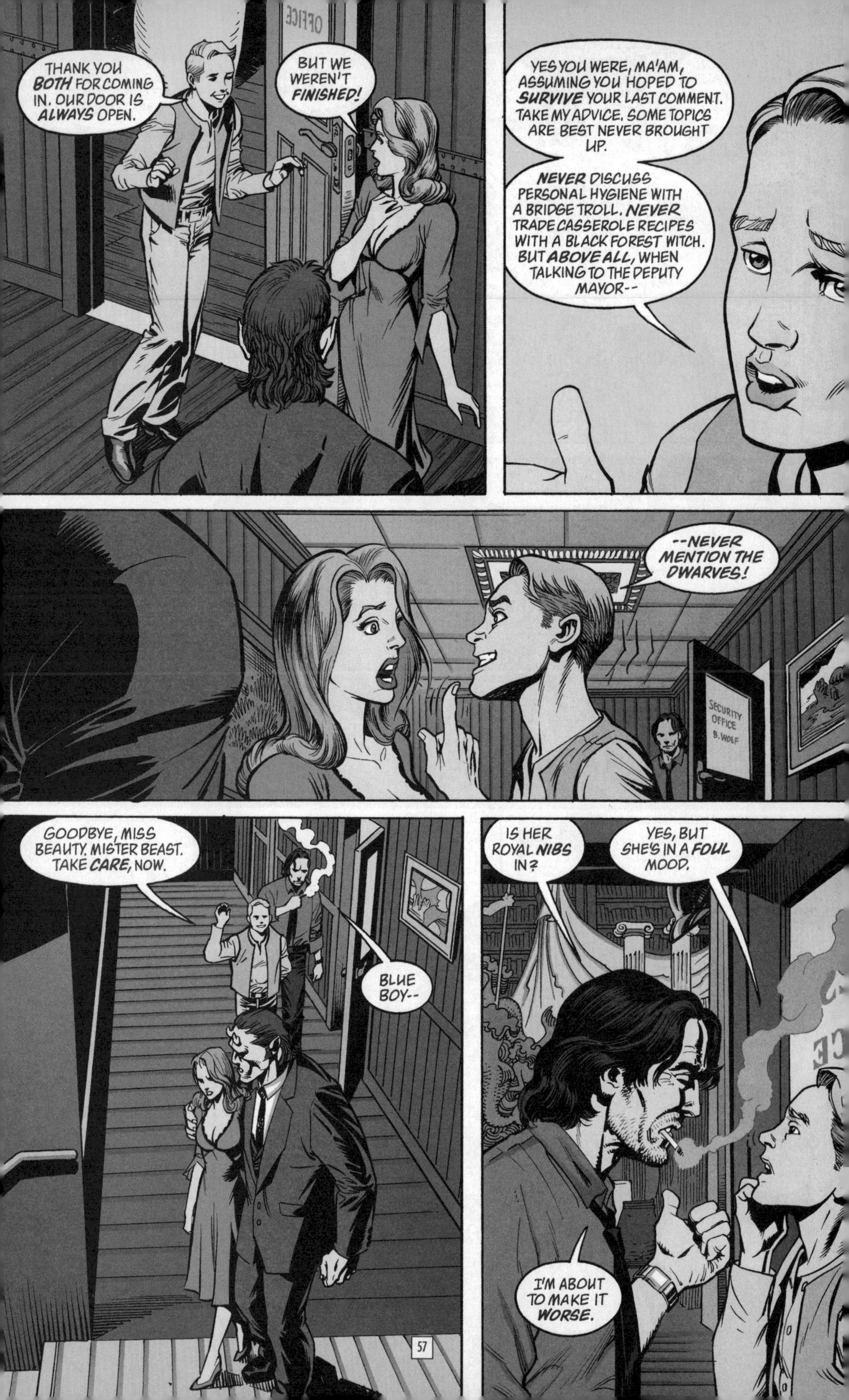
THANK YOU BOTH FOR COMING IN. OUR DOOR IS ALWAYS OPEN.
BUT WE WEREN'T FINISHED!
OFFICE
YES YOU WERE, MA'AM, ASSUMING YOU HOPED TO SURVIVE YOUR LAST COMMENT. TAKE MY ADVICE. SOME TOPICS ARE BEST NEVER BROUGHT UP.
NEVER DISCUSS PERSONAL HYGIENE WITH A BRIDGE TROLL. NEVER TRADE CASSEROLE RECIPES WITH A BLACK FOREST WITCH. BUT ABOVE ALL, WHEN TALKING TO THE DEPUTY MAYOR--
--NEVER MENTION THE DWARVES!
SECURITY OFFICE B. WOLF
GOODBYE, MISS BEAUTY. MISTER BEAST. TAKE CARE, NOW.
BLUE BOY--
IS HER ROYAL NIBS IN?
YES, BUT SHE'S IN A FOUL MOOD.
I'M ABOUT TO MAKE IT WORSE.

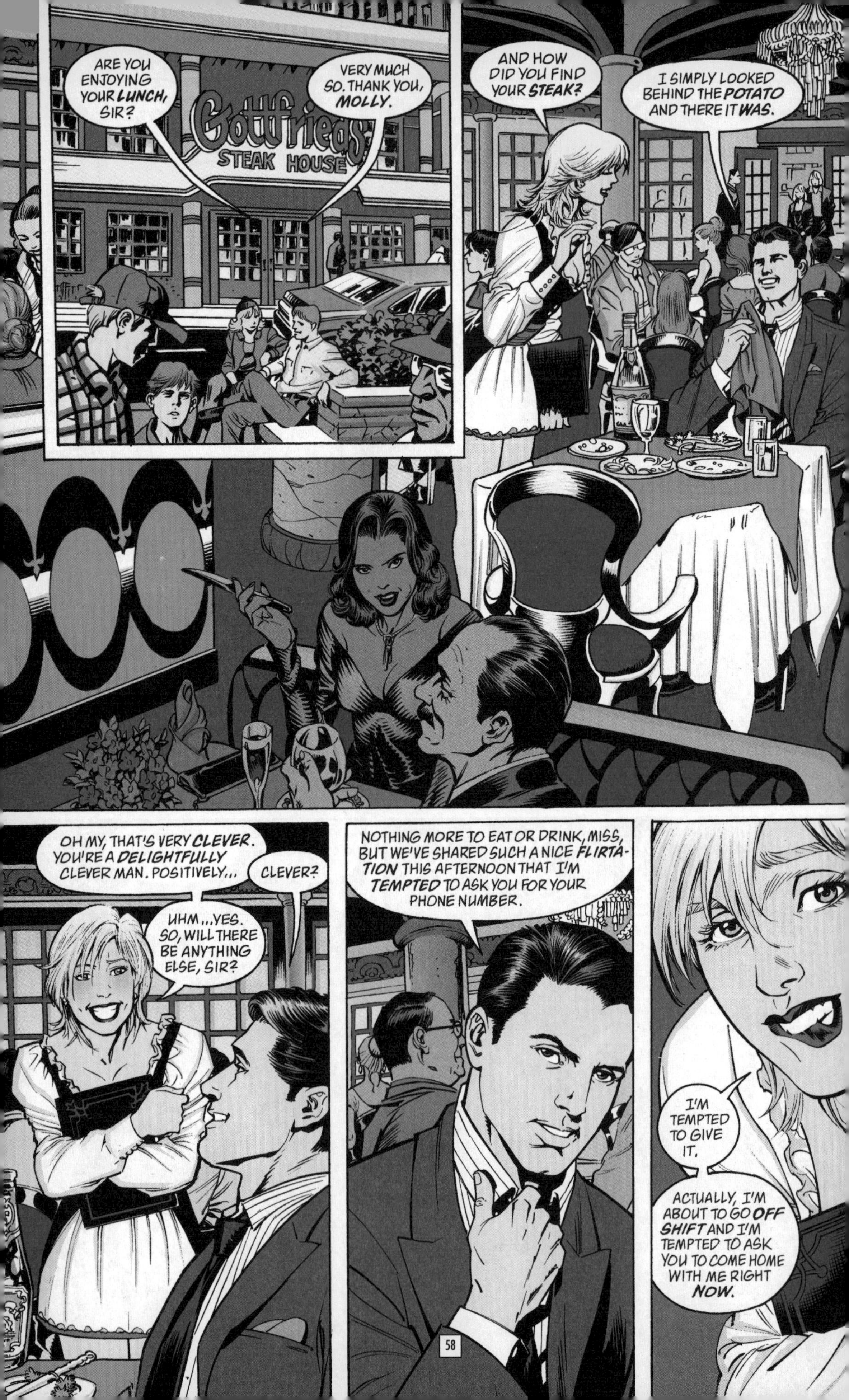
ARE YOU ENJOYING YOUR LUNCH, SIR?
Gottfrieds STEAK HOUSE
VERY MUCH SO. THANK YOU, MOLLY.
AND HOW DID YOU FIND YOUR STEAK?
I SIMPLY LOOKED BEHIND THE POTATO AND THERE IT WAS.
OH MY, THAT'S VERY CLEVER. YOU'RE A DELIGHTFULLY CLEVER MAN. POSITIVELY...
CLEVER?
UHM...YES. SO, WILL THERE BE ANYTHING ELSE, SIR?
NOTHING MORE TO EAT OR DRINK, MISS, BUT WE'VE SHARED SUCH A NICE FLIRTATION THIS AFTERNOON THAT I'M TEMPTED TO ASK YOU FOR YOUR PHONE NUMBER.
I'M TEMPTED TO GIVE IT.
ACTUALLY, I'M ABOUT TO GO OFF SHIFT AND I'M TEMPTED TO ASK YOU TO COME HOME WITH ME RIGHT NOW.

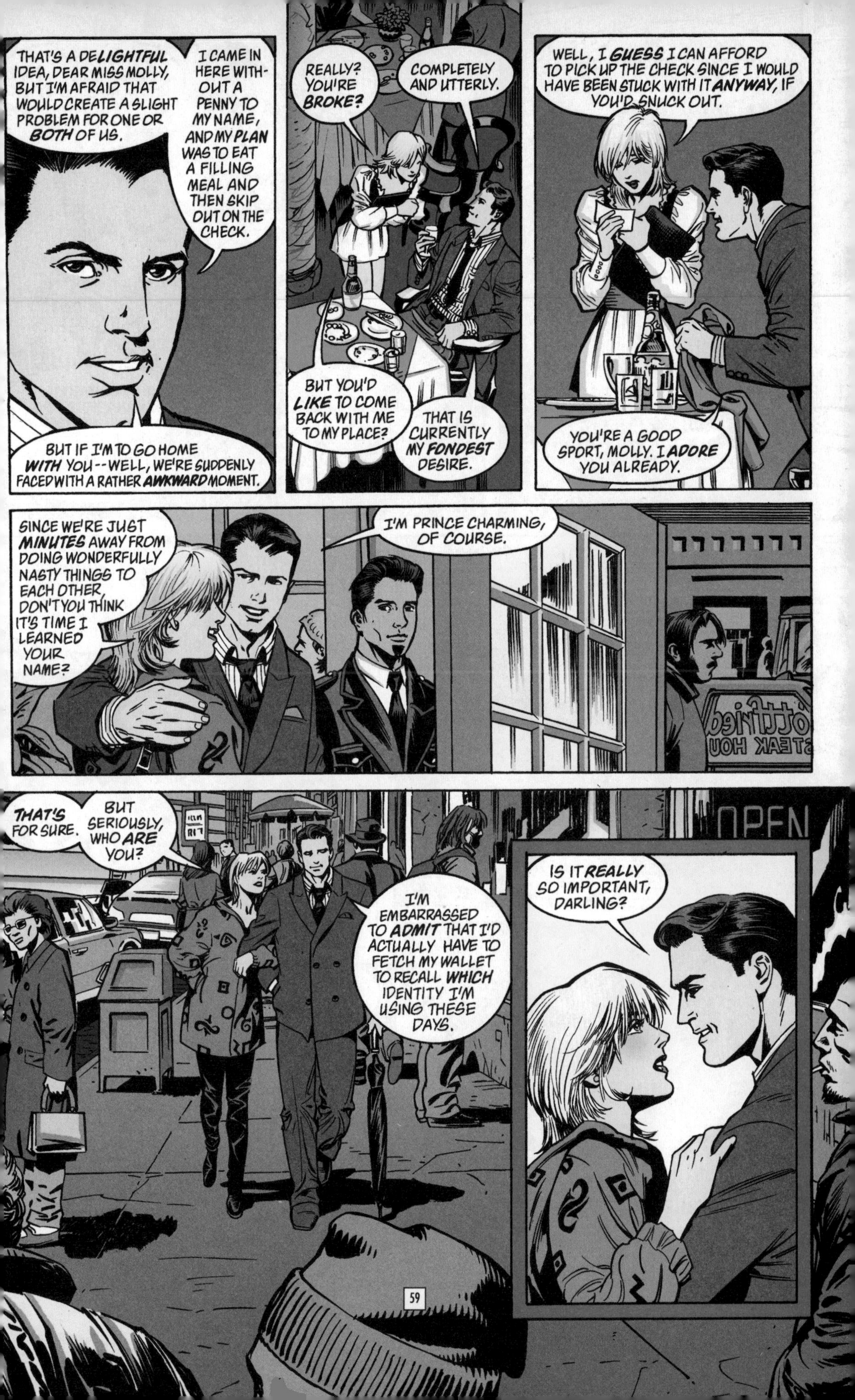

THAT'S A DELIGHTFUL IDEA, DEAR MISS MOLLY, BUT I'M AFRAID THAT WOULD CREATE A SLIGHT PROBLEM FOR ONE OR BOTH OF US.
I CAME IN HERE WITH-OUT A PENNY TO MY NAME, AND MY PLAN WAS TO EAT A FILLING MEAL AND THEN SKIP OUT ON THE CHECK.
BUT IF I'M TO GO HOME WITH YOU--WELL, WE'RE SUDDENLY FACED WITH A RATHER AWKWARD MOMENT.
REALLY? YOU'RE BROKE?
COMPLETELY AND UTTERLY.
BUT YOU'D LIKE TO COME BACK WITH ME TO MY PLACE?
THAT IS CURRENTLY MY FONDEST DESIRE.
WELL, I GUESS I CAN AFFORD TO PICK UP THE CHECK SINCE I WOULD HAVE BEEN STUCK WITH IT ANYWAY, IF YOU'D SNUCK OUT.
YOU'RE A GOOD SPORT, MOLLY. I ADORE YOU ALREADY.
SINCE WE'RE JUST MINUTES AWAY FROM DOING WONDERFULLY NASTY THINGS TO EACH OTHER, DON'T YOU THINK IT'S TIME I LEARNED YOUR NAME?
I'M PRINCE CHARMING, OF COURSE.
THAT'S FOR SURE.
BUT SERIOUSLY, WHO ARE YOU?
I'M EMBARRASSED TO ADMIT THAT I'D ACTUALLY HAVE TO FETCH MY WALLET TO RECALL WHICH IDENTITY I'M USING THESE DAYS.
IS IT REALLY SO IMPORTANT, DARLING?
OPEN

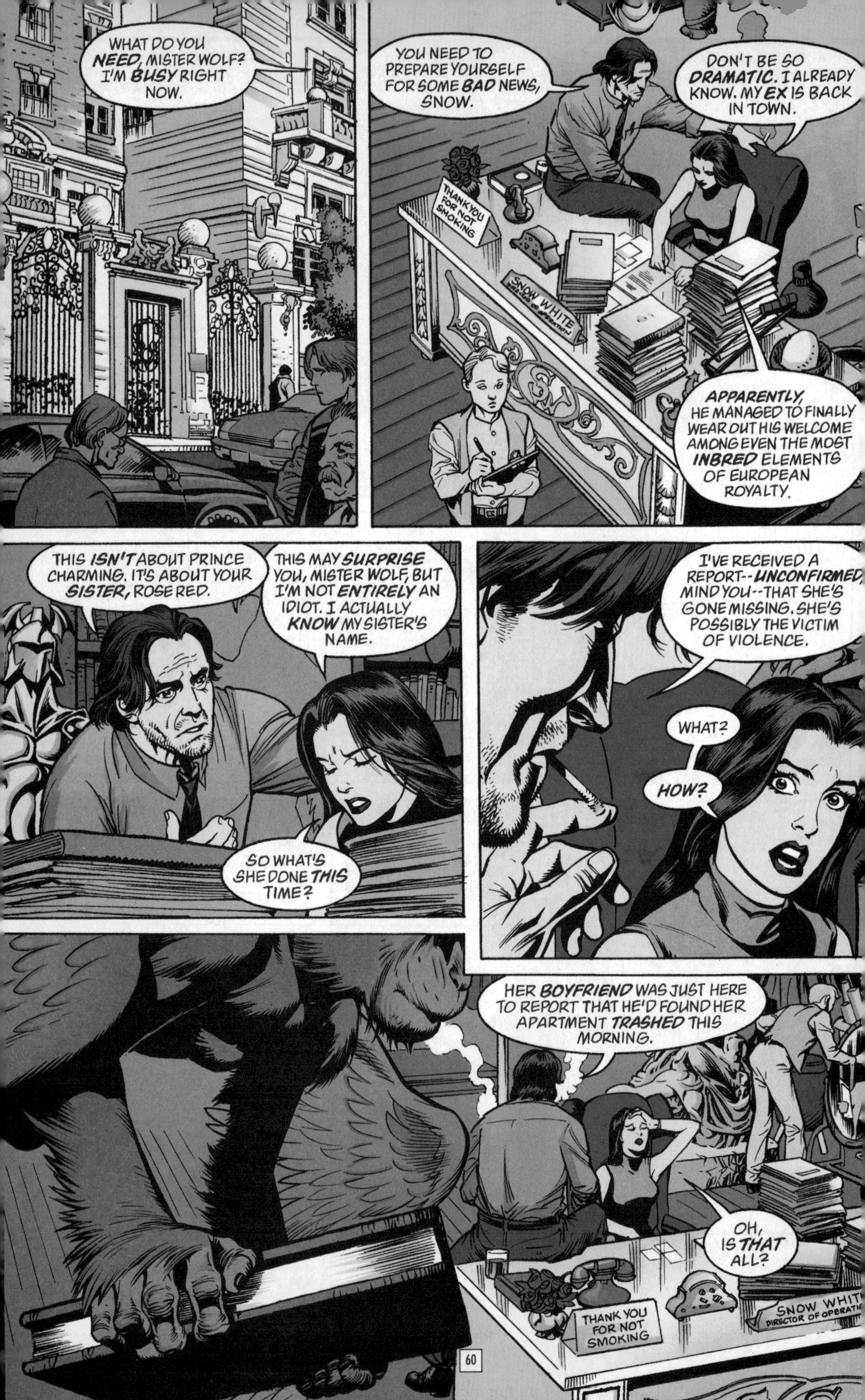
WHAT DO YOU NEED, MISTER WOLF? I'M BUSY RIGHT NOW.
YOU NEED TO PREPARE YOURSELF FOR SOME BAD NEWS, SNOW.
DON'T BE SO DRAMATIC. I ALREADY KNOW. MY EX IS BACK IN TOWN.
THANK YOU FOR NOT SMOKING
SNOW WHITE
APPARENTLY, HE MANAGED TO FINALLY WEAR OUT HIS WELCOME AMONG EVEN THE MOST INBRED ELEMENTS OF EUROPEAN ROYALTY.
THIS ISN'T ABOUT PRINCE CHARMING. IT'S ABOUT YOUR SISTER, ROSE RED.
THIS MAY SURPRISE YOU, MISTER WOLF, BUT I'M NOT ENTIRELY AN IDIOT. I ACTUALLY KNOW MY SISTER'S NAME.
SO WHAT'S SHE DONE THIS TIME?
I'VE RECEIVED A REPORT--UNCONFIRMED, MIND YOU--THAT SHE'S GONE MISSING. SHE'S POSSIBLY THE VICTIM OF VIOLENCE.
WHAT?
HOW?
HER BOYFRIEND WAS JUST HERE TO REPORT THAT HE'D FOUND HER APARTMENT TRASHED THIS MORNING.
OH, IS THAT ALL?
THANK YOU FOR NOT SMOKING
SNOW WHIT
DIRECTOR OF OPERATI

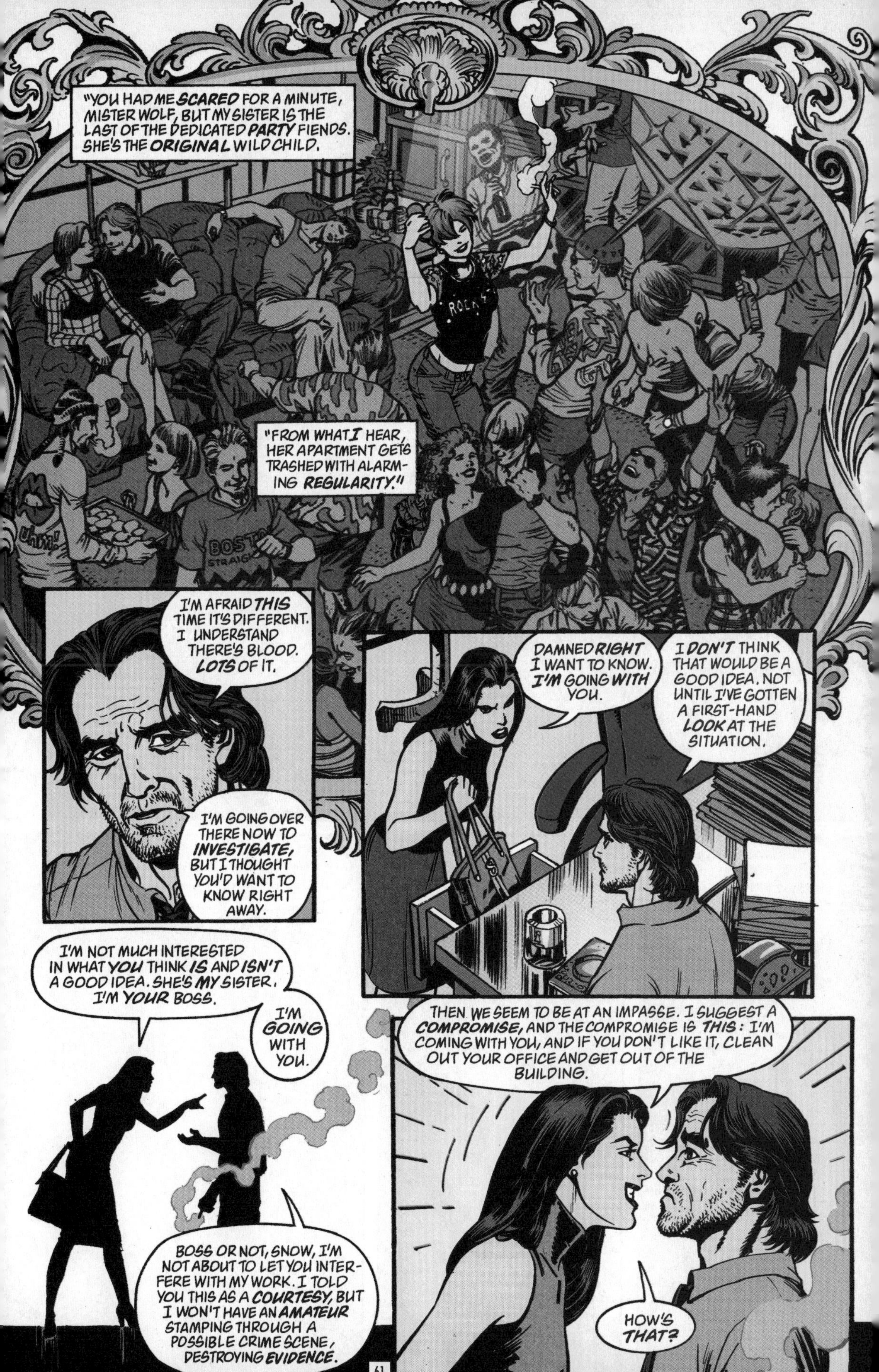
"YOU HAD ME SCARED FOR A MINUTE, MISTER WOLF, BUT MY SISTER IS THE LAST OF THE DEDICATED PARTY FIENDS. SHE'S THE ORIGINAL WILD CHILD.
ROCK
BOST
STRAIG
"FROM WHAT I HEAR, HER APARTMENT GETS TRASHED WITH ALARMING REGULARITY."
I'M AFRAID THIS TIME IT'S DIFFERENT. I UNDERSTAND THERE'S BLOOD. LOTS OF IT.
I'M GOING OVER THERE NOW TO INVESTIGATE, BUT I THOUGHT YOU'D WANT TO KNOW RIGHT AWAY.
DAMNED RIGHT I WANT TO KNOW. I'M GOING WITH YOU.
I DON'T THINK THAT WOULD BE A GOOD IDEA. NOT UNTIL I'VE GOTTEN A FIRST-HAND LOOK AT THE SITUATION.
I'M NOT MUCH INTERESTED IN WHAT YOU THINK IS AND ISN'T A GOOD IDEA. SHE'S MY SISTER. I'M YOUR BOSS.
I'M GOING WITH YOU.
BOSS OR NOT, SNOW, I'M NOT ABOUT TO LET YOU INTERFERE WITH MY WORK. I TOLD YOU THIS AS A COURTESY, BUT I WON'T HAVE AN AMATEUR STAMPING THROUGH A POSSIBLE CRIME SCENE, DESTROYING EVIDENCE.
THEN WE SEEM TO BE AT AN IMPASSE. I SUGGEST A COMPROMISE, AND THE COMPROMISE IS THIS: I'M COMING WITH YOU, AND IF YOU DON'T LIKE IT, CLEAN OUT YOUR OFFICE AND GET OUT OF THE BUILDING.
HOW'S THAT?

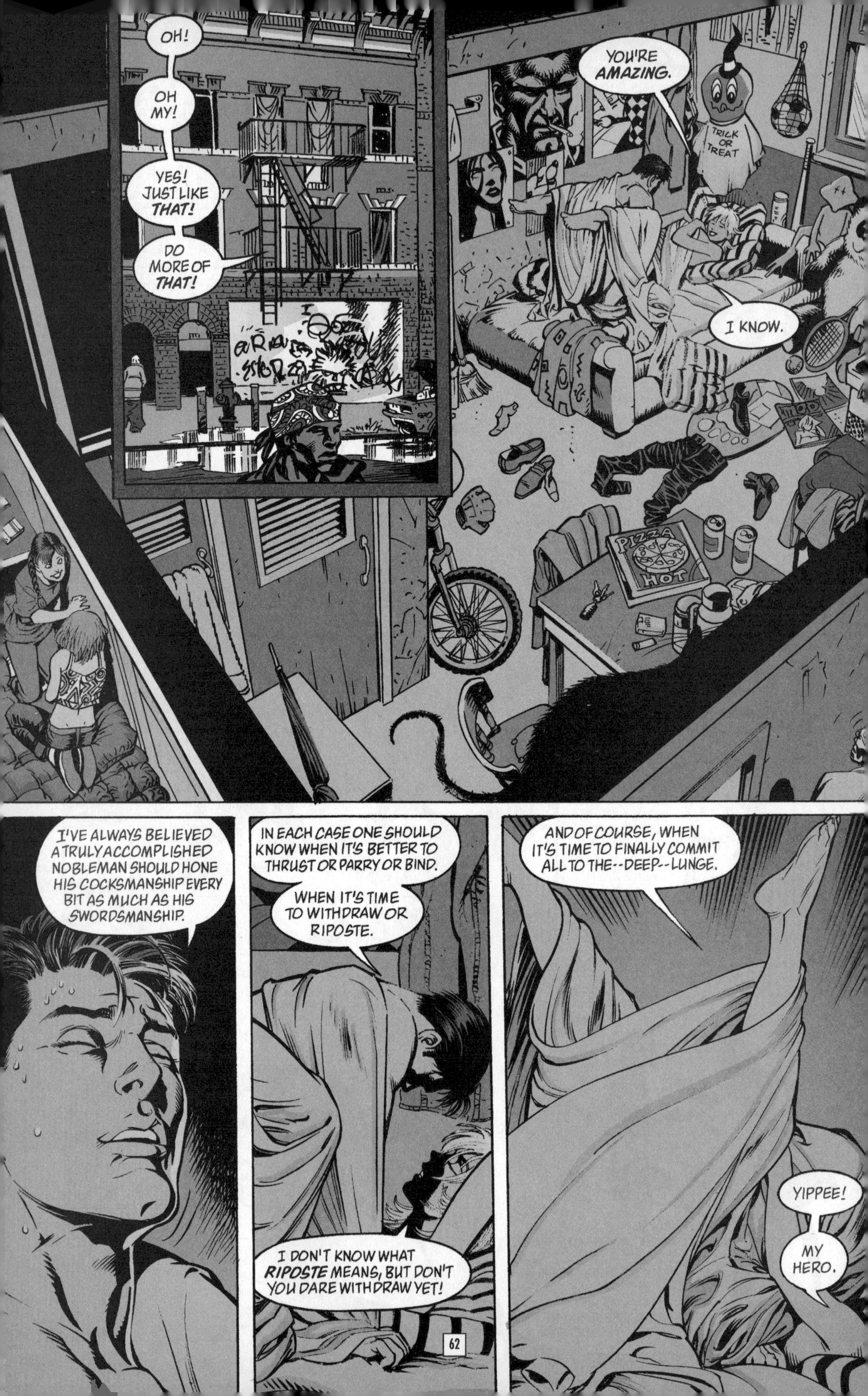
OH!
OH MY!
YES! JUST LIKE THAT!
DO MORE OF THAT!
YOU'RE AMAZING.
TRICK OR TREAT
I KNOW.
PIZZA HOT
I'VE ALWAYS BELIEVED A TRULY ACCOMPLISHED NOBLEMAN SHOULD HONE HIS COCKSMANSHIP EVERY BIT AS MUCH AS HIS SWORDSMANSHIP.
IN EACH CASE ONE SHOULD KNOW WHEN IT'S BETTER TO THRUST OR PARRY OR BIND.
WHEN IT'S TIME TO WITHDRAW OR RIPOSTE.
I DON'T KNOW WHAT RIPOSTE MEANS, BUT DON'T YOU DARE WITHDRAW YET!
AND OF COURSE, WHEN IT'S TIME TO FINALLY COMMIT ALL TO THE--DEEP--LUNGE.
YIPPEE!
MY HERO.

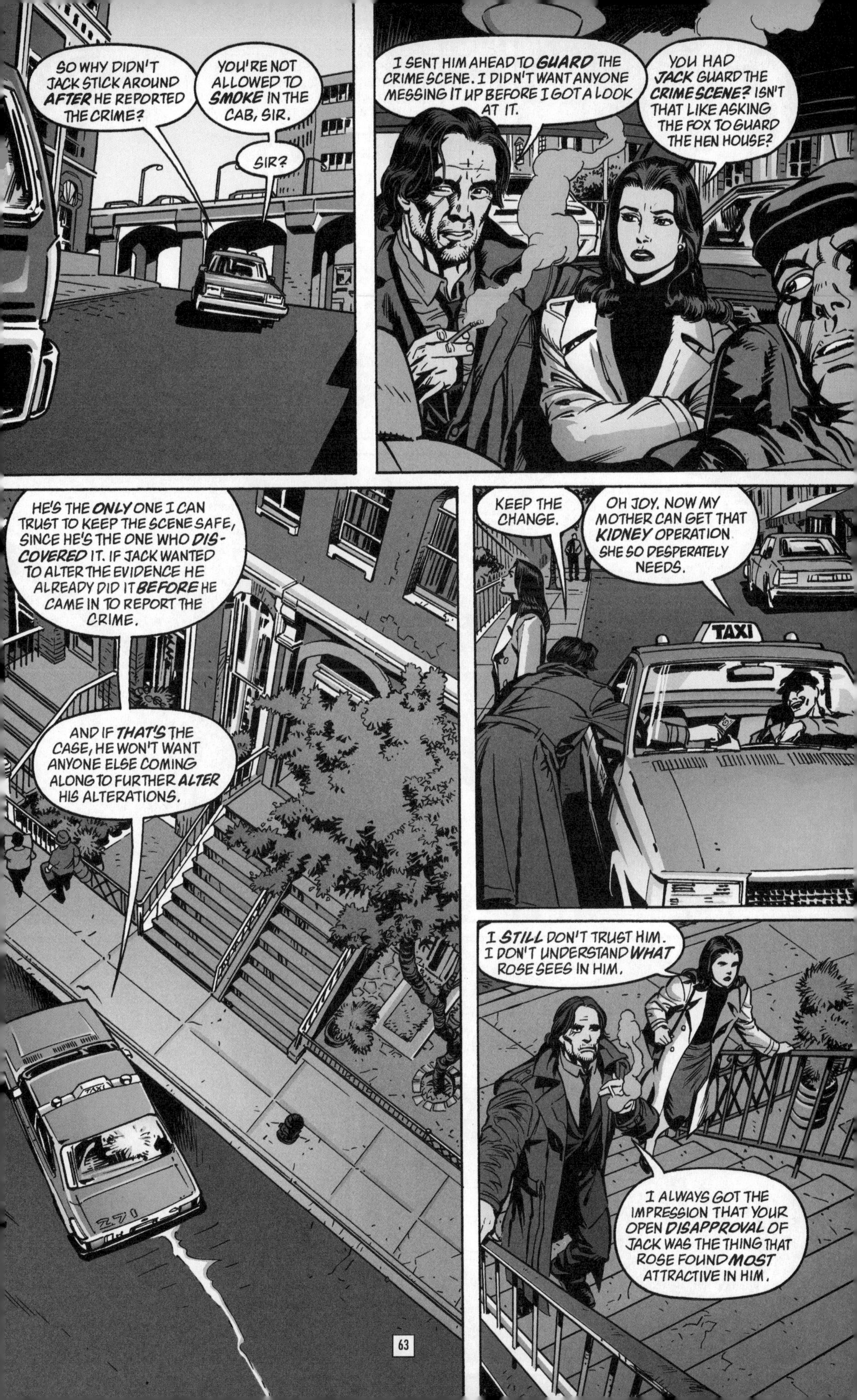
SO WHY DIDN'T JACK STICK AROUND AFTER HE REPORTED THE CRIME?
YOU'RE NOT ALLOWED TO SMOKE IN THE CAB, SIR.
SIR?
I SENT HIM AHEAD TO GUARD THE CRIME SCENE. I DIDN'T WANT ANYONE MESSING IT UP BEFORE I GOT A LOOK AT IT.
YOU HAD JACK GUARD THE CRIME SCENE? ISN'T THAT LIKE ASKING THE FOX TO GUARD THE HEN HOUSE?
HE'S THE ONLY ONE I CAN TRUST TO KEEP THE SCENE SAFE, SINCE HE'S THE ONE WHO DISCOVERED IT. IF JACK WANTED TO ALTER THE EVIDENCE HE ALREADY DID IT BEFORE HE CAME IN TO REPORT THE CRIME.
AND IF THAT'S THE CASE, HE WON'T WANT ANYONE ELSE COMING ALONG TO FURTHER ALTER HIS ALTERATIONS.
KEEP THE CHANGE.
OH JOY. NOW MY MOTHER CAN GET THAT KIDNEY OPERATION SHE SO DESPERATELY NEEDS.
TAXI
I STILL DON'T TRUST HIM. I DON'T UNDERSTAND WHAT ROSE SEES IN HIM.
I ALWAYS GOT THE IMPRESSION THAT YOUR OPEN DISAPPROVAL OF JACK WAS THE THING THAT ROSE FOUND MOST ATTRACTIVE IN HIM.

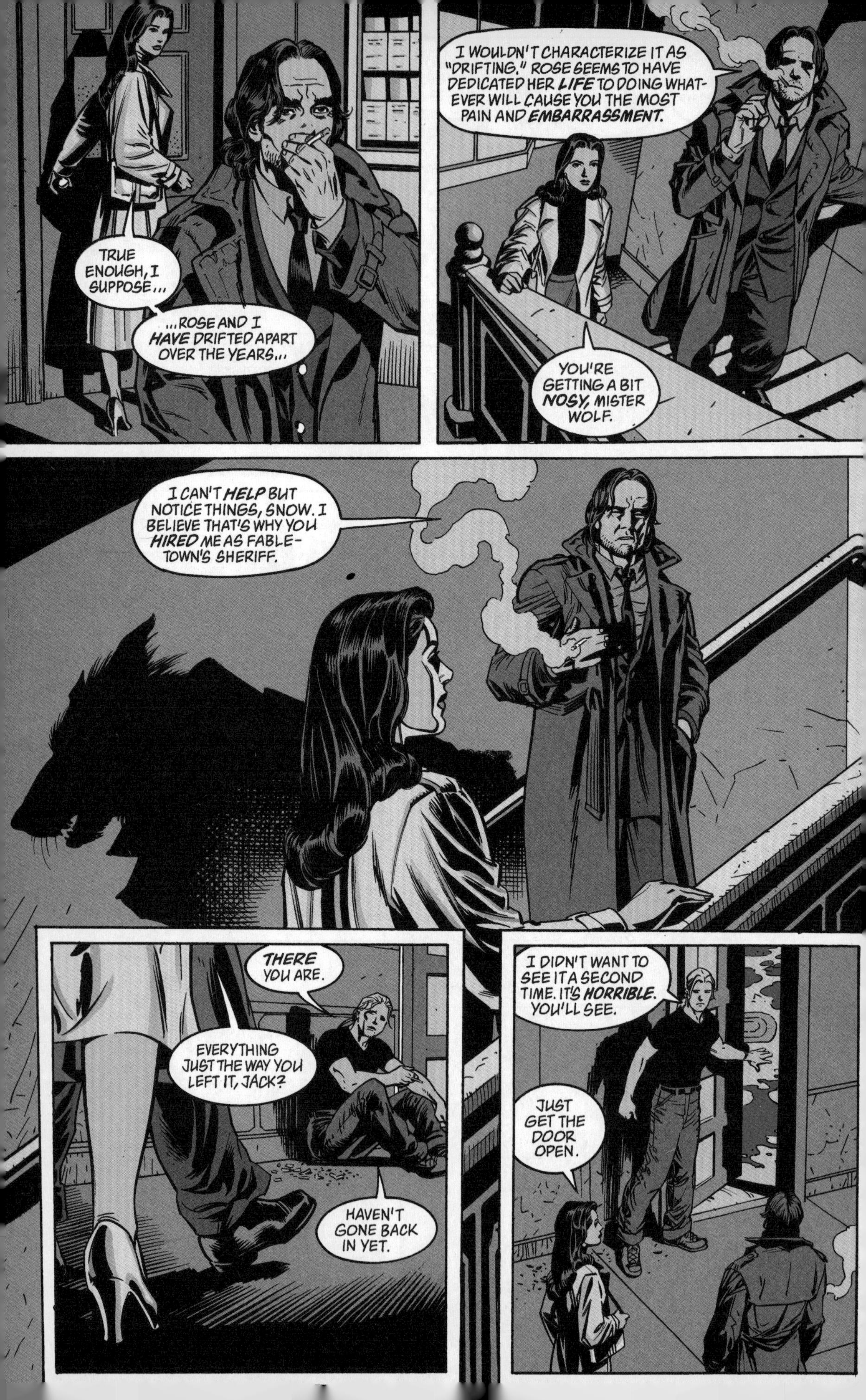
TRUE ENOUGH, I SUPPOSE...
...ROSE AND I HAVE DRIFTED APART OVER THE YEARS...
I WOULDN'T CHARACTERIZE IT AS "DRIFTING." ROSE SEEMS TO HAVE DEDICATED HER LIFE TO DOING WHATEVER WILL CAUSE YOU THE MOST PAIN AND EMBARRASSMENT.
YOU'RE GETTING A BIT NOSY, MISTER WOLF.
I CAN'T HELP BUT NOTICE THINGS, SNOW. I BELIEVE THAT'S WHY YOU HIRED ME AS FABLE-TOWN'S SHERIFF.
THERE YOU ARE.
EVERYTHING JUST THE WAY YOU LEFT IT, JACK?
HAVEN'T GONE BACK IN YET.
I DIDN'T WANT TO SEE IT A SECOND TIME. IT'S HORRIBLE. YOU'LL SEE.
JUST GET THE DOOR OPEN.

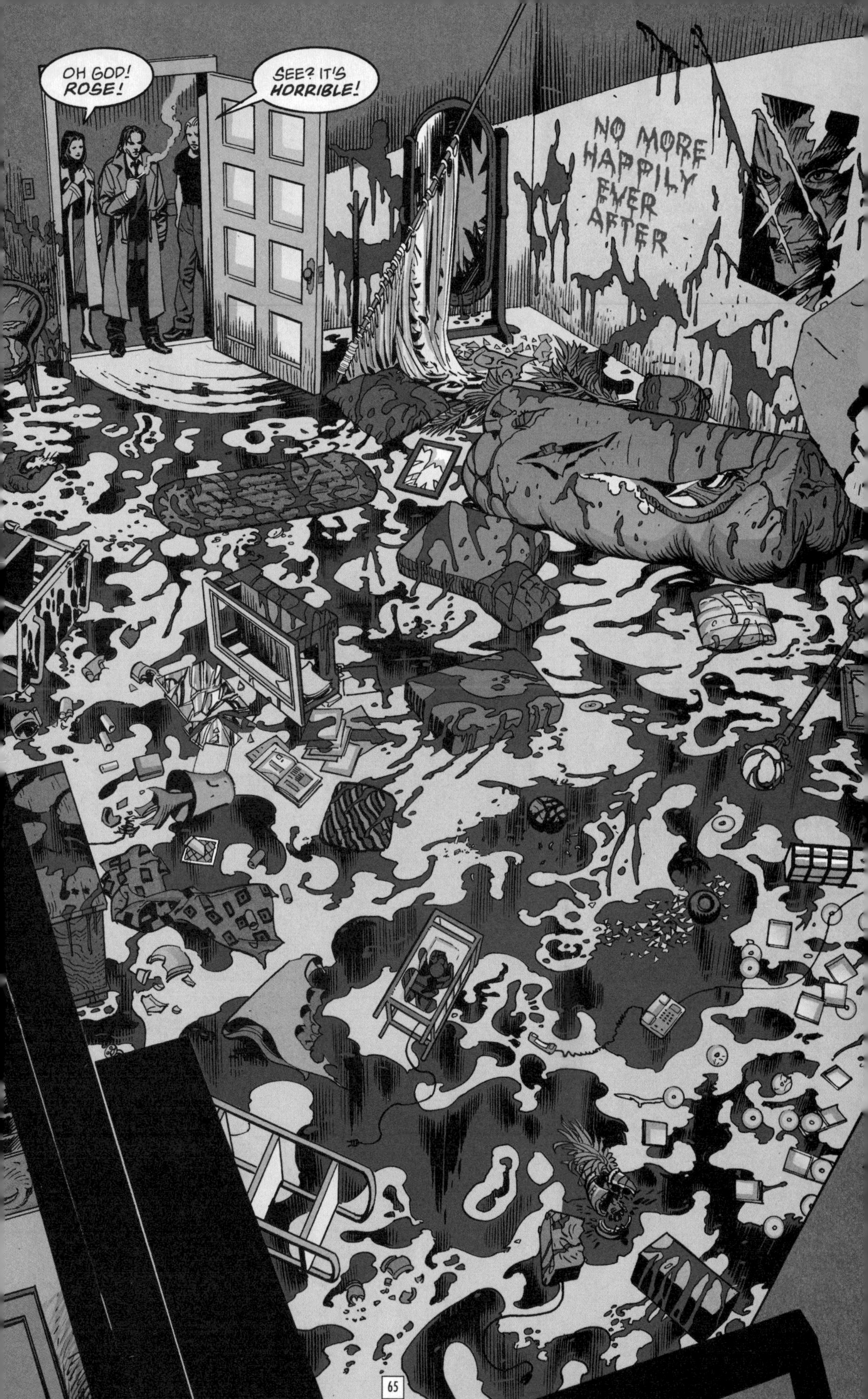
OH GOD! ROSE!
SEE? IT'S HORRIBLE!
NO MORE HAPPILY EVER AFTER

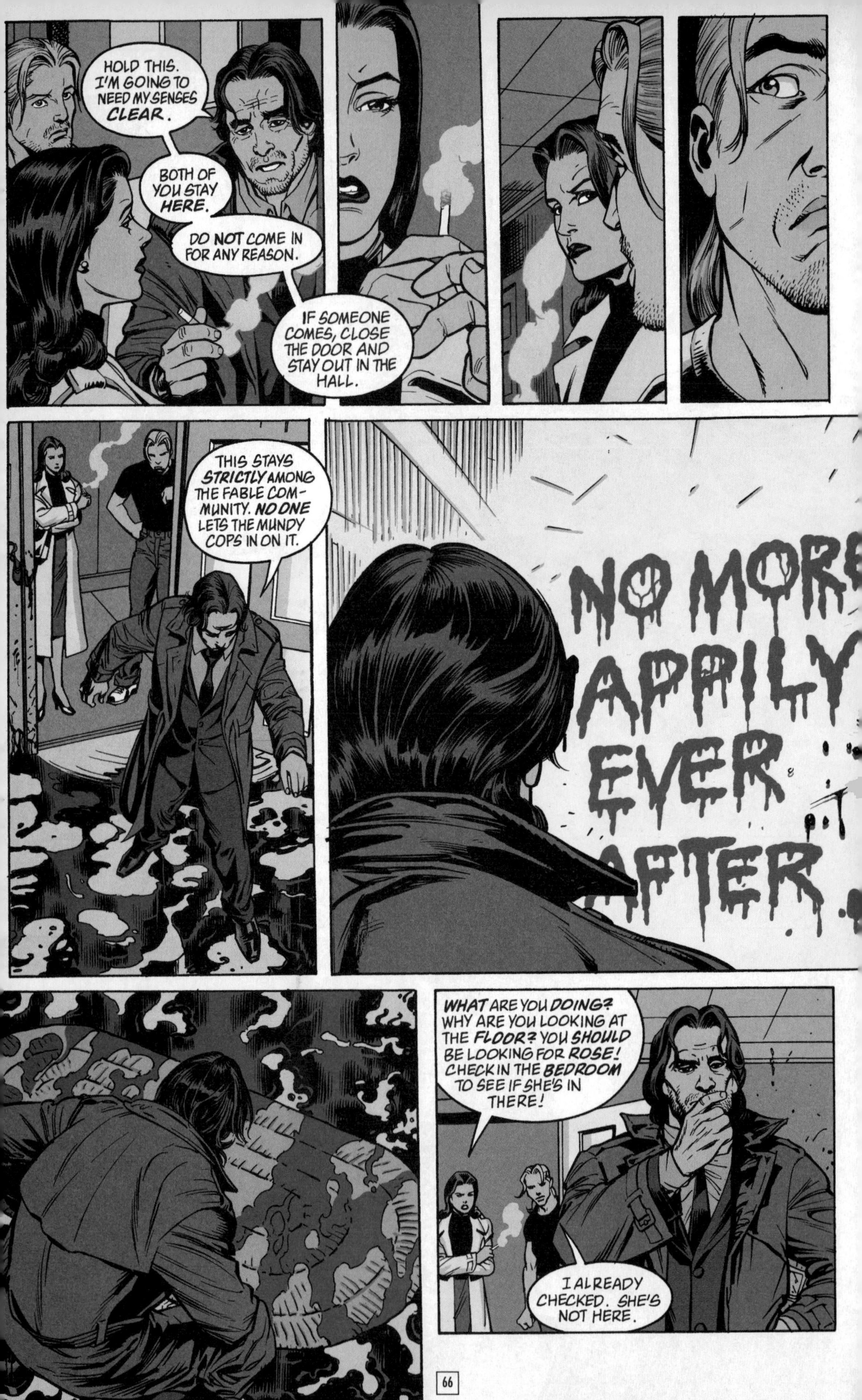
HOLD THIS. I'M GOING TO NEED MY SENSES CLEAR.
BOTH OF YOU STAY HERE.
DO NOT COME IN FOR ANY REASON.
IF SOMEONE COMES, CLOSE THE DOOR AND STAY OUT IN THE HALL.
THIS STAYS STRICTLY AMONG THE FABLE COMMUNITY. NO ONE LETS THE MUNDY COPS IN ON IT.
NO MORE HAPPILY EVER AFTER
WHAT ARE YOU DOING? WHY ARE YOU LOOKING AT THE FLOOR? YOU SHOULD BE LOOKING FOR ROSE! CHECK IN THE BEDROOM TO SEE IF SHE'S IN THERE!
I ALREADY CHECKED. SHE'S NOT HERE.

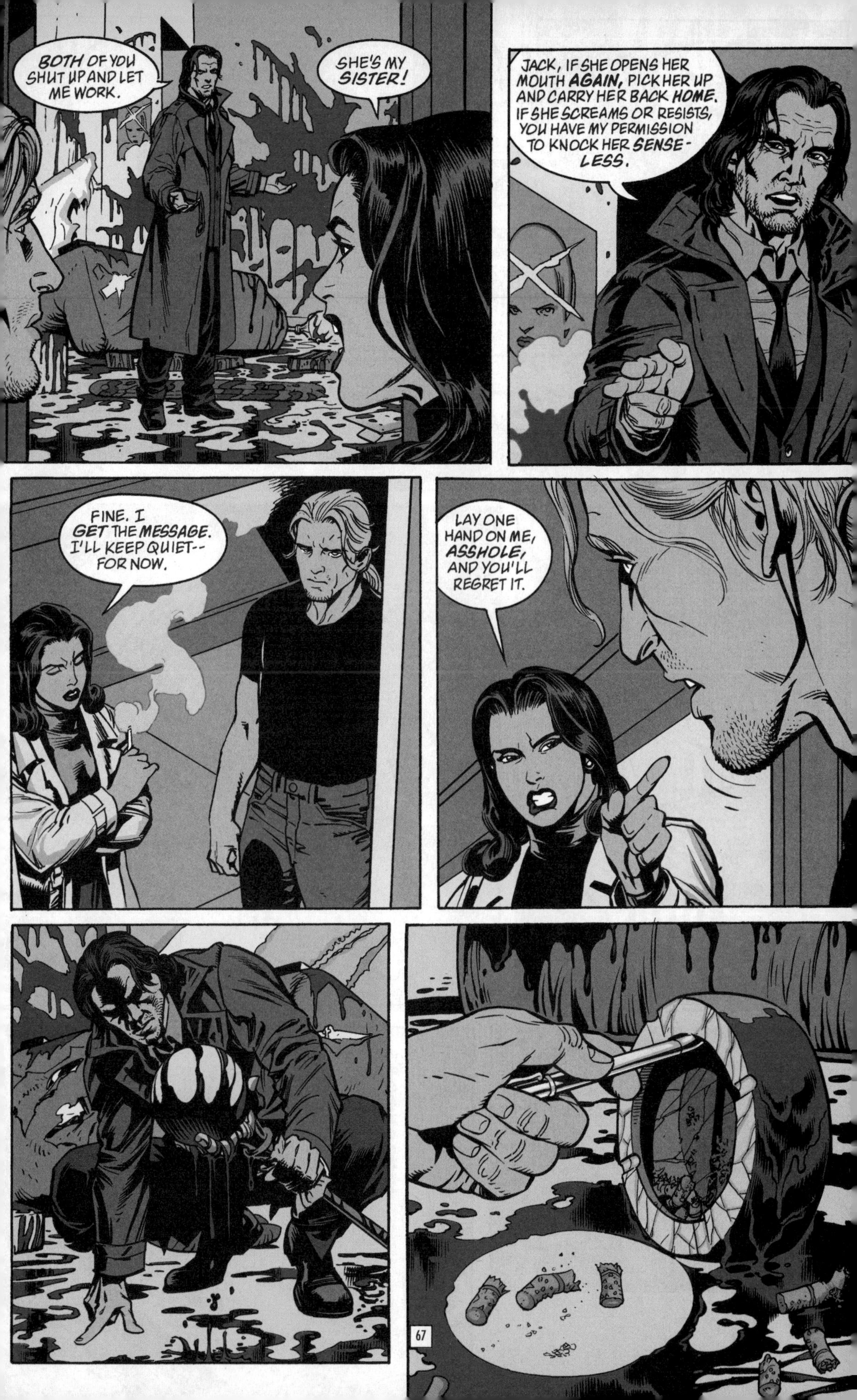
BOTH OF YOU SHUT UP AND LET ME WORK.
SHE'S MY SISTER!
JACK, IF SHE OPENS HER MOUTH AGAIN, PICK HER UP AND CARRY HER BACK HOME. IF SHE SCREAMS OR RESISTS, YOU HAVE MY PERMISSION TO KNOCK HER SENSE-LESS.
FINE. I GET THE MESSAGE. I'LL KEEP QUIET-- FOR NOW.
LAY ONE HAND ON ME, ASSHOLE, AND YOU'LL REGRET IT.

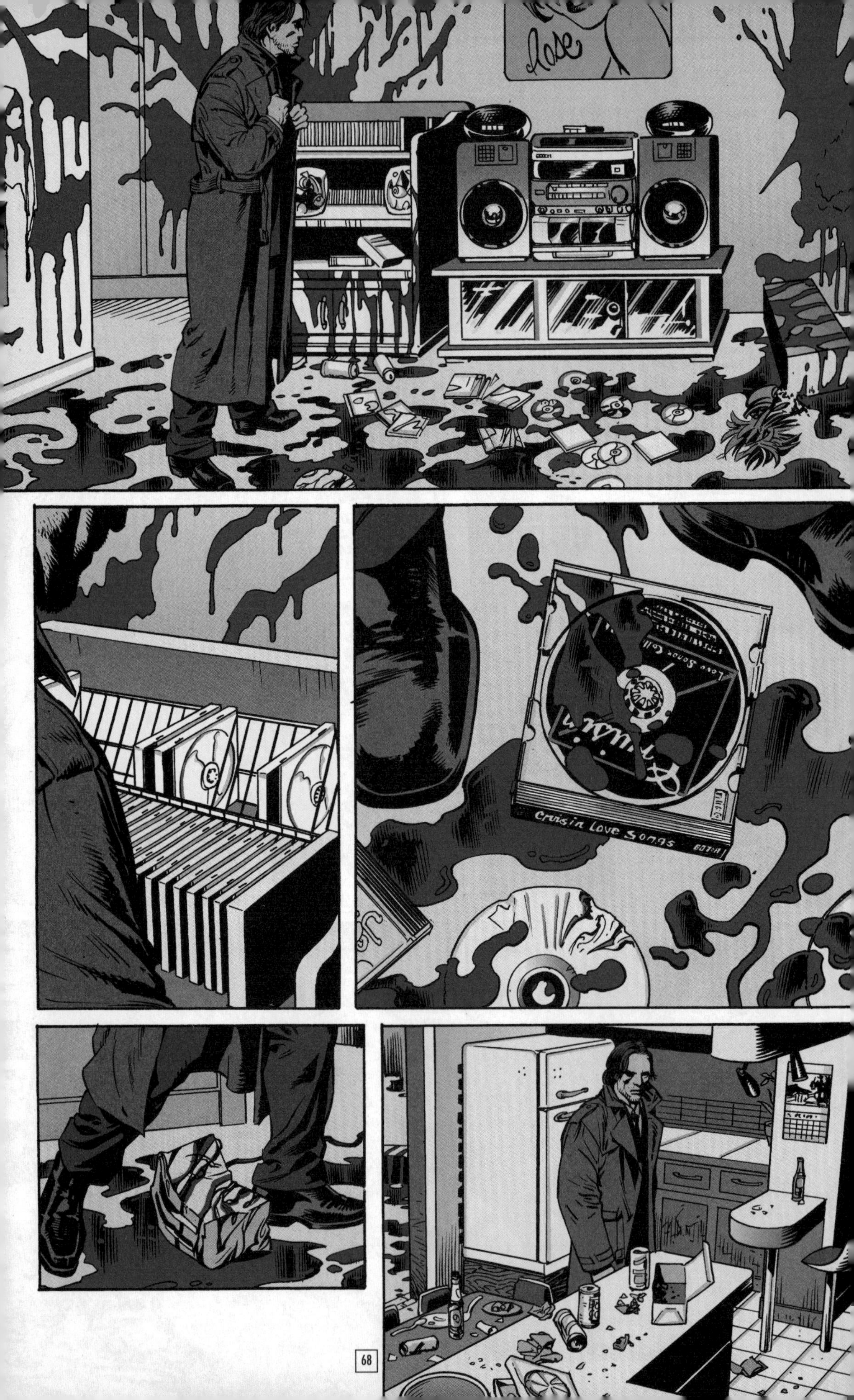
Cruisin Love Songs

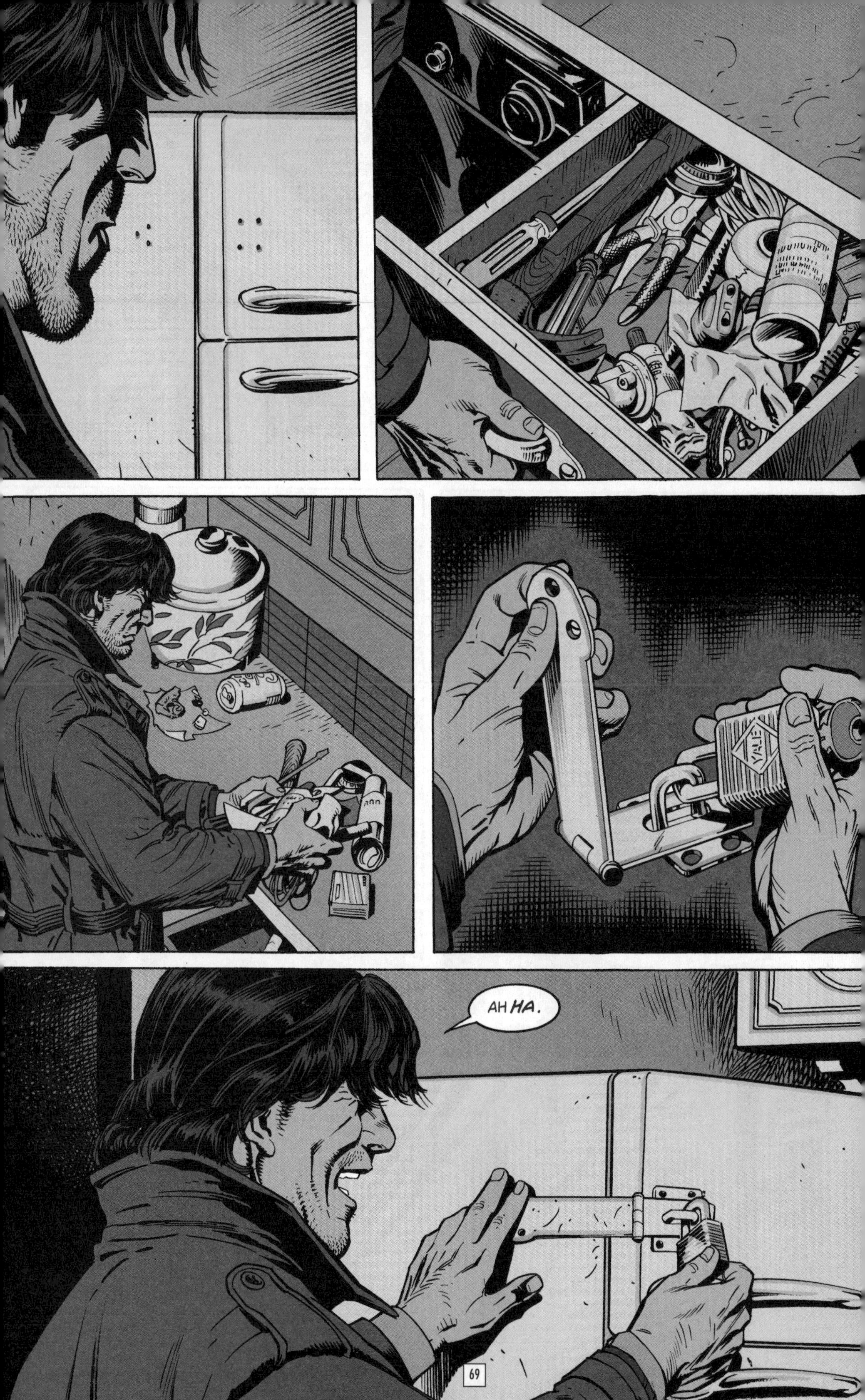
Artline
YALE
AH HA.

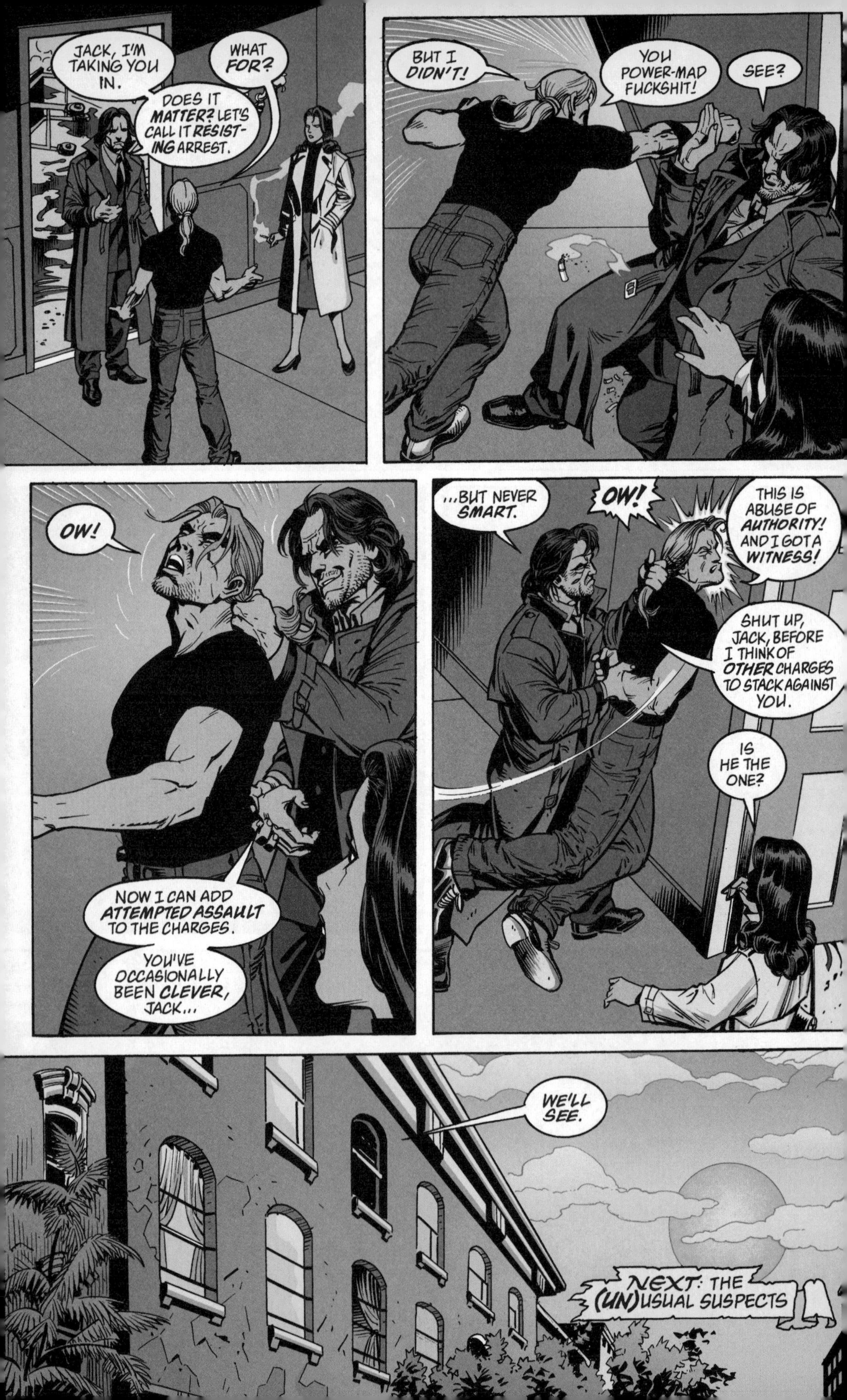
JACK, I'M TAKING YOU IN.
WHAT FOR?
DOES IT MATTER? LET'S CALL IT RESISTING ARREST.
BUT I DIDN'T!
YOU POWER-MAD FUCKSHIT!
SEE?
OW!
NOW I CAN ADD ATTEMPTED ASSAULT TO THE CHARGES.
YOU'VE OCCASIONALLY BEEN CLEVER, JACK...
...BUT NEVER SMART.
OW!
THIS IS ABUSE OF AUTHORITY! AND I GOT A WITNESS!
SHUT UP, JACK, BEFORE I THINK OF OTHER CHARGES TO STACK AGAINST YOU.
IS HE THE ONE?
WE'LL SEE.
NEXT: THE (UN)USUAL SUSPECTS

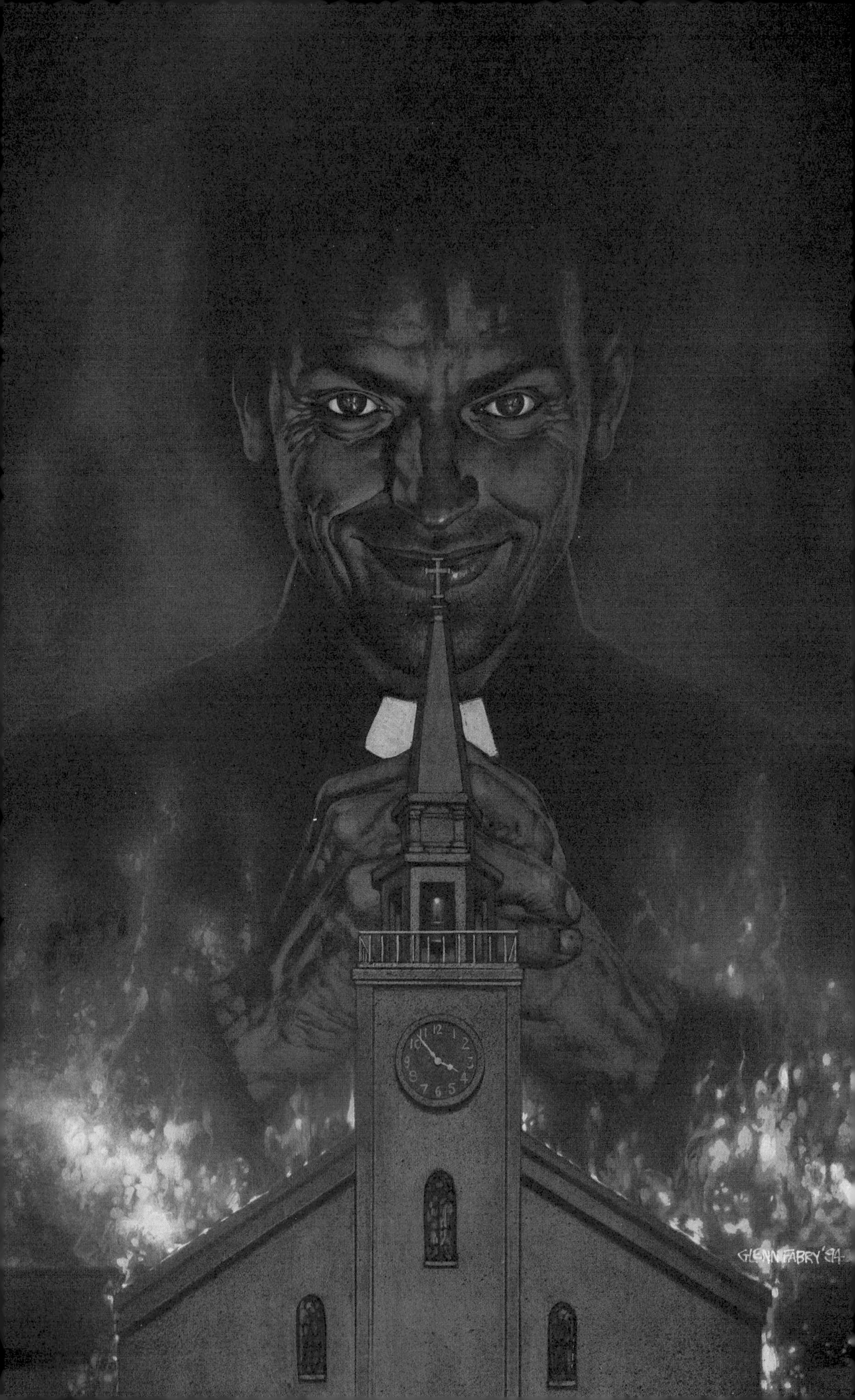
GLENN FABRY '94

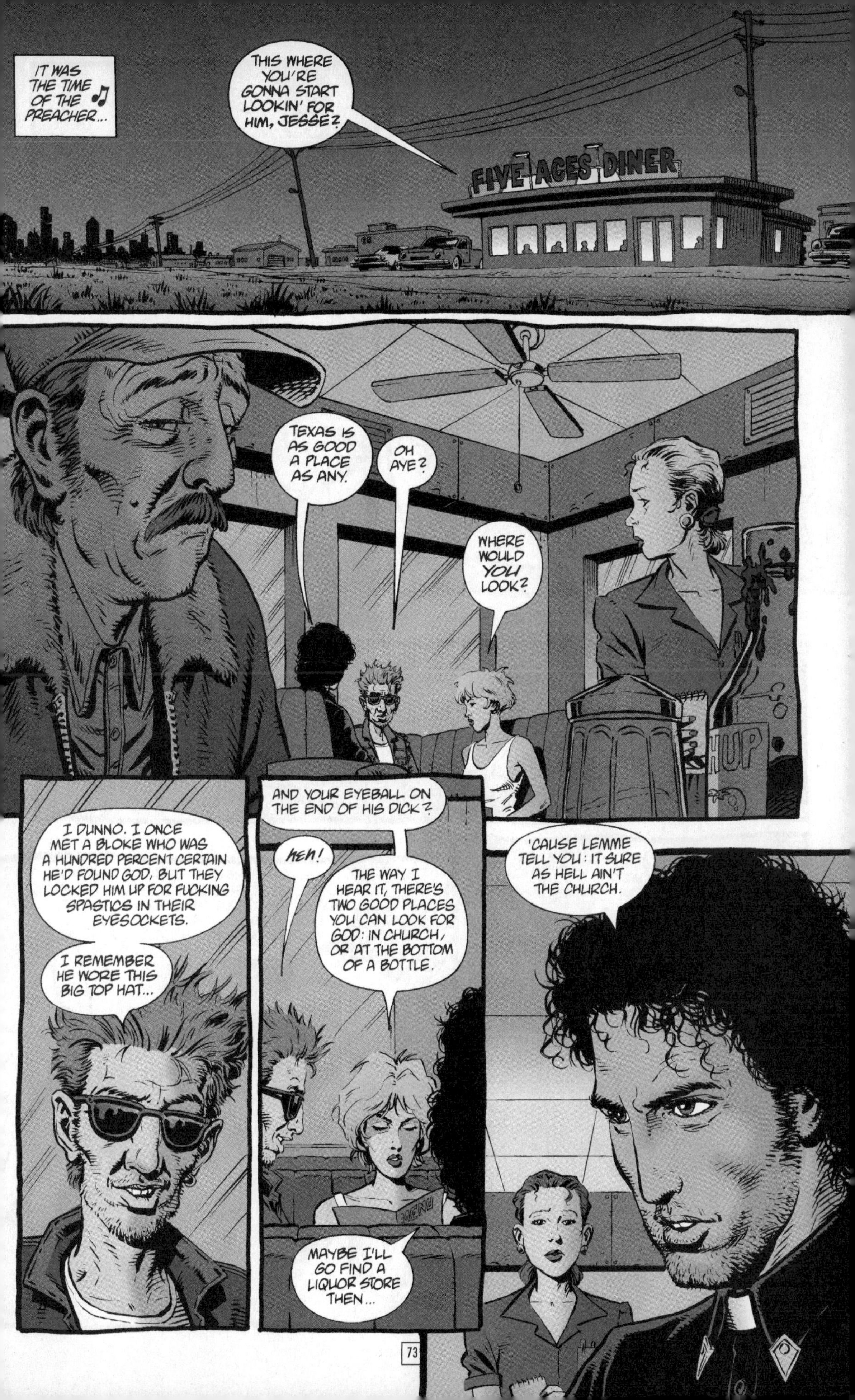

IT WAS THE TIME OF THE PREACHER...
THIS WHERE YOU'RE GONNA START LOOKIN' FOR HIM, JESSE?
FIVE ACES DINER
TEXAS IS AS GOOD A PLACE AS ANY.
OH AYE?
WHERE WOULD YOU LOOK?
I DUNNO. I ONCE MET A BLOKE WHO WAS A HUNDRED PERCENT CERTAIN HE'D FOUND GOD, BUT THEY LOCKED HIM UP FOR FUCKING SPASTICS IN THEIR EYESOCKETS.
I REMEMBER HE WORE THIS BIG TOP HAT...
AND YOUR EYEBALL ON THE END OF HIS DICK?
HEH!
THE WAY I HEAR IT, THERE'S TWO GOOD PLACES YOU CAN LOOK FOR GOD: IN CHURCH, OR AT THE BOTTOM OF A BOTTLE.
MAYBE I'LL GO FIND A LIQUOR STORE THEN...
'CAUSE LEMME TELL YOU: IT SURE AS HELL AIN'T THE CHURCH.

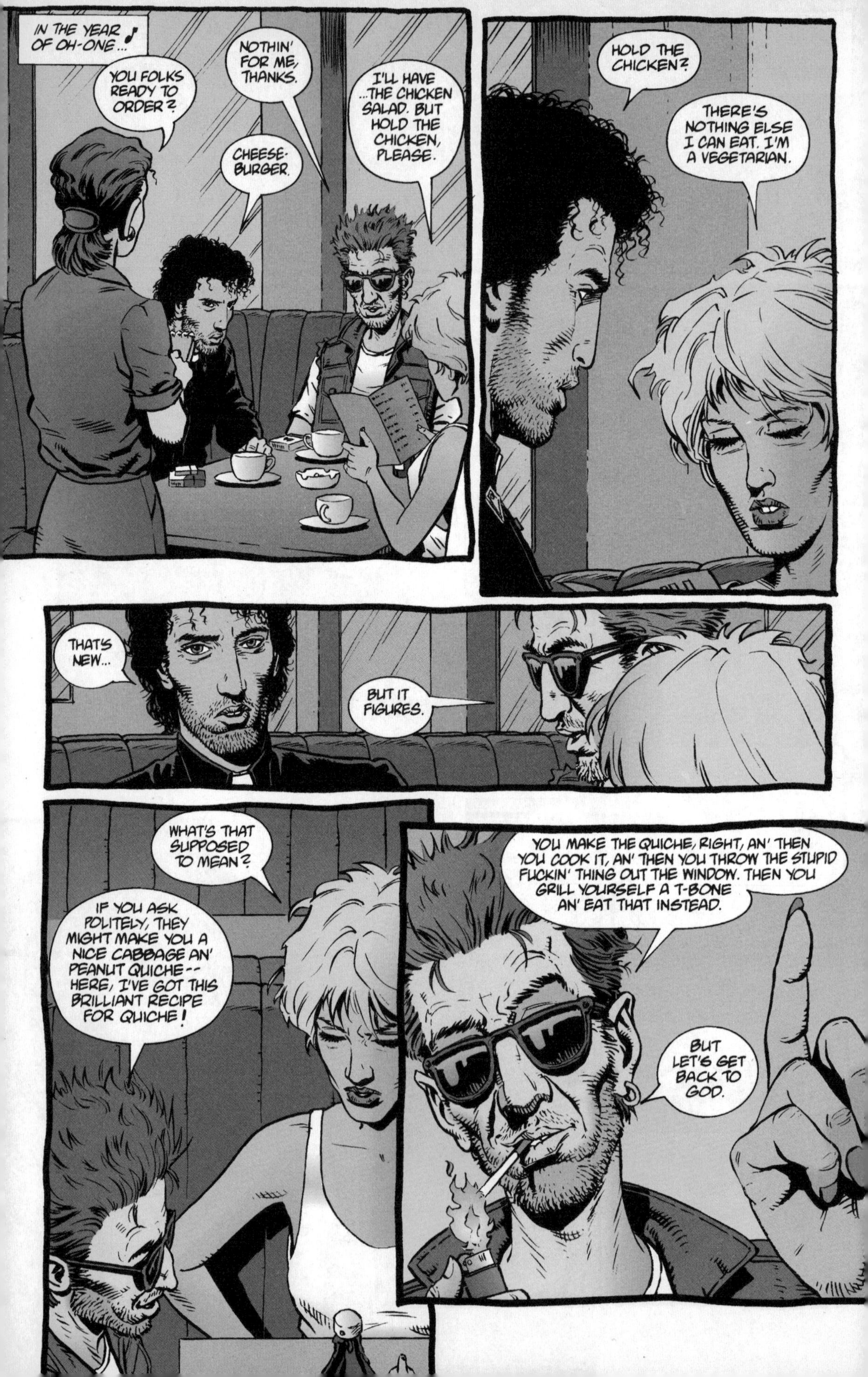
IN THE YEAR OF OH-ONE...
YOU FOLKS READY TO ORDER?
NOTHIN' FOR ME, THANKS.
CHEESE-BURGER.
I'LL HAVE ...THE CHICKEN SALAD. BUT HOLD THE CHICKEN, PLEASE.
HOLD THE CHICKEN?
THERE'S NOTHING ELSE I CAN EAT. I'M A VEGETARIAN.
THAT'S NEW...
BUT IT FIGURES.
WHAT'S THAT SUPPOSED TO MEAN?
IF YOU ASK POLITELY, THEY MIGHT MAKE YOU A NICE CABBAGE AN' PEANUT QUICHE-- HERE, I'VE GOT THIS BRILLIANT RECIPE FOR QUICHE!
YOU MAKE THE QUICHE, RIGHT, AN' THEN YOU COOK IT, AN' THEN YOU THROW THE STUPID FUCKIN' THING OUT THE WINDOW. THEN YOU GRILL YOURSELF A T-BONE AN' EAT THAT INSTEAD.
BUT LET'S GET BACK TO GOD.

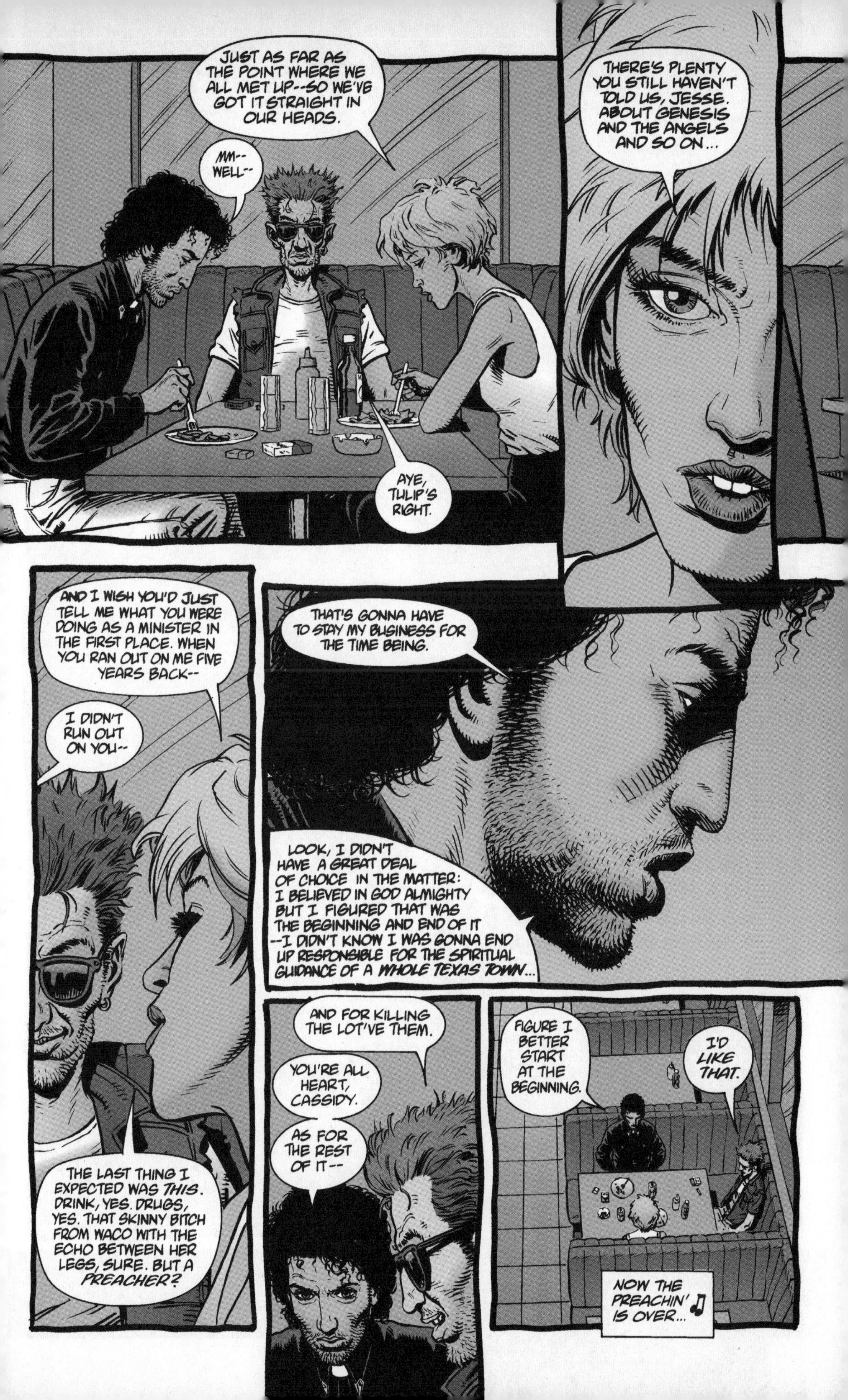
JUST AS FAR AS THE POINT WHERE WE ALL MET UP--SO WE'VE GOT IT STRAIGHT IN OUR HEADS.
MM--WELL--
AYE, TULIP'S RIGHT.
THERE'S PLENTY YOU STILL HAVEN'T TOLD US, JESSE. ABOUT GENESIS AND THE ANGELS AND SO ON...
AND I WISH YOU'D JUST TELL ME WHAT YOU WERE DOING AS A MINISTER IN THE FIRST PLACE. WHEN YOU RAN OUT ON ME FIVE YEARS BACK--
I DIDN'T RUN OUT ON YOU--
THE LAST THING I EXPECTED WAS THIS. DRINK, YES. DRUGS, YES. THAT SKINNY BITCH FROM WACO WITH THE ECHO BETWEEN HER LEGS, SURE. BUT A PREACHER?
THAT'S GONNA HAVE TO STAY MY BUSINESS FOR THE TIME BEING.
LOOK, I DIDN'T HAVE A GREAT DEAL OF CHOICE IN THE MATTER: I BELIEVED IN GOD ALMIGHTY BUT I FIGURED THAT WAS THE BEGINNING AND END OF IT --I DIDN'T KNOW I WAS GONNA END UP RESPONSIBLE FOR THE SPIRITUAL GUIDANCE OF A WHOLE TEXAS TOWN...
AND FOR KILLING THE LOT'VE THEM.
YOU'RE ALL HEART, CASSIDY.
AS FOR THE REST OF IT--
FIGURE I BETTER START AT THE BEGINNING.
I'D LIKE THAT.
NOW THE PREACHIN' IS OVER...♫

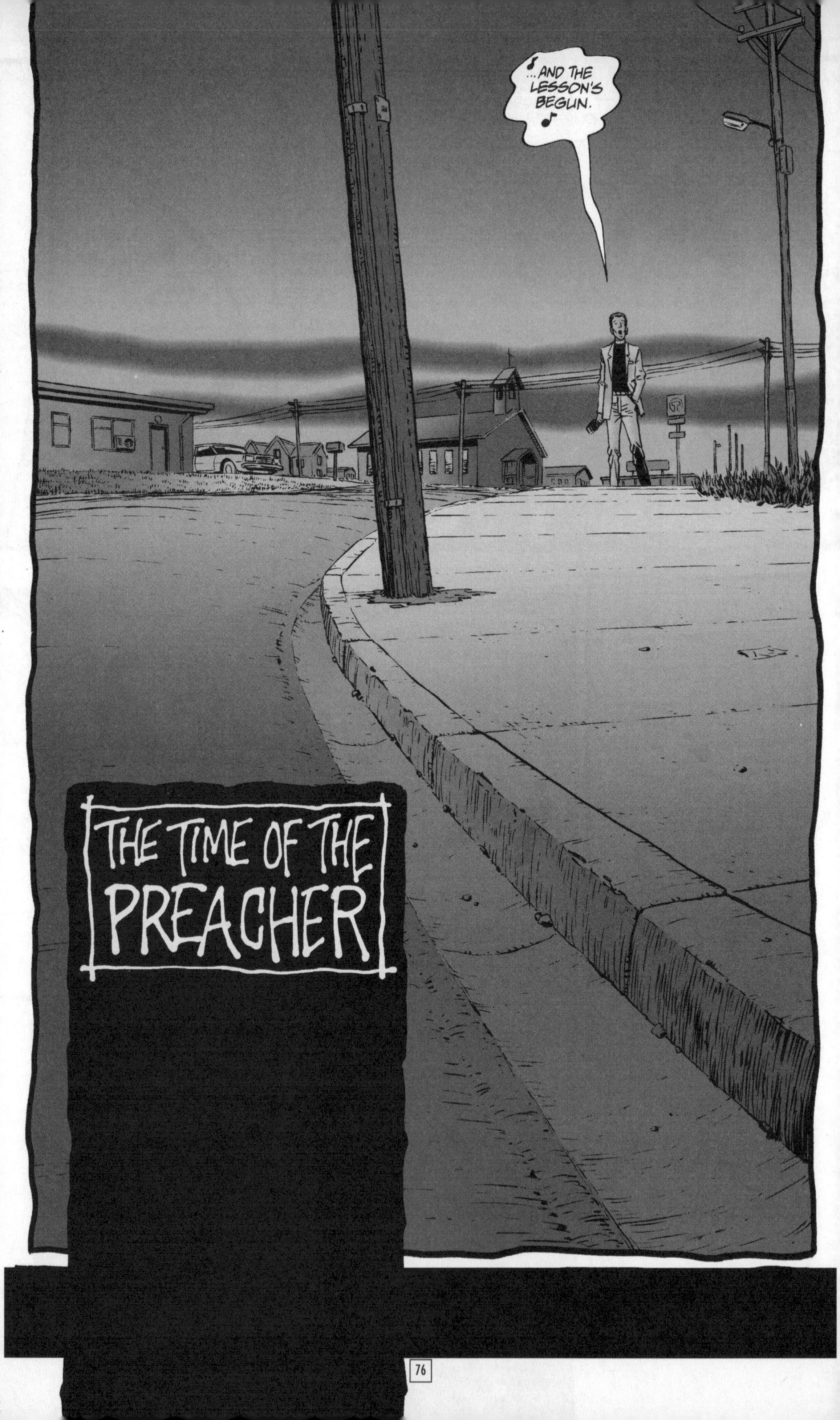
...AND THE LESSON'S BEGUN.
THE TIME OF THE PREACHER

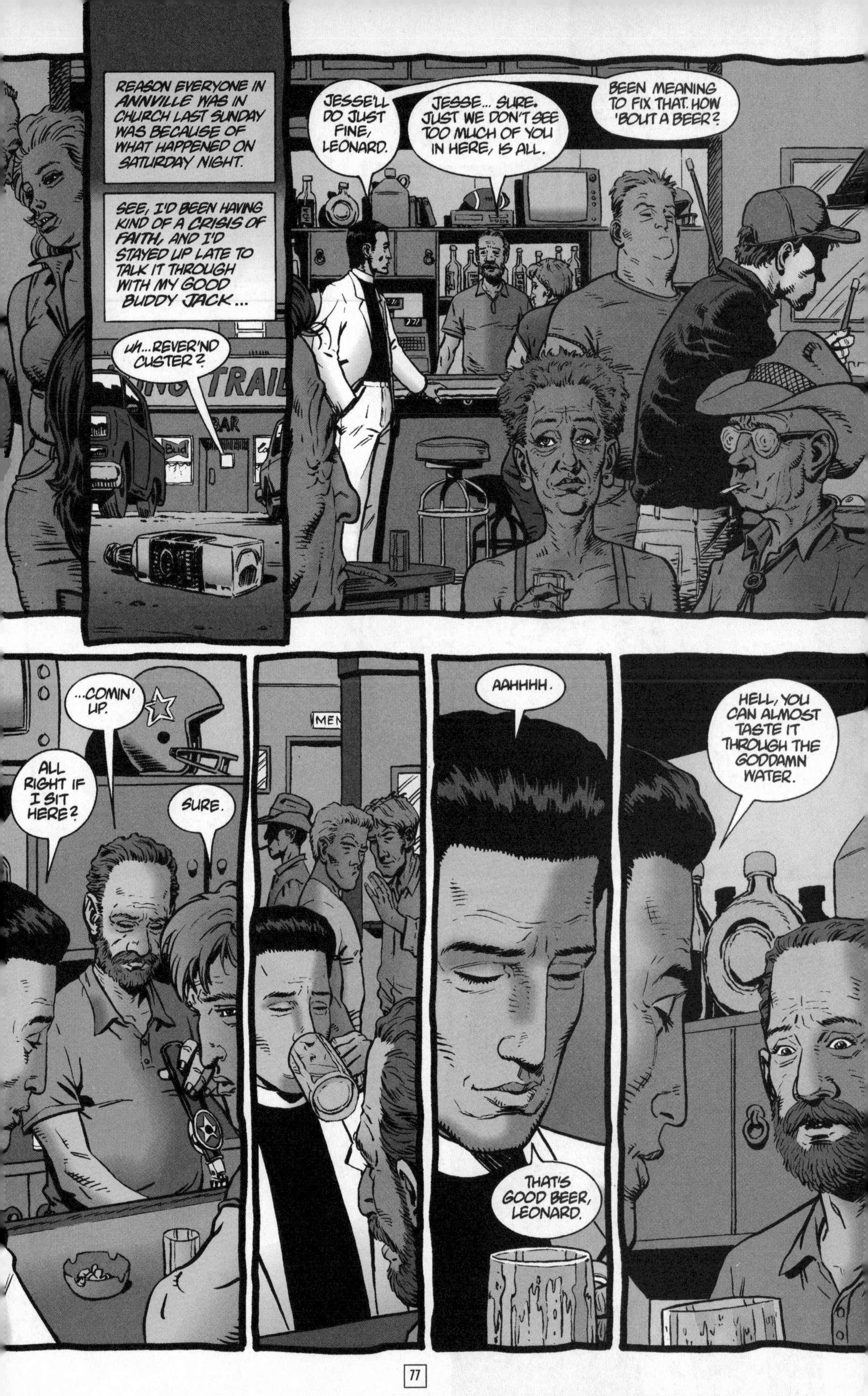
REASON EVERYONE IN ANNVILLE WAS IN CHURCH LAST SUNDAY WAS BECAUSE OF WHAT HAPPENED ON SATURDAY NIGHT.
SEE, I'D BEEN HAVING KIND OF A CRISIS OF FAITH, AND I'D STAYED UP LATE TO TALK IT THROUGH WITH MY GOOD BUDDY JACK...
uh...REVER'ND CUSTER?
JESSE'LL DO JUST FINE, LEONARD.
JESSE... SURE. JUST WE DON'T SEE TOO MUCH OF YOU IN HERE, IS ALL.
BEEN MEANING TO FIX THAT. HOW 'BOUT A BEER?
ALL RIGHT IF I SIT HERE?
...COMIN' UP.
SURE.
AAHHHH.
THAT'S GOOD BEER, LEONARD.
HELL, YOU CAN ALMOST TASTE IT THROUGH THE GODDAMN WATER.

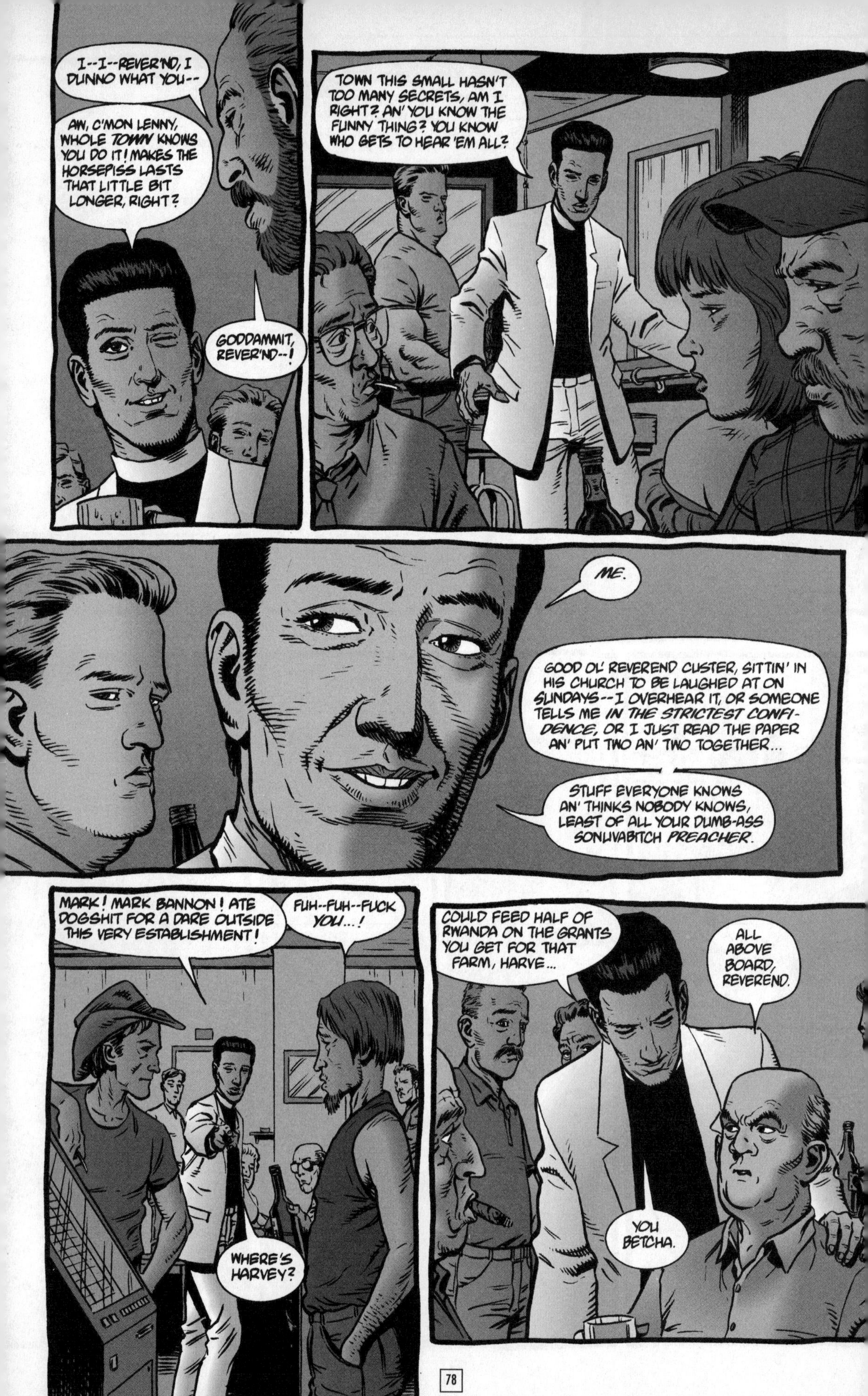
I--I--REVER'ND, I DUNNO WHAT YOU--
AW, C'MON LENNY, WHOLE TOWN KNOWS YOU DO IT! MAKES THE HORSEPISS LASTS THAT LITTLE BIT LONGER, RIGHT?
GODDAMMIT, REVER'ND--!
TOWN THIS SMALL HASN'T TOO MANY SECRETS, AM I RIGHT? AN' YOU KNOW THE FUNNY THING? YOU KNOW WHO GETS TO HEAR 'EM ALL?
ME.
GOOD OL' REVEREND CUSTER, SITTIN' IN HIS CHURCH TO BE LAUGHED AT ON SUNDAYS--I OVERHEAR IT, OR SOMEONE TELLS ME IN THE STRICTEST CONFI-DENCE, OR I JUST READ THE PAPER AN' PUT TWO AN' TWO TOGETHER...
STUFF EVERYONE KNOWS AN' THINKS NOBODY KNOWS, LEAST OF ALL YOUR DUMB-ASS SONUVABITCH PREACHER.
MARK! MARK BANNON! ATE DOGSHIT FOR A DARE OUTSIDE THIS VERY ESTABLISHMENT!
FUH--FUH--FUCK YOU...!
WHERE'S HARVEY?
COULD FEED HALF OF RWANDA ON THE GRANTS YOU GET FOR THAT FARM, HARVE...
ALL ABOVE BOARD, REVEREND.
YOU BETCHA.

LIKE THE MOVIE KATE SHOT IN YOUR BARN, HUH? JUST HER AN' A PIEBALD STALLION-- WENT STRAIGHT TO VIDEO, WAY I HEAR IT.

I'VE NEVER SEEN THIS WOMAN BEFORE IN MY LIFE--

uh--

BUT LEAVIN' ASIDE MICHAEL HERE--WHO'S GOTTA BE THE ONLY MAN FROM ANNVILLE THAT EVER WENT TO CALIFORNIA --LET'S MEET THE STARS OF THE SHOW...

REVER'ND, YOU'VE HAD A LITTLE TOO MUCH TO--REVER'ND--

PAT AN' TERRY MORROW.

NOW YOU BETTER JUST WATCH YOUR FUCKIN' MOUTH, CUSTER...

WHO RAPED THAT HITCHER GIRL NO MATTER WHAT THEIR DADDY PAID JUDGE SHEBIN.

OR HOW MANY TIMES THIS TOWN CAN CHANGE THE GODDAMN SUBJECT.

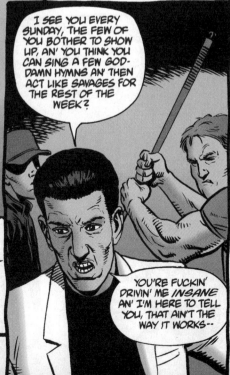

I SEE YOU EVERY SUNDAY, THE FEW OF YOU BOTHER TO SHOW UP, AN' YOU THINK YOU CAN SING A FEW GOD- DAMN HYMNS AN' THEN ACT LIKE SAVAGES FOR THE REST OF THE WEEK?

YOU'RE FUCKIN' DRIVIN' ME INSANE AN' I'M HERE TO TELL YOU, THAT AIN'T THE WAY IT WORKS--

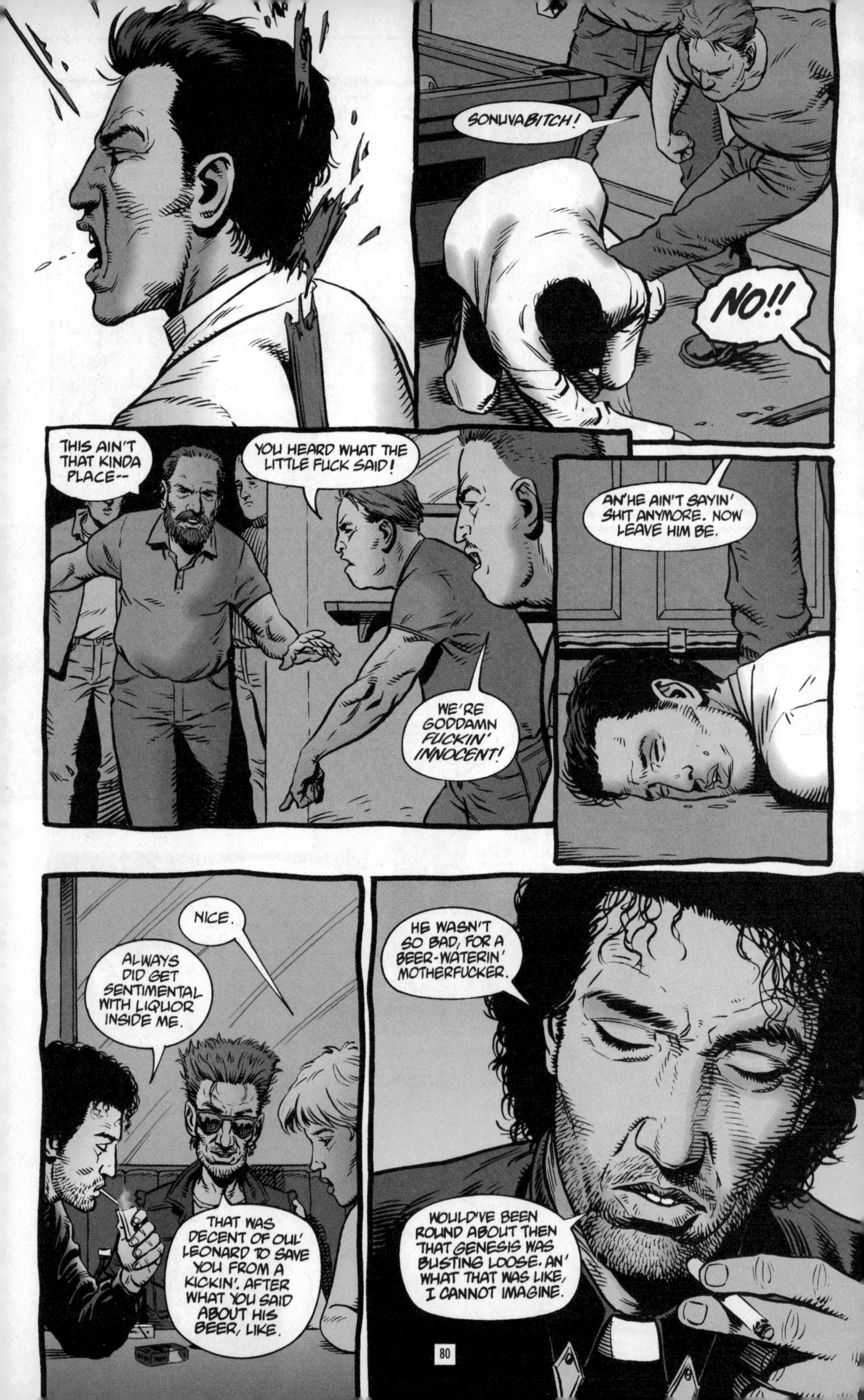
SONUVABITCH!
NO!!
THIS AIN'T THAT KINDA PLACE--
YOU HEARD WHAT THE LITTLE FUCK SAID!
WE'RE GODDAMN FUCKIN' INNOCENT!
AN'HE AIN'T SAYIN' SHIT ANYMORE. NOW LEAVE HIM BE.
NICE.
ALWAYS DID GET SENTIMENTAL WITH LIQUOR INSIDE ME.
THAT WAS DECENT OF OUL' LEONARD TO SAVE YOU FROM A KICKIN', AFTER WHAT YOU SAID ABOUT HIS BEER, LIKE.
HE WASN'T SO BAD, FOR A BEER-WATERIN' MOTHERFUCKER.
WOULD'VE BEEN ROUND ABOUT THEN THAT GENESIS WAS BUSTING LOOSE. AN' WHAT THAT WAS LIKE, I CANNOT IMAGINE.

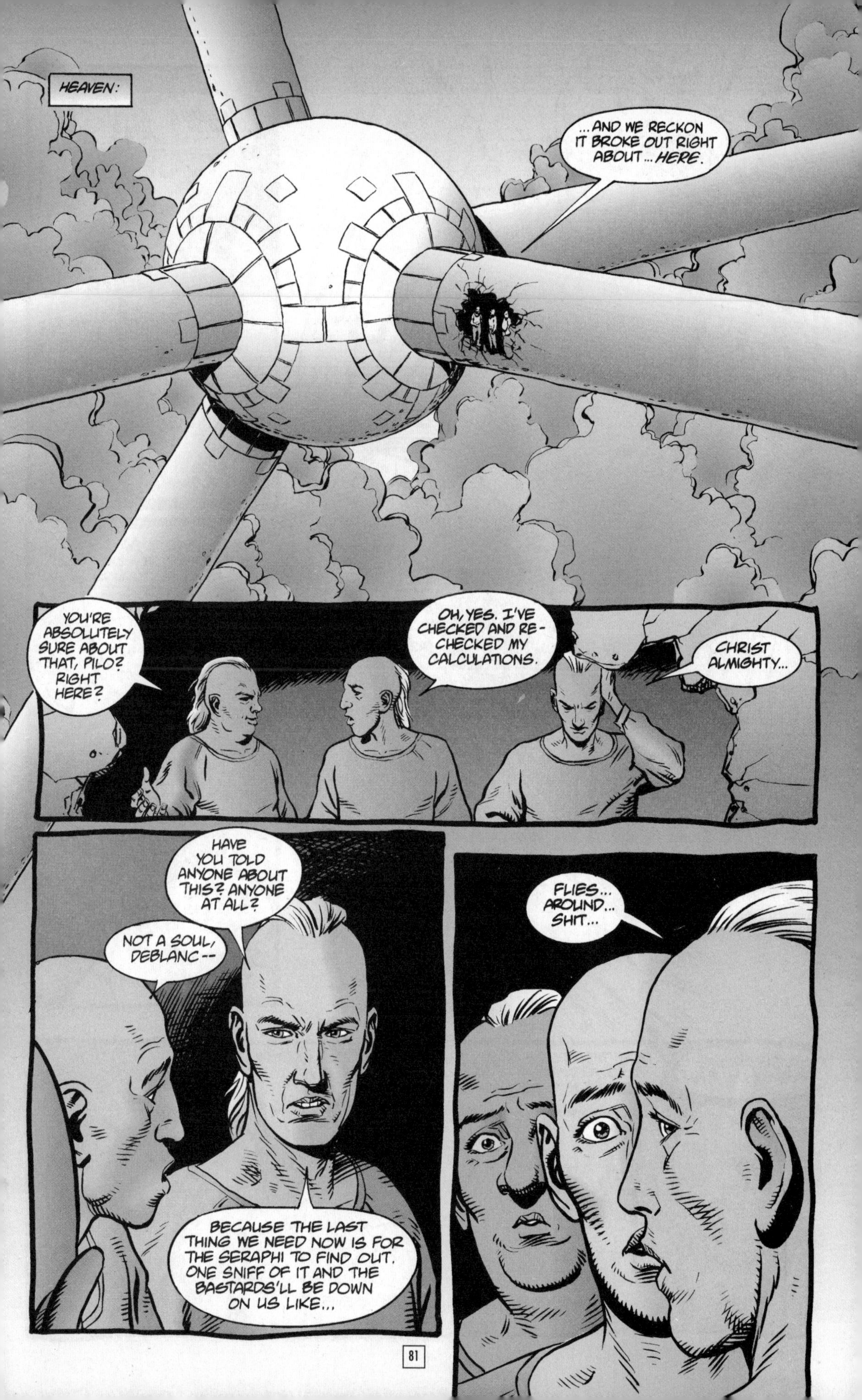
HEAVEN:
...AND WE RECKON IT BROKE OUT RIGHT ABOUT... *HERE*.
YOU'RE ABSOLUTELY SURE ABOUT THAT, PILO? RIGHT HERE?
OH, YES. I'VE CHECKED AND RE-CHECKED MY CALCULATIONS.
CHRIST ALMIGHTY...
HAVE YOU TOLD ANYONE ABOUT THIS? ANYONE AT ALL?
NOT A SOUL, DEBLANC--
BECAUSE THE LAST THING WE NEED NOW IS FOR THE SERAPHI TO FIND OUT. ONE SNIFF OF IT AND THE BASTARDS'LL BE DOWN ON US LIKE...
FLIES... AROUND... SHIT...

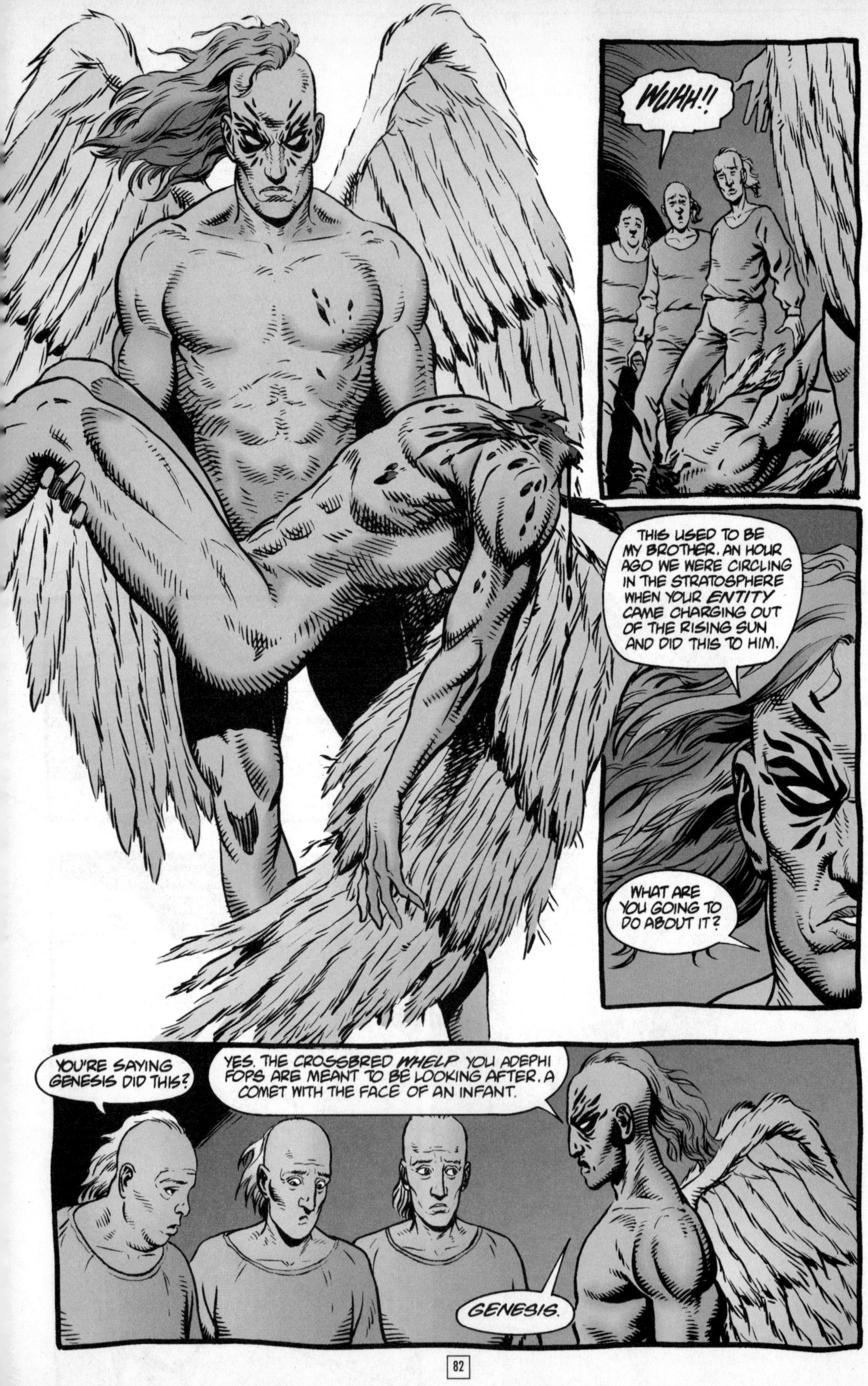
WUHH!!
THIS USED TO BE MY BROTHER. AN HOUR AGO WE WERE CIRCLING IN THE STRATOSPHERE WHEN YOUR *ENTITY* CAME CHARGING OUT OF THE RISING SUN AND DID THIS TO HIM.
WHAT ARE YOU GOING TO DO ABOUT IT?
YOU'RE SAYING GENESIS DID THIS?
YES. THE CROSSBRED *WHELP* YOU ADEPHI FOPS ARE MEANT TO BE LOOKING AFTER. A COMET WITH THE FACE OF AN INFANT.
GENESIS.

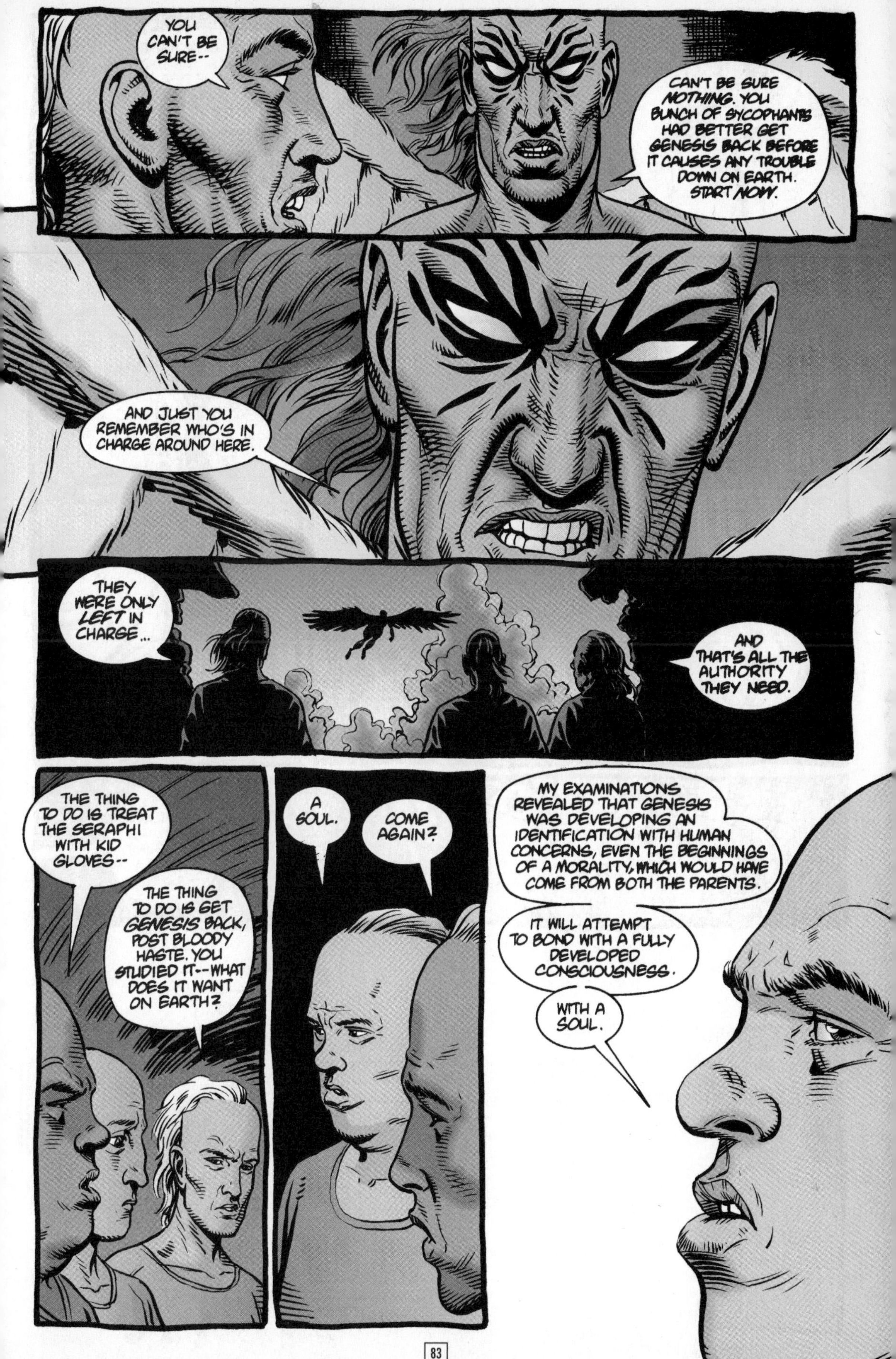
YOU CAN'T BE SURE--
CAN'T BE SURE NOTHING. YOU BUNCH OF SYCOPHANTS HAD BETTER GET GENESIS BACK BEFORE IT CAUSES ANY TROUBLE DOWN ON EARTH. START NOW.
AND JUST YOU REMEMBER WHO'S IN CHARGE AROUND HERE.
THEY WERE ONLY LEFT IN CHARGE...
AND THAT'S ALL THE AUTHORITY THEY NEED.
THE THING TO DO IS TREAT THE SERAPHI WITH KID GLOVES--
THE THING TO DO IS GET GENESIS BACK, POST BLOODY HASTE. YOU STUDIED IT--WHAT DOES IT WANT ON EARTH?
A SOUL.
COME AGAIN?
MY EXAMINATIONS REVEALED THAT GENESIS WAS DEVELOPING AN IDENTIFICATION WITH HUMAN CONCERNS, EVEN THE BEGINNINGS OF A MORALITY, WHICH WOULD HAVE COME FROM BOTH THE PARENTS.
IT WILL ATTEMPT TO BOND WITH A FULLY DEVELOPED CONSCIOUSNESS.
WITH A SOUL.

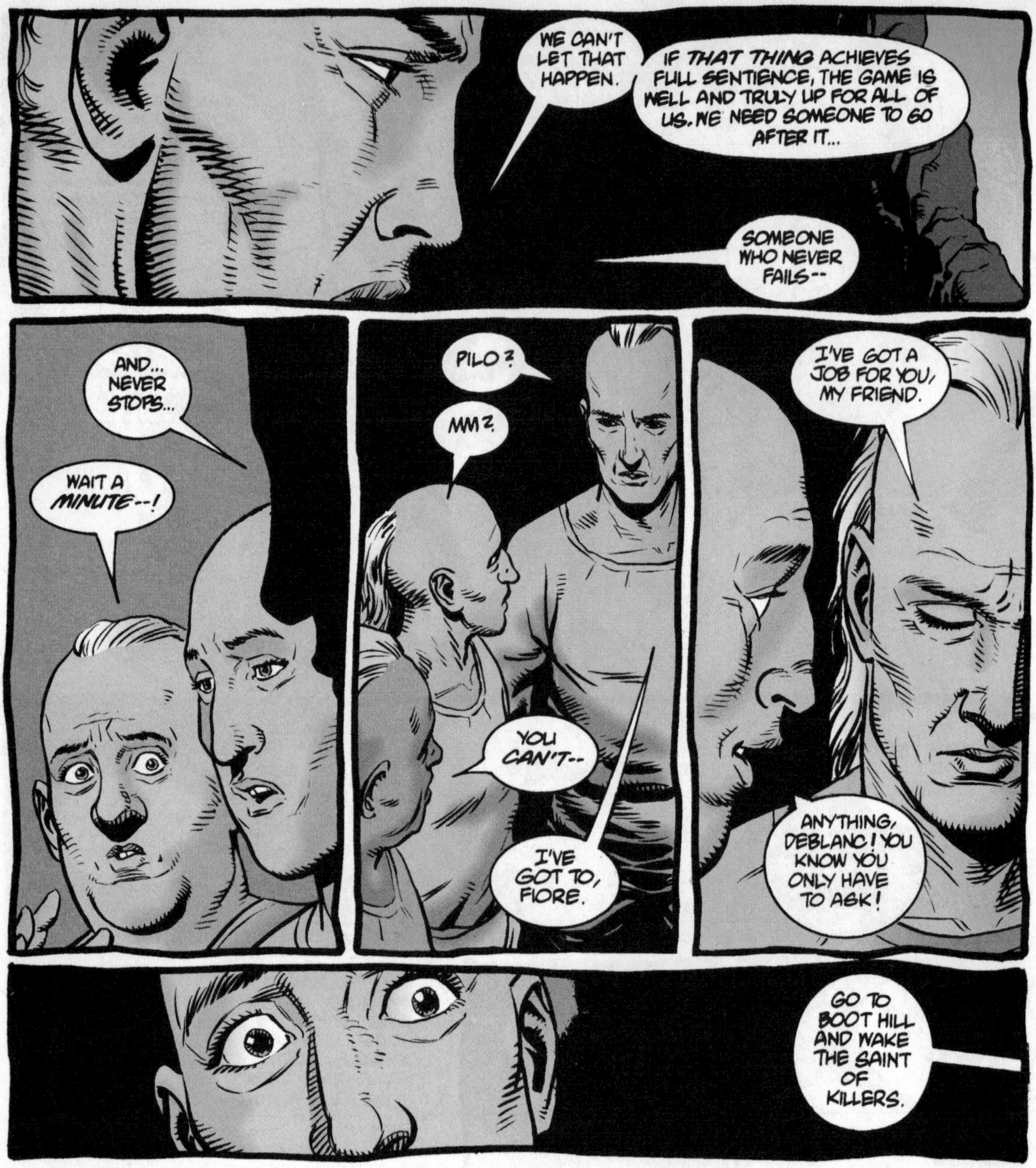
WE CAN'T LET THAT HAPPEN.
IF *THAT THING* ACHIEVES FULL SENTIENCE, THE GAME IS WELL AND TRULY UP FOR ALL OF US. WE NEED SOMEONE TO GO AFTER IT...
SOMEONE WHO NEVER FAILS--
AND... NEVER STOPS...
WAIT A *MINUTE*--!
PILO?
MM?
YOU *CAN'T*--
I'VE GOT TO, FIORE.
I'VE GOT A JOB FOR YOU, MY FRIEND.
ANYTHING, DEBLANC! YOU KNOW YOU ONLY HAVE TO ASK!
GO TO BOOT HILL AND WAKE THE SAINT OF KILLERS.

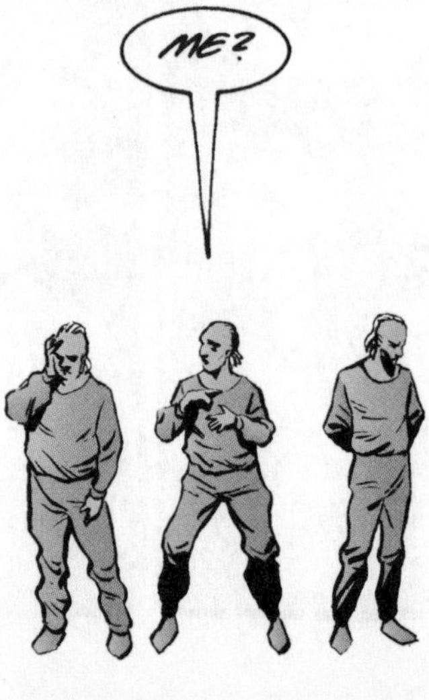
ME?

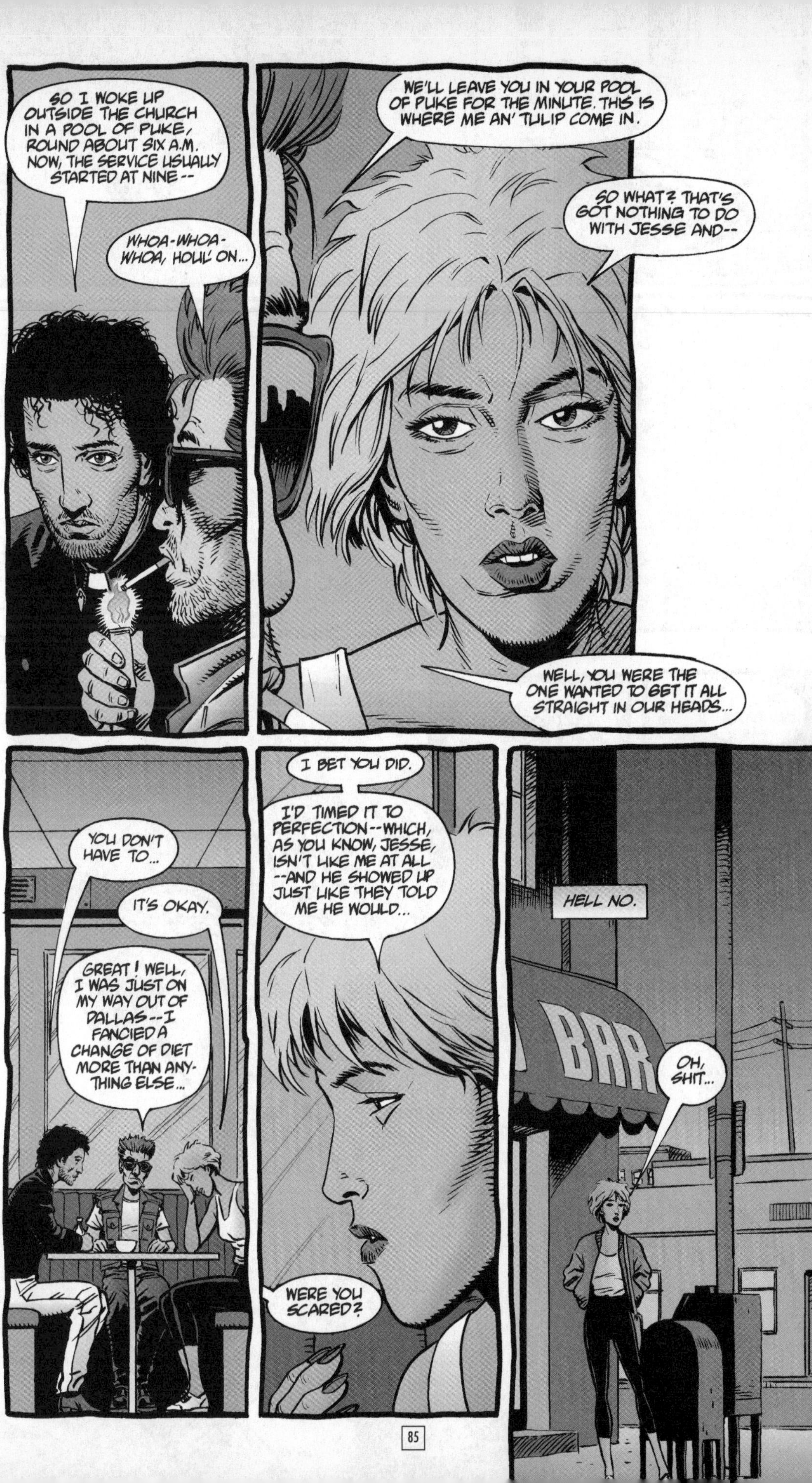
SO I WOKE UP OUTSIDE THE CHURCH IN A POOL OF PUKE, ROUND ABOUT SIX A.M. NOW, THE SERVICE USUALLY STARTED AT NINE --
WHOA-WHOA-WHOA, HOUL' ON...
WE'LL LEAVE YOU IN YOUR POOL OF PUKE FOR THE MINUTE. THIS IS WHERE ME AN' TULIP COME IN.
SO WHAT? THAT'S GOT NOTHING TO DO WITH JESSE AND--
WELL, YOU WERE THE ONE WANTED TO GET IT ALL STRAIGHT IN OUR HEADS...
YOU DON'T HAVE TO...
IT'S OKAY.
GREAT! WELL, I WAS JUST ON MY WAY OUT OF DALLAS--I FANCIED A CHANGE OF DIET MORE THAN ANYTHING ELSE...
I BET YOU DID.
I'D TIMED IT TO PERFECTION--WHICH, AS YOU KNOW, JESSE, ISN'T LIKE ME AT ALL --AND HE SHOWED UP JUST LIKE THEY TOLD ME HE WOULD...
WERE YOU SCARED?
HELL NO.
BAR
OH, SHIT...

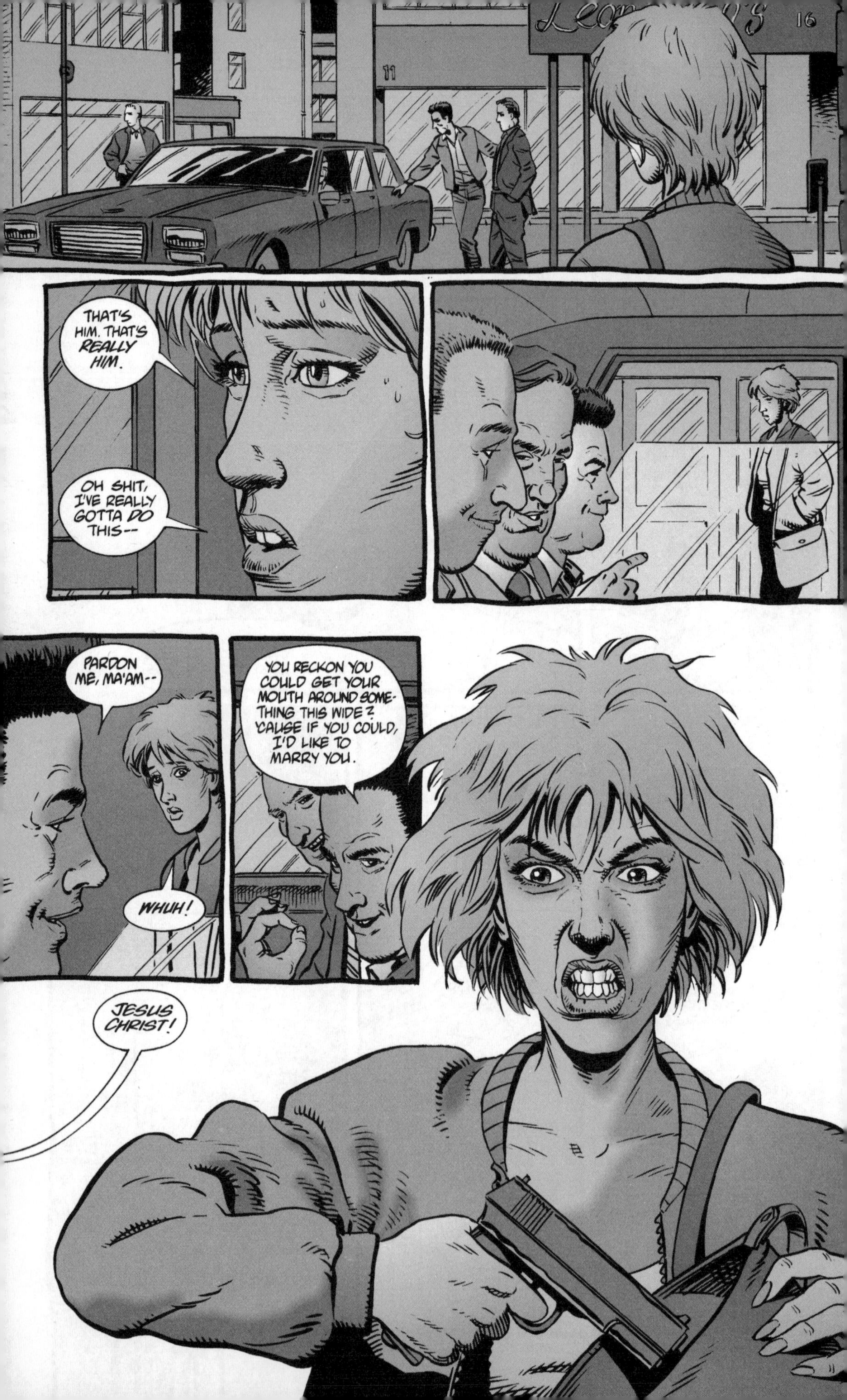

THAT'S HIM. THAT'S REALLY HIM.
OH SHIT, I'VE REALLY GOTTA DO THIS--
PARDON ME, MA'AM--
WHUH!
YOU RECKON YOU COULD GET YOUR MOUTH AROUND SOMETHING THIS WIDE? 'CAUSE IF YOU COULD, I'D LIKE TO MARRY YOU.
JESUS CHRIST!

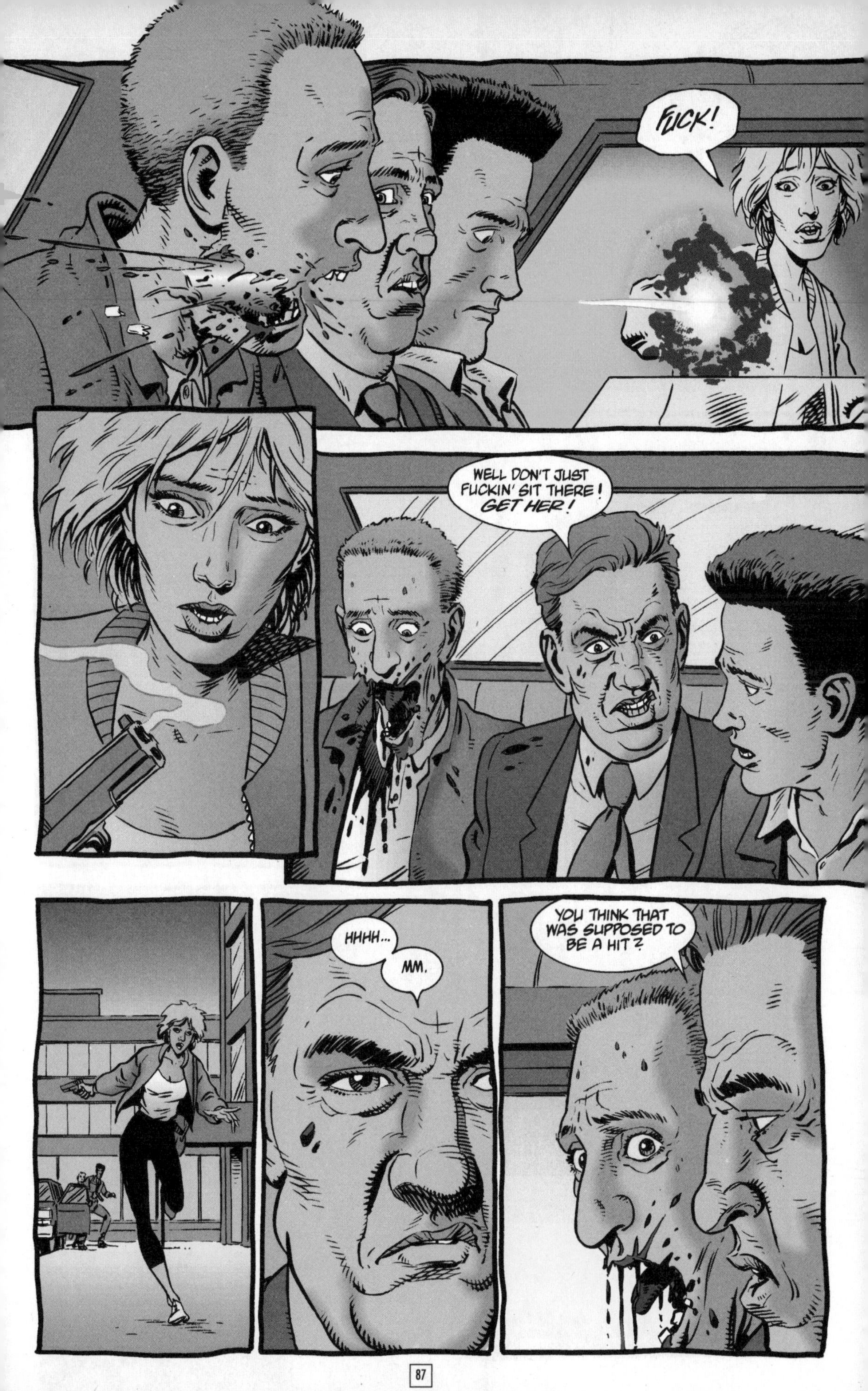
FUCK!
WELL DON'T JUST FUCKIN' SIT THERE! GET HER!
HHHH...
MM.
YOU THINK THAT WAS SUPPOSED TO BE A HIT?

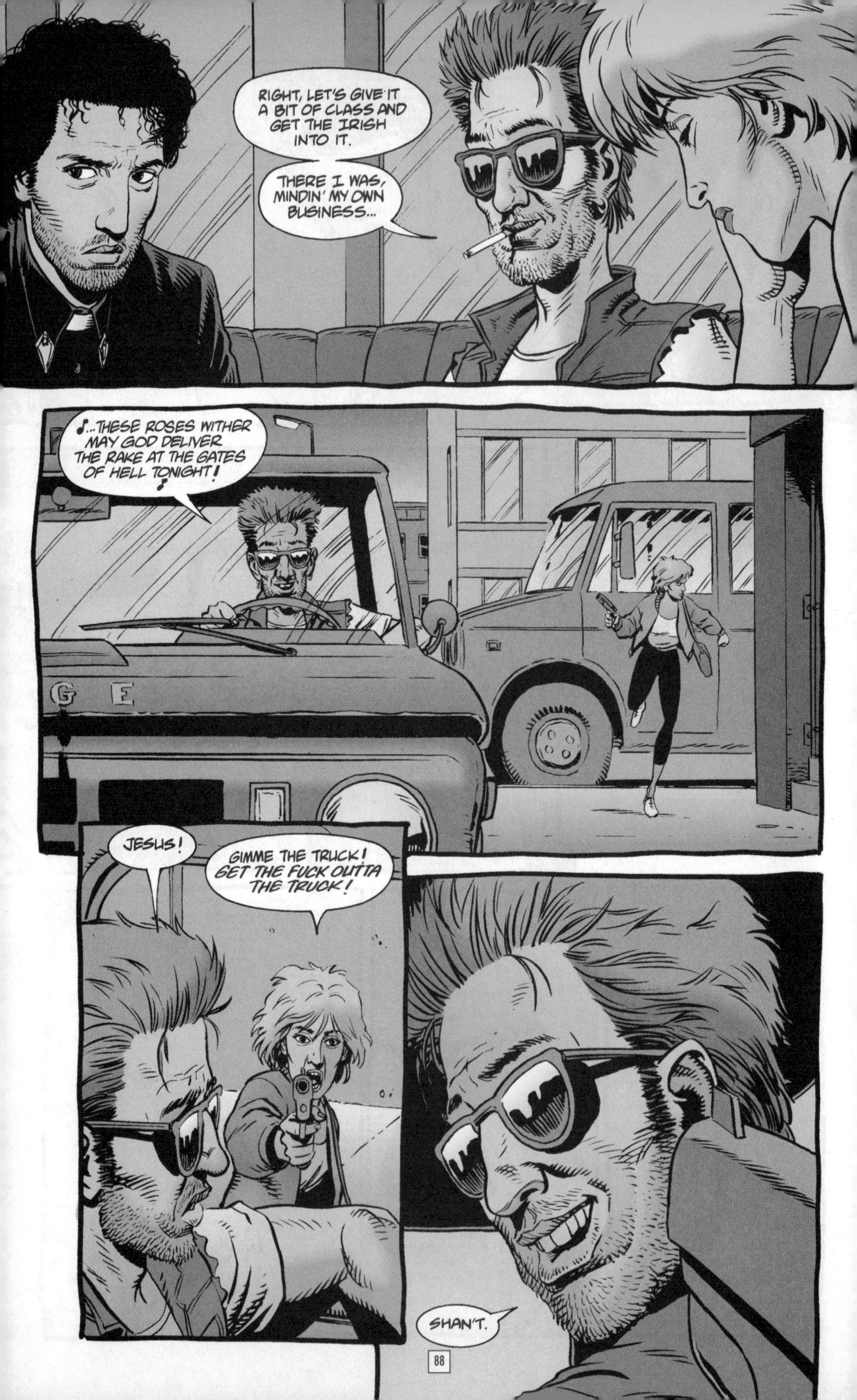
RIGHT, LET'S GIVE IT A BIT OF CLASS AND GET THE IRISH INTO IT.
THERE I WAS, MINDIN' MY OWN BUSINESS...
♪...THESE ROSES WITHER MAY GOD DELIVER THE RAKE AT THE GATES OF HELL TONIGHT! ♪
JESUS!
GIMME THE TRUCK! GET THE FUCK OUTTA THE TRUCK!
SHAN'T.

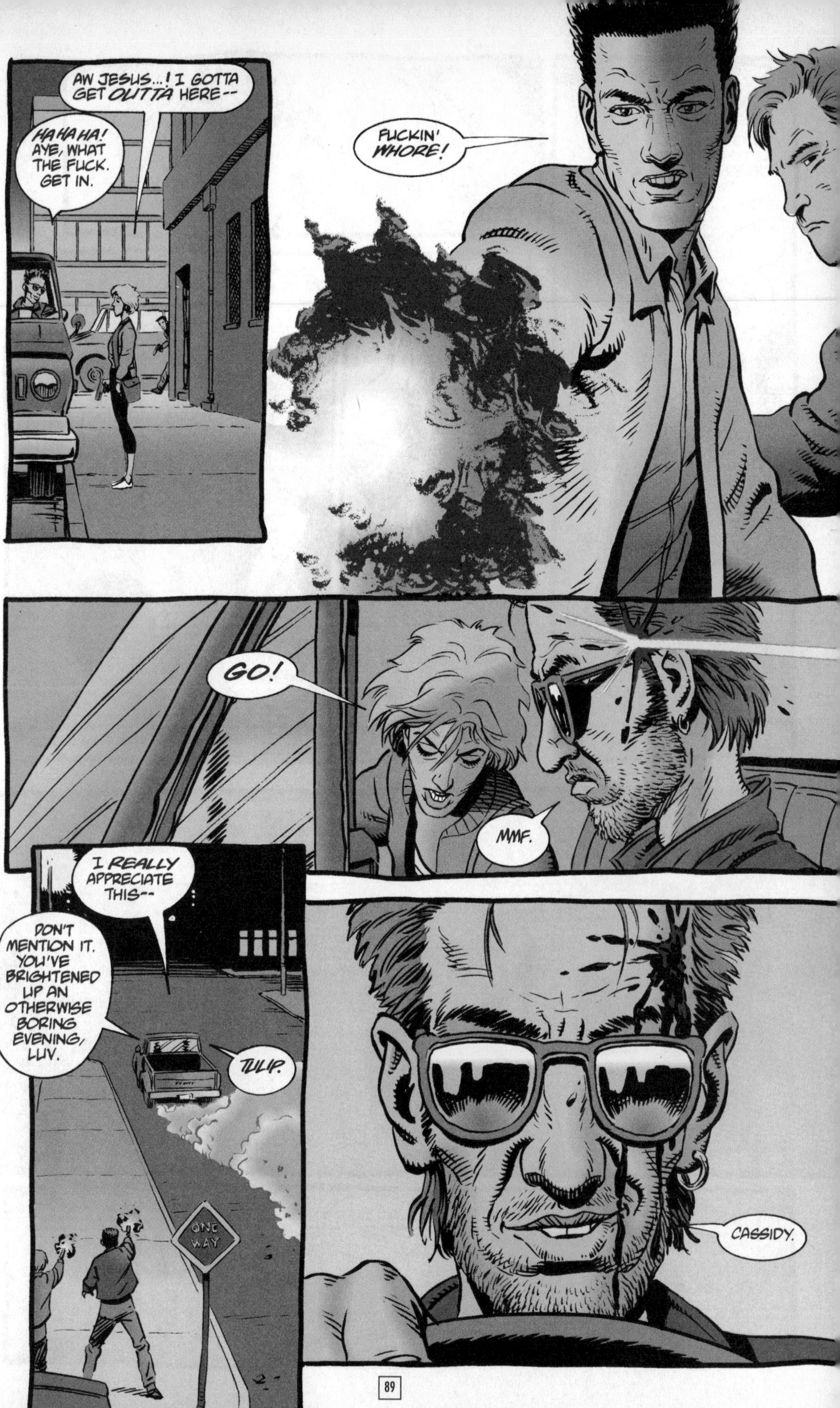
AW JESUS...! I GOTTA GET OUTTA HERE--
HA HA HA! AYE, WHAT THE FUCK. GET IN.
FUCKIN' WHORE!
GO!
MMF.
I REALLY APPRECIATE THIS--
DON'T MENTION IT. YOU'VE BRIGHTENED UP AN OTHERWISE BORING EVENING, LUV.
TULIP.
CASSIDY.
ONE WAY

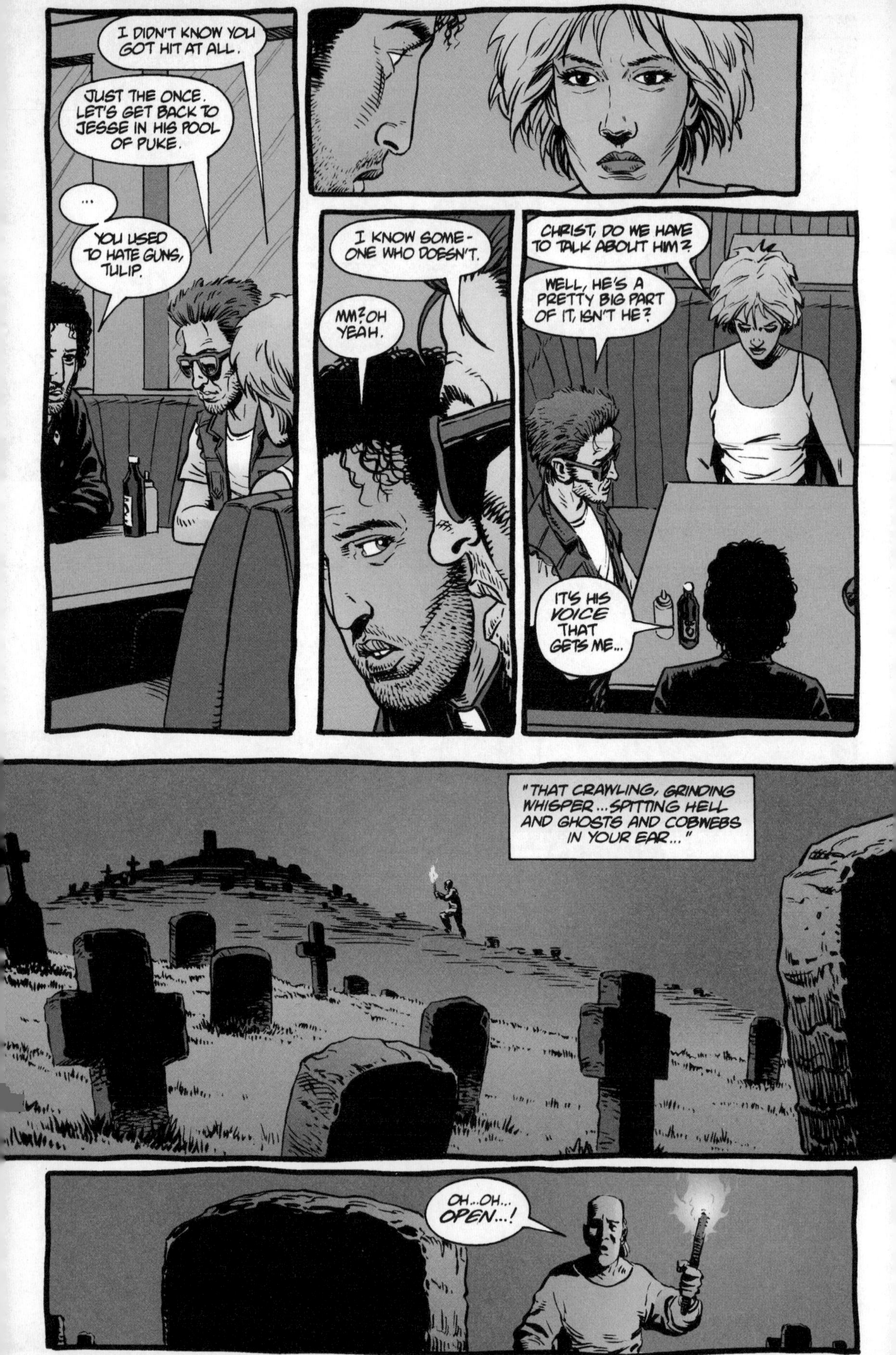
I DIDN'T KNOW YOU GOT HIT AT ALL.
JUST THE ONCE. LET'S GET BACK TO JESSE IN HIS POOL OF PUKE.
...
YOU USED TO HATE GUNS, TULIP.
I KNOW SOME-ONE WHO DOESN'T.
MM? OH YEAH.
CHRIST, DO WE HAVE TO TALK ABOUT HIM?
WELL, HE'S A PRETTY BIG PART OF IT, ISN'T HE?
IT'S HIS VOICE THAT GETS ME...
"THAT CRAWLING, GRINDING WHISPER... SPITTING HELL AND GHOSTS AND COBWEBS IN YOUR EAR..."
OH...OH... OPEN...!

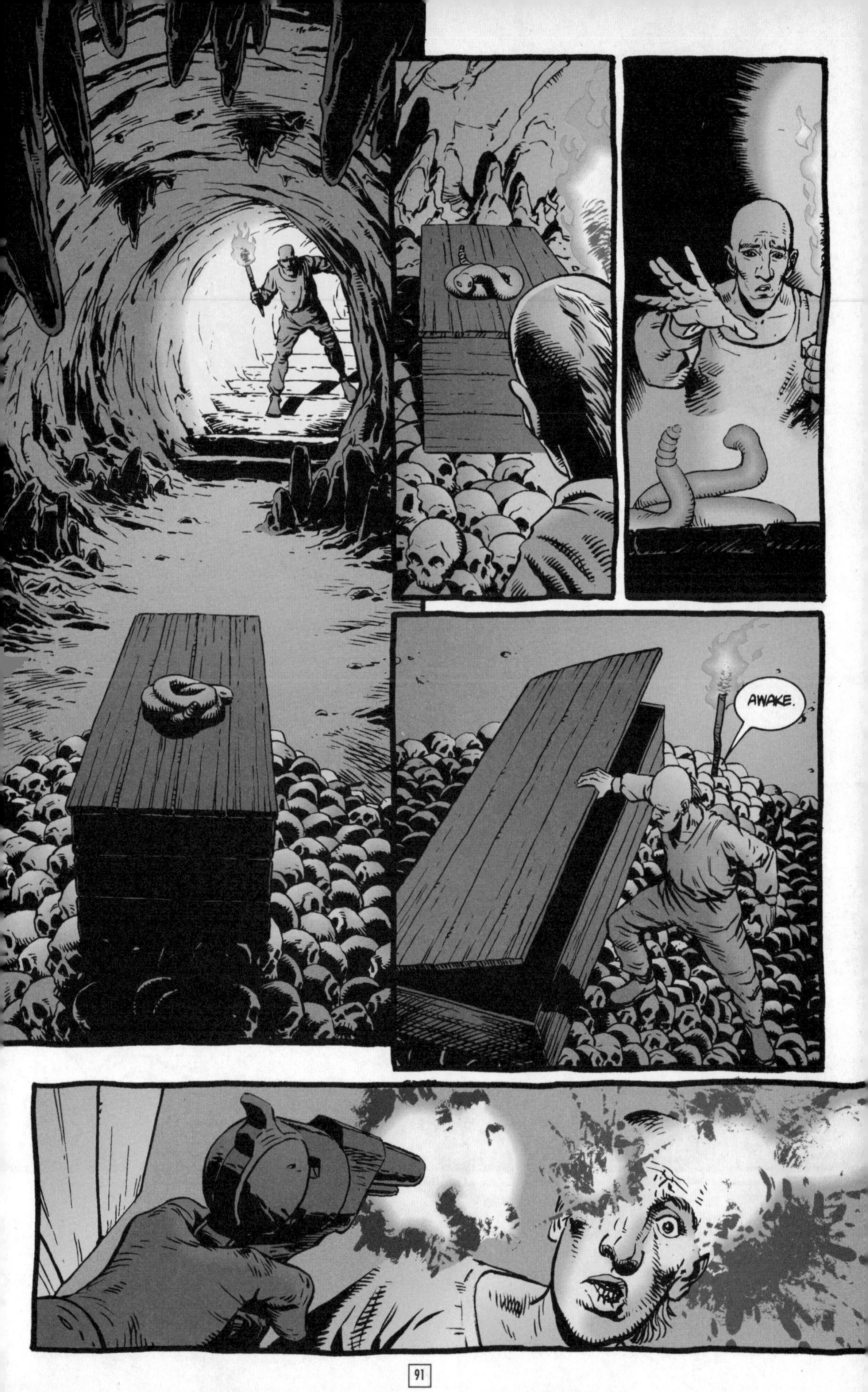
AWAKE.

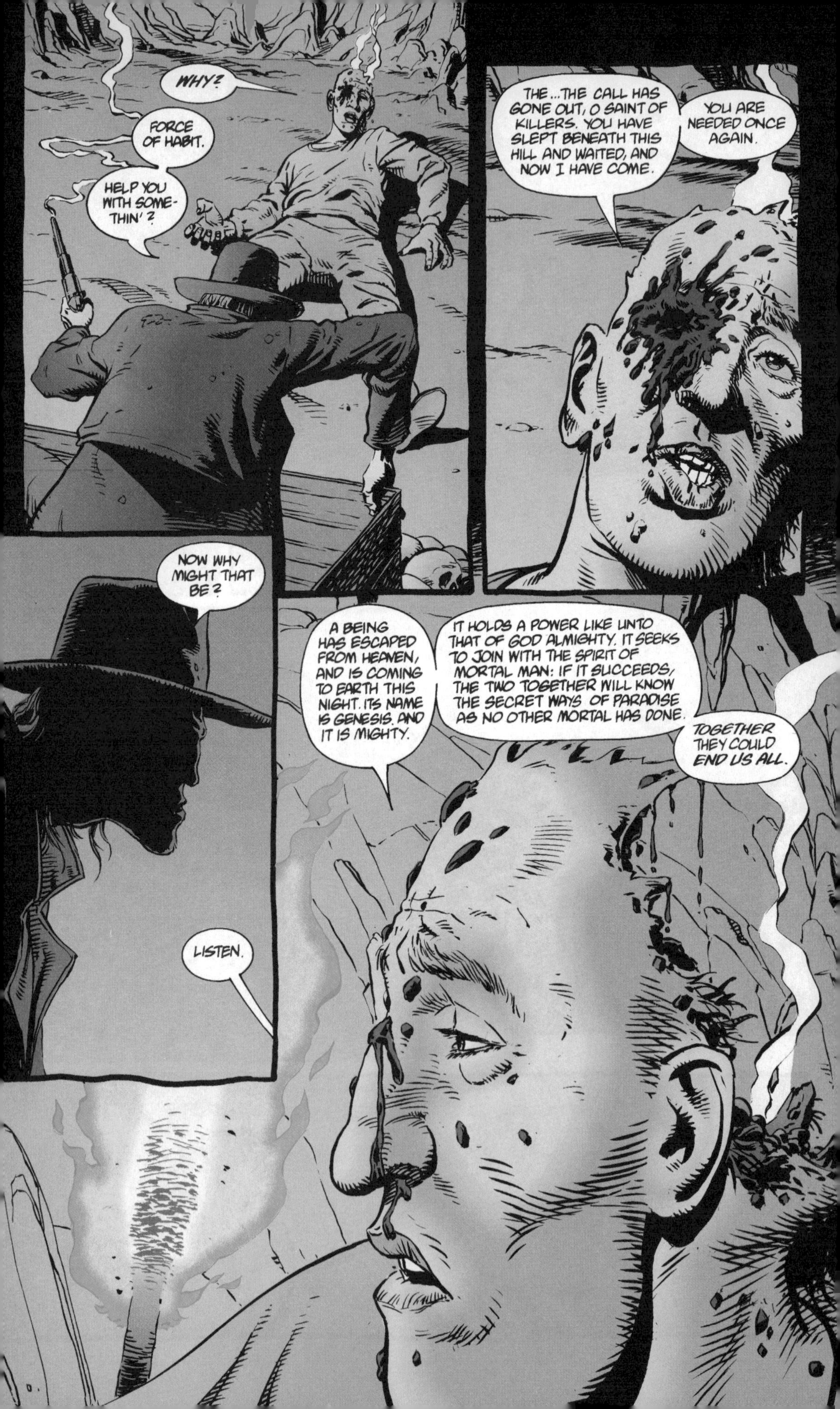
WHY?
FORCE OF HABIT.
HELP YOU WITH SOME-THIN'?
THE ...THE CALL HAS GONE OUT, O SAINT OF KILLERS. YOU HAVE SLEPT BENEATH THIS HILL AND WAITED, AND NOW I HAVE COME.
YOU ARE NEEDED ONCE AGAIN.
NOW WHY MIGHT THAT BE?
LISTEN.
A BEING HAS ESCAPED FROM HEAVEN, AND IS COMING TO EARTH THIS NIGHT. ITS NAME IS GENESIS. AND IT IS MIGHTY.
IT HOLDS A POWER LIKE UNTO THAT OF GOD ALMIGHTY. IT SEEKS TO JOIN WITH THE SPIRIT OF MORTAL MAN: IF IT SUCCEEDS, THE TWO TOGETHER WILL KNOW THE SECRET WAYS OF PARADISE AS NO OTHER MORTAL HAS DONE.
TOGETHER THEY COULD END US ALL.

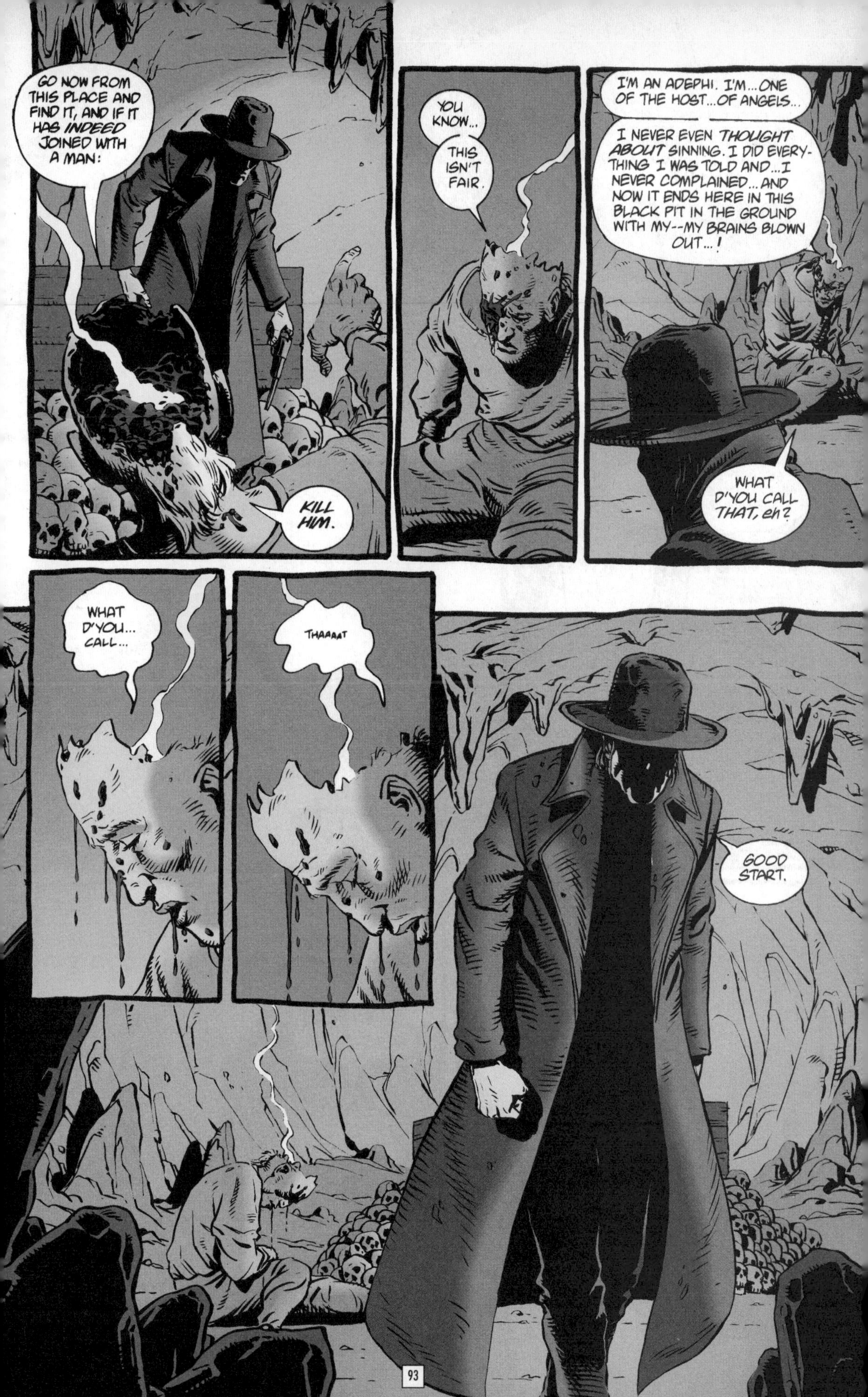
GO NOW FROM THIS PLACE AND FIND IT, AND IF IT HAS *INDEED* JOINED WITH A MAN:
KILL HIM.
YOU KNOW...
THIS ISN'T FAIR.
I'M AN ADEPHI. I'M... ONE OF THE HOST... OF ANGELS...
I NEVER EVEN *THOUGHT ABOUT* SINNING. I DID EVERYTHING I WAS TOLD AND... I NEVER COMPLAINED... AND NOW IT ENDS HERE IN THIS BLACK PIT IN THE GROUND WITH MY--MY BRAINS BLOWN OUT...!
WHAT D'YOU CALL THAT, eh?
WHAT D'YOU... CALL...
THAAAAT
GOOD START.

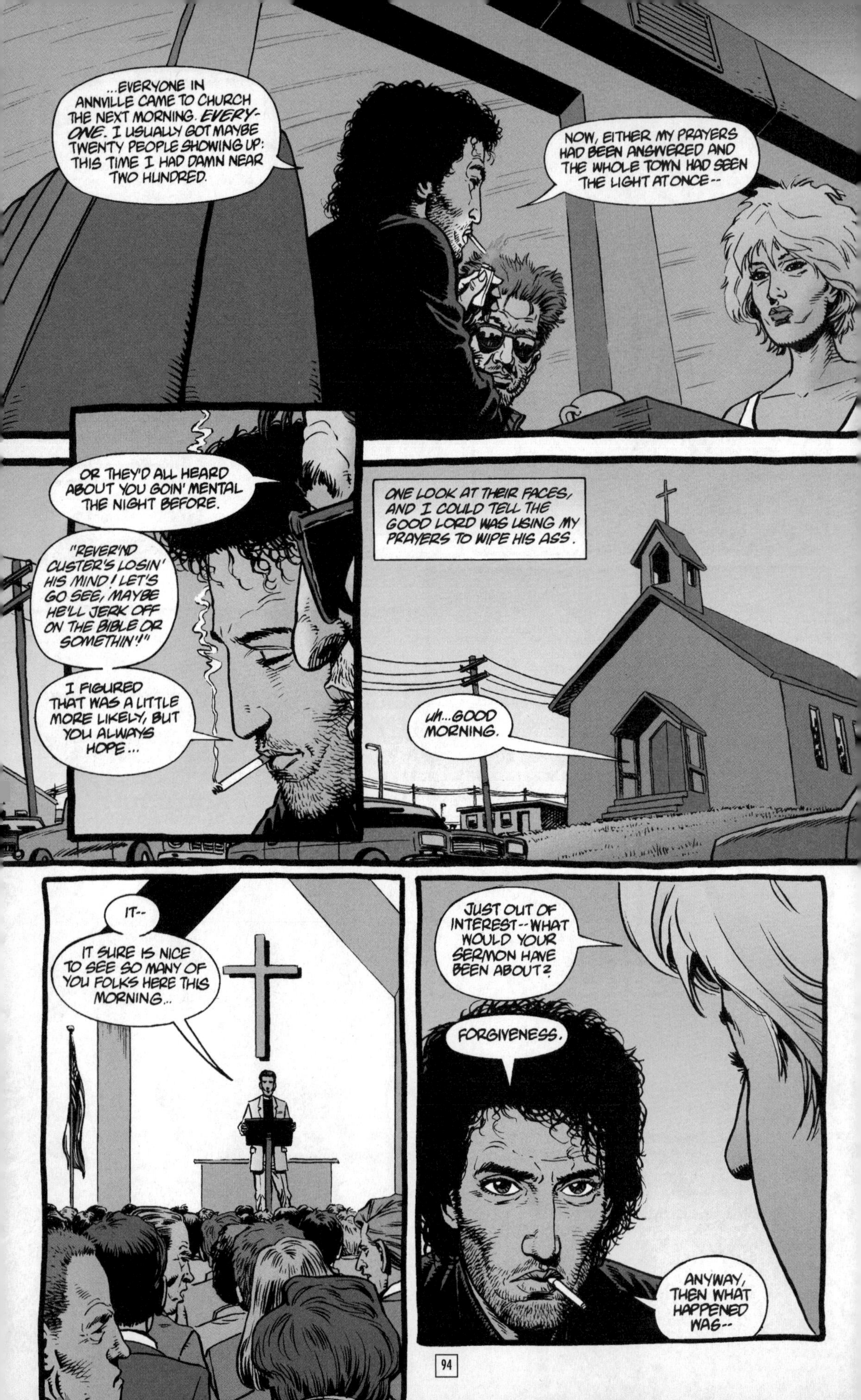

...EVERYONE IN ANNVILLE CAME TO CHURCH THE NEXT MORNING. EVERY-ONE. I USUALLY GOT MAYBE TWENTY PEOPLE SHOWING UP: THIS TIME I HAD DAMN NEAR TWO HUNDRED.
NOW, EITHER MY PRAYERS HAD BEEN ANSWERED AND THE WHOLE TOWN HAD SEEN THE LIGHT AT ONCE--
OR THEY'D ALL HEARD ABOUT YOU GOIN' MENTAL THE NIGHT BEFORE.
"REVER'ND CUSTER'S LOSIN' HIS MIND! LET'S GO SEE, MAYBE HE'LL JERK OFF ON THE BIBLE OR SOMETHIN'!"
I FIGURED THAT WAS A LITTLE MORE LIKELY, BUT YOU ALWAYS HOPE...
ONE LOOK AT THEIR FACES, AND I COULD TELL THE GOOD LORD WAS USING MY PRAYERS TO WIPE HIS ASS.
uh...GOOD MORNING.
IT--
IT SURE IS NICE TO SEE SO MANY OF YOU FOLKS HERE THIS MORNING...
JUST OUT OF INTEREST--WHAT WOULD YOUR SERMON HAVE BEEN ABOUT?
FORGIVENESS.
ANYWAY, THEN WHAT HAPPENED WAS--

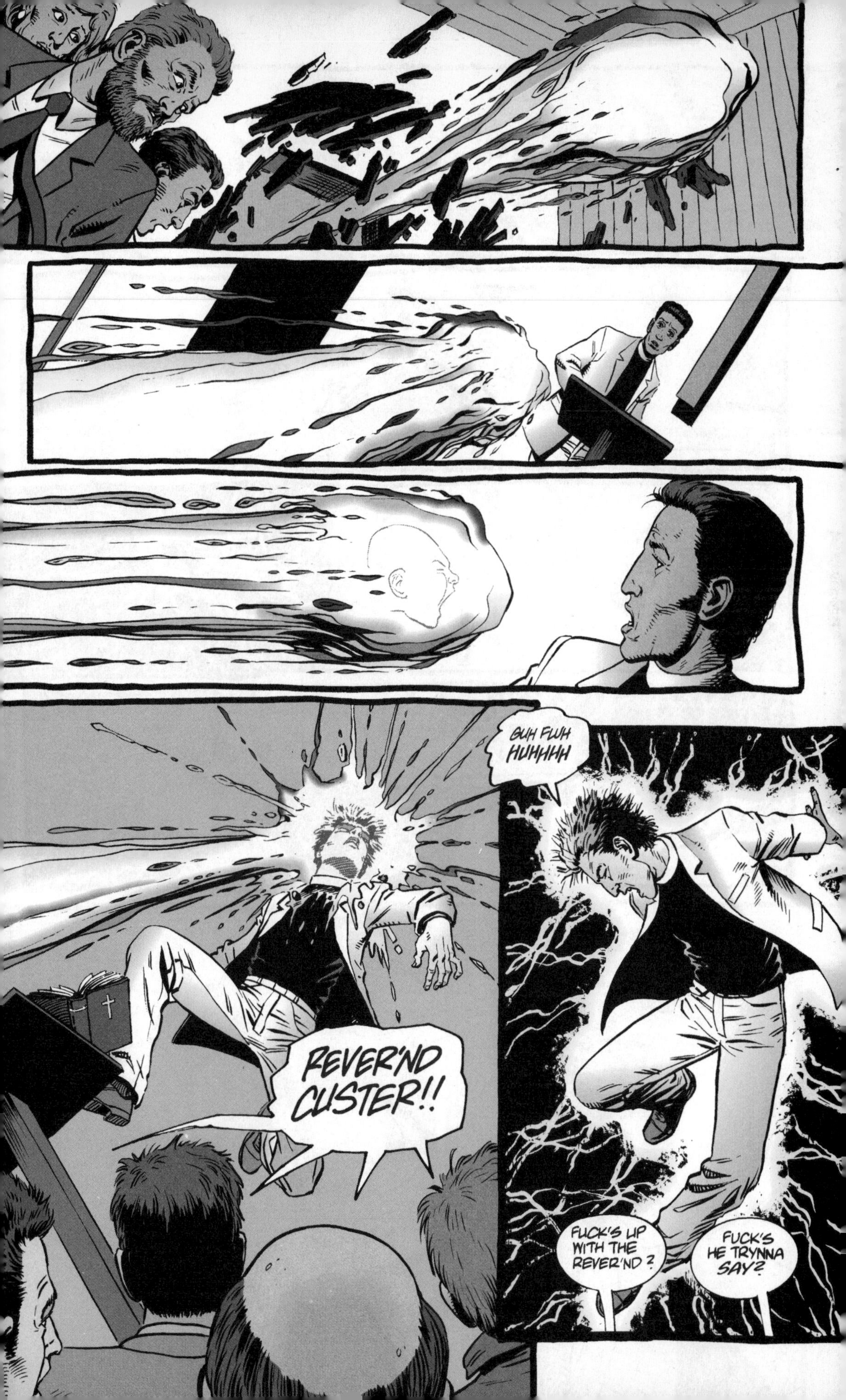
REVER'ND CUSTER!!
GUH FLUH HUHHHH
FUCK'S UP WITH THE REVER'ND?
FUCK'S HE TRYNNA SAY?

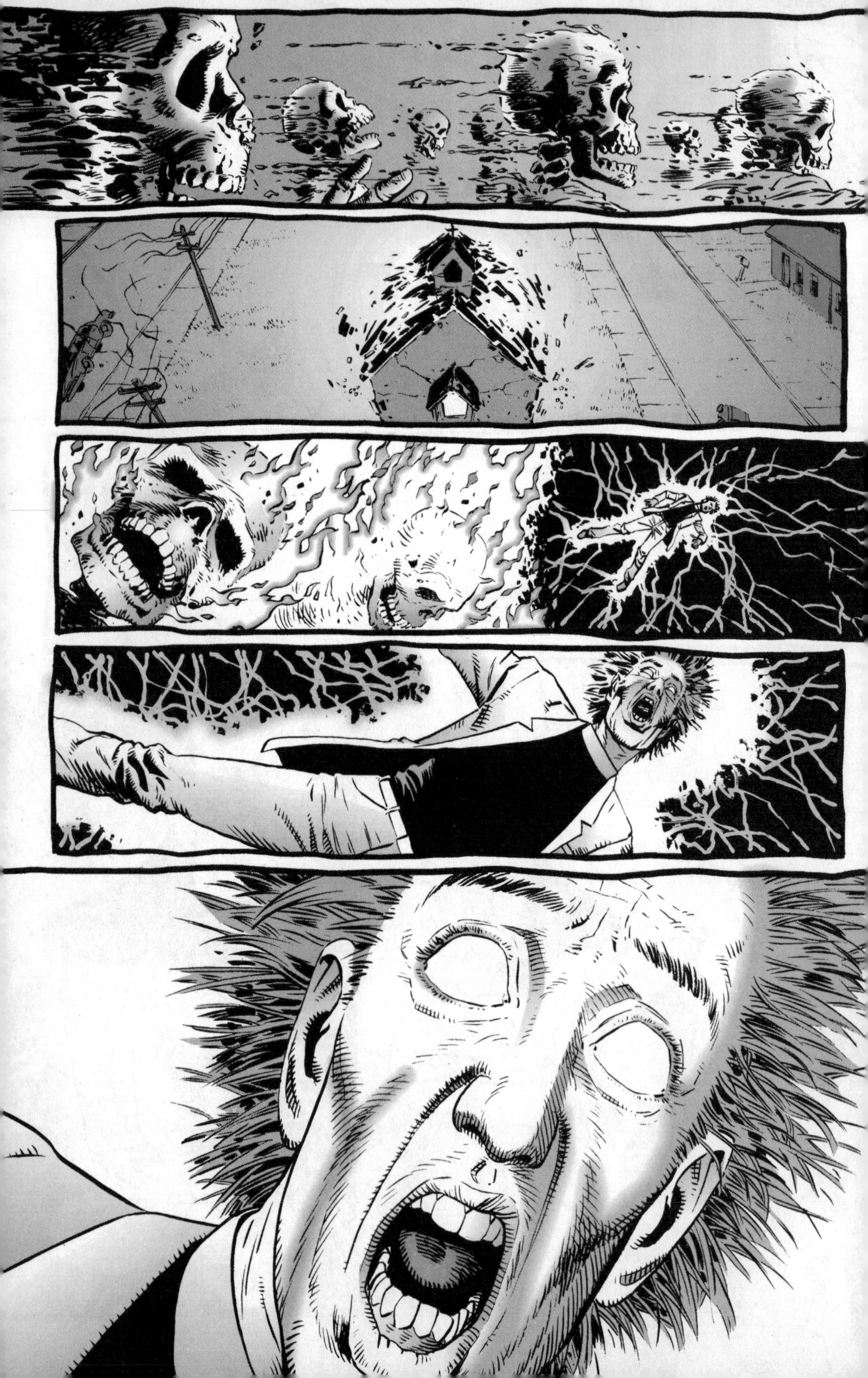

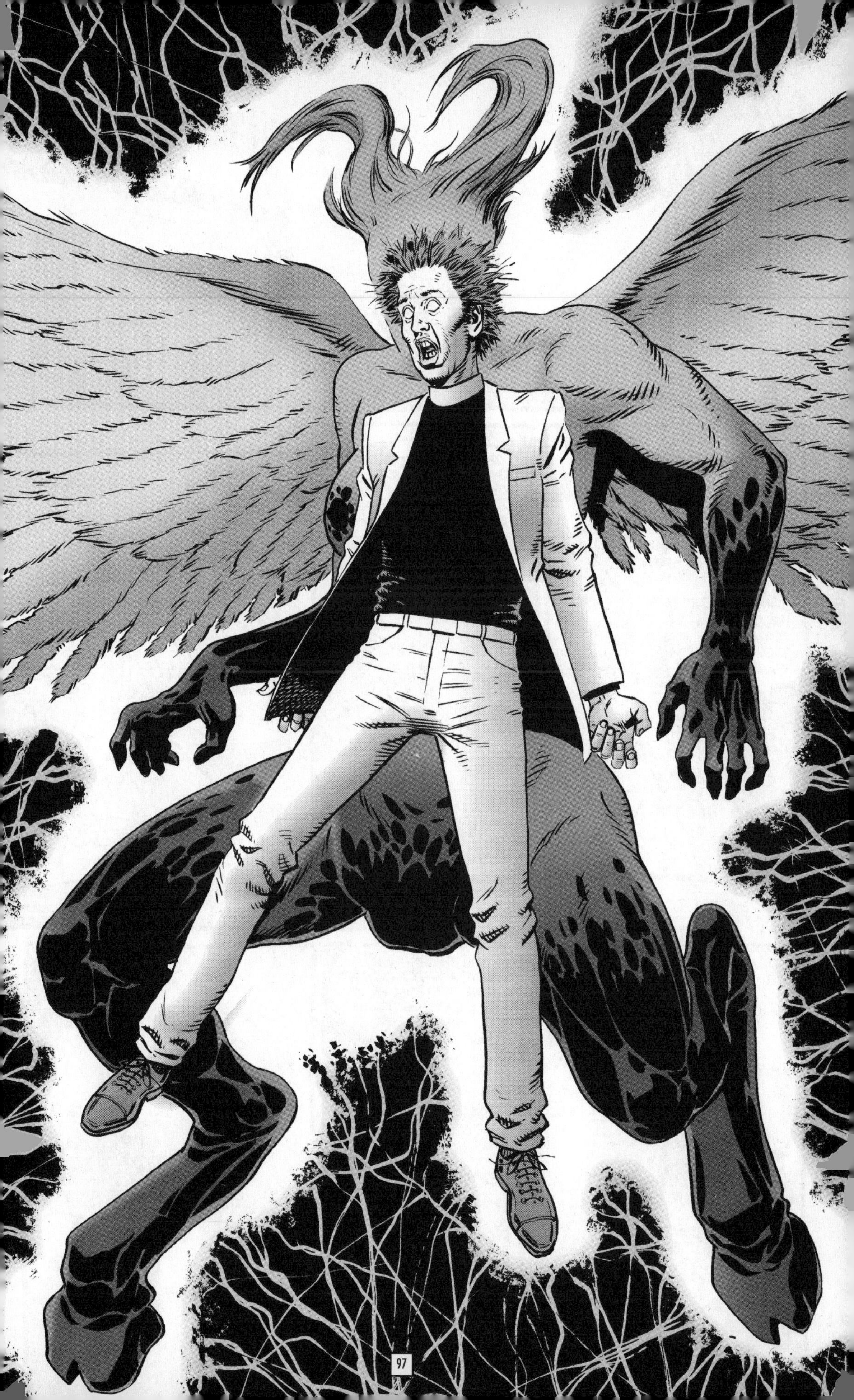

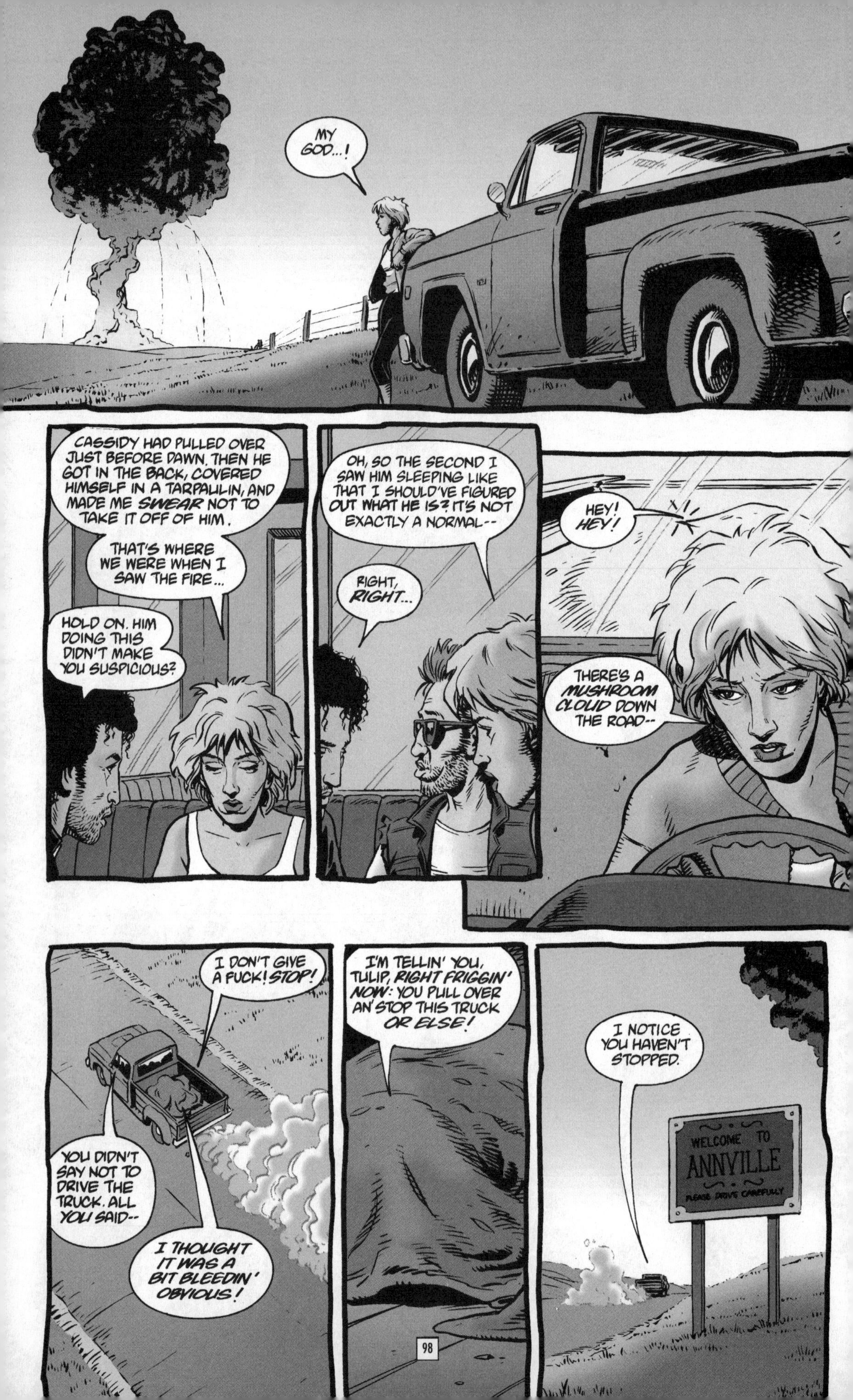
MY GOD...!
CASSIDY HAD PULLED OVER JUST BEFORE DAWN. THEN HE GOT IN THE BACK, COVERED HIMSELF IN A TARPAULIN, AND MADE ME SWEAR NOT TO TAKE IT OFF OF HIM.
THAT'S WHERE WE WERE WHEN I SAW THE FIRE...
HOLD ON. HIM DOING THIS DIDN'T MAKE YOU SUSPICIOUS?
OH, SO THE SECOND I SAW HIM SLEEPING LIKE THAT I SHOULD'VE FIGURED OUT WHAT HE IS? IT'S NOT EXACTLY A NORMAL--
RIGHT, RIGHT...
HEY! HEY!
THERE'S A MUSHROOM CLOUD DOWN THE ROAD--
I DON'T GIVE A FUCK! STOP!
YOU DIDN'T SAY NOT TO DRIVE THE TRUCK. ALL YOU SAID--
I THOUGHT IT WAS A BIT BLEEDIN' OBVIOUS!
I'M TELLIN' YOU, TULIP, RIGHT FRIGGIN' NOW: YOU PULL OVER AN' STOP THIS TRUCK OR ELSE!
I NOTICE YOU HAVEN'T STOPPED.
WELCOME TO
ANNVILLE
PLEASE DRIVE CAREFULLY

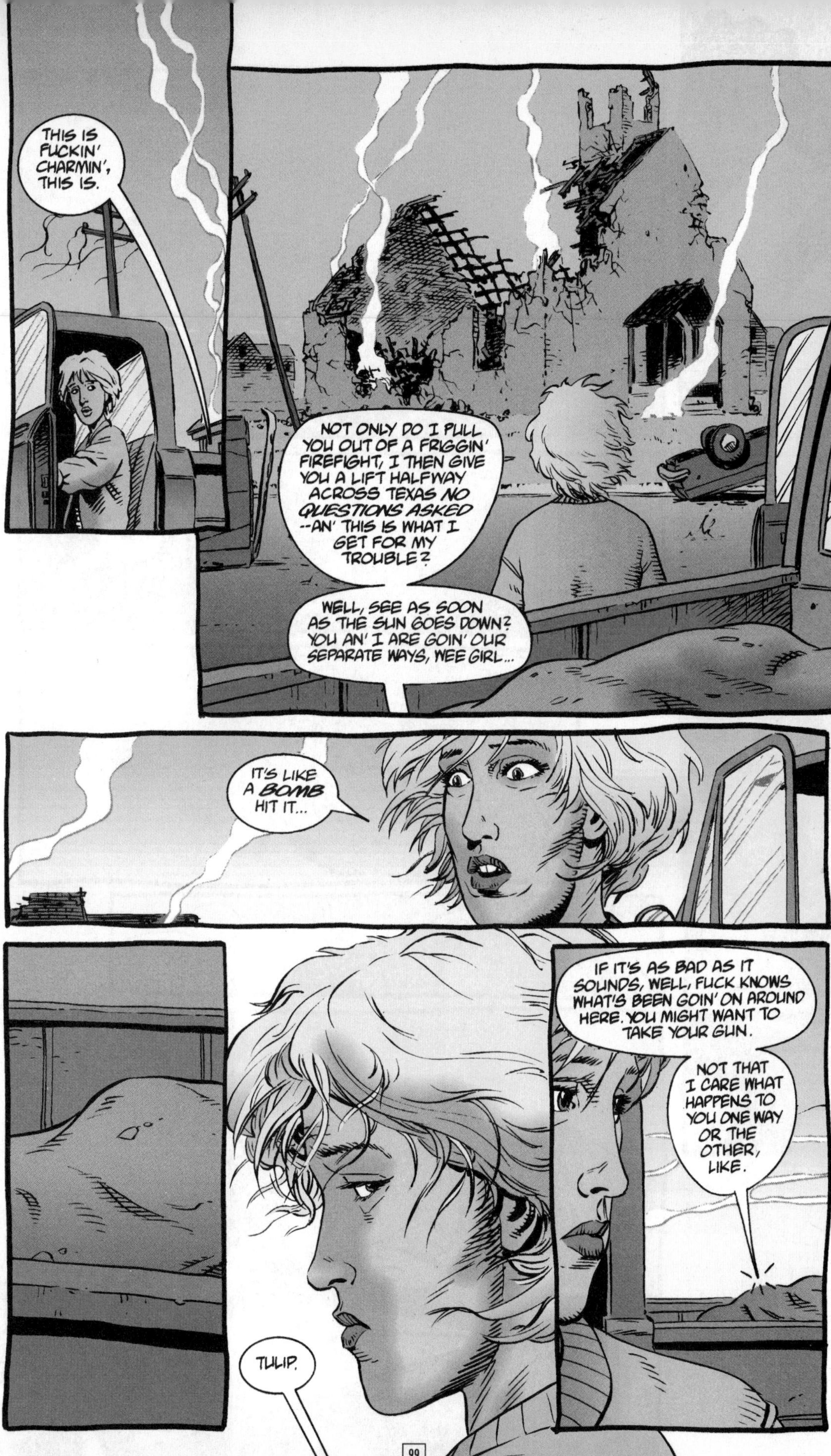
THIS IS FUCKIN' CHARMIN', THIS IS.
NOT ONLY DO I PULL YOU OUT OF A FRIGGIN' FIREFIGHT, I THEN GIVE YOU A LIFT HALFWAY ACROSS TEXAS NO QUESTIONS ASKED --AN' THIS IS WHAT I GET FOR MY TROUBLE?
WELL, SEE AS SOON AS THE SUN GOES DOWN? YOU AN' I ARE GOIN' OUR SEPARATE WAYS, WEE GIRL...
IT'S LIKE A BOMB HIT IT...
IF IT'S AS BAD AS IT SOUNDS, WELL, FUCK KNOWS WHAT'S BEEN GOIN' ON AROUND HERE. YOU MIGHT WANT TO TAKE YOUR GUN.
NOT THAT I CARE WHAT HAPPENS TO YOU ONE WAY OR THE OTHER, LIKE.
TULIP.

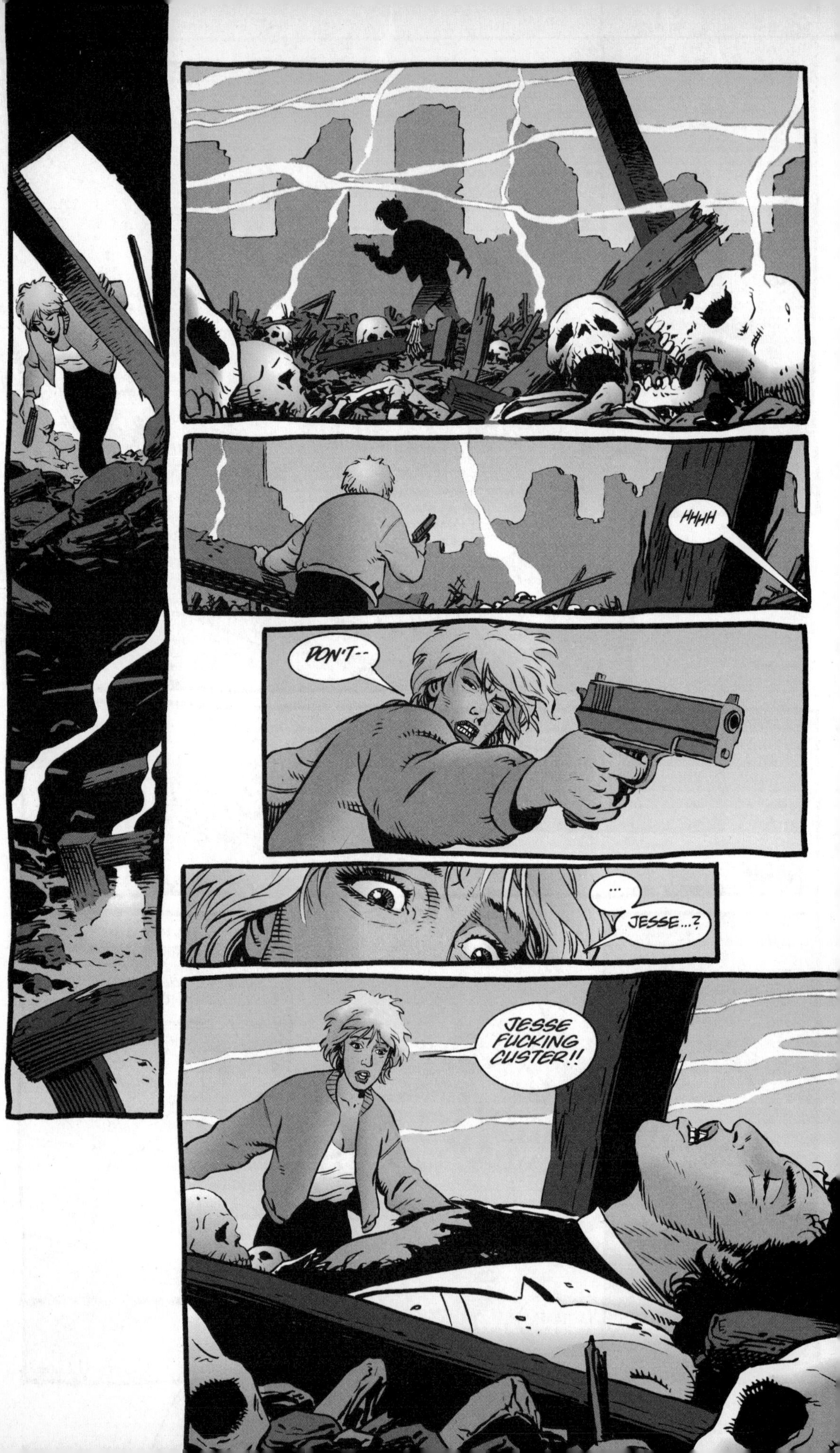
HHHH
DON'T--
...
JESSE...?
JESSE FUCKING CUSTER!!

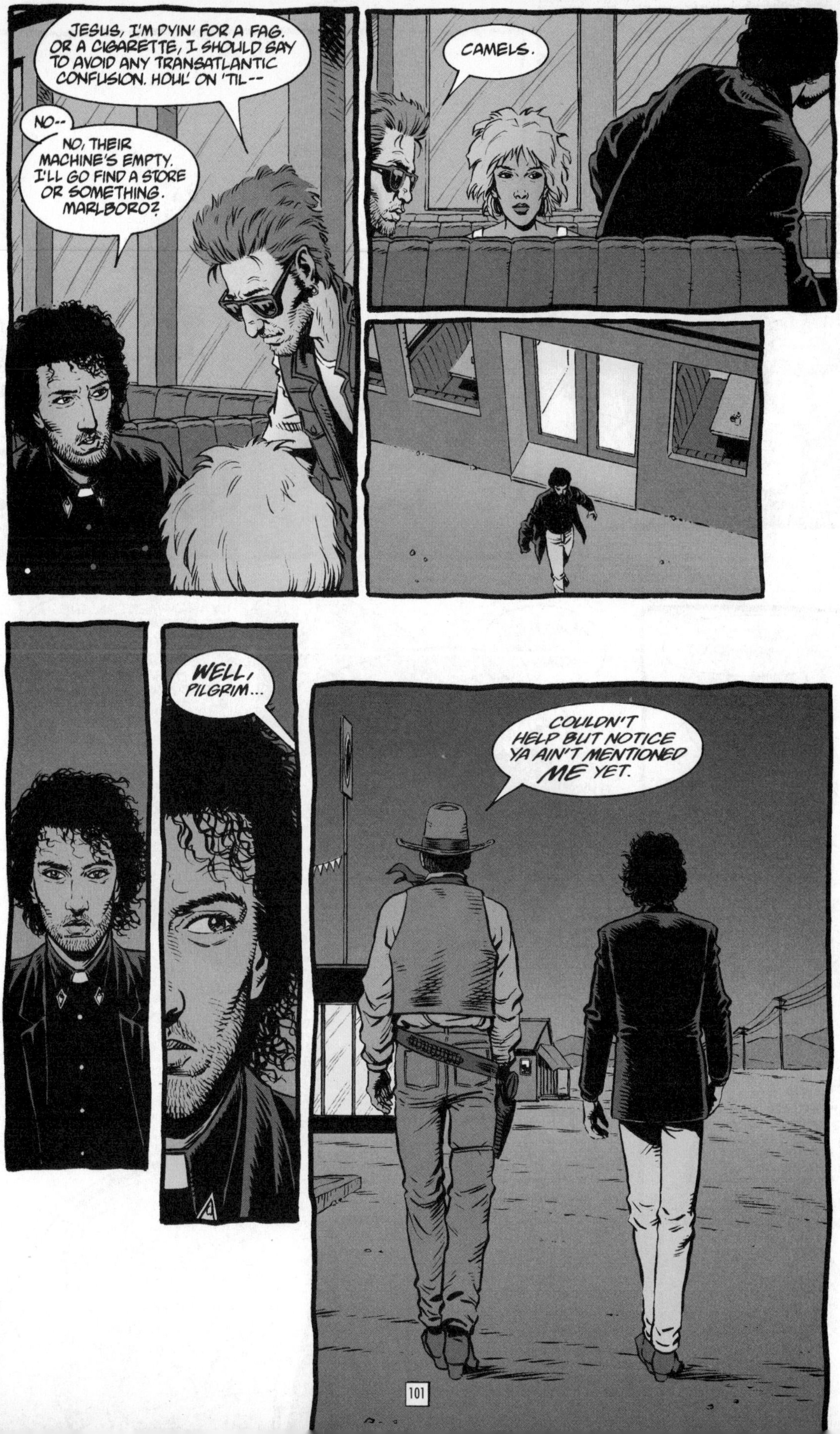
JESUS, I'M DYIN' FOR A FAG. OR A CIGARETTE, I SHOULD SAY TO AVOID ANY TRANSATLANTIC CONFUSION. HOUL' ON 'TIL--
NO--
NO, THEIR MACHINE'S EMPTY. I'LL GO FIND A STORE OR SOMETHING. MARLBORO?
CAMELS.
WELL, PILGRIM...
COULDN'T HELP BUT NOTICE YA AIN'T MENTIONED ME YET.

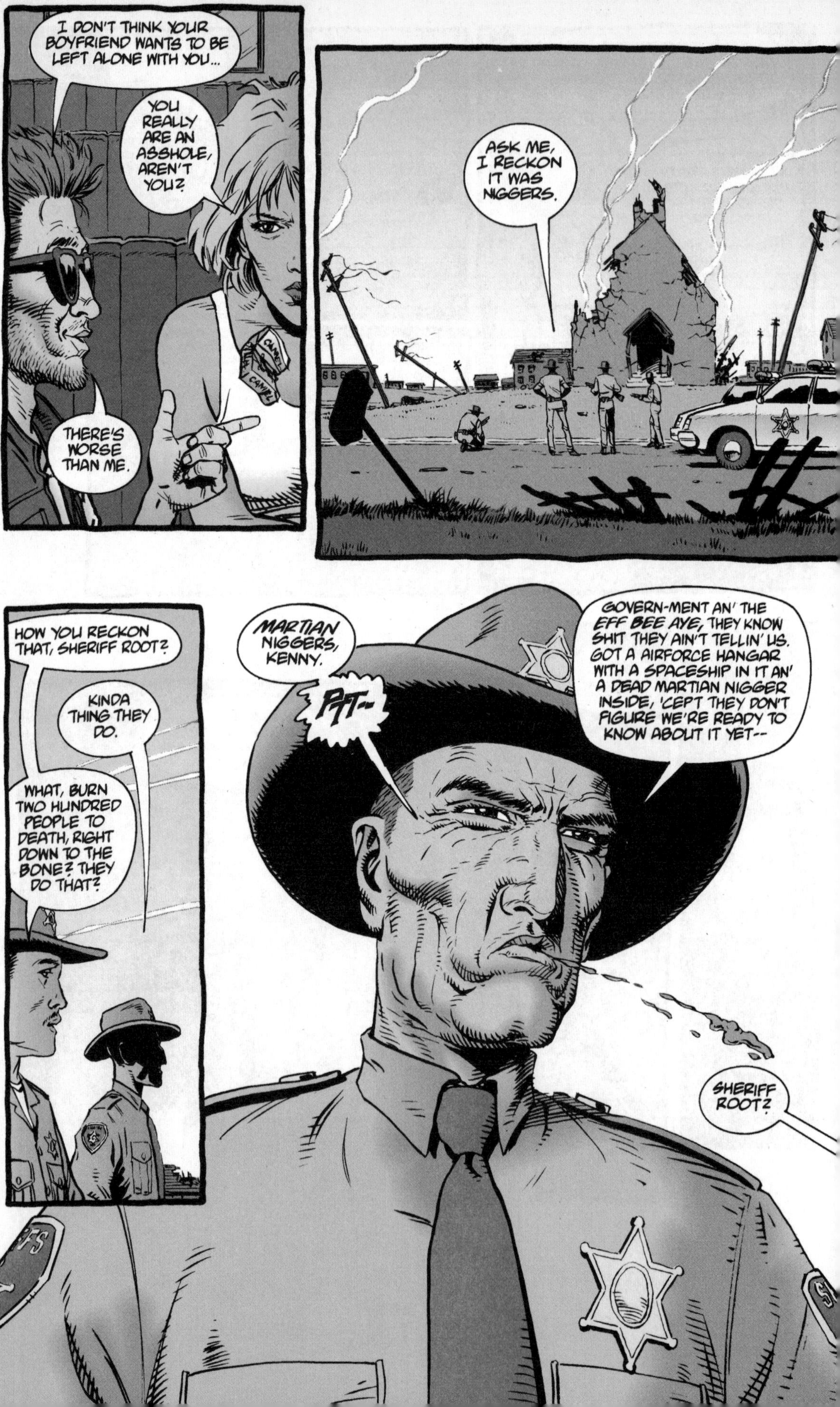

I DON'T THINK YOUR BOYFRIEND WANTS TO BE LEFT ALONE WITH YOU...
YOU REALLY ARE AN ASSHOLE, AREN'T YOU?
THERE'S WORSE THAN ME.
ASK ME, I RECKON IT WAS NIGGERS.
HOW YOU RECKON THAT, SHERIFF ROOT?
KINDA THING THEY DO.
WHAT, BURN TWO HUNDRED PEOPLE TO DEATH, RIGHT DOWN TO THE BONE? THEY DO THAT?
MARTIAN NIGGERS, KENNY.
PTT--
GOVERN-MENT AN' THE EFF BEE AYE, THEY KNOW SHIT THEY AIN'T TELLIN' US. GOT A AIRFORCE HANGAR WITH A SPACESHIP IN IT AN' A DEAD MARTIAN NIGGER INSIDE, 'CEPT THEY DON'T FIGURE WE'RE READY TO KNOW ABOUT IT YET--
SHERIFF ROOT?

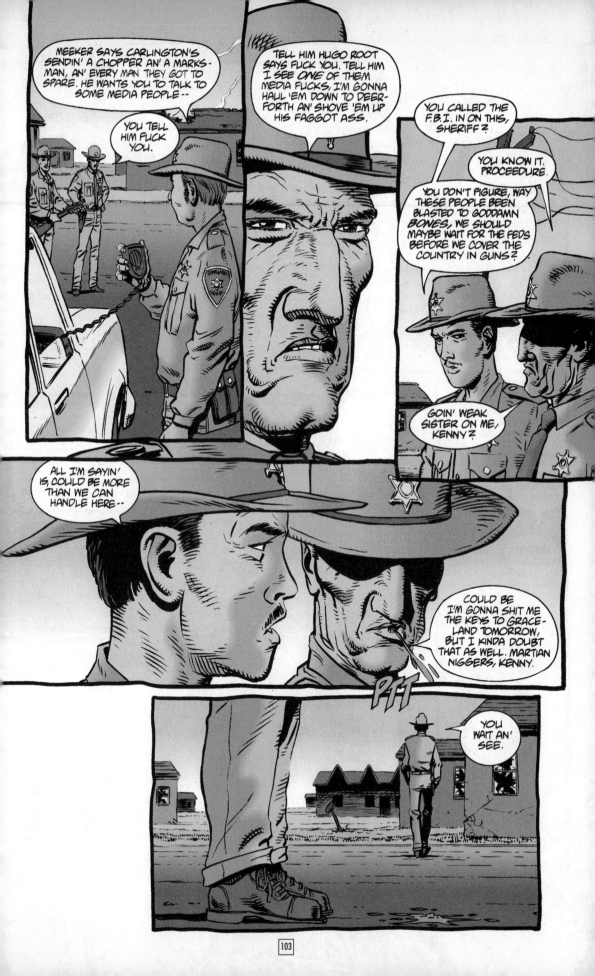

MEEKER SAYS CARLINGTON'S SENDIN' A CHOPPER AN' A MARKS-MAN, AN' EVERY MAN THEY GOT TO SPARE. HE WANTS YOU TO TALK TO SOME MEDIA PEOPLE--

YOU TELL HIM FUCK YOU.

TELL HIM HUGO ROOT SAYS FUCK YOU. TELL HIM I SEE *ONE* OF THEM MEDIA FUCKS, I'M GONNA HAUL 'EM DOWN TO DEER-FORTH AN' SHOVE 'EM UP HIS FAGGOT ASS.

YOU CALLED THE F.B.I. IN ON THIS, SHERIFF?

YOU KNOW IT. PROCEEDURE.

YOU DON'T FIGURE, WAY THESE PEOPLE BEEN BLASTED TO GODDAMN *BONES*, WE SHOULD MAYBE WAIT FOR THE FEDS BEFORE WE COVER THE COUNTRY IN GUNS?

GOIN' WEAK SISTER ON ME, KENNY?

ALL I'M SAYIN' IS, COULD BE MORE THAN WE CAN HANDLE HERE--

COULD BE I'M GONNA SHIT ME THE KEYS TO GRACE-LAND TOMORROW, BUT I KINDA DOUBT THAT AS WELL. MARTIAN NIGGERS, KENNY.

PTT

YOU WAIT AN' SEE.

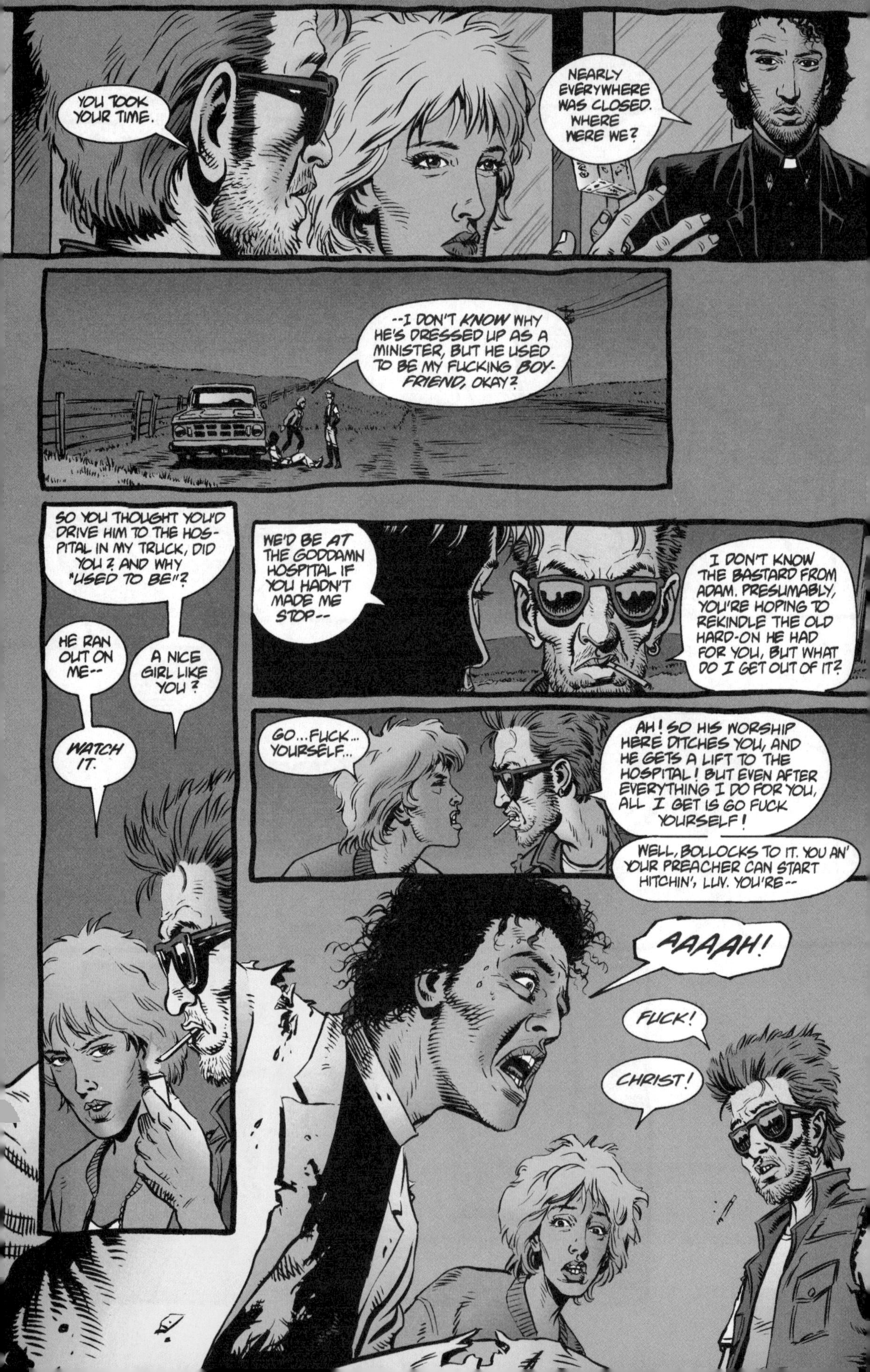
YOU TOOK YOUR TIME.
NEARLY EVERYWHERE WAS CLOSED. WHERE WERE WE?
--I DON'T *KNOW* WHY HE'S DRESSED UP AS A MINISTER, BUT HE USED TO BE MY FUCKING *BOY-FRIEND*, OKAY?
SO YOU THOUGHT YOU'D DRIVE HIM TO THE HOS-PITAL IN MY TRUCK, DID YOU? AND WHY "*USED TO BE*"?
HE RAN OUT ON ME--
A NICE GIRL LIKE YOU?
WATCH IT.
WE'D BE AT THE GODDAMN HOSPITAL IF YOU HADN'T MADE ME STOP--
I DON'T KNOW THE BASTARD FROM ADAM. PRESUMABLY, YOU'RE HOPING TO REKINDLE THE OLD HARD-ON HE HAD FOR YOU, BUT WHAT DO I GET OUT OF IT?
GO...FUCK... YOURSELF...
AH! SO HIS WORSHIP HERE DITCHES YOU, AND HE GETS A LIFT TO THE HOSPITAL! BUT EVEN AFTER EVERYTHING I DO FOR YOU, ALL I GET IS GO FUCK YOURSELF!
WELL, BOLLOCKS TO IT. YOU AN' YOUR PREACHER CAN START HITCHIN', LUV. YOU'RE--
AAAAH!
FUCK!
CHRIST!

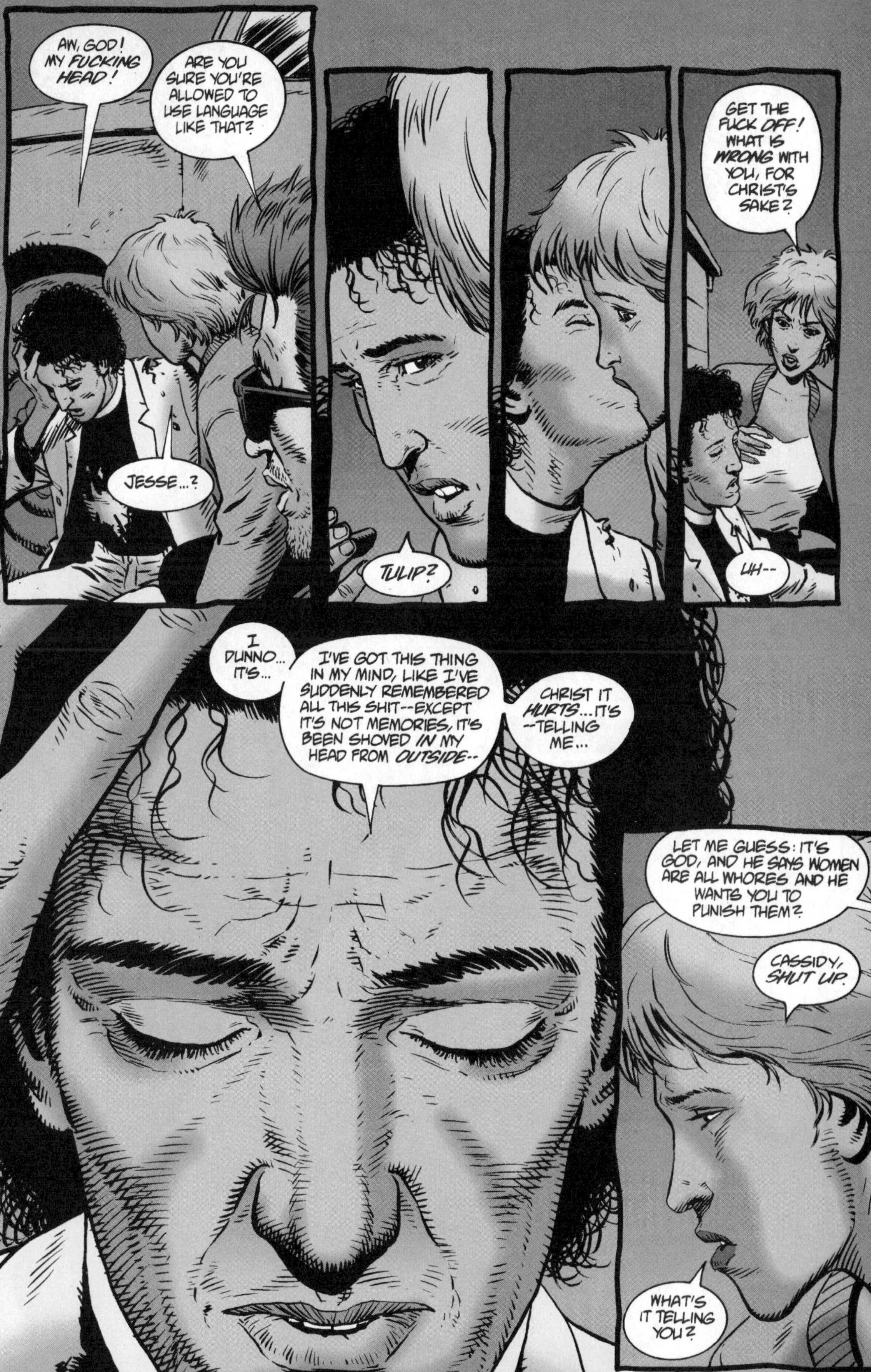
AW, GOD! MY FUCKING HEAD!
ARE YOU SURE YOU'RE ALLOWED TO USE LANGUAGE LIKE THAT?
JESSE...?
TULIP?
GET THE FUCK OFF! WHAT IS WRONG WITH YOU, FOR CHRIST'S SAKE?
UH--
I DUNNO... IT'S...
I'VE GOT THIS THING IN MY MIND, LIKE I'VE SUDDENLY REMEMBERED ALL THIS SHIT--EXCEPT IT'S NOT MEMORIES, IT'S BEEN SHOVED IN MY HEAD FROM OUTSIDE--
CHRIST IT HURTS... IT'S --TELLING ME...
LET ME GUESS: IT'S GOD, AND HE SAYS WOMEN ARE ALL WHORES AND HE WANTS YOU TO PUNISH THEM?
CASSIDY, SHUT UP.
WHAT'S IT TELLING YOU?

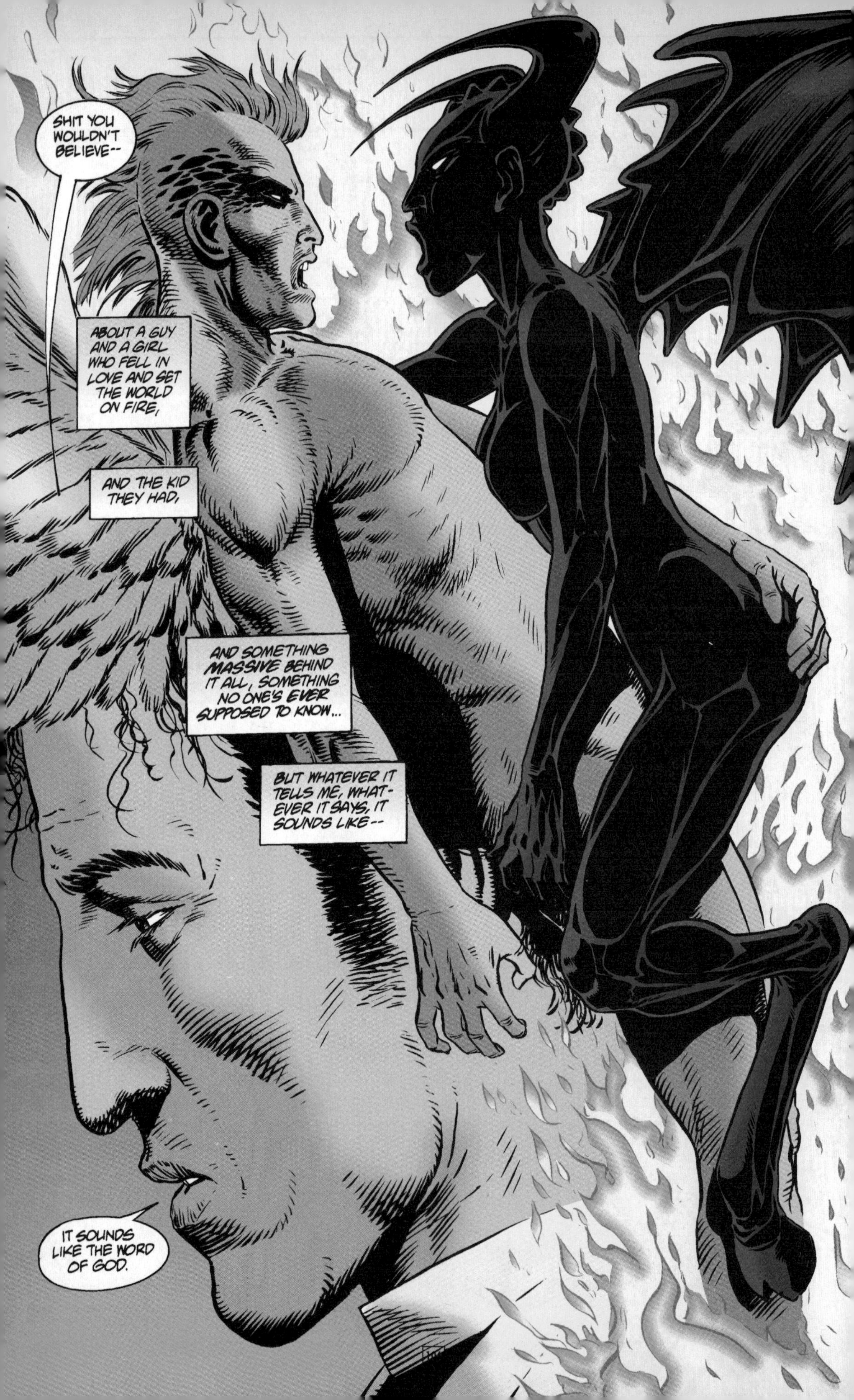
SHIT YOU WOULDN'T BELIEVE--
ABOUT A GUY AND A GIRL WHO FELL IN LOVE AND SET THE WORLD ON FIRE,
AND THE KID THEY HAD,
AND SOMETHING MASSIVE BEHIND IT ALL, SOMETHING NO ONE'S EVER SUPPOSED TO KNOW...
BUT WHATEVER IT TELLS ME, WHATEVER IT SAYS, IT SOUNDS LIKE--
IT SOUNDS LIKE THE WORD OF GOD.

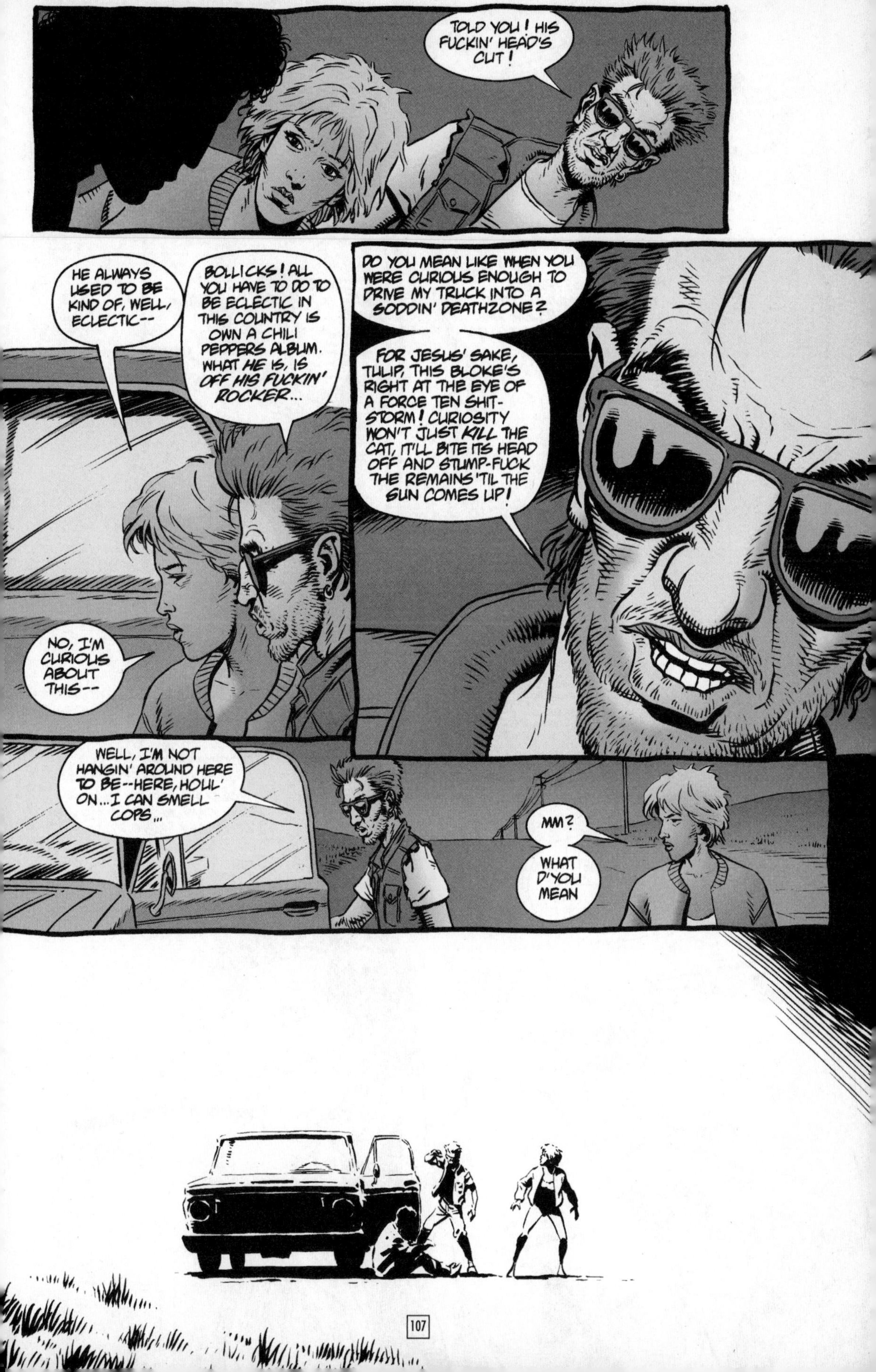
TOLD YOU! HIS FUCKIN' HEAD'S CUT!
HE ALWAYS USED TO BE KIND OF, WELL, ECLECTIC--
BOLLICKS! ALL YOU HAVE TO DO TO BE ECLECTIC IN THIS COUNTRY IS OWN A CHILI PEPPERS ALBUM. WHAT HE IS, IS OFF HIS FUCKIN' ROCKER...
NO, I'M CURIOUS ABOUT THIS--
DO YOU MEAN LIKE WHEN YOU WERE CURIOUS ENOUGH TO DRIVE MY TRUCK INTO A SODDIN' DEATHZONE?
FOR JESUS' SAKE, TULIP, THIS BLOKE'S RIGHT AT THE EYE OF A FORCE TEN SHIT-STORM! CURIOSITY WON'T JUST KILL THE CAT, IT'LL BITE ITS HEAD OFF AND STUMP-FUCK THE REMAINS 'TIL THE SUN COMES UP!
WELL, I'M NOT HANGIN' AROUND HERE TO BE--HERE, HOUL' ON...I CAN SMELL COPS...
MM?
WHAT D'YOU MEAN

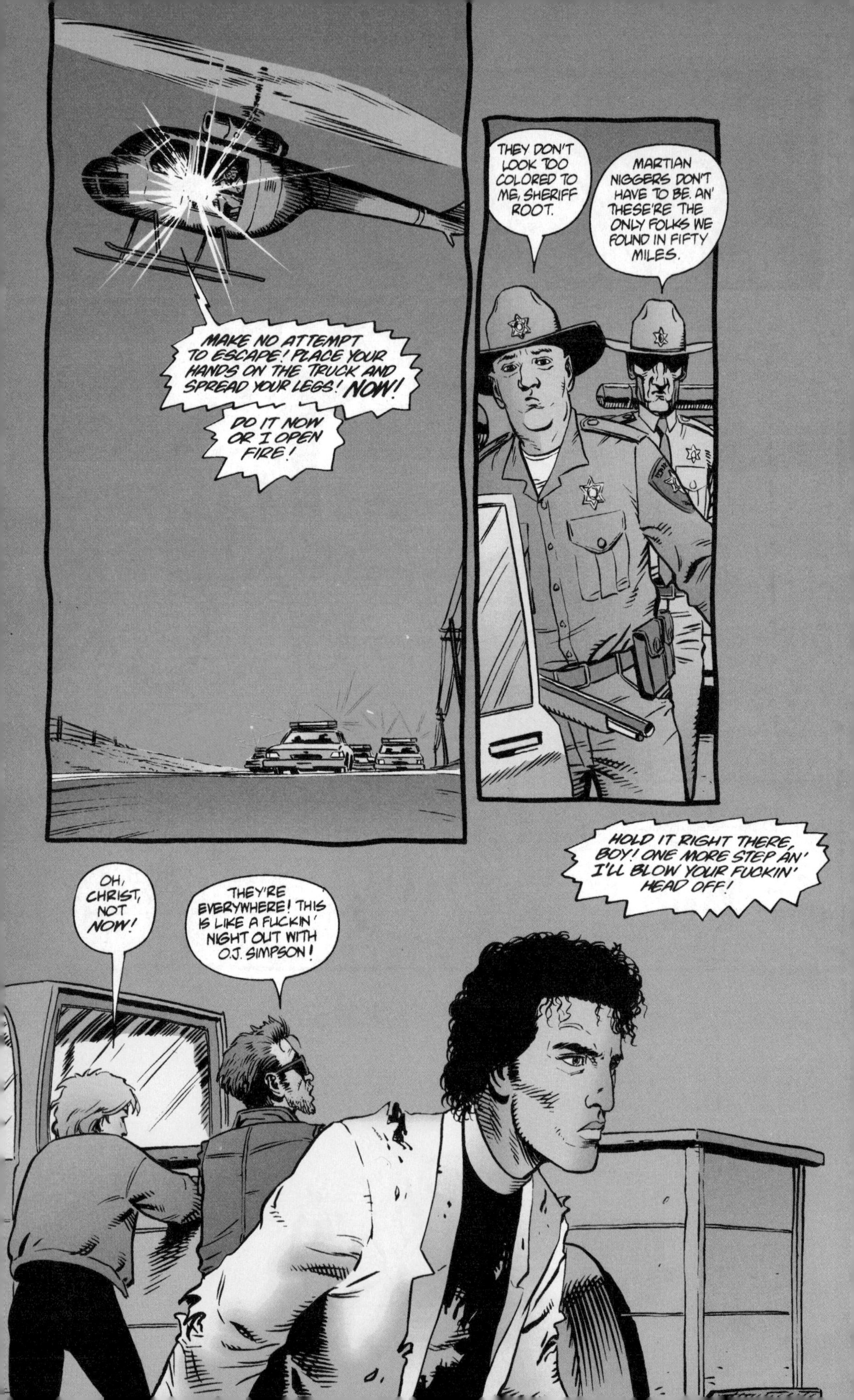
MAKE NO ATTEMPT TO ESCAPE! PLACE YOUR HANDS ON THE TRUCK AND SPREAD YOUR LEGS! NOW!
DO IT NOW OR I OPEN FIRE!
THEY DON'T LOOK TOO COLORED TO ME, SHERIFF ROOT.
MARTIAN NIGGERS DON'T HAVE TO BE. AN' THESE'RE THE ONLY FOLKS WE FOUND IN FIFTY MILES.
HOLD IT RIGHT THERE, BOY! ONE MORE STEP AN' I'LL BLOW YOUR FUCKIN' HEAD OFF!
OH, CHRIST, NOT NOW!
THEY'RE EVERYWHERE! THIS IS LIKE A FUCKIN' NIGHT OUT WITH O.J. SIMPSON!

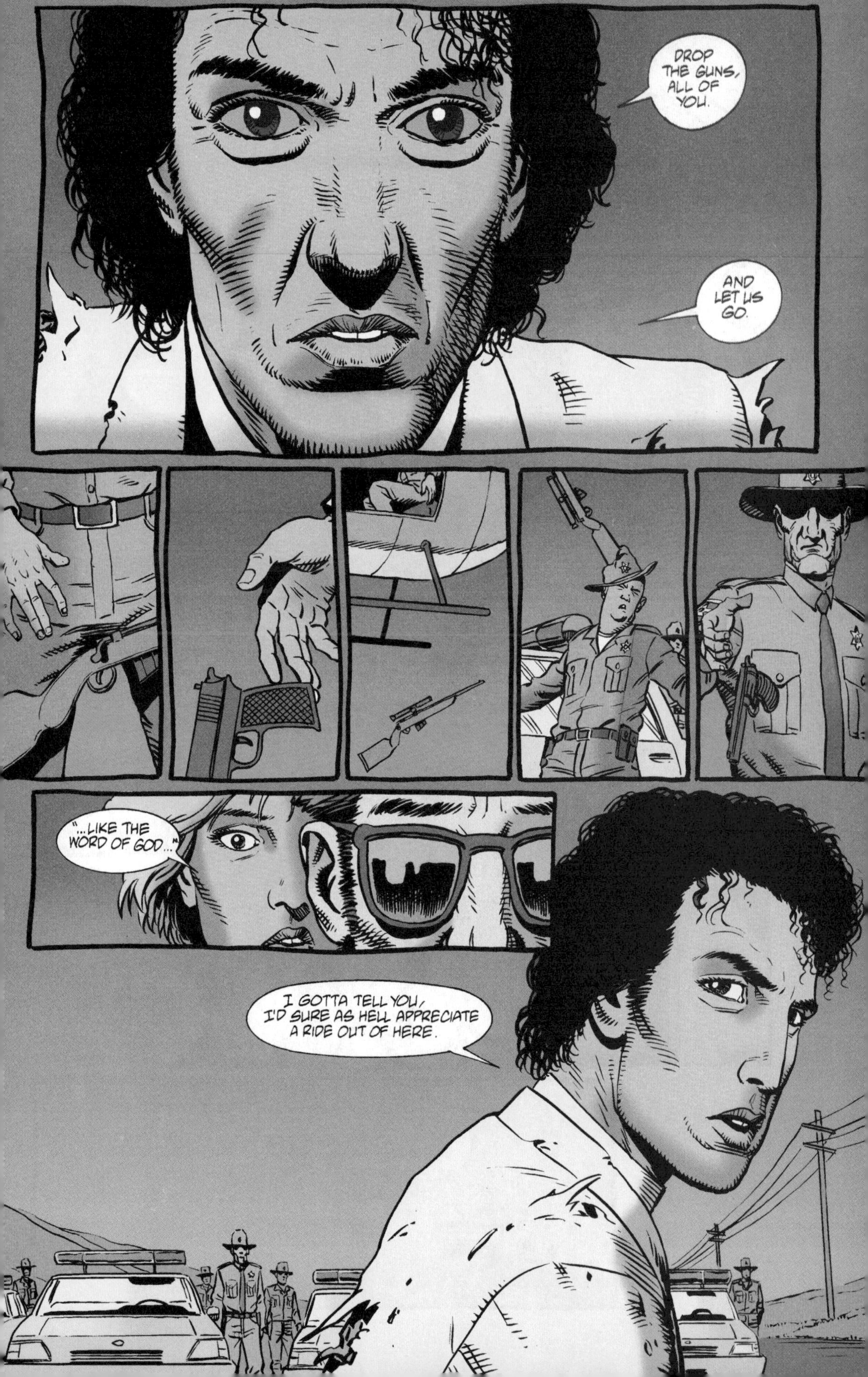
DROP THE GUNS, ALL OF YOU.
AND LET US GO.
"...LIKE THE WORD OF GOD..."
I GOTTA TELL YOU, I'D SURE AS HELL APPRECIATE A RIDE OUT OF HERE.

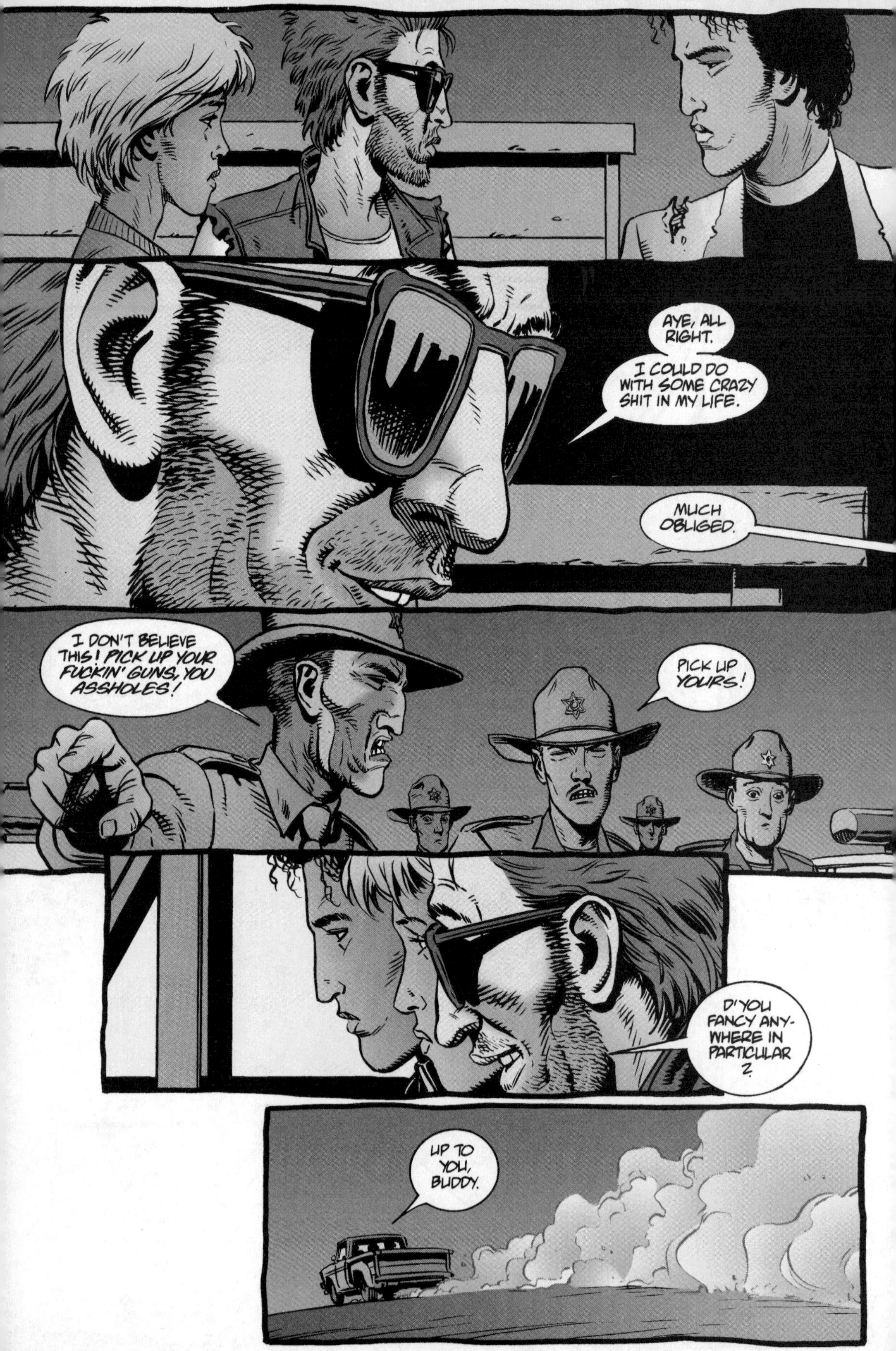
AYE, ALL RIGHT.
I COULD DO WITH SOME CRAZY SHIT IN MY LIFE.
MUCH OBLIGED.
I DON'T BELIEVE THIS! PICK UP YOUR FUCKIN' GUNS, YOU ASSHOLES!
PICK UP YOURS!
D'YOU FANCY ANY-WHERE IN PARTICULAR ?
UP TO YOU, BUDDY.

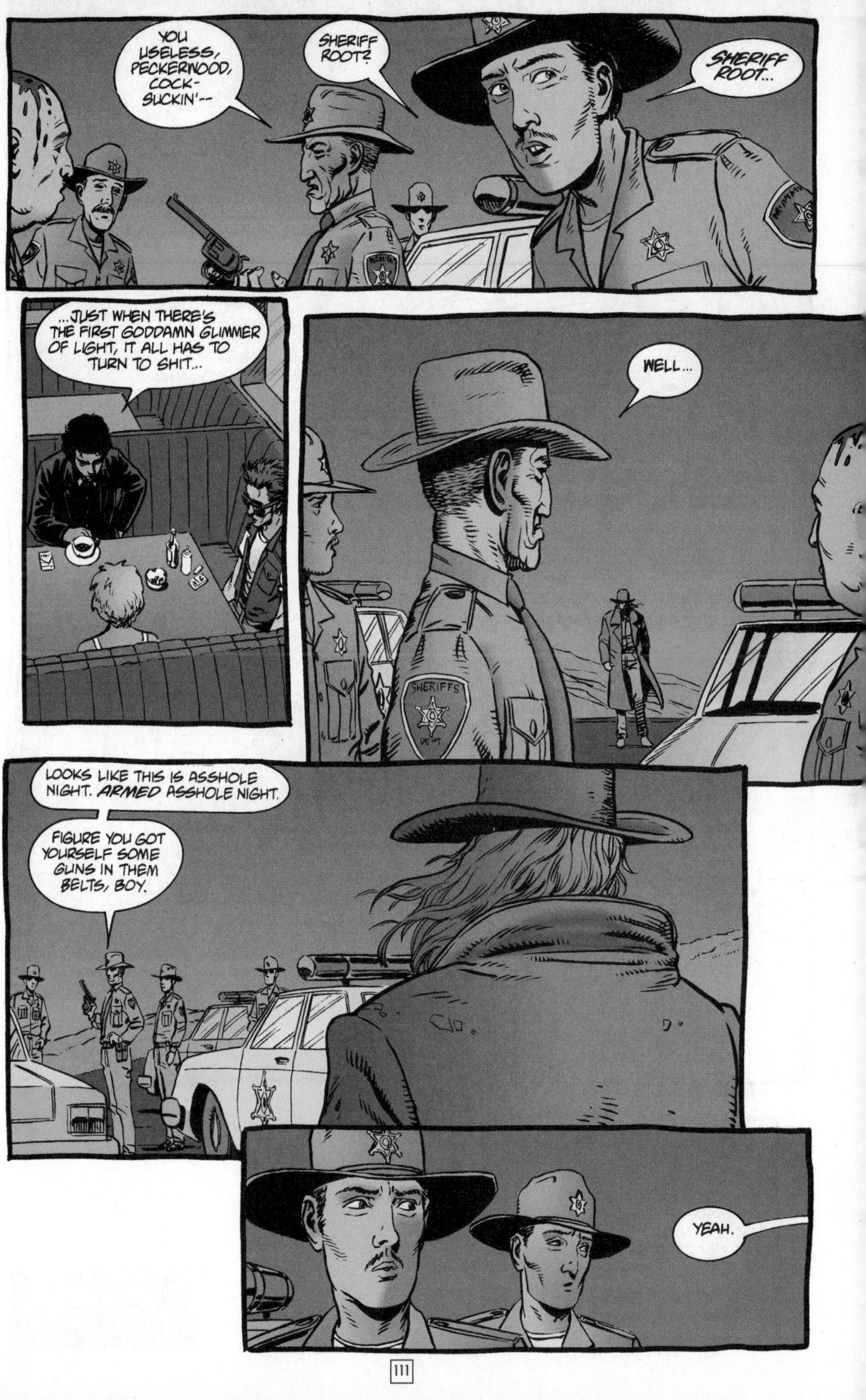

YOU USELESS, PECKERWOOD, COCK-SUCKIN'--
SHERIFF ROOT?
SHERIFF ROOT...
...JUST WHEN THERE'S THE FIRST GODDAMN GLIMMER OF LIGHT, IT ALL HAS TO TURN TO SHIT...
WELL...
SHERIFFS DEPT.
LOOKS LIKE THIS IS ASSHOLE NIGHT. ARMED ASSHOLE NIGHT.
FIGURE YOU GOT YOURSELF SOME GUNS IN THEM BELTS, BOY.
YEAH.

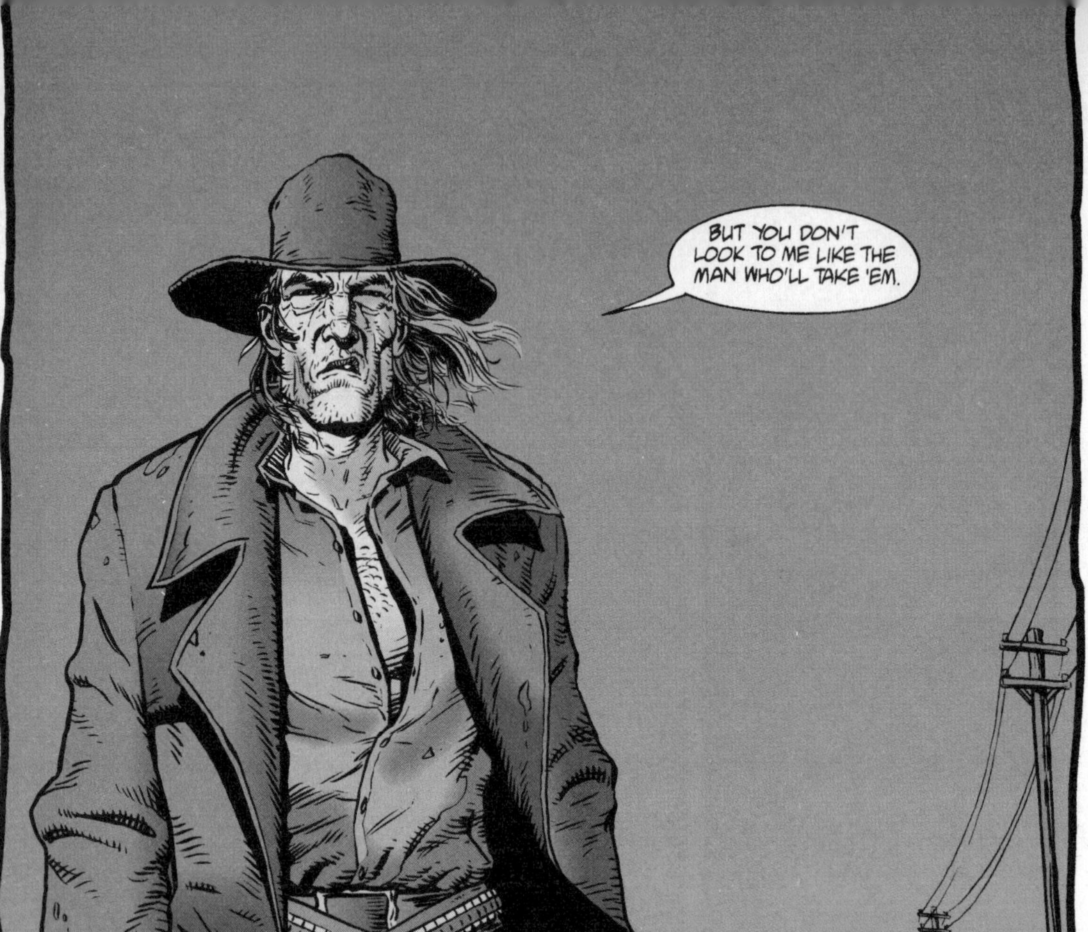
BUT YOU DON'T LOOK TO ME LIKE THE MAN WHO'LL TAKE 'EM.

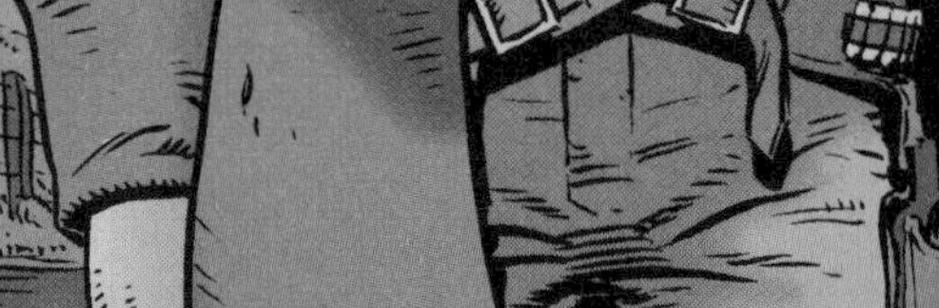
BANG.

NEXT: JUST A FEW COPS

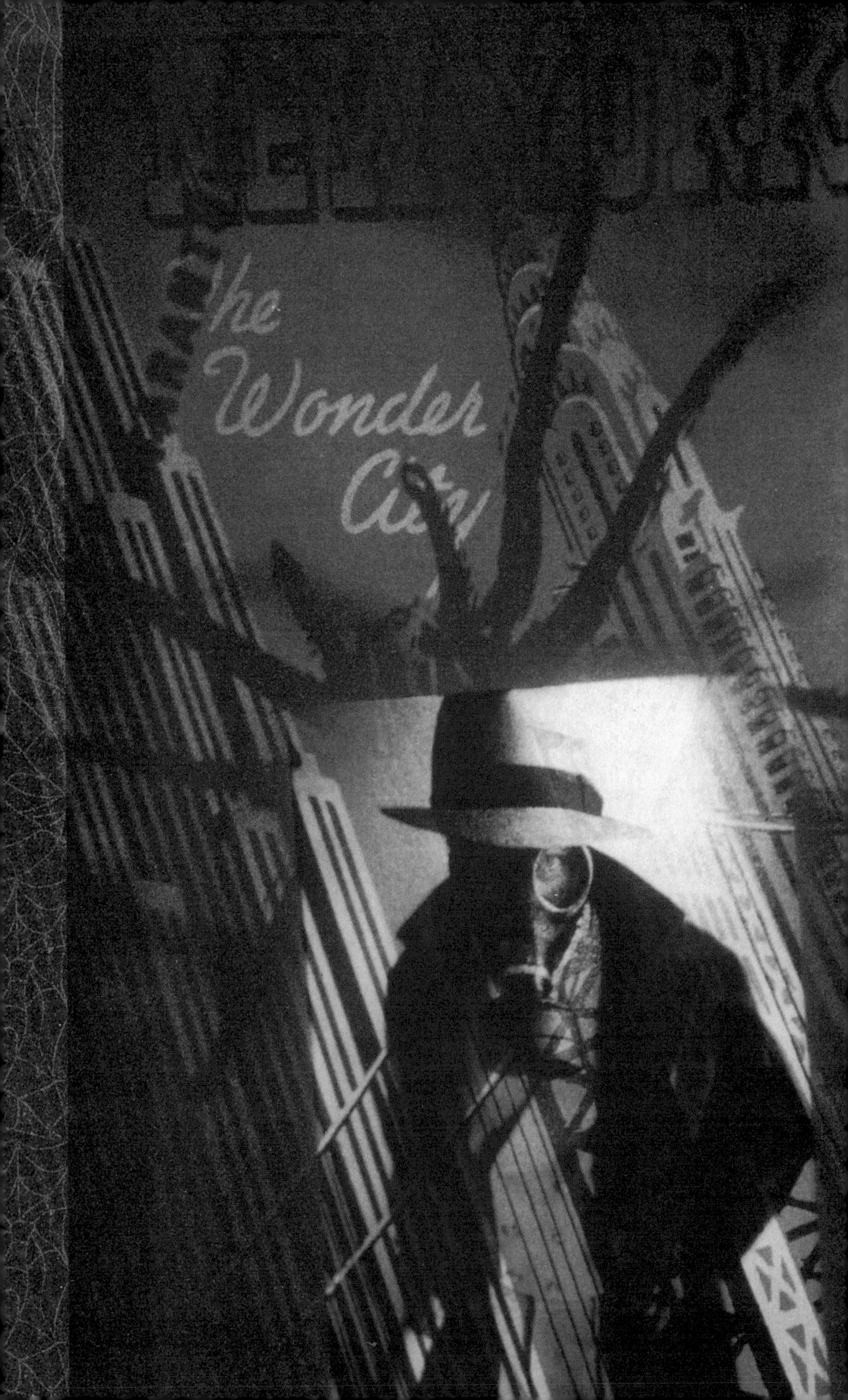
Wonder

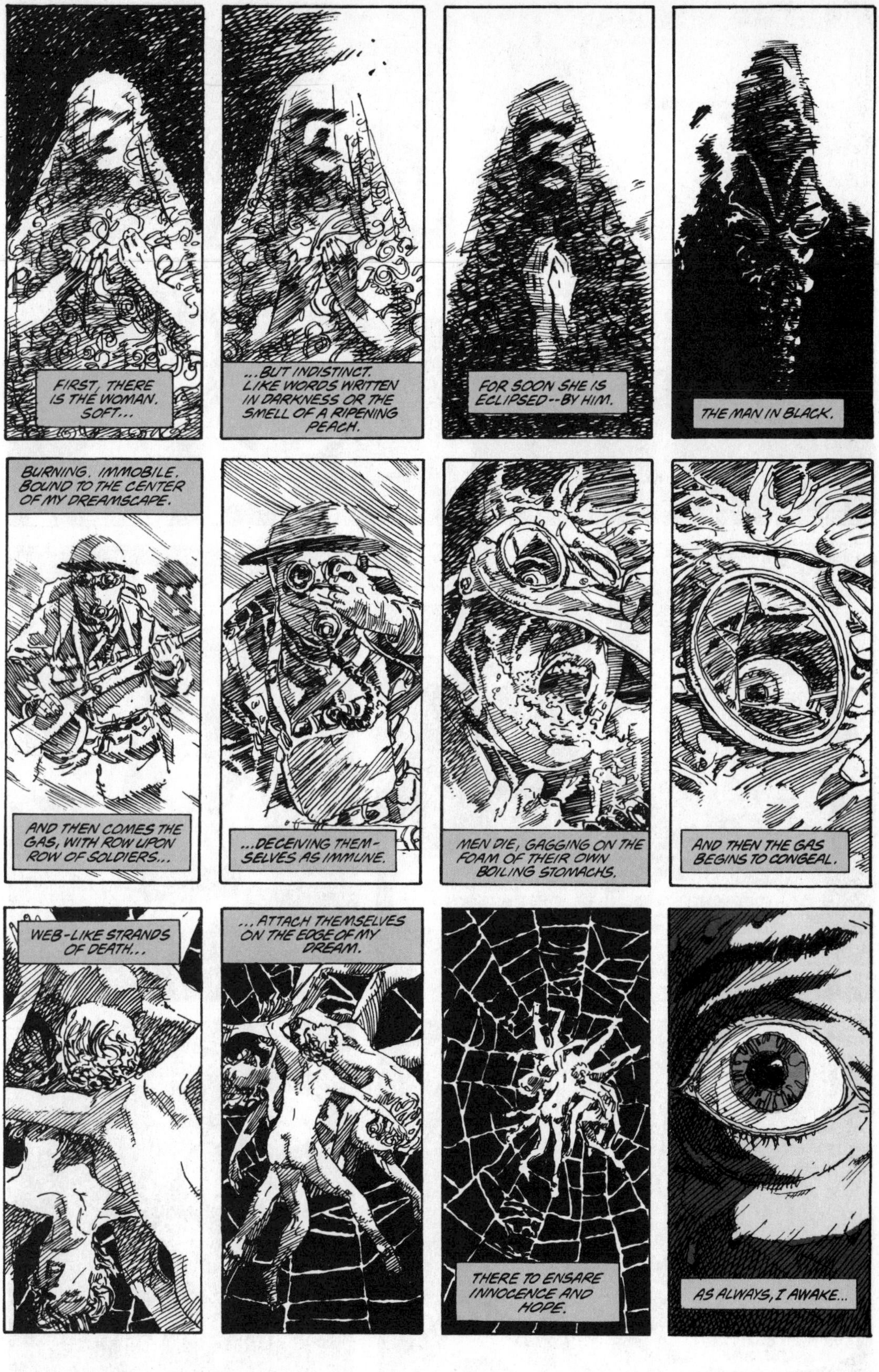
FIRST, THERE IS THE WOMAN. SOFT...
...BUT INDISTINCT. LIKE WORDS WRITTEN IN DARKNESS OR THE SMELL OF A RIPENING PEACH.
FOR SOON SHE IS ECLIPSED--BY HIM.
THE MAN IN BLACK.
BURNING. IMMOBILE. BOUND TO THE CENTER OF MY DREAMSCAPE.
AND THEN COMES THE GAS, WITH ROW UPON ROW OF SOLDIERS...
...DECEIVING THEM-SELVES AS IMMUNE.
MEN DIE, GAGGING ON THE FOAM OF THEIR OWN BOILING STOMACHS.
AND THEN THE GAS BEGINS TO CONGEAL.
WEB-LIKE STRANDS OF DEATH...
...ATTACH THEMSELVES ON THE EDGE OF MY DREAM.
THERE TO ENSARE INNOCENCE AND HOPE.
AS ALWAYS, I AWAKE...

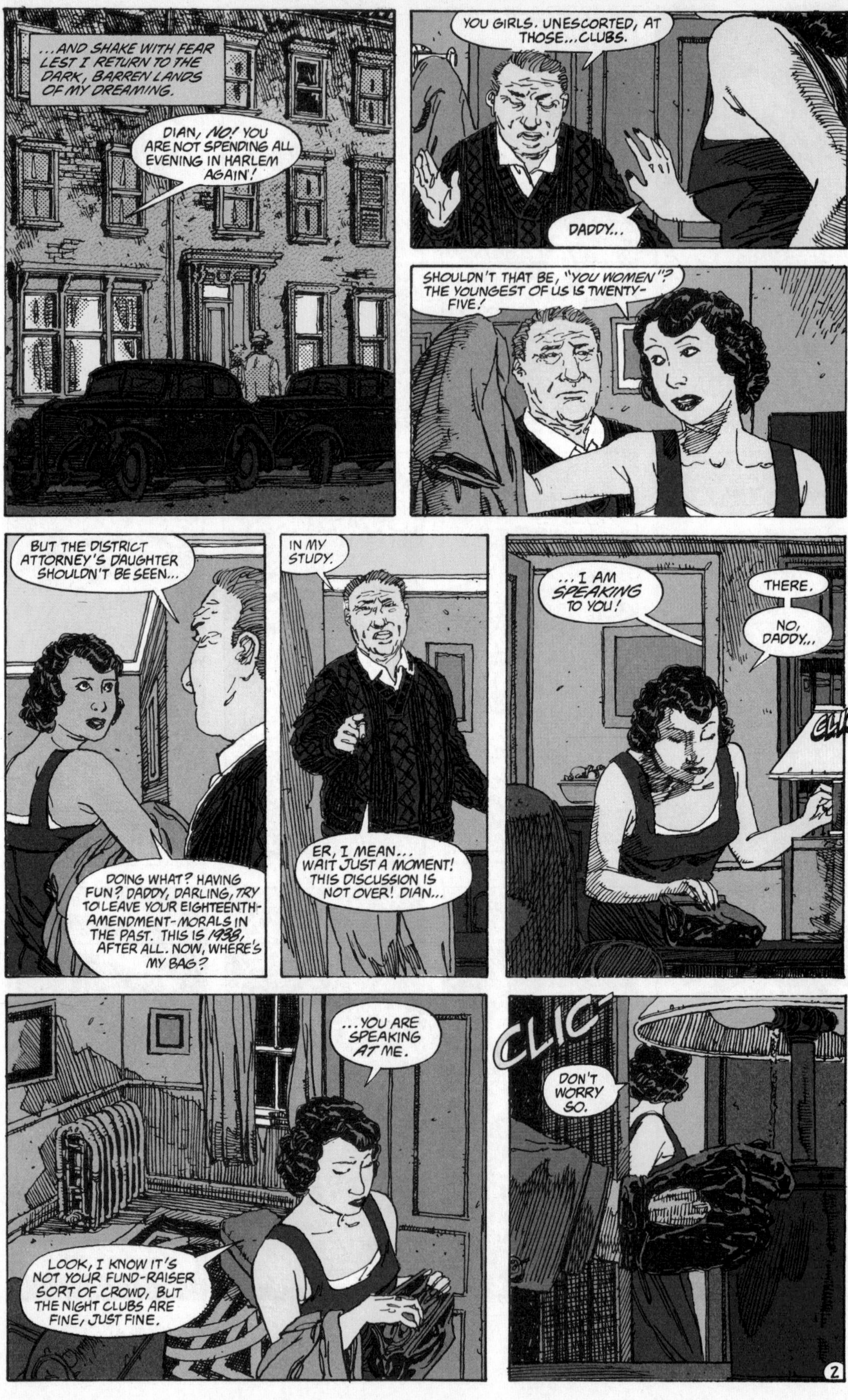
...AND SHAKE WITH FEAR LEST I RETURN TO THE DARK, BARREN LANDS OF MY DREAMING.
DIAN, NO! YOU ARE NOT SPENDING ALL EVENING IN HARLEM AGAIN!
YOU GIRLS. UNESCORTED, AT THOSE...CLUBS.
DADDY...
SHOULDN'T THAT BE, "YOU WOMEN"? THE YOUNGEST OF US IS TWENTY-FIVE!
BUT THE DISTRICT ATTORNEY'S DAUGHTER SHOULDN'T BE SEEN...
DOING WHAT? HAVING FUN? DADDY, DARLING, TRY TO LEAVE YOUR EIGHTEENTH-AMENDMENT-MORALS IN THE PAST. THIS IS 1938, AFTER ALL. NOW, WHERE'S MY BAG?
IN MY STUDY.
ER, I MEAN... WAIT JUST A MOMENT! THIS DISCUSSION IS NOT OVER! DIAN...
...I AM SPEAKING TO YOU!
THERE.
NO, DADDY...
CLIC
...YOU ARE SPEAKING AT ME.
LOOK, I KNOW IT'S NOT YOUR FUND-RAISER SORT OF CROWD, BUT THE NIGHT CLUBS ARE FINE, JUST FINE.
CLIC-
DON'T WORRY SO.
2

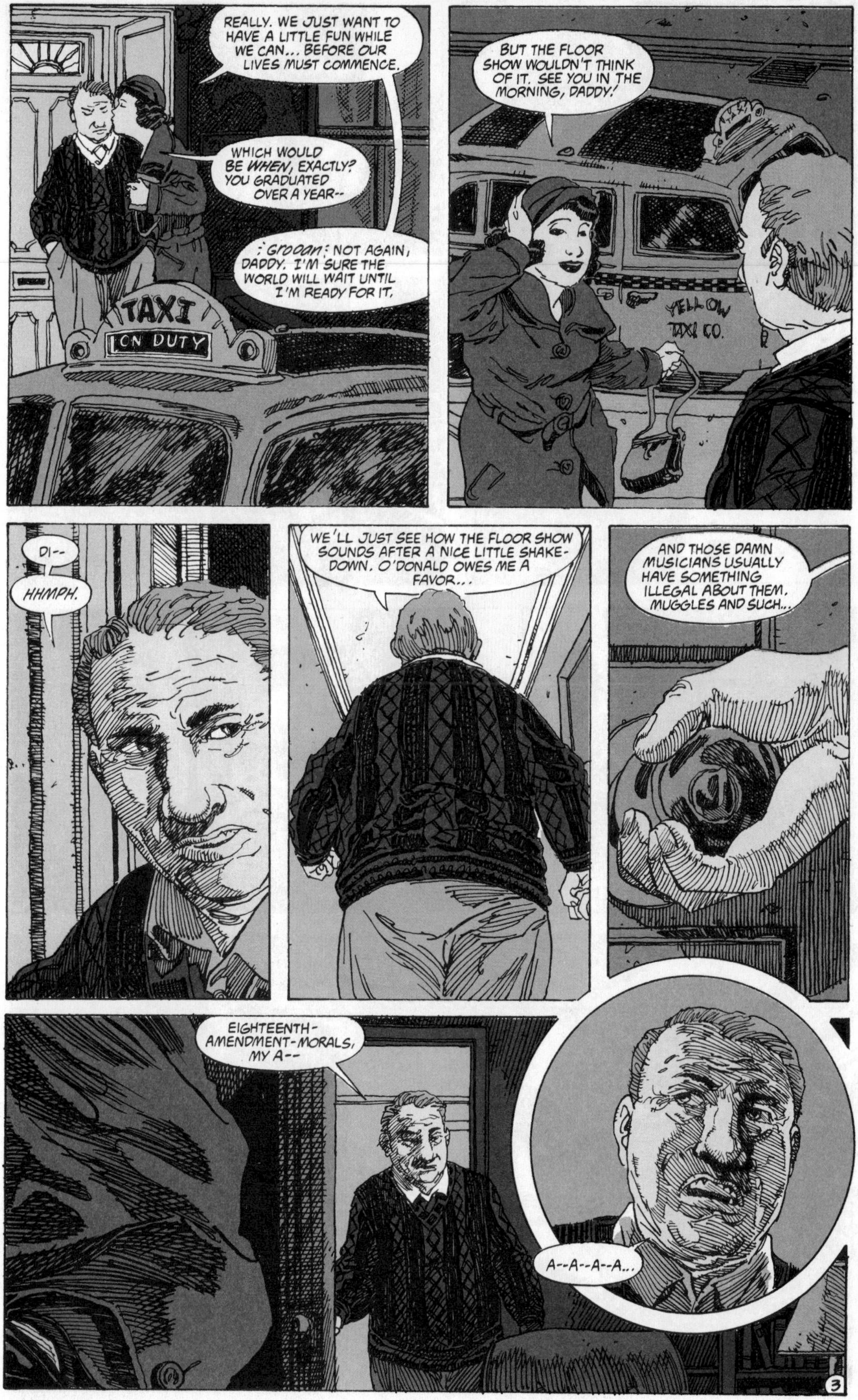
REALLY. WE JUST WANT TO HAVE A LITTLE FUN WHILE WE CAN... BEFORE OUR LIVES MUST COMMENCE.
WHICH WOULD BE *WHEN*, EXACTLY? YOU GRADUATED OVER A YEAR--
:*GROAN*: NOT AGAIN, DADDY. I'M SURE THE WORLD WILL WAIT UNTIL I'M READY FOR IT.
TAXI
ON DUTY
BUT THE FLOOR SHOW WOULDN'T THINK OF IT. SEE YOU IN THE MORNING, DADDY!
YELLOW TAXI CO.
DI--
HHMPH.
WE'LL JUST SEE HOW THE FLOOR SHOW SOUNDS AFTER A NICE LITTLE SHAKE-DOWN. O'DONALD OWES ME A FAVOR...
AND THOSE DAMN MUSICIANS USUALLY HAVE SOMETHING ILLEGAL ABOUT THEM. MUGGLES AND SUCH...
EIGHTEENTH-AMENDMENT-MORALS, MY A--
A--A--A--A...
3

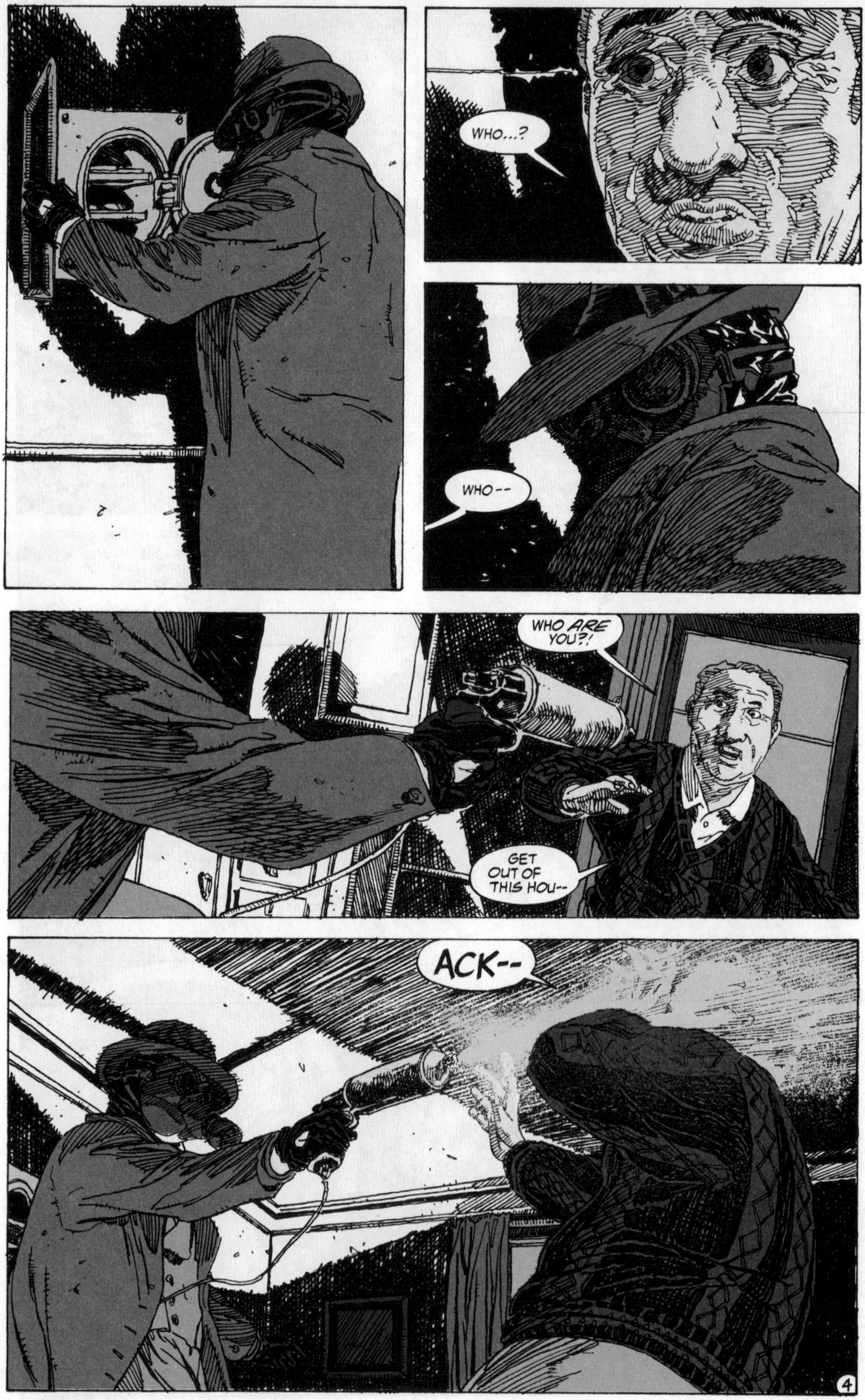
WHO...?
WHO--
WHO *ARE* YOU?!
GET OUT OF THIS HOU--
ACK--
4

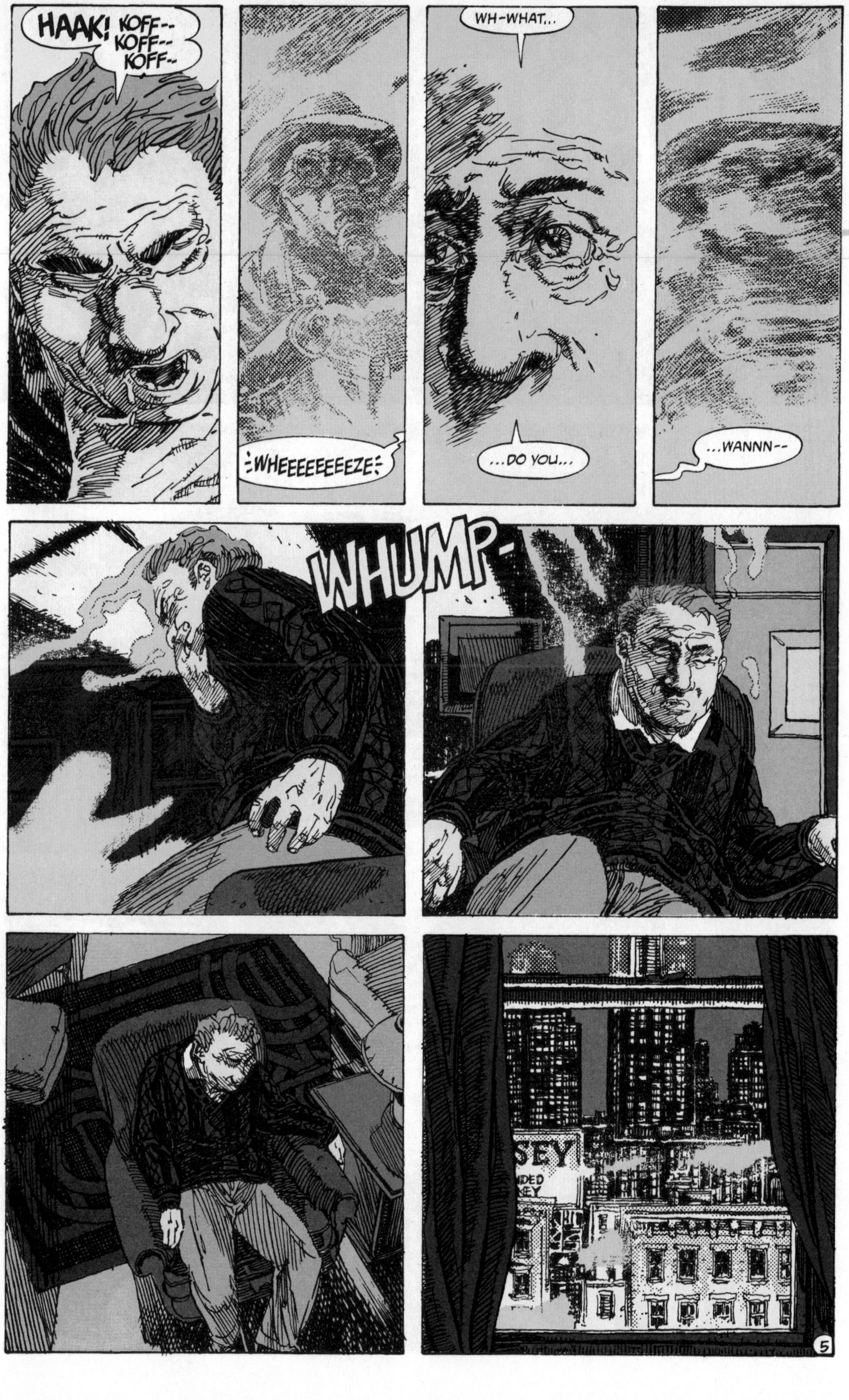
HAAK! KOFF-- KOFF-- KOFF--
WHEEEEEEEEZE
WH-WHAT...
...DO YOU...
...WANNN--
WHUMP-
SEY
NDED
KEY
5

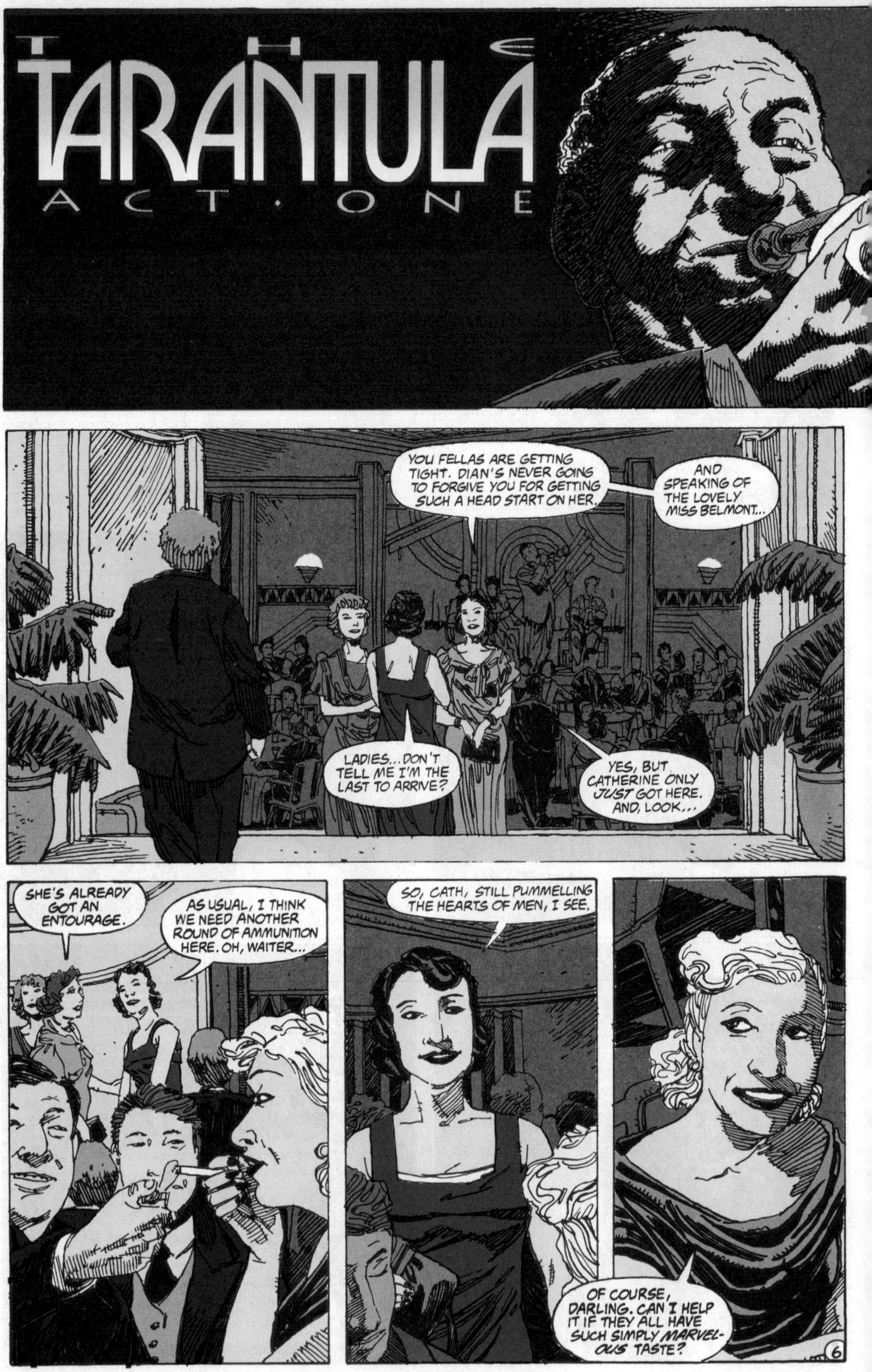
THE TARANTULA
ACT·ONE
YOU FELLAS ARE GETTING TIGHT. DIAN'S NEVER GOING TO FORGIVE YOU FOR GETTING SUCH A HEAD START ON HER.
AND SPEAKING OF THE LOVELY MISS BELMONT...
LADIES... DON'T TELL ME I'M THE LAST TO ARRIVE?
YES, BUT CATHERINE ONLY JUST GOT HERE. AND, LOOK...
SHE'S ALREADY GOT AN ENTOURAGE.
AS USUAL, I THINK WE NEED ANOTHER ROUND OF AMMUNITION HERE. OH, WAITER...
SO, CATH, STILL PUMMELLING THE HEARTS OF MEN, I SEE.
OF COURSE, DARLING. CAN I HELP IT IF THEY ALL HAVE SUCH SIMPLY MARVEL-OUS TASTE?
6

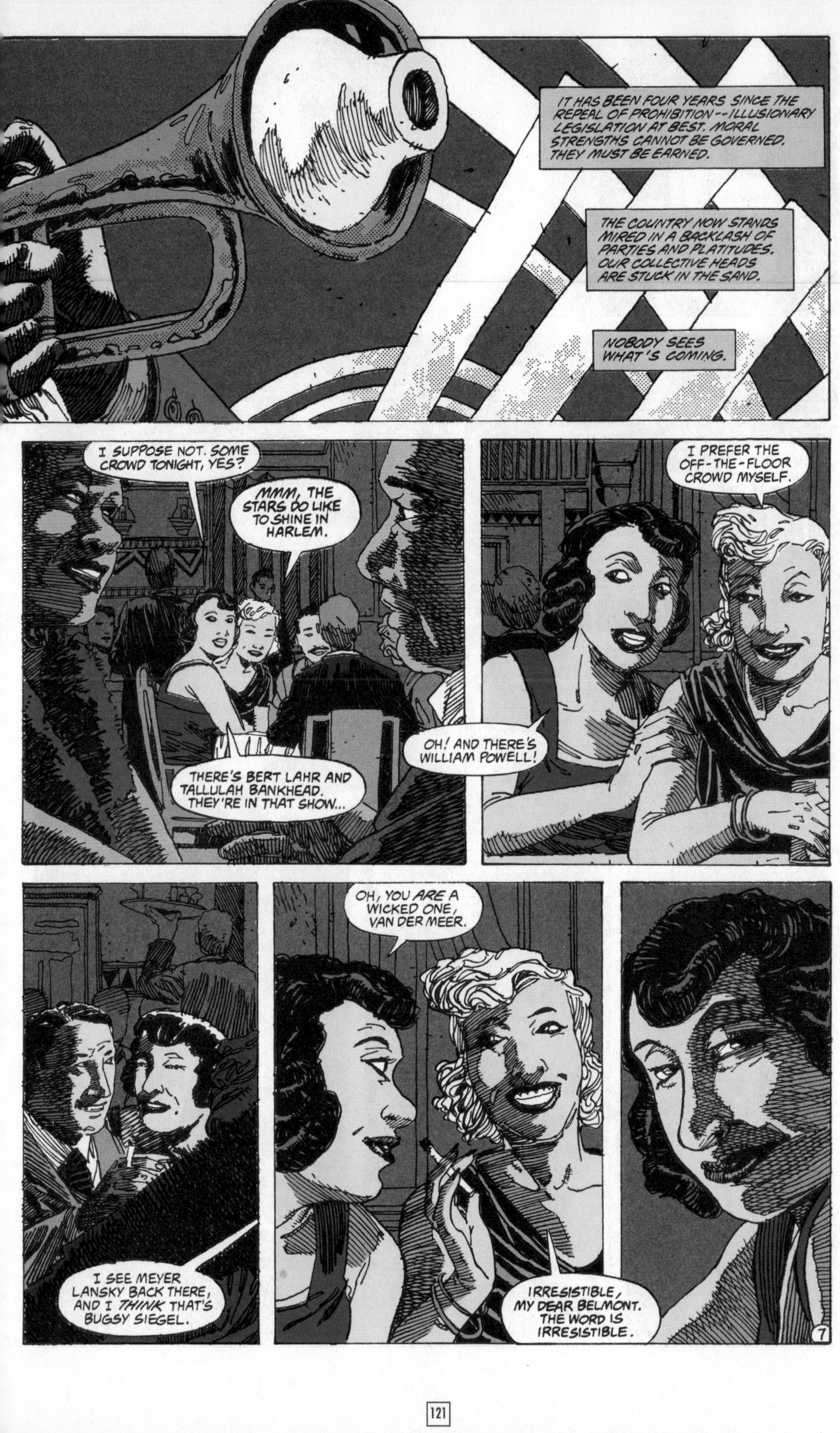
IT HAS BEEN FOUR YEARS SINCE THE REPEAL OF PROHIBITION -- ILLUSIONARY LEGISLATION AT BEST. MORAL STRENGTHS CANNOT BE GOVERNED. THEY MUST BE EARNED.
THE COUNTRY NOW STANDS MIRED IN A BACKLASH OF PARTIES AND PLATITUDES. OUR COLLECTIVE HEADS ARE STUCK IN THE SAND.
NOBODY SEES WHAT'S COMING.
I SUPPOSE NOT. SOME CROWD TONIGHT, YES?
MMM, THE STARS DO LIKE TO SHINE IN HARLEM.
THERE'S BERT LAHR AND TALLULAH BANKHEAD. THEY'RE IN THAT SHOW...
OH! AND THERE'S WILLIAM POWELL!
I PREFER THE OFF-THE-FLOOR CROWD MYSELF.
I SEE MEYER LANSKY BACK THERE, AND I THINK THAT'S BUGSY SIEGEL.
OH, YOU ARE A WICKED ONE, VAN DER MEER.
IRRESISTIBLE, MY DEAR BELMONT. THE WORD IS IRRESISTIBLE.
7

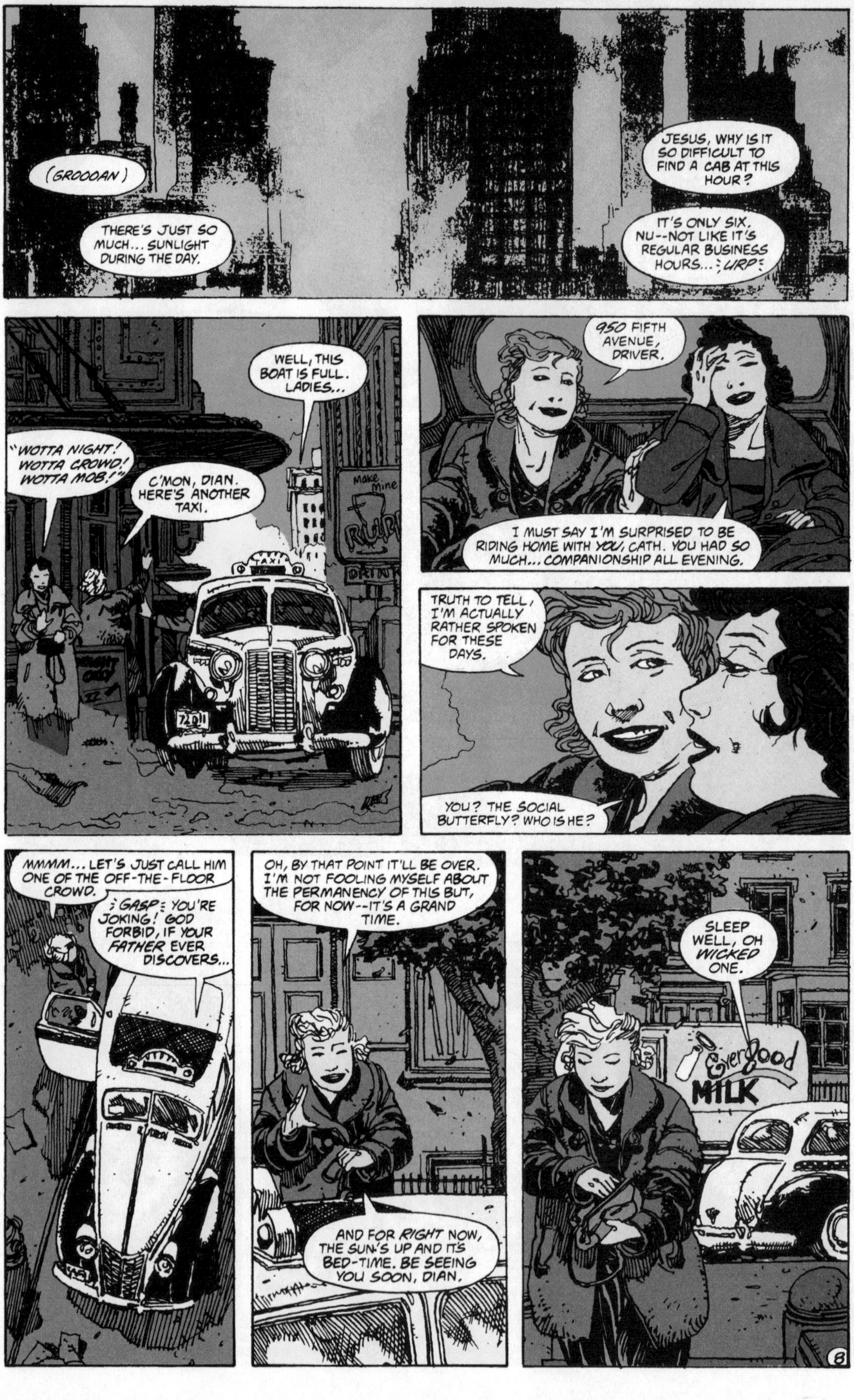
(GROOOAN)
THERE'S JUST SO MUCH... SUNLIGHT DURING THE DAY.
JESUS, WHY IS IT SO DIFFICULT TO FIND A CAB AT THIS HOUR?
IT'S ONLY SIX, NU--NOT LIKE IT'S REGULAR BUSINESS HOURS... ;URP;
WELL, THIS BOAT IS FULL. LADIES...
"WOTTA NIGHT! WOTTA CROWD! WOTTA MOB!"
C'MON, DIAN. HERE'S ANOTHER TAXI.
950 FIFTH AVENUE, DRIVER.
I MUST SAY I'M SURPRISED TO BE RIDING HOME WITH YOU, CATH. YOU HAD SO MUCH... COMPANIONSHIP ALL EVENING.
TRUTH TO TELL, I'M ACTUALLY RATHER SPOKEN FOR THESE DAYS.
YOU? THE SOCIAL BUTTERFLY? WHO IS HE?
MMMM... LET'S JUST CALL HIM ONE OF THE OFF-THE-FLOOR CROWD.
;GASP; YOU'RE JOKING! GOD FORBID, IF YOUR FATHER EVER DISCOVERS...
OH, BY THAT POINT IT'LL BE OVER. I'M NOT FOOLING MYSELF ABOUT THE PERMANENCY OF THIS BUT, FOR NOW--IT'S A GRAND TIME.
AND FOR RIGHT NOW, THE SUN'S UP AND IT'S BED-TIME. BE SEEING YOU SOON, DIAN.
SLEEP WELL, OH WICKED ONE.
Ever Good MILK
8

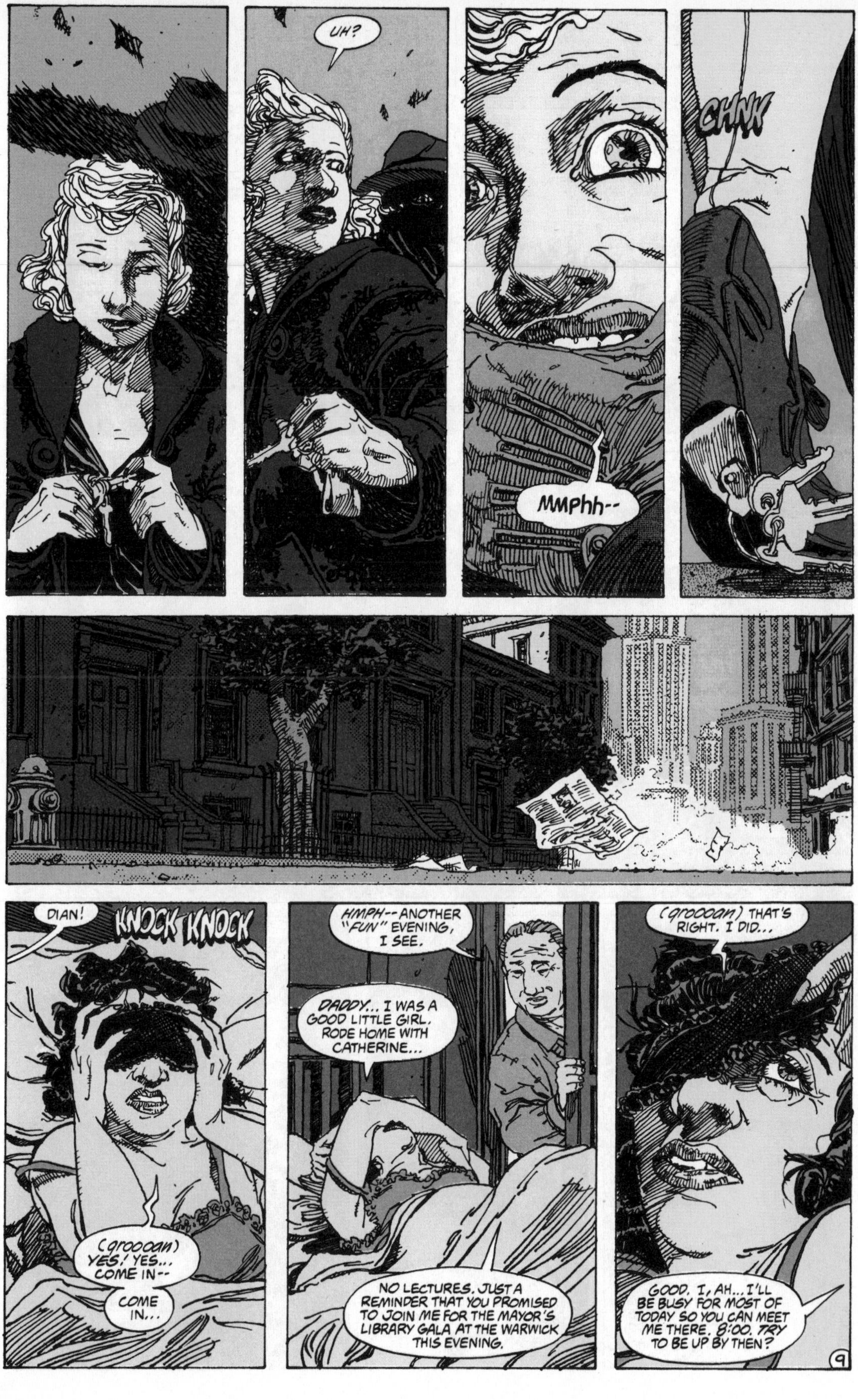
UH?
CHNK
MMPhh--
DIAN!
KNOCK KNOCK
(grooaan) YES! YES... COME IN--
COME IN...
HMPH--ANOTHER "FUN" EVENING, I SEE.
DADDY... I WAS A GOOD LITTLE GIRL. RODE HOME WITH CATHERINE...
NO LECTURES. JUST A REMINDER THAT YOU PROMISED TO JOIN ME FOR THE MAYOR'S LIBRARY GALA AT THE WARWICK THIS EVENING.
(grooaan) THAT'S RIGHT. I DID...
GOOD. I, AH... I'LL BE BUSY FOR MOST OF TODAY SO YOU CAN MEET ME THERE. 8:00. TRY TO BE UP BY THEN?
9

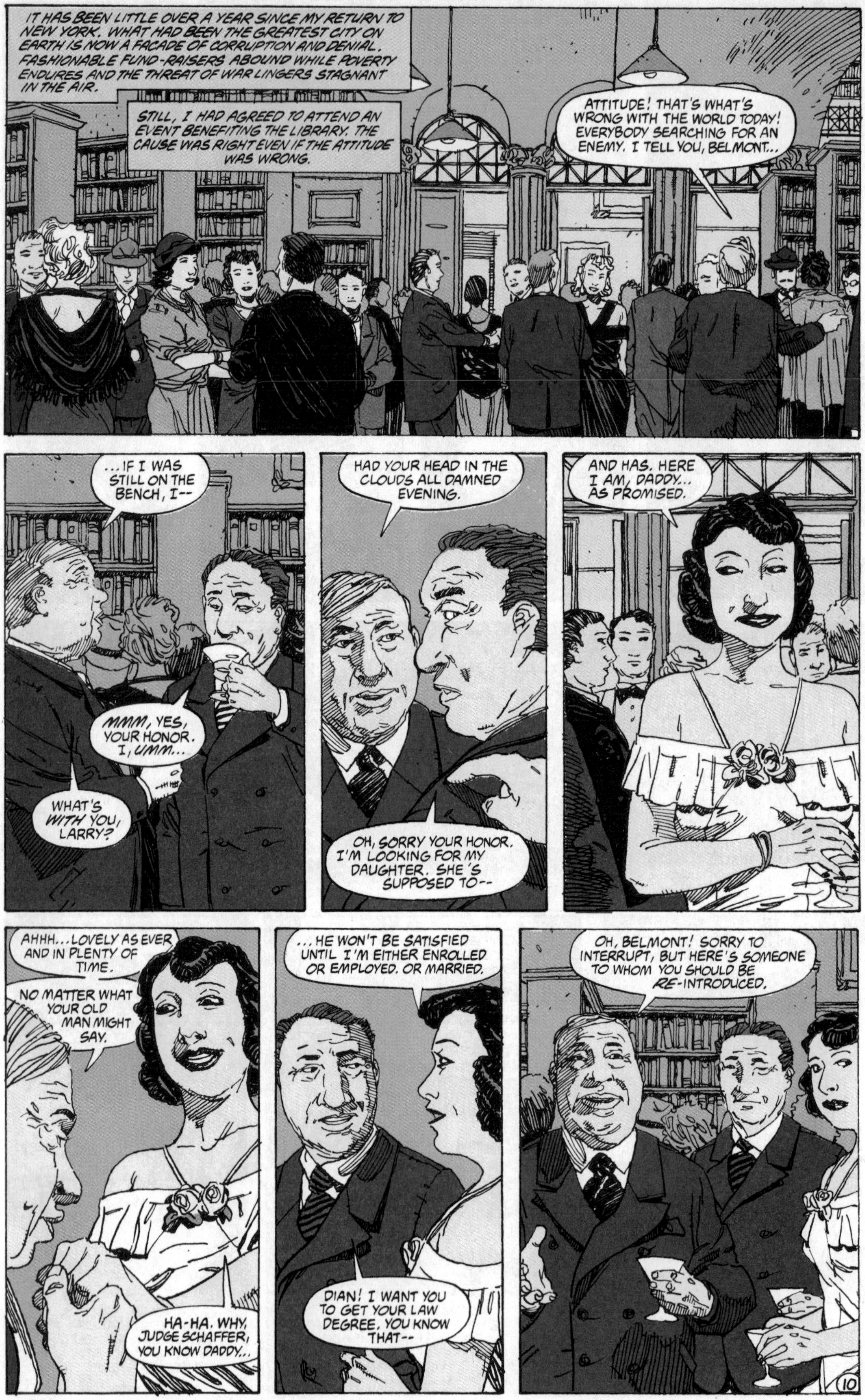
IT HAS BEEN LITTLE OVER A YEAR SINCE MY RETURN TO NEW YORK. WHAT HAD BEEN THE GREATEST CITY ON EARTH IS NOW A FACADE OF CORRUPTION AND DENIAL. FASHIONABLE FUND-RAISERS ABOUND WHILE POVERTY ENDURES AND THE THREAT OF WAR LINGERS STAGNANT IN THE AIR.
STILL, I HAD AGREED TO ATTEND AN EVENT BENEFITING THE LIBRARY. THE CAUSE WAS RIGHT EVEN IF THE ATTITUDE WAS WRONG.
ATTITUDE! THAT'S WHAT'S WRONG WITH THE WORLD TODAY! EVERYBODY SEARCHING FOR AN ENEMY. I TELL YOU, BELMONT...
...IF I WAS STILL ON THE BENCH, I--
MMM, YES, YOUR HONOR. I, UMM...
WHAT'S WITH YOU, LARRY?
HAD YOUR HEAD IN THE CLOUDS ALL DAMNED EVENING.
OH, SORRY YOUR HONOR. I'M LOOKING FOR MY DAUGHTER. SHE'S SUPPOSED TO--
AND HAS. HERE I AM, DADDY... AS PROMISED.
AHHH... LOVELY AS EVER AND IN PLENTY OF TIME.
NO MATTER WHAT YOUR OLD MAN MIGHT SAY.
HA-HA. WHY, JUDGE SCHAFFER, YOU KNOW DADDY...
...HE WON'T BE SATISFIED UNTIL I'M EITHER ENROLLED OR EMPLOYED. OR MARRIED.
DIAN! I WANT YOU TO GET YOUR LAW DEGREE. YOU KNOW THAT--
OH, BELMONT! SORRY TO INTERRUPT, BUT HERE'S SOMEONE TO WHOM YOU SHOULD BE RE-INTRODUCED.
10

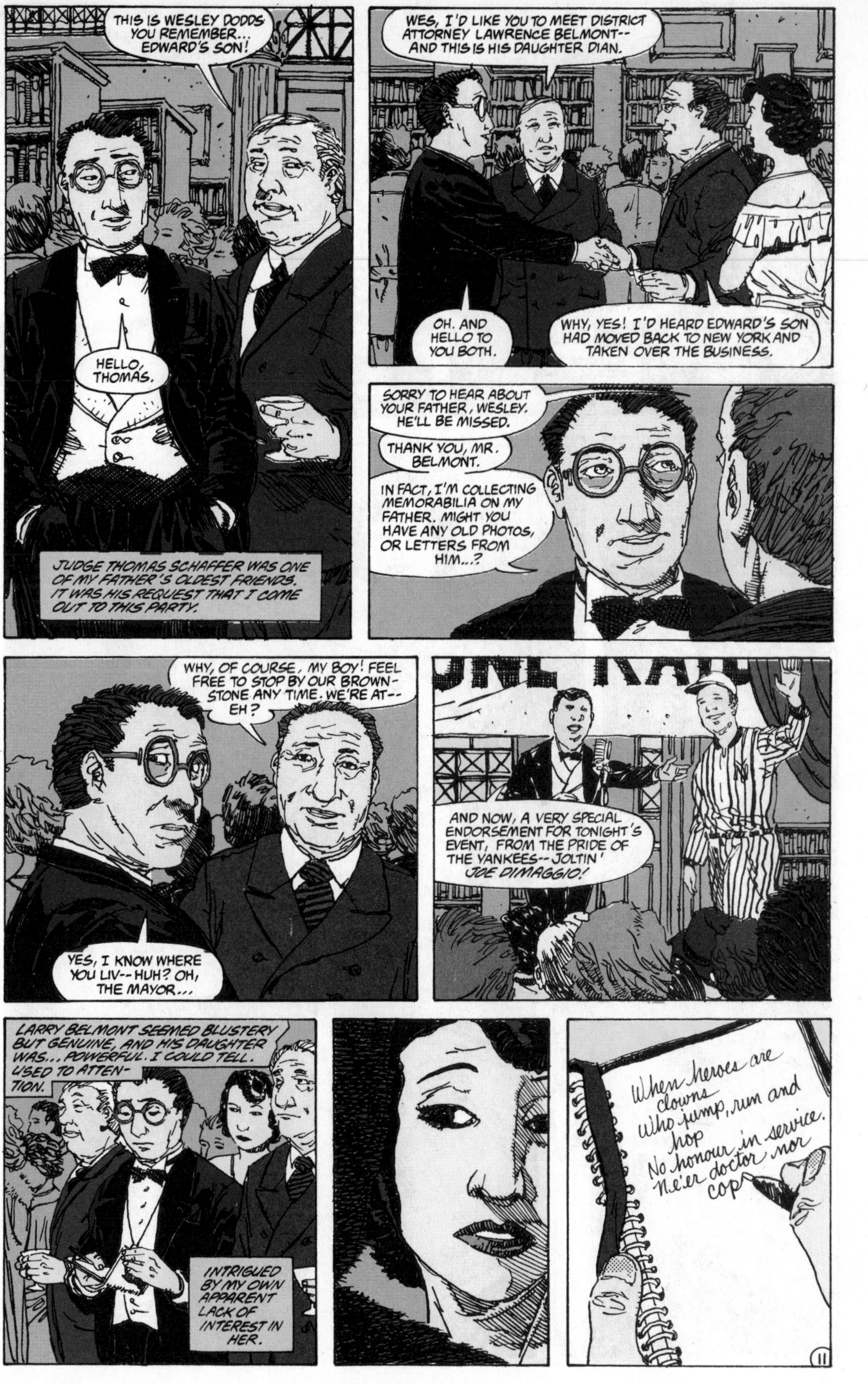
THIS IS WESLEY DODDS YOU REMEMBER... EDWARD'S SON!
HELLO, THOMAS.
JUDGE THOMAS SCHAFFER WAS ONE OF MY FATHER'S OLDEST FRIENDS. IT WAS HIS REQUEST THAT I COME OUT TO THIS PARTY.
WES, I'D LIKE YOU TO MEET DISTRICT ATTORNEY LAWRENCE BELMONT-- AND THIS IS HIS DAUGHTER DIAN.
OH. AND HELLO TO YOU BOTH.
WHY, YES! I'D HEARD EDWARD'S SON HAD MOVED BACK TO NEW YORK AND TAKEN OVER THE BUSINESS.
SORRY TO HEAR ABOUT YOUR FATHER, WESLEY. HE'LL BE MISSED.
THANK YOU, MR. BELMONT.
IN FACT, I'M COLLECTING MEMORABILIA ON MY FATHER. MIGHT YOU HAVE ANY OLD PHOTOS, OR LETTERS FROM HIM...?
WHY, OF COURSE, MY BOY! FEEL FREE TO STOP BY OUR BROWNSTONE ANY TIME. WE'RE AT-- EH?
YES, I KNOW WHERE YOU LIV-- HUH? OH, THE MAYOR...
AND NOW, A VERY SPECIAL ENDORSEMENT FOR TONIGHT'S EVENT, FROM THE PRIDE OF THE YANKEES--JOLTIN' JOE DIMAGGIO!
LARRY BELMONT SEEMED BLUSTERY BUT GENUINE, AND HIS DAUGHTER WAS... POWERFUL. I COULD TELL. USED TO ATTENTION.
INTRIGUED BY MY OWN APPARENT LACK OF INTEREST IN HER.
When heroes are clowns
Who jump, run and hop
No honour in service
Ne'er doctor nor cop
11

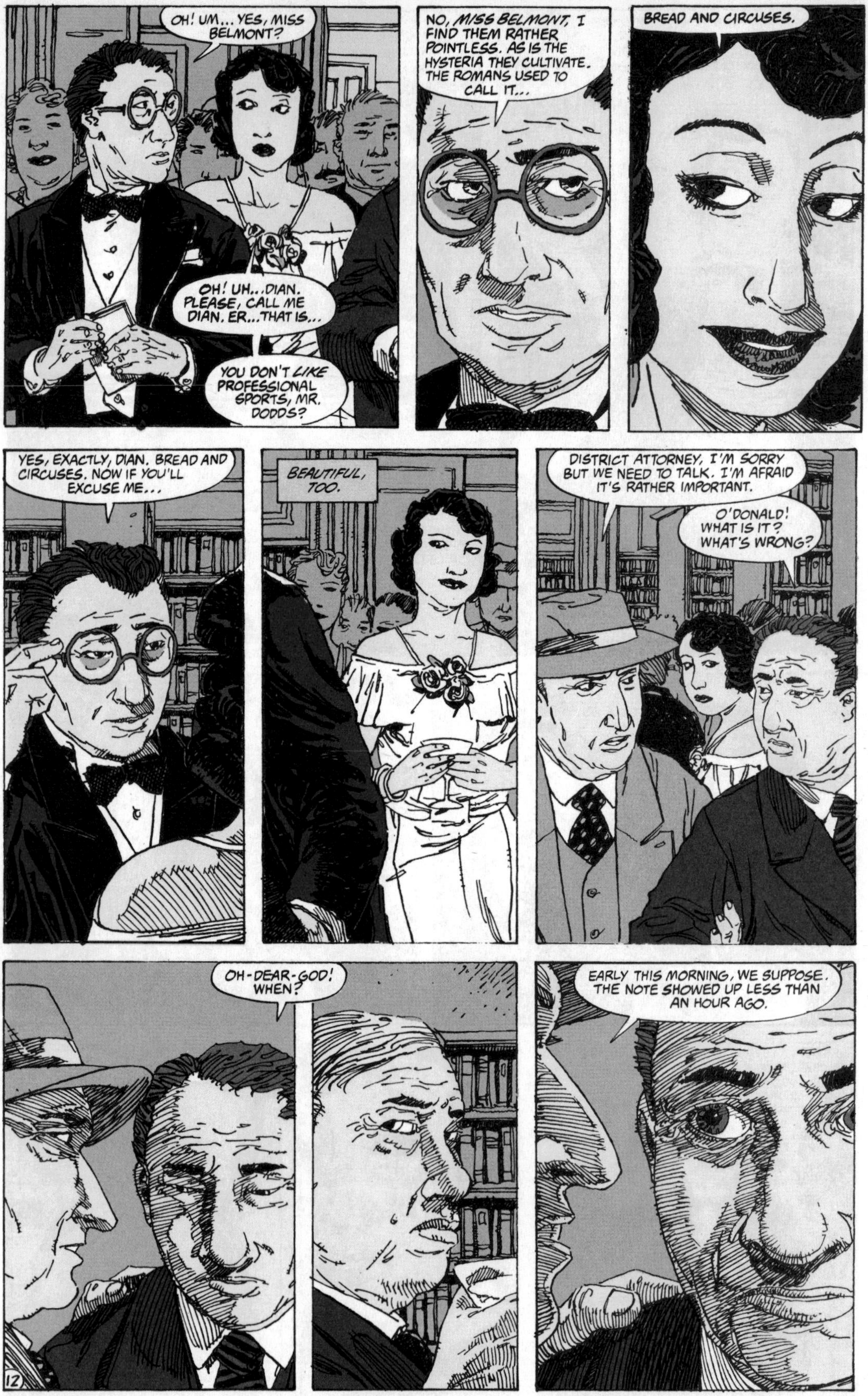
OH! UM... YES, MISS BELMONT?
OH! UH...DIAN. PLEASE, CALL ME DIAN. ER...THAT IS...
YOU DON'T LIKE PROFESSIONAL SPORTS, MR. DODDS?
NO, MISS BELMONT, I FIND THEM RATHER POINTLESS. AS IS THE HYSTERIA THEY CULTIVATE. THE ROMANS USED TO CALL IT...
BREAD AND CIRCUSES.
YES, EXACTLY, DIAN. BREAD AND CIRCUSES. NOW IF YOU'LL EXCUSE ME...
BEAUTIFUL, TOO.
DISTRICT ATTORNEY, I'M SORRY BUT WE NEED TO TALK. I'M AFRAID IT'S RATHER IMPORTANT.
O'DONALD! WHAT IS IT? WHAT'S WRONG?
OH-DEAR-GOD! WHEN?
EARLY THIS MORNING, WE SUPPOSE. THE NOTE SHOWED UP LESS THAN AN HOUR AGO.
12

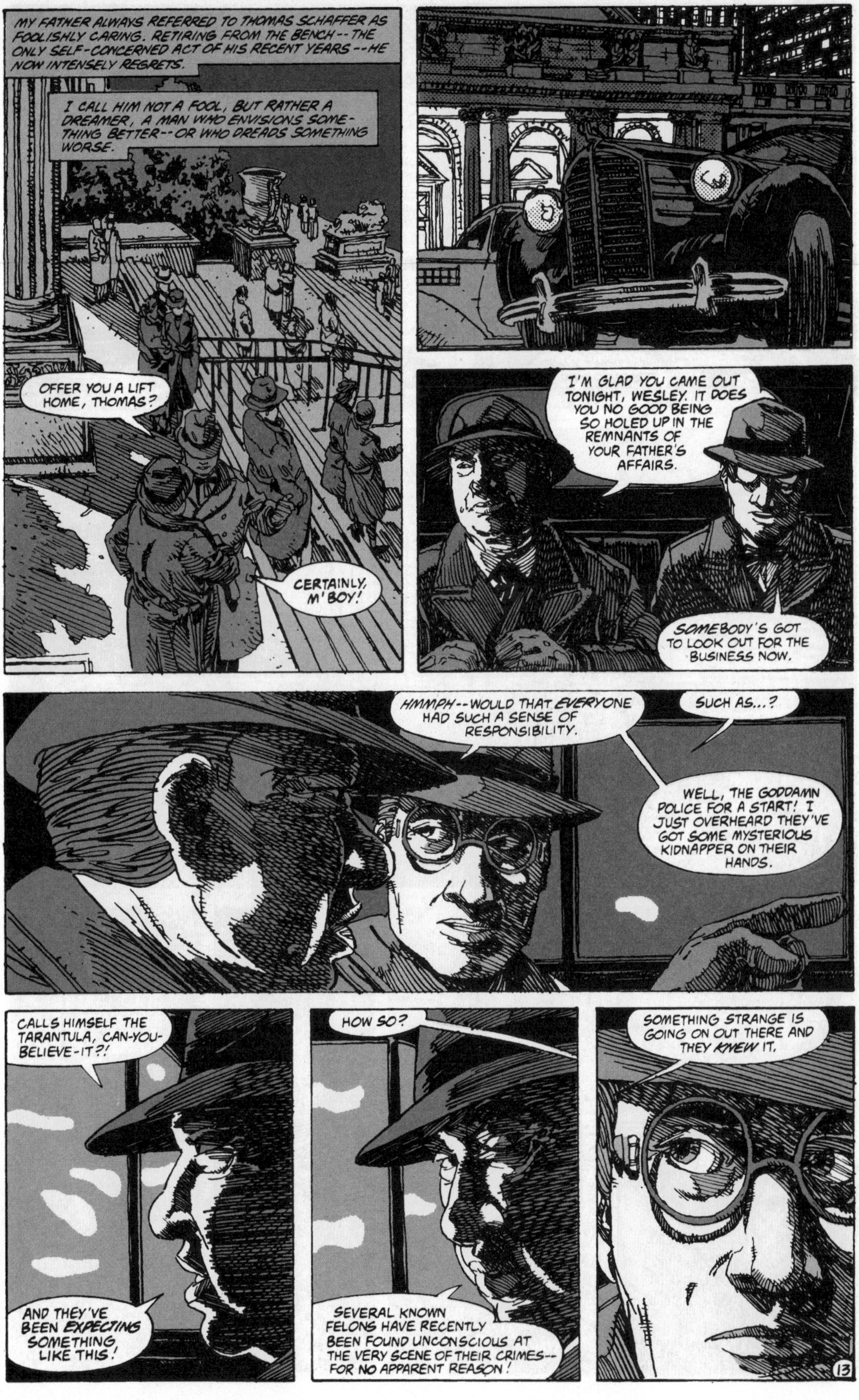
MY FATHER ALWAYS REFERRED TO THOMAS SCHAFFER AS FOOLISHLY CARING. RETIRING FROM THE BENCH--THE ONLY SELF-CONCERNED ACT OF HIS RECENT YEARS--HE NOW INTENSELY REGRETS.
I CALL HIM NOT A FOOL, BUT RATHER A DREAMER, A MAN WHO ENVISIONS SOMETHING BETTER--OR WHO DREADS SOMETHING WORSE.
OFFER YOU A LIFT HOME, THOMAS?
CERTAINLY, M'BOY!
I'M GLAD YOU CAME OUT TONIGHT, WESLEY. IT DOES YOU NO GOOD BEING SO HOLED UP IN THE REMNANTS OF YOUR FATHER'S AFFAIRS.
SOMEBODY'S GOT TO LOOK OUT FOR THE BUSINESS NOW.
HMMPH--WOULD THAT EVERYONE HAD SUCH A SENSE OF RESPONSIBILITY.
SUCH AS...?
WELL, THE GODDAMN POLICE FOR A START! I JUST OVERHEARD THEY'VE GOT SOME MYSTERIOUS KIDNAPPER ON THEIR HANDS.
CALLS HIMSELF THE TARANTULA, CAN-YOU-BELIEVE-IT?!
AND THEY'VE BEEN EXPECTING SOMETHING LIKE THIS!
HOW SO?
SEVERAL KNOWN FELONS HAVE RECENTLY BEEN FOUND UNCONSCIOUS AT THE VERY SCENE OF THEIR CRIMES--FOR NO APPARENT REASON!
SOMETHING STRANGE IS GOING ON OUT THERE AND THEY KNEW IT.
13

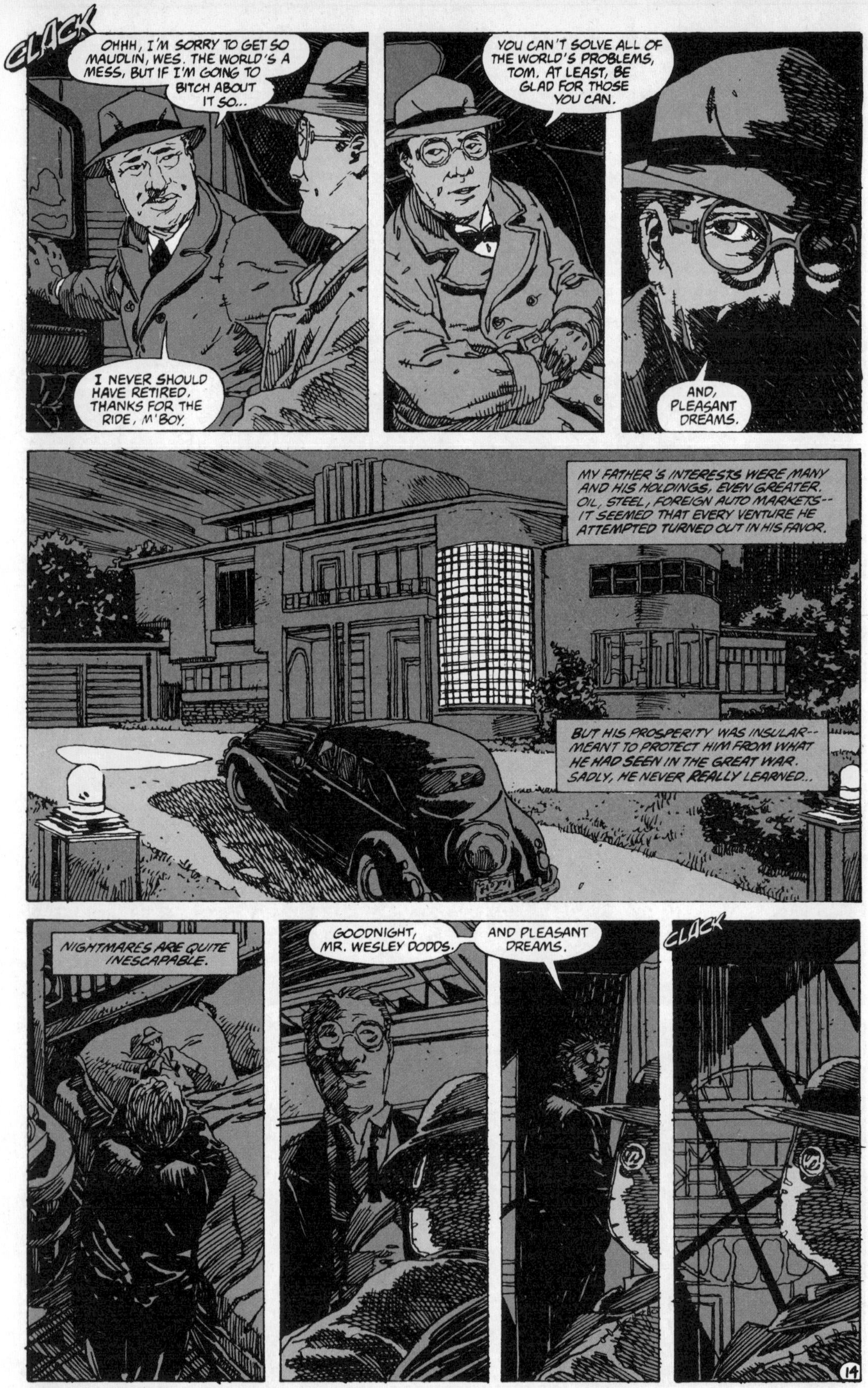
CLACK
OHHH, I'M SORRY TO GET SO MAUDLIN, WES. THE WORLD'S A MESS, BUT IF I'M GOING TO BITCH ABOUT IT SO...
I NEVER SHOULD HAVE RETIRED. THANKS FOR THE RIDE, M'BOY.
YOU CAN'T SOLVE ALL OF THE WORLD'S PROBLEMS, TOM. AT LEAST, BE GLAD FOR THOSE YOU CAN.
AND, PLEASANT DREAMS.
MY FATHER'S INTERESTS WERE MANY AND HIS HOLDINGS, EVEN GREATER. OIL, STEEL, FOREIGN AUTO MARKETS-- IT SEEMED THAT EVERY VENTURE HE ATTEMPTED TURNED OUT IN HIS FAVOR.
BUT HIS PROSPERITY WAS INSULAR-- MEANT TO PROTECT HIM FROM WHAT HE HAD SEEN IN THE GREAT WAR. SADLY, HE NEVER REALLY LEARNED...
NIGHTMARES ARE QUITE INESCAPABLE.
GOODNIGHT, MR. WESLEY DODDS.
AND PLEASANT DREAMS.
CLACK
14

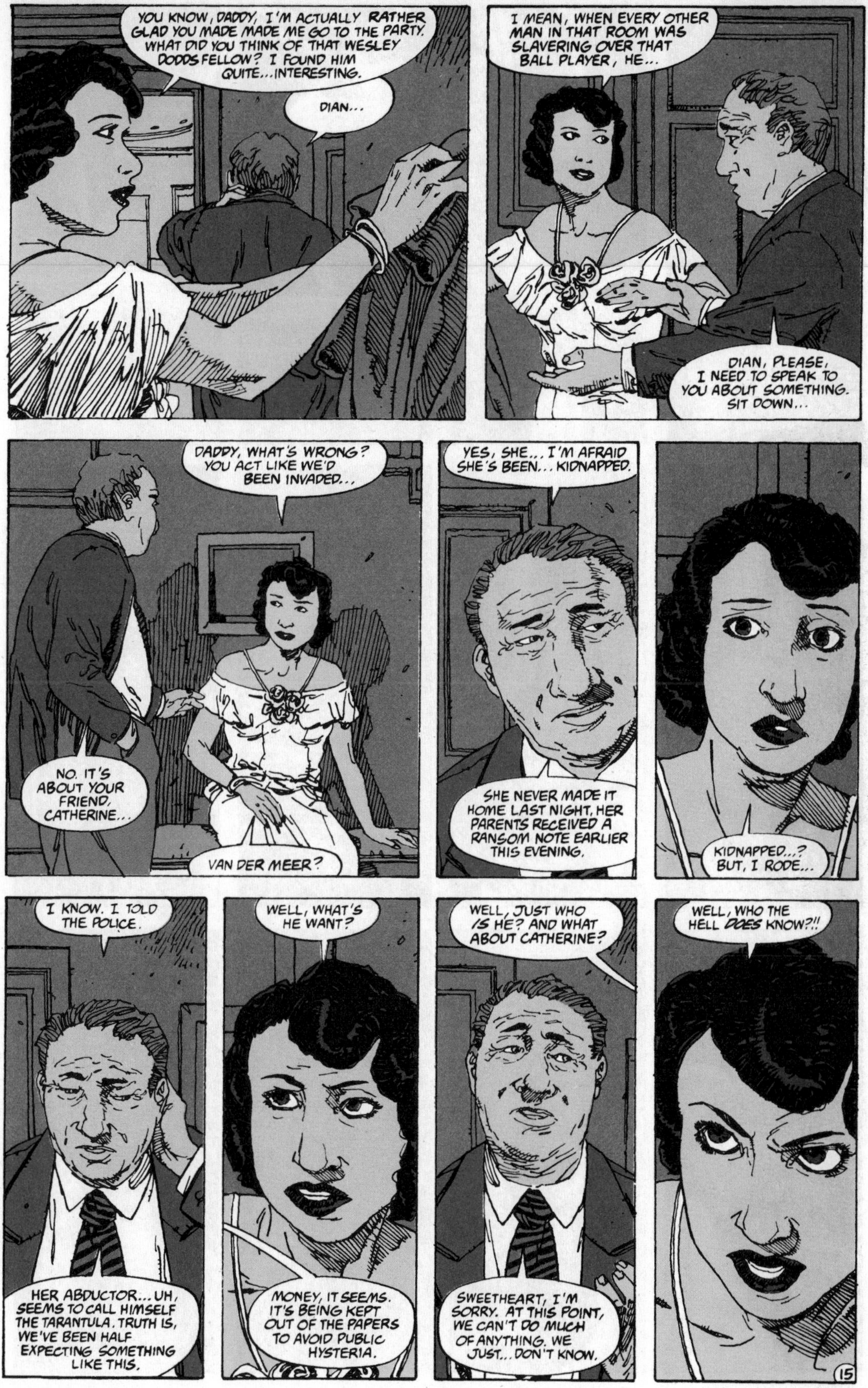
YOU KNOW, DADDY, I'M ACTUALLY RATHER GLAD YOU MADE ME GO TO THE PARTY. WHAT DID YOU THINK OF THAT WESLEY DODDS FELLOW? I FOUND HIM QUITE... INTERESTING.
DIAN...
I MEAN, WHEN EVERY OTHER MAN IN THAT ROOM WAS SLAVERING OVER THAT BALL PLAYER, HE...
DIAN, PLEASE, I NEED TO SPEAK TO YOU ABOUT SOMETHING. SIT DOWN...
DADDY, WHAT'S WRONG? YOU ACT LIKE WE'D BEEN INVADED...
NO. IT'S ABOUT YOUR FRIEND, CATHERINE...
VAN DER MEER?
YES, SHE... I'M AFRAID SHE'S BEEN... KIDNAPPED.
SHE NEVER MADE IT HOME LAST NIGHT. HER PARENTS RECEIVED A RANSOM NOTE EARLIER THIS EVENING.
KIDNAPPED...? BUT, I RODE...
I KNOW. I TOLD THE POLICE.
HER ABDUCTOR... UH, SEEMS TO CALL HIMSELF THE TARANTULA. TRUTH IS, WE'VE BEEN HALF EXPECTING SOMETHING LIKE THIS.
WELL, WHAT'S HE WANT?
MONEY, IT SEEMS. IT'S BEING KEPT OUT OF THE PAPERS TO AVOID PUBLIC HYSTERIA.
WELL, JUST WHO IS HE? AND WHAT ABOUT CATHERINE?
SWEETHEART, I'M SORRY. AT THIS POINT, WE CAN'T DO MUCH OF ANYTHING. WE JUST... DON'T KNOW.
WELL, WHO THE HELL DOES KNOW?!!
15

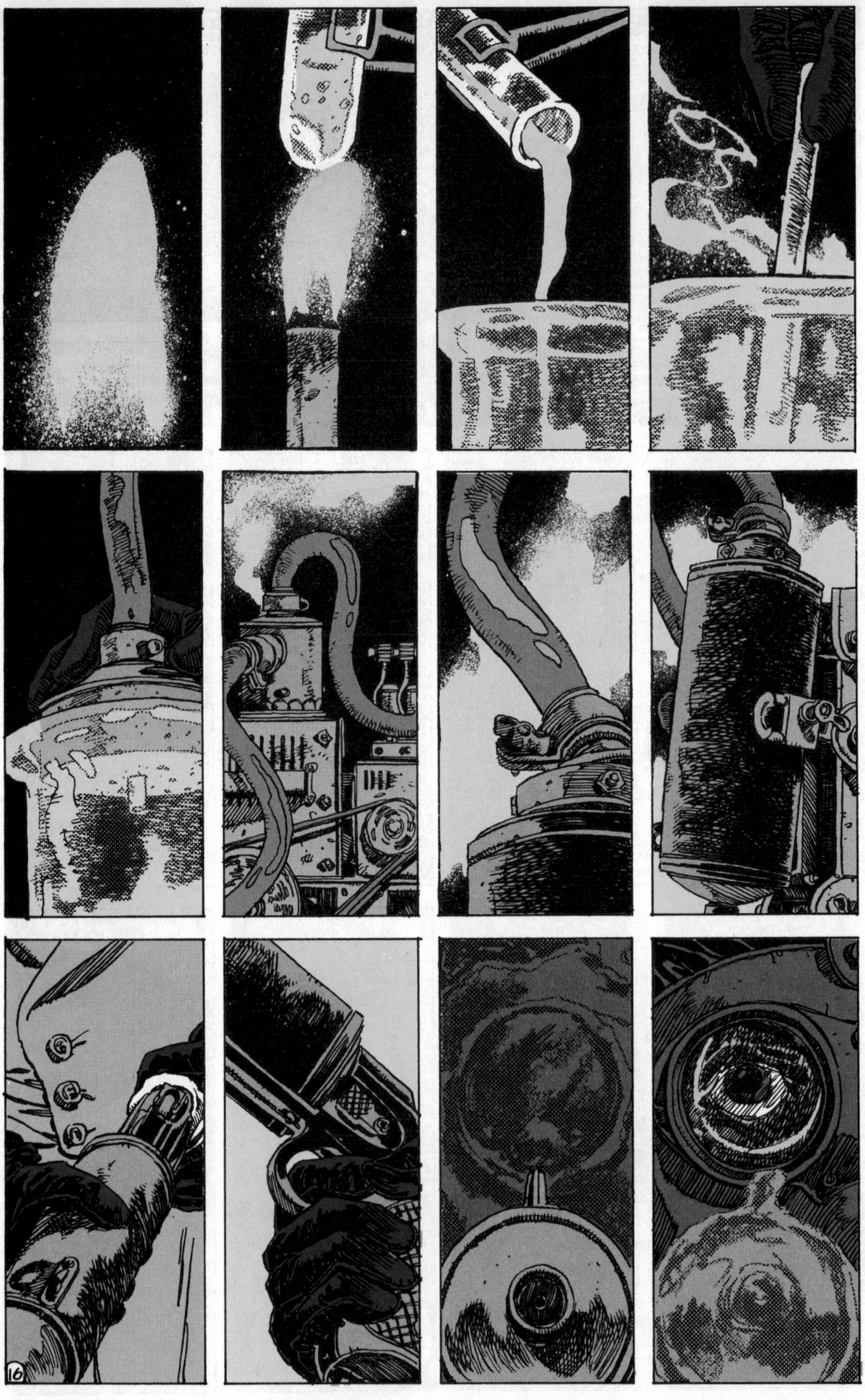
16

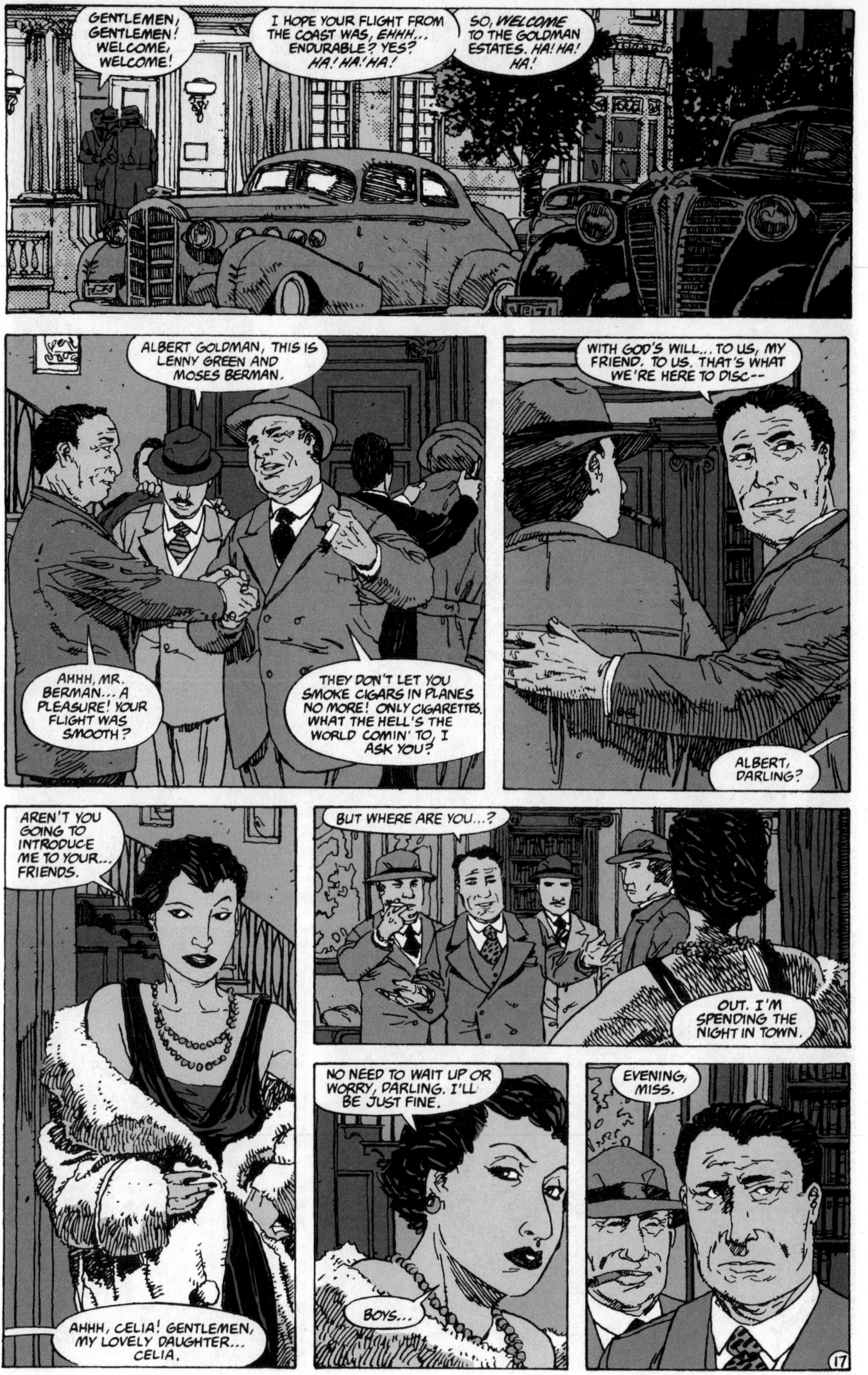

GENTLEMEN, GENTLEMEN! WELCOME, WELCOME!
I HOPE YOUR FLIGHT FROM THE COAST WAS, EHHH... ENDURABLE? YES? HA! HA! HA!
SO, WELCOME TO THE GOLDMAN ESTATES. HA! HA! HA!
ALBERT GOLDMAN, THIS IS LENNY GREEN AND MOSES BERMAN.
AHHH, MR. BERMAN... A PLEASURE! YOUR FLIGHT WAS SMOOTH?
THEY DON'T LET YOU SMOKE CIGARS IN PLANES NO MORE! ONLY CIGARETTES. WHAT THE HELL'S THE WORLD COMIN' TO, I ASK YOU?
WITH GOD'S WILL... TO US, MY FRIEND. TO US. THAT'S WHAT WE'RE HERE TO DISC--
ALBERT, DARLING?
AREN'T YOU GOING TO INTRODUCE ME TO YOUR... FRIENDS.
AHHH, CELIA! GENTLEMEN, MY LOVELY DAUGHTER... CELIA.
BUT WHERE ARE YOU...?
OUT. I'M SPENDING THE NIGHT IN TOWN.
NO NEED TO WAIT UP OR WORRY, DARLING. I'LL BE JUST FINE.
BOYS...
EVENING, MISS.
17

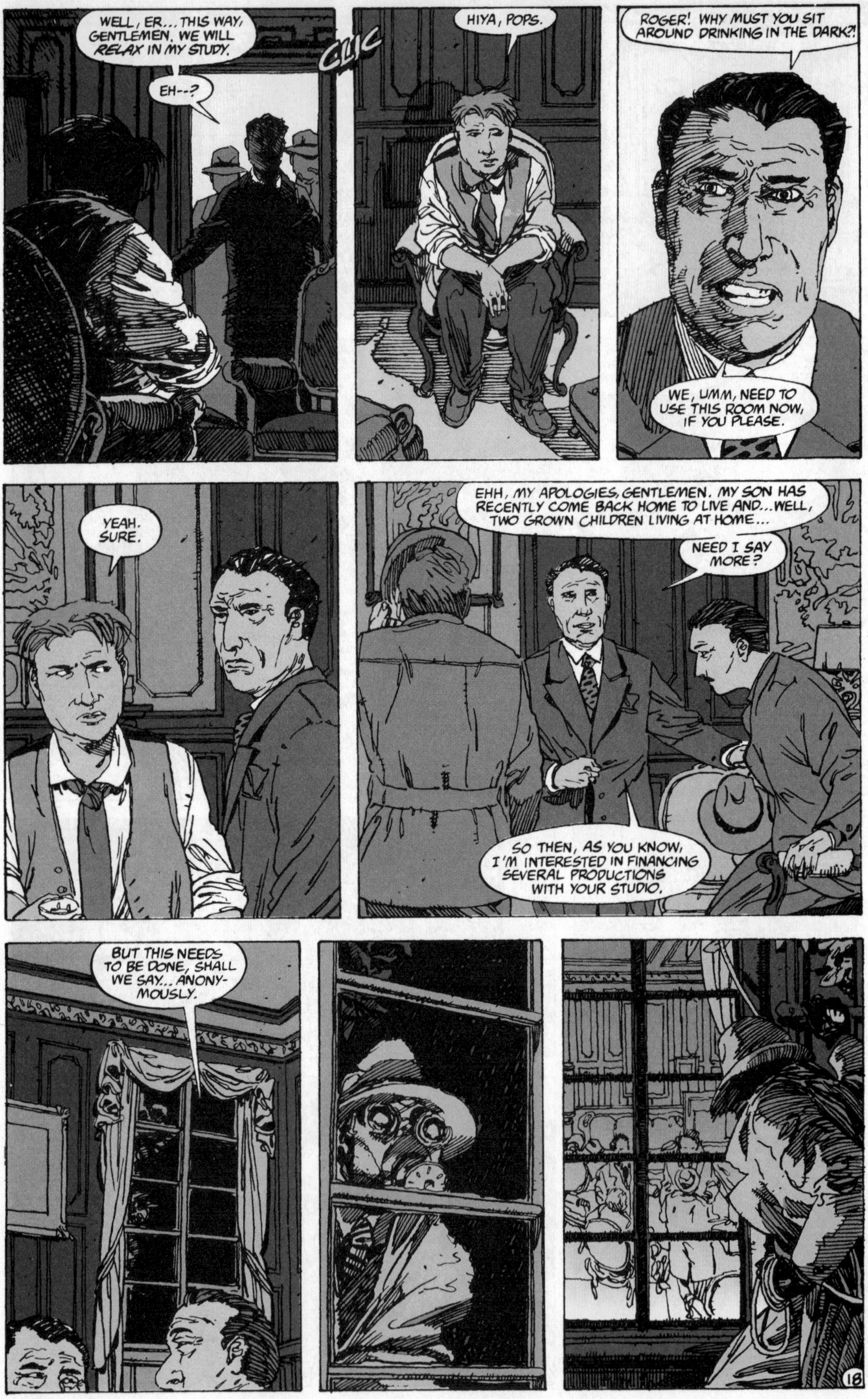
WELL, ER... THIS WAY, GENTLEMEN. WE WILL RELAX IN MY STUDY.
CLIC
EH--?
HIYA, POPS.
ROGER! WHY MUST YOU SIT AROUND DRINKING IN THE DARK?!
WE, UMM, NEED TO USE THIS ROOM NOW, IF YOU PLEASE.
YEAH. SURE.
EHH, MY APOLOGIES, GENTLEMEN. MY SON HAS RECENTLY COME BACK HOME TO LIVE AND... WELL, TWO GROWN CHILDREN LIVING AT HOME...
NEED I SAY MORE?
SO THEN, AS YOU KNOW, I'M INTERESTED IN FINANCING SEVERAL PRODUCTIONS WITH YOUR STUDIO.
BUT THIS NEEDS TO BE DONE, SHALL WE SAY... ANONY-MOUSLY.
18

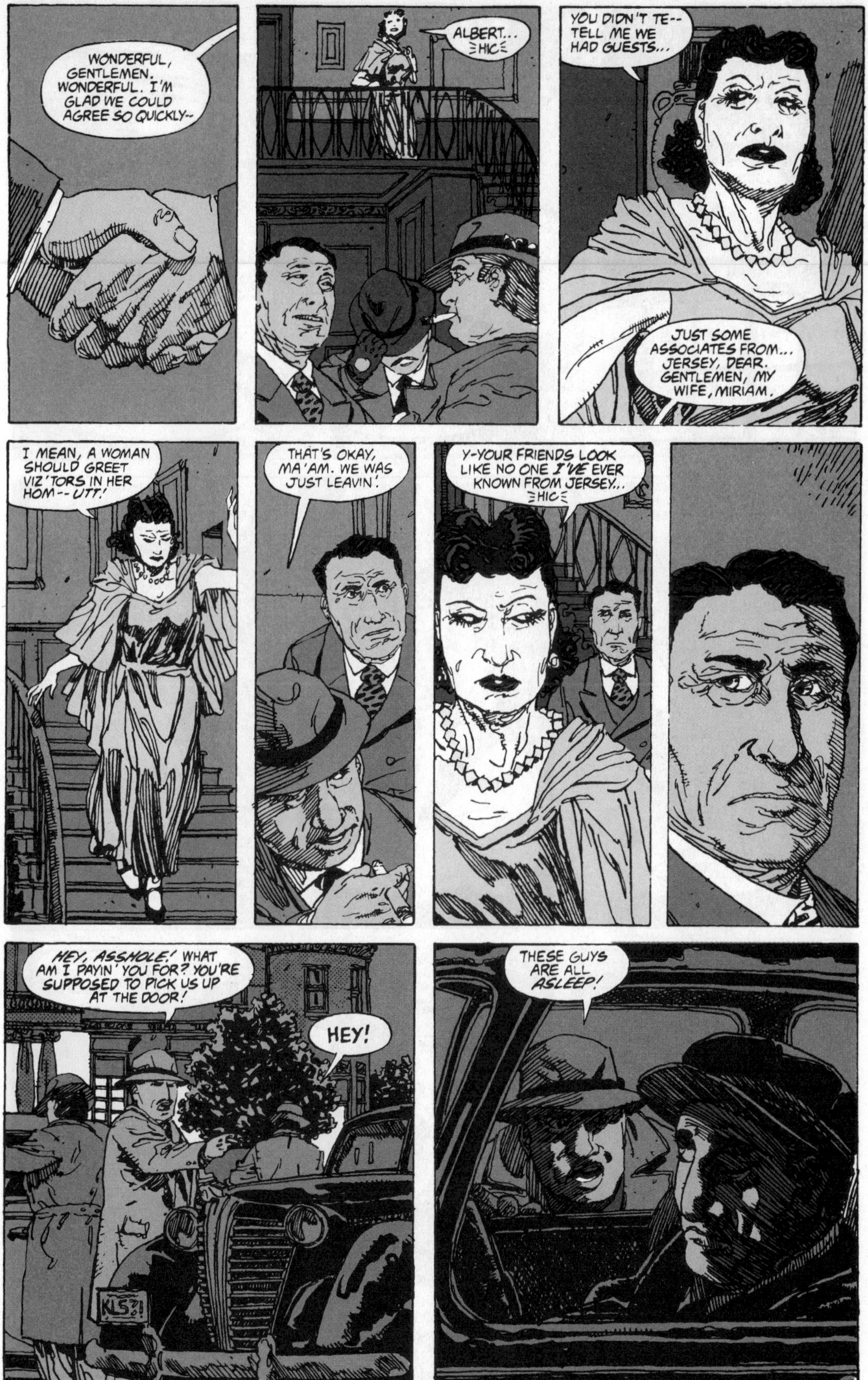
WONDERFUL, GENTLEMEN. WONDERFUL. I'M GLAD WE COULD AGREE SO QUICKLY--
ALBERT... HIC
YOU DIDN'T TE-- TELL ME WE HAD GUESTS...
JUST SOME ASSOCIATES FROM... JERSEY, DEAR. GENTLEMEN, MY WIFE, MIRIAM.
I MEAN, A WOMAN SHOULD GREET VIZ'TORS IN HER HOM--UTT.'
THAT'S OKAY, MA'AM. WE WAS JUST LEAVIN'.
Y-YOUR FRIENDS LOOK LIKE NO ONE I'VE EVER KNOWN FROM JERSEY... HIC
HEY, ASSHOLE! WHAT AM I PAYIN' YOU FOR? YOU'RE SUPPOSED TO PICK US UP AT THE DOOR!
HEY!
KLS?!
THESE GUYS ARE ALL ASLEEP!
19

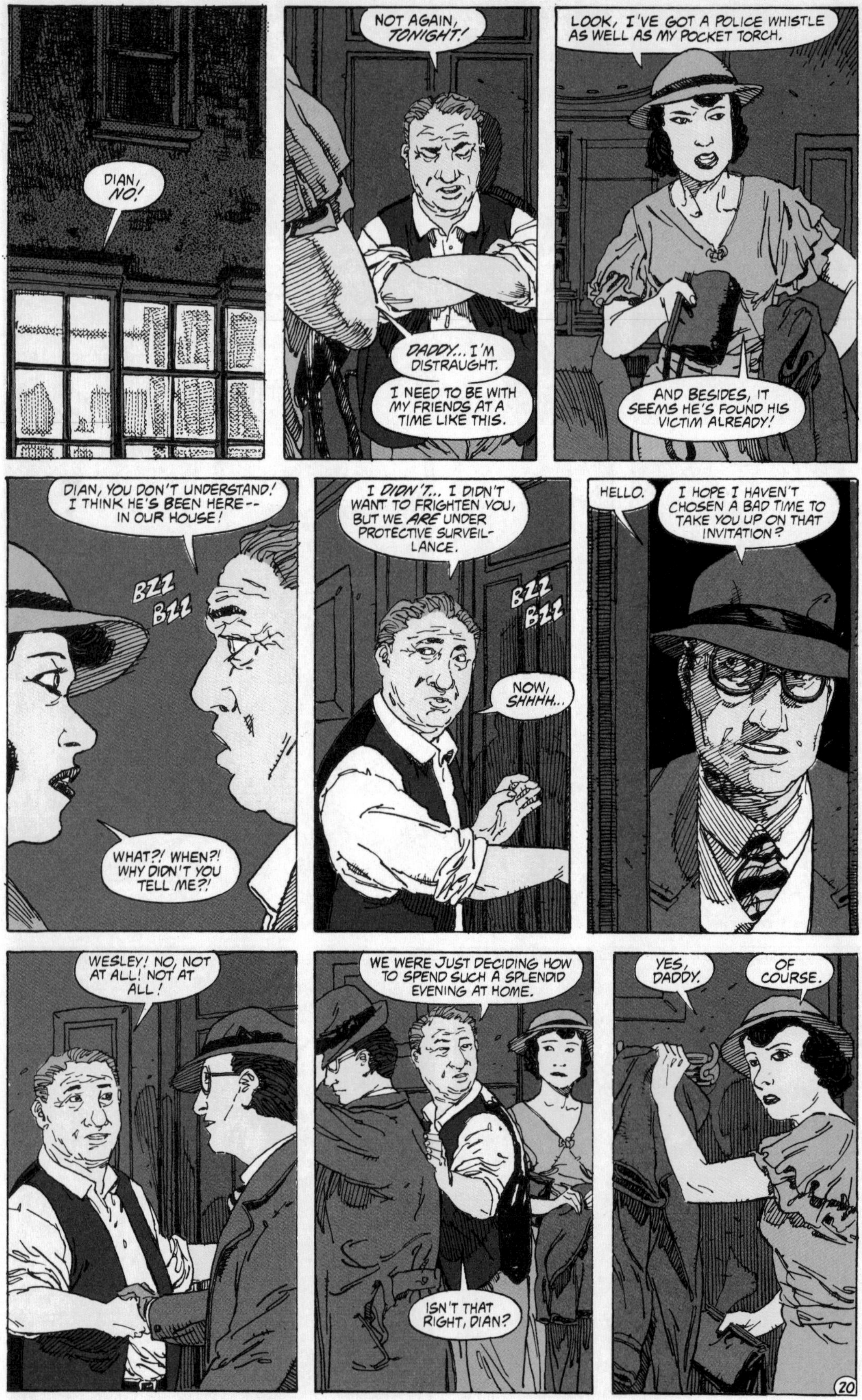
DIAN, NO!
NOT AGAIN, TONIGHT!
DADDY... I'M DISTRAUGHT.
I NEED TO BE WITH MY FRIENDS AT A TIME LIKE THIS.
LOOK, I'VE GOT A POLICE WHISTLE AS WELL AS MY POCKET TORCH.
AND BESIDES, IT SEEMS HE'S FOUND HIS VICTIM ALREADY!
DIAN, YOU DON'T UNDERSTAND! I THINK HE'S BEEN HERE-- IN OUR HOUSE!
BZZ BZZ
WHAT?! WHEN?! WHY DIDN'T YOU TELL ME?!
I DIDN'T... I DIDN'T WANT TO FRIGHTEN YOU, BUT WE ARE UNDER PROTECTIVE SURVEIL-LANCE.
BZZ BZZ
NOW, SHHHH...
HELLO.
I HOPE I HAVEN'T CHOSEN A BAD TIME TO TAKE YOU UP ON THAT INVITATION?
WESLEY! NO, NOT AT ALL! NOT AT ALL!
WE WERE JUST DECIDING HOW TO SPEND SUCH A SPLENDID EVENING AT HOME.
ISN'T THAT RIGHT, DIAN?
YES, DADDY.
OF COURSE.
20

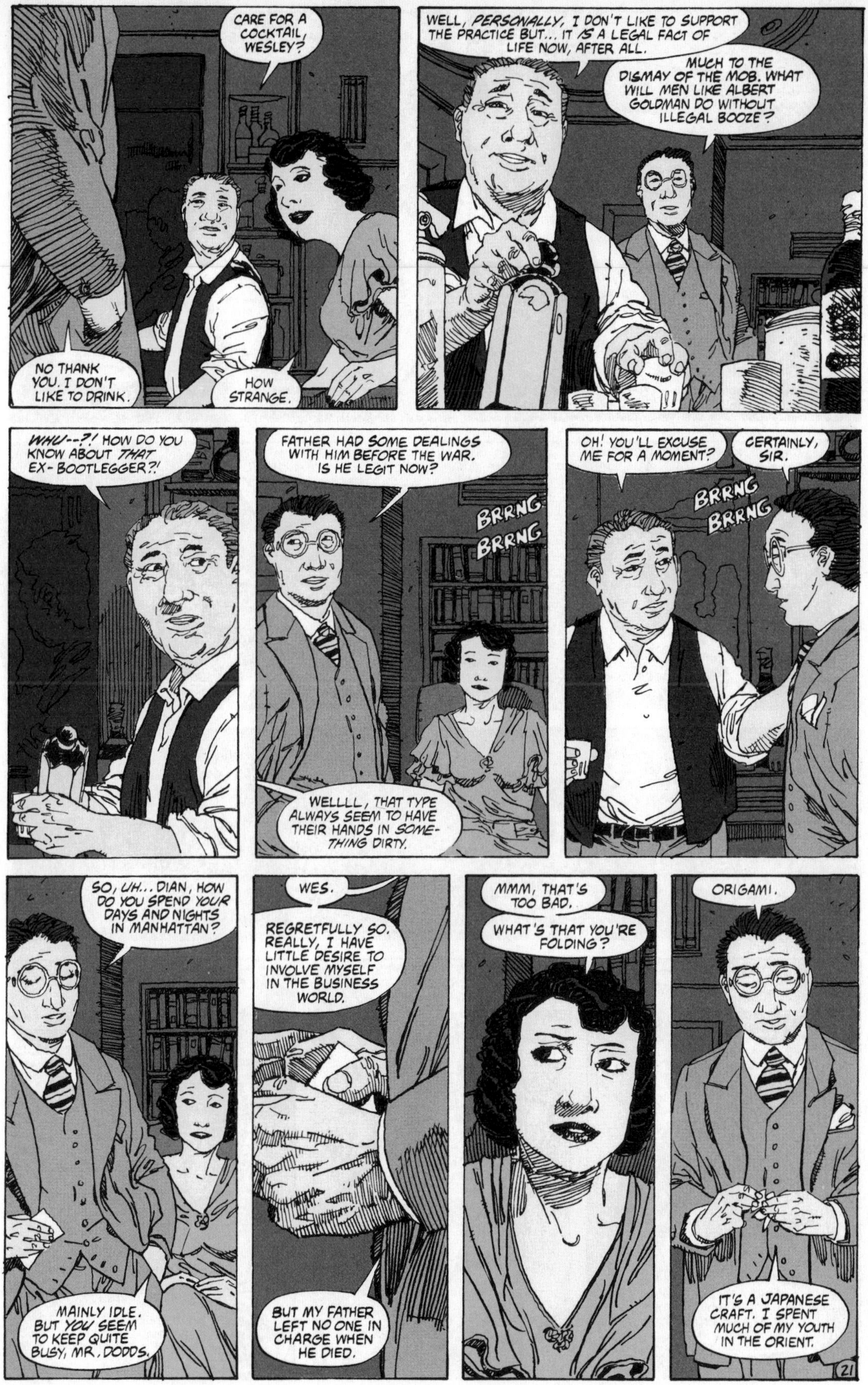
CARE FOR A COCKTAIL, WESLEY?
NO THANK YOU. I DON'T LIKE TO DRINK.
HOW STRANGE.
WELL, PERSONALLY, I DON'T LIKE TO SUPPORT THE PRACTICE BUT... IT IS A LEGAL FACT OF LIFE NOW, AFTER ALL.
MUCH TO THE DISMAY OF THE MOB. WHAT WILL MEN LIKE ALBERT GOLDMAN DO WITHOUT ILLEGAL BOOZE?
WHU--?! HOW DO YOU KNOW ABOUT THAT EX-BOOTLEGGER?!
FATHER HAD SOME DEALINGS WITH HIM BEFORE THE WAR. IS HE LEGIT NOW?
BRRNG BRRNG
WELLLL, THAT TYPE ALWAYS SEEM TO HAVE THEIR HANDS IN SOME-THING DIRTY.
OH! YOU'LL EXCUSE ME FOR A MOMENT?
CERTAINLY, SIR.
BRRNG BRRNG
SO, UH... DIAN, HOW DO YOU SPEND YOUR DAYS AND NIGHTS IN MANHATTAN?
MAINLY IDLE. BUT YOU SEEM TO KEEP QUITE BUSY, MR. DODDS.
WES.
REGRETFULLY SO. REALLY, I HAVE LITTLE DESIRE TO INVOLVE MYSELF IN THE BUSINESS WORLD.
BUT MY FATHER LEFT NO ONE IN CHARGE WHEN HE DIED.
MMM, THAT'S TOO BAD.
WHAT'S THAT YOU'RE FOLDING?
ORIGAMI.
IT'S A JAPANESE CRAFT. I SPENT MUCH OF MY YOUTH IN THE ORIENT.
21

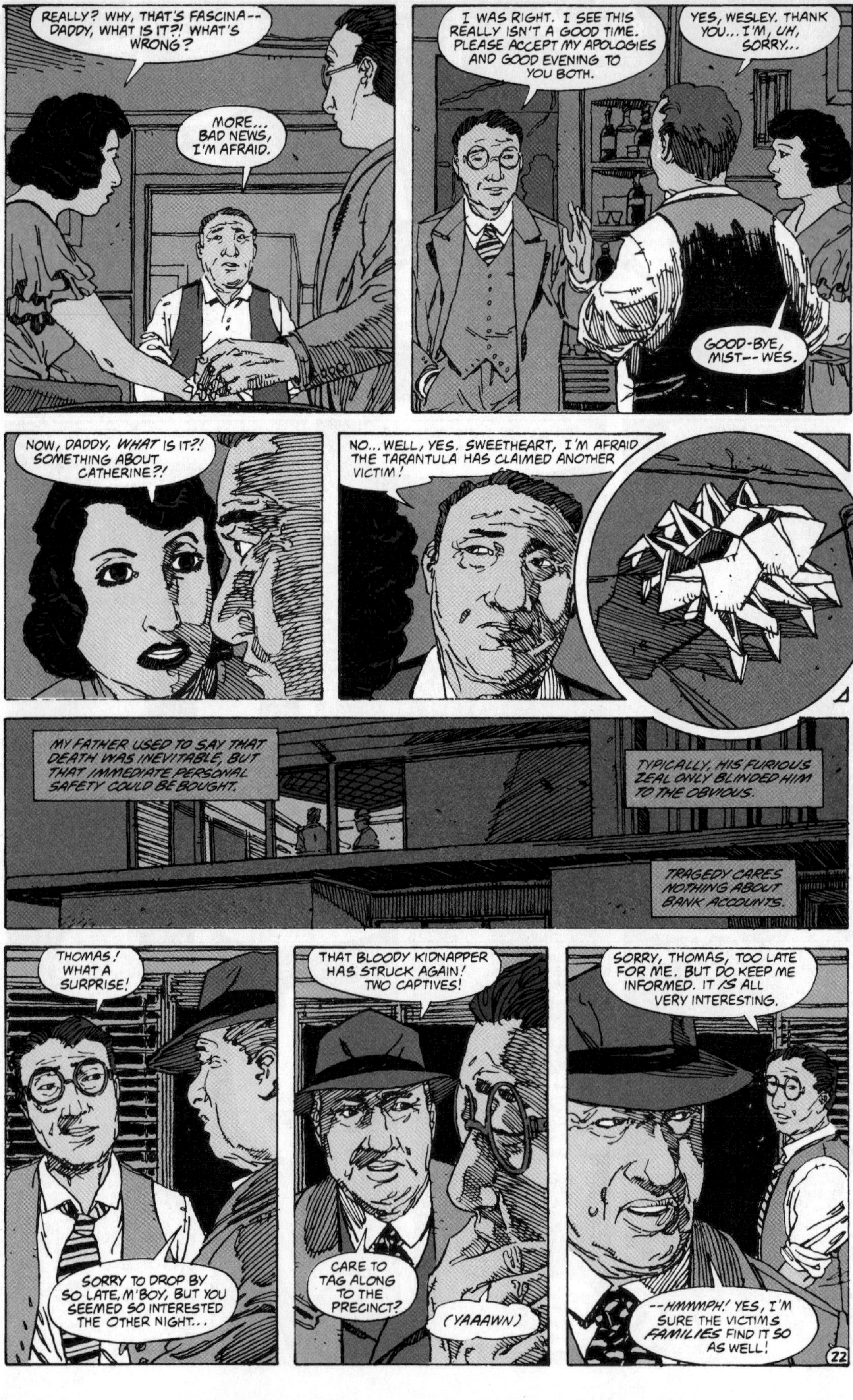
REALLY? WHY, THAT'S FASCINA-- DADDY, WHAT IS IT?! WHAT'S WRONG?
MORE... BAD NEWS, I'M AFRAID.
I WAS RIGHT. I SEE THIS REALLY ISN'T A GOOD TIME. PLEASE ACCEPT MY APOLOGIES AND GOOD EVENING TO YOU BOTH.
YES, WESLEY. THANK YOU... I'M, UH, SORRY...
GOOD-BYE, MIST--WES.
NOW, DADDY, WHAT IS IT?! SOMETHING ABOUT CATHERINE?!
NO... WELL, YES. SWEETHEART, I'M AFRAID THE TARANTULA HAS CLAIMED ANOTHER VICTIM!
MY FATHER USED TO SAY THAT DEATH WAS INEVITABLE, BUT THAT IMMEDIATE PERSONAL SAFETY COULD BE BOUGHT.
TYPICALLY, HIS FURIOUS ZEAL ONLY BLINDED HIM TO THE OBVIOUS.
TRAGEDY CARES NOTHING ABOUT BANK ACCOUNTS.
THOMAS! WHAT A SURPRISE!
SORRY TO DROP BY SO LATE, M'BOY, BUT YOU SEEMED SO INTERESTED THE OTHER NIGHT...
THAT BLOODY KIDNAPPER HAS STRUCK AGAIN! TWO CAPTIVES!
CARE TO TAG ALONG TO THE PRECINCT?
(YAAAAWN)
SORRY, THOMAS, TOO LATE FOR ME. BUT DO KEEP ME INFORMED. IT IS ALL VERY INTERESTING.
--HMMMPH! YES, I'M SURE THE VICTIMS FAMILIES FIND IT SO AS WELL!
22

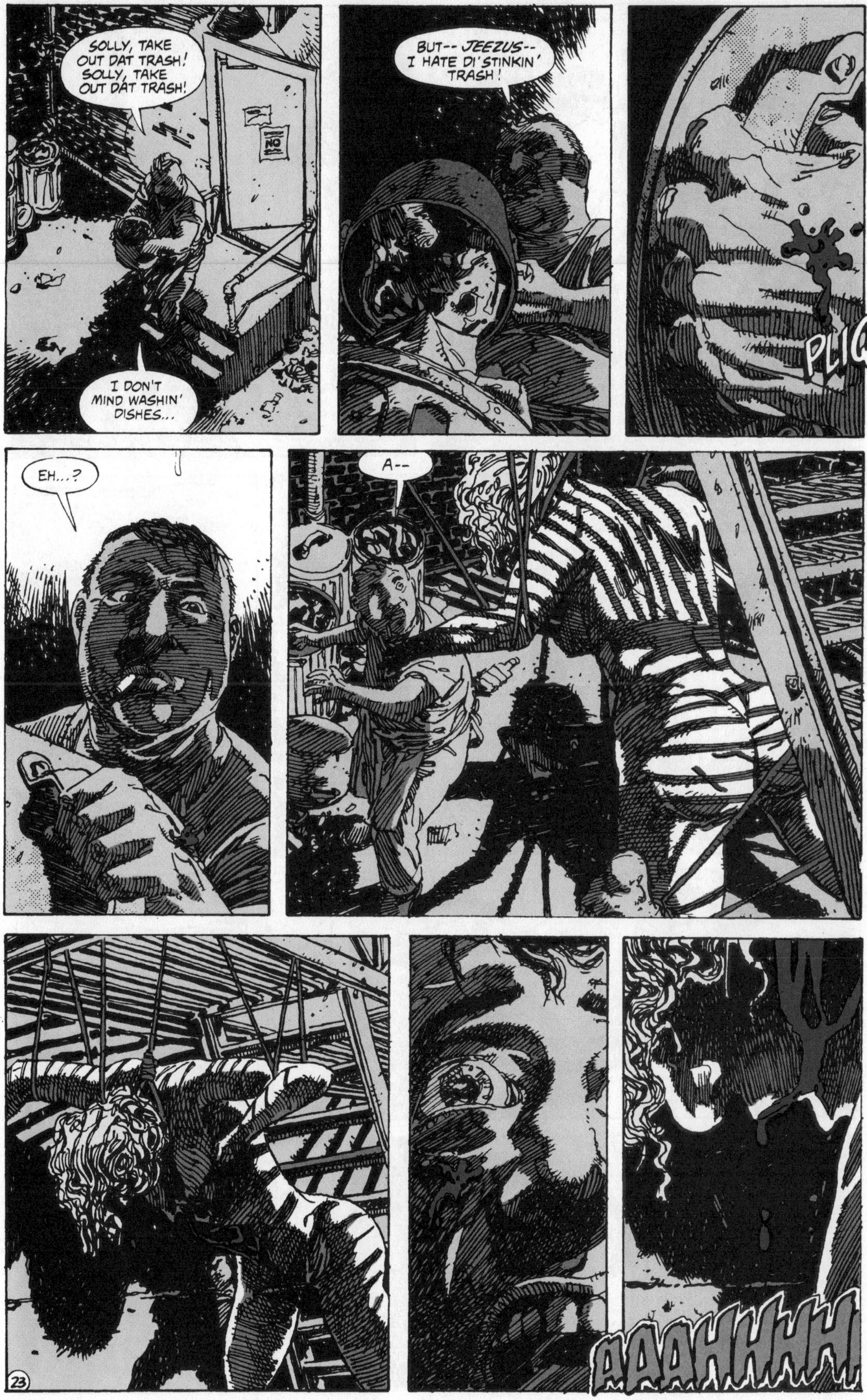
SOLLY, TAKE OUT DAT TRASH! SOLLY, TAKE OUT DAT TRASH!
I DON'T MIND WASHIN' DISHES...
BUT-- JEEZUS-- I HATE DI'STINKIN' TRASH!
PLIQ
EH...?
A--
23
AAAHHHH

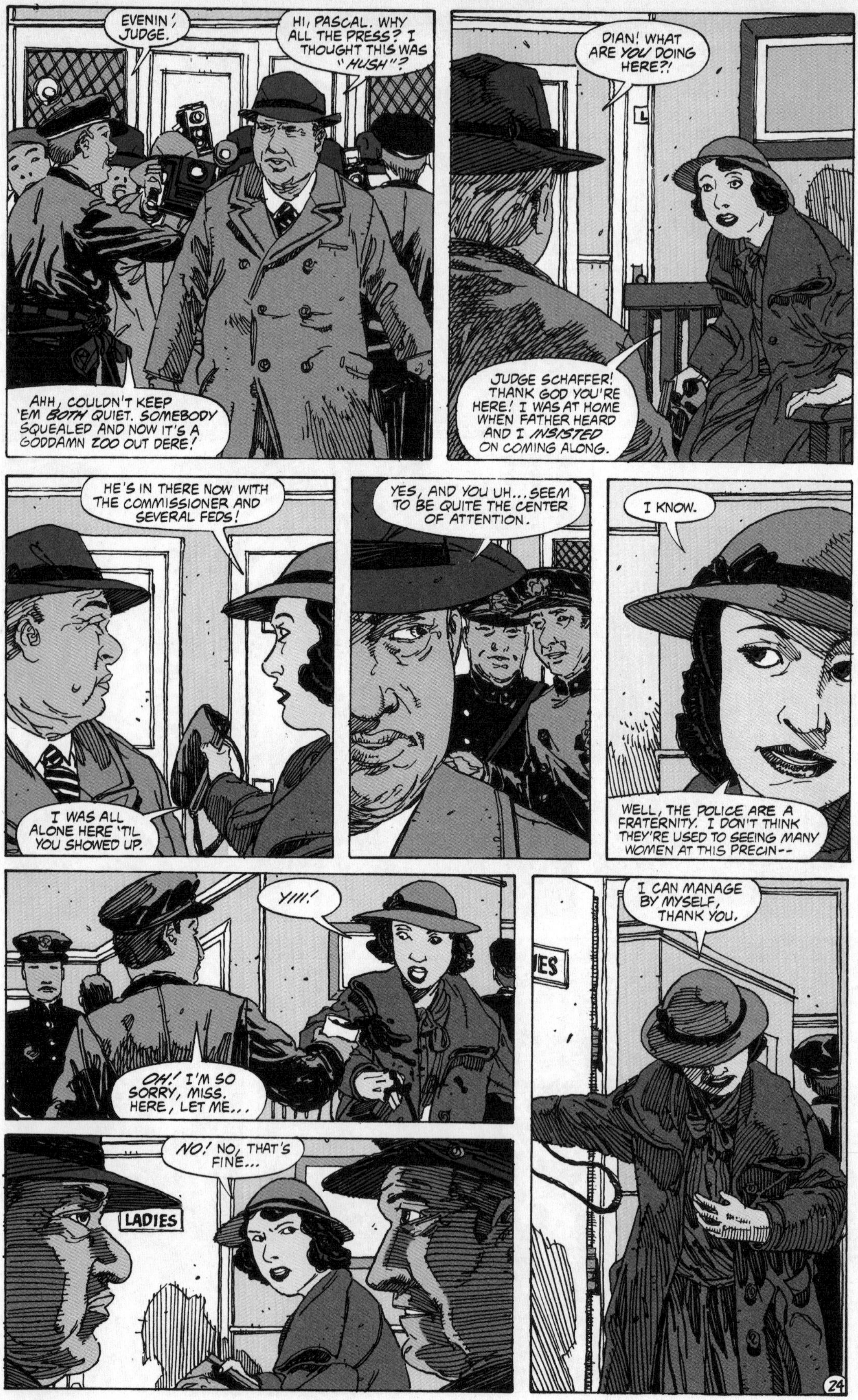
EVENIN', JUDGE.
HI, PASCAL. WHY ALL THE PRESS? I THOUGHT THIS WAS "HUSH"?
AHH, COULDN'T KEEP 'EM BOTH QUIET. SOMEBODY SQUEALED AND NOW IT'S A GODDAMN ZOO OUT DERE!
DIAN! WHAT ARE YOU DOING HERE?!
JUDGE SCHAFFER! THANK GOD YOU'RE HERE! I WAS AT HOME WHEN FATHER HEARD AND I INSISTED ON COMING ALONG.
HE'S IN THERE NOW WITH THE COMMISSIONER AND SEVERAL FEDS!
I WAS ALL ALONE HERE 'TIL YOU SHOWED UP.
YES, AND YOU UH... SEEM TO BE QUITE THE CENTER OF ATTENTION.
I KNOW.
WELL, THE POLICE ARE A FRATERNITY. I DON'T THINK THEY'RE USED TO SEEING MANY WOMEN AT THIS PRECIN--
YIII!
OH! I'M SO SORRY, MISS. HERE, LET ME...
I CAN MANAGE BY MYSELF, THANK YOU.
IES
NO! NO, THAT'S FINE...
LADIES
24

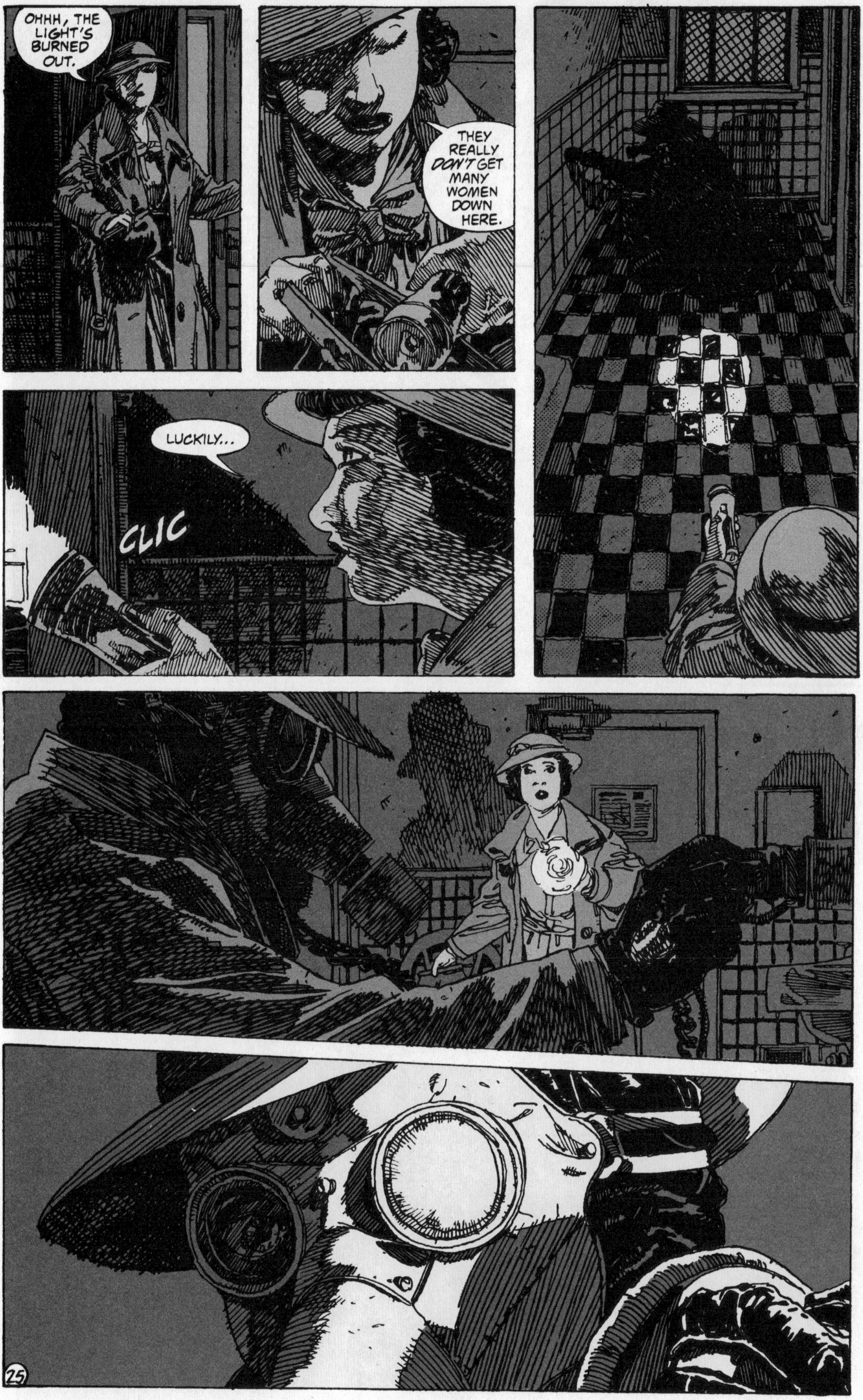
OHHH, THE LIGHT'S BURNED OUT.
THEY REALLY DON'T GET MANY WOMEN DOWN HERE.
LUCKILY...
CLIC
25

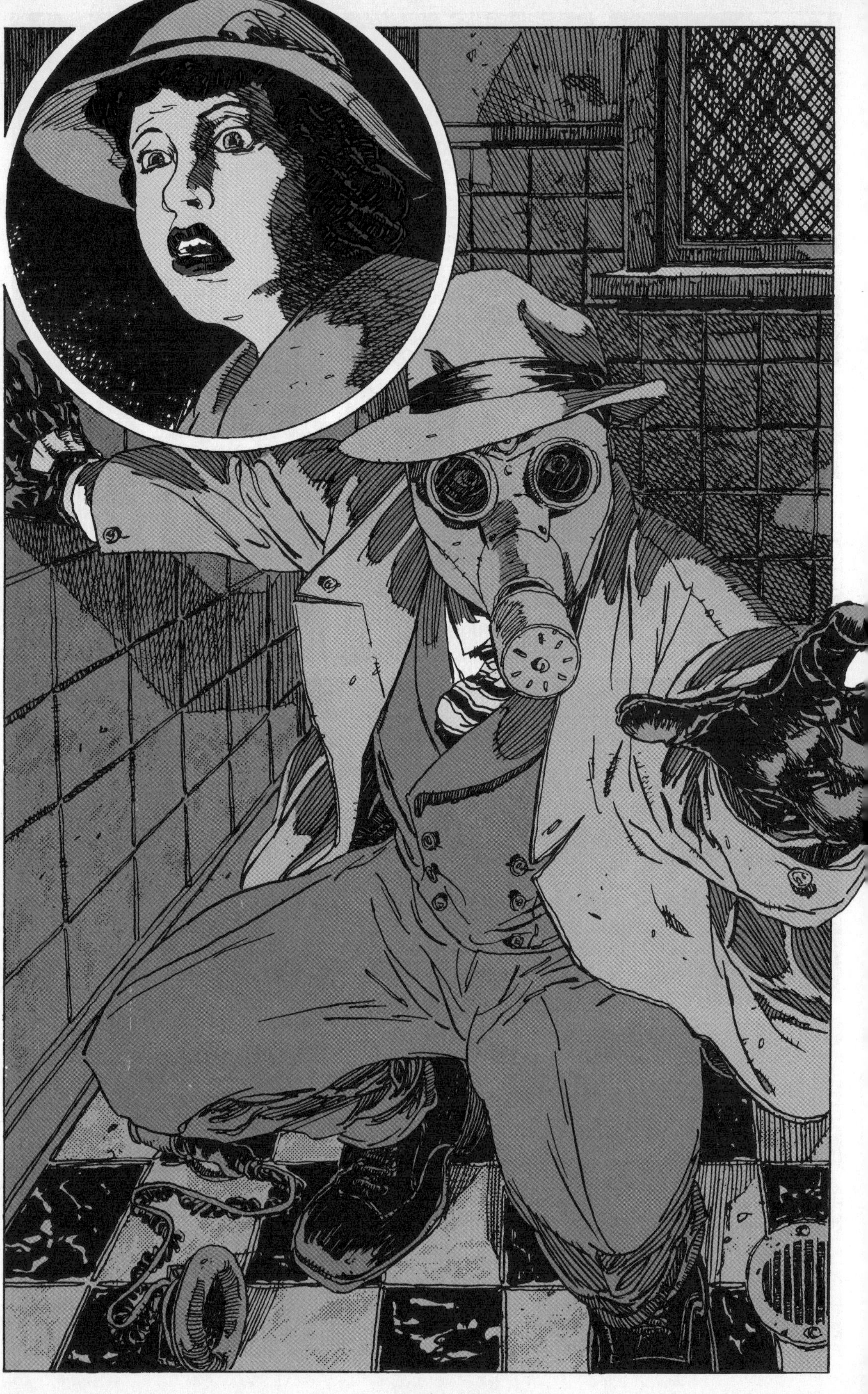

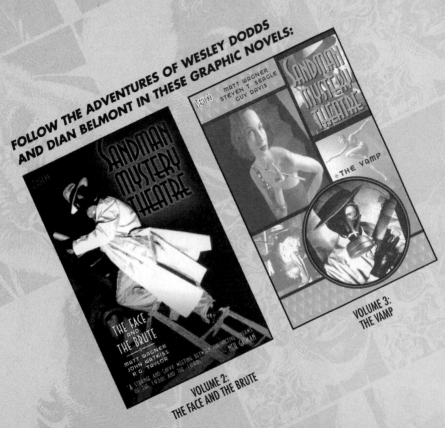

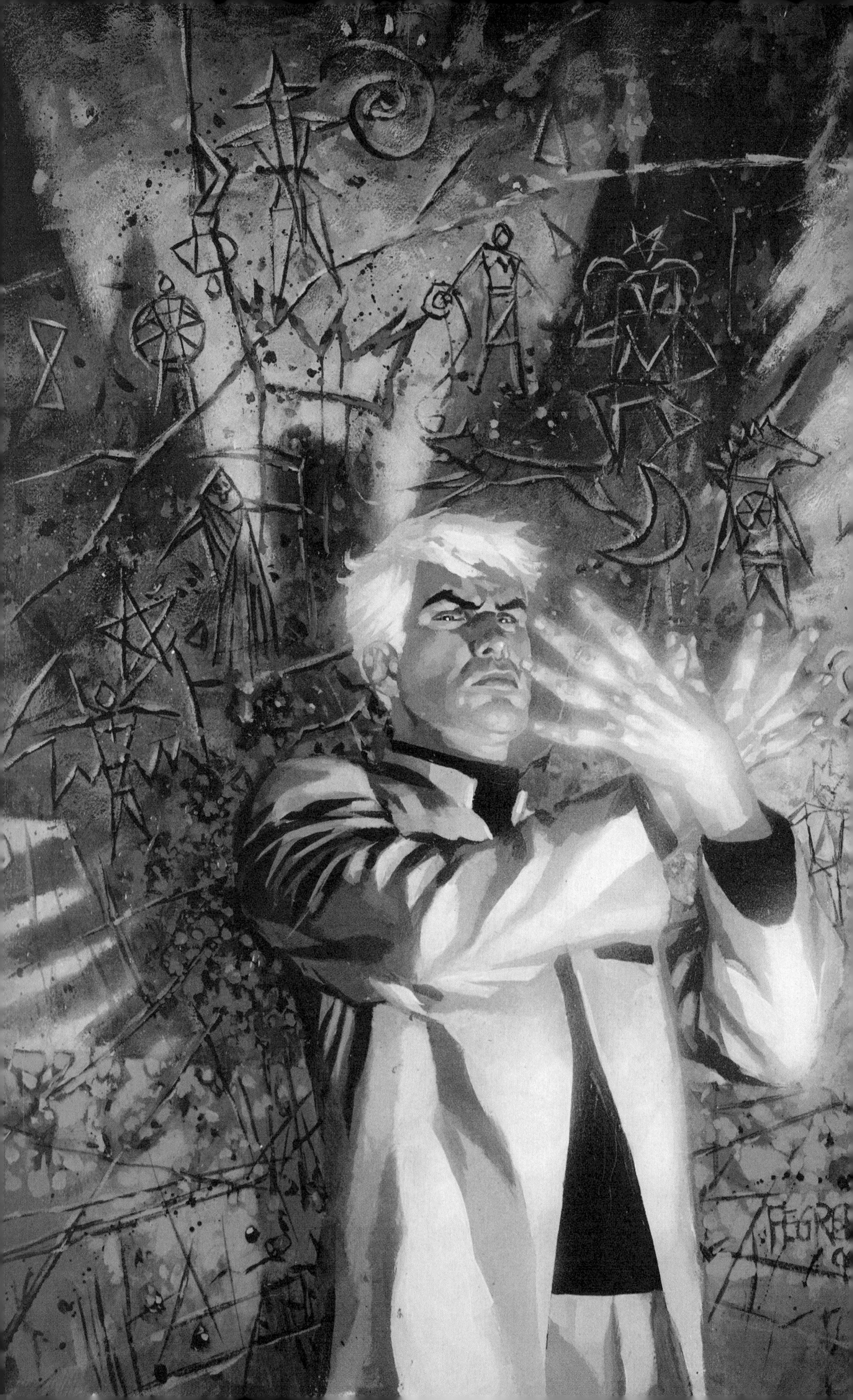

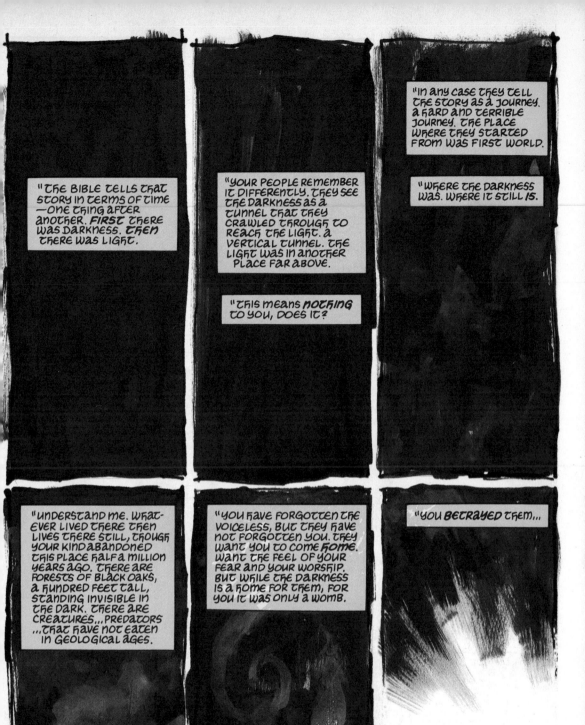

"THE BIBLE TELLS THAT STORY IN TERMS OF TIME —ONE THING AFTER ANOTHER. *FIRST* THERE WAS DARKNESS. *THEN* THERE WAS LIGHT.

"YOUR PEOPLE REMEMBER IT DIFFERENTLY. THEY SEE THE DARKNESS AS A TUNNEL THAT THEY CRAWLED THROUGH TO REACH THE LIGHT. A VERTICAL TUNNEL. THE LIGHT WAS IN ANOTHER PLACE FAR ABOVE.

"THIS MEANS *NOTHING* TO YOU, DOES IT?

"IN ANY CASE THEY TELL THE STORY AS A JOURNEY. A HARD AND TERRIBLE JOURNEY. THE PLACE WHERE THEY STARTED FROM WAS FIRST WORLD.

"WHERE THE DARKNESS WAS. WHERE IT STILL *IS*.

"UNDERSTAND ME. WHAT-EVER LIVED THERE THEN LIVES THERE STILL, THOUGH YOUR KIND ABANDONED THIS PLACE HALF A MILLION YEARS AGO. THERE ARE FORESTS OF BLACK OAKS, A HUNDRED FEET TALL, STANDING INVISIBLE IN THE DARK. THERE ARE CREATURES...PREDATORS ...THAT HAVE NOT EATEN IN GEOLOGICAL AGES.

"YOU HAVE FORGOTTEN THE VOICELESS, BUT THEY HAVE NOT FORGOTTEN YOU. THEY WANT YOU TO COME *HOME*. WANT THE FEEL OF YOUR FEAR AND YOUR WORSHIP. BUT WHILE THE DARKNESS IS A HOME FOR THEM, FOR YOU IT WAS ONLY A WOMB.

"YOU *BETRAYED* THEM...

"...WHEN YOU WERE BORN INTO THE *LIGHT*."

143

NO ASYMMETRY, BUT THE PUPILLARY DILATION *IS* ON THE SLOW SIDE.

IT'S OKAY, PAUL, THE LIGHT WON'T HURT YOU.

SEE THE PICTURE? THE BOY'S PLAYING WITH A *TRUCK*, ISN'T HE? CAN YOU POINT TO THE *TRUCK*? TRY TO POINT TO THE *TRUCK*, PAUL.

...AUL HAS A *TRUCK*

...RY RIDES A

LET'S FEEL THOSE FINGERS. OH, GOOD GRIP, PAUL. NICE GRIP. HE'S LEFT-HANDED, ISN'T HE? LET'S TRY THE OTHER SIDE.

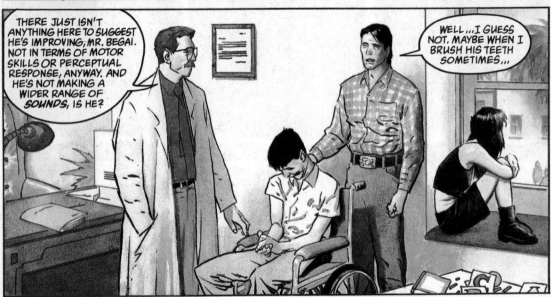

THERE JUST ISN'T ANYTHING HERE TO SUGGEST HE'S IMPROVING, MR. BEGAI. NOT IN TERMS OF MOTOR SKILLS OR PERCEPTUAL RESPONSE, ANYWAY. AND HE'S NOT MAKING A WIDER RANGE OF *SOUNDS*, IS HE?

WELL ... I GUESS NOT. MAYBE WHEN I BRUSH HIS TEETH SOMETIMES ...

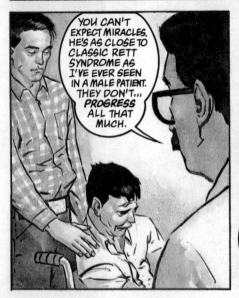

YOU CAN'T EXPECT MIRACLES. HE'S AS CLOSE TO CLASSIC RETT SYNDROME AS I'VE EVER SEEN IN A MALE PATIENT. THEY DON'T ... *PROGRESS* ALL THAT MUCH.

I WAS THINKIN' ... I DUNNO ... THAT HE WAS *LOOKIN'* AT ME MORE. LIKE HE WANTED TO TALK TO ME, ALMOST. YOU THINK THAT COULD EVER ...?

NO. PUT THAT OUT OF YOUR MIND.

YOU SAID THE FITS ARE ACTUALLY WORSE NOW. DOES THAT MEAN LONGER OR MORE INTENSE?

WELL, BOTH.

I CAN UP THE DOSAGE ON THE LAMOTRIGINE BUT TRY USING THE RECTAL VALIUM TOO, AS A PREVENTATIVE...

"HE'S YOUR BROTHER. YOU'D WANT TO BE THERE FOR YOUR BROTHER, WOULDN'T YOU RACHEL?"

"YEAH, DAD, FINE. IT'S JUST A SCHOOL DAY. I'LL JUST MISS IT. NO PROBLEM. MY TIME IS YOURS."

"...OBVIOUSLY."

HEY, DAD--THERE'S SOME WEIRD WOMAN HANGING 'ROUND YOUR CAR.

I TOLD YOU NOT TO PARK THERE.

SHE'S ACTING REAL CRAZY. SHE'S WAVING THIS FLOWER AROUND LIKE SHE'S DIRECTING TRAFFIC. AND I THINK SHE'S CRYING.

MY GOD, HE *LOVES* ME! HE REALLY *LOVES* ME! OH JESUS, SWEET JESUS!

LOOK! I FOUND THIS!

THAT'S NICE. TAKE CARE. TAKE CARE, NOW.

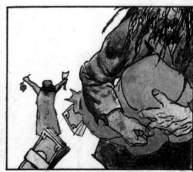

LOCAL MAN JERRY RUFINO SPRAYED HIS BOSS WITH SHAVING FOAM WHEN HE WON THE STATE LOTTERY YESTERDAY, BUT TWELVE HOURS LATER HE WAS ASKING FOR HIS OLD JOB BACK...

I DUNNO ABOUT USIN' MORE OF THAT LAMOTRIGINE STUFF. IT ALWAYS LEAVES 'IM DOPEY. WHAT D'YOU RECKON, RACH?

...BECAUSE A STAGGERING EIGHT HUNDRED PEOPLE PICKED THE WINNING NUMBERS, EACH COLLECTING LESS THAN THREE THOUSAND DOLLARS! DON'T GIVE UP YOUR DAY JOB, JER.

WELL IF IT'S A CHOICE BETWEEN DOPEY AND FRENZY, I KNOW WHICH DWARF I'D GO FOR.

WHAT'S THAT, FLOWER?

NOTHING, DAD.

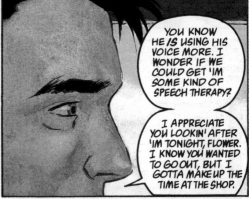

YOU KNOW HE IS USING HIS VOICE MORE. I WONDER IF WE COULD GET 'IM SOME KIND OF SPEECH THERAPY?

I APPRECIATE YOU LOOKIN' AFTER 'IM TONIGHT, FLOWER. I KNOW YOU WANTED TO GO OUT, BUT I GOTTA MAKE UP THE TIME AT THE SHOP.

NO PROBLEM. ALL PART OF THE SERVICE.

TCH. COME ON, PAUL, MOST CHICKS WON'T EVEN LOOK AT A GUY WITH DROOL ON HIS CHIN.

"THEN AGAIN, MOM LOOKED AT DAD.

"SO I GUESS THERE'S HOPE FOR ALL OF US."

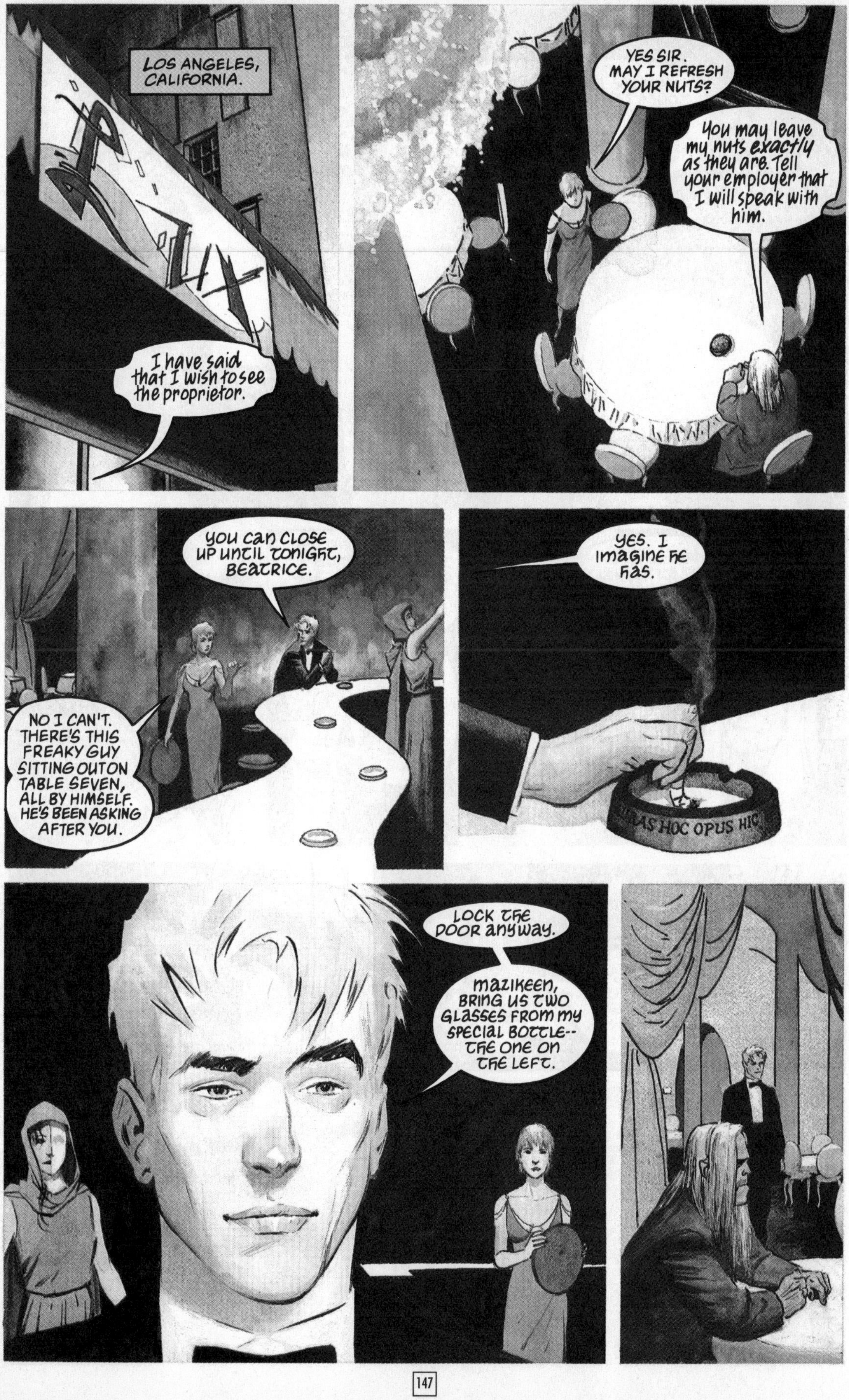
LOS ANGELES, CALIFORNIA.
I have said that I wish to see the proprietor.
YES SIR. MAY I REFRESH YOUR NUTS?
You may leave my nuts exactly as they are. Tell your employer that I will speak with him.
YOU CAN CLOSE UP UNTIL TONIGHT, BEATRICE.
NO I CAN'T. THERE'S THIS FREAKY GUY SITTING OUT ON TABLE SEVEN, ALL BY HIMSELF. HE'S BEEN ASKING AFTER YOU.
YES. I IMAGINE HE HAS.
...RAS HOC OPUS HIC...
LOCK THE DOOR ANYWAY.
MAZIKEEN, BRING US TWO GLASSES FROM MY SPECIAL BOTTLE-- THE ONE ON THE LEFT.

"WHOSE FEET MAY NOT TOUCH THE GROUND, NOR ANY FOULNESS STAIN THEIR GARMENTS, FOR THEY ARE OF THE SEVENTH SPHERE WHICH IS ABOVE CORRUPTION."

The devil can cite scripture for his purpose. Good day to you, Lucifer Morningstar.

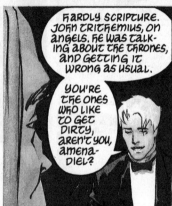

HARDLY SCRIPTURE. JOHN TRITHEMIUS, ON ANGELS. HE WAS TALKING ABOUT THE THRONES, AND GETTING IT WRONG AS USUAL.

YOU'RE THE ONES WHO LIKE TO GET DIRTY, AREN'T YOU, AMENA-DIEL?

There is no room for doubt or scruple in the service of the name. If you'd realized that you might still be of the host.

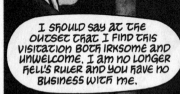

I SHOULD SAY AT THE OUTSET THAT I FIND THIS VISITATION BOTH IRKSOME AND UNWELCOME. I AM NO LONGER HELL'S RULER AND YOU HAVE NO BUSINESS WITH ME.

And how are you finding your retirement, Prince of the East?

RESTFUL.

148

I would have thought you'd be bored. It's difficult to let go of power when you've been used to exercising it.

To settle down and grow roses up the door.

And yet here I am.

And the old firm is in new hands. And the world goes on.

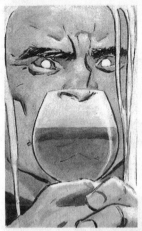

That's an eighty-year-old Janneau Armagnac. If I'd known you were going to waste it on melodrama I'd have given you the '78.

The world is on fire, Lucifer Morningstar. I wanted to make that point forcefully.

Otherwise we could squander the whole evening in stale repartee.

I've no desire to trespass on your evening at all, Amenadiel, I'm sure there are many places where your company would be almost welcome.

No need, Mazikeen. Leave it.

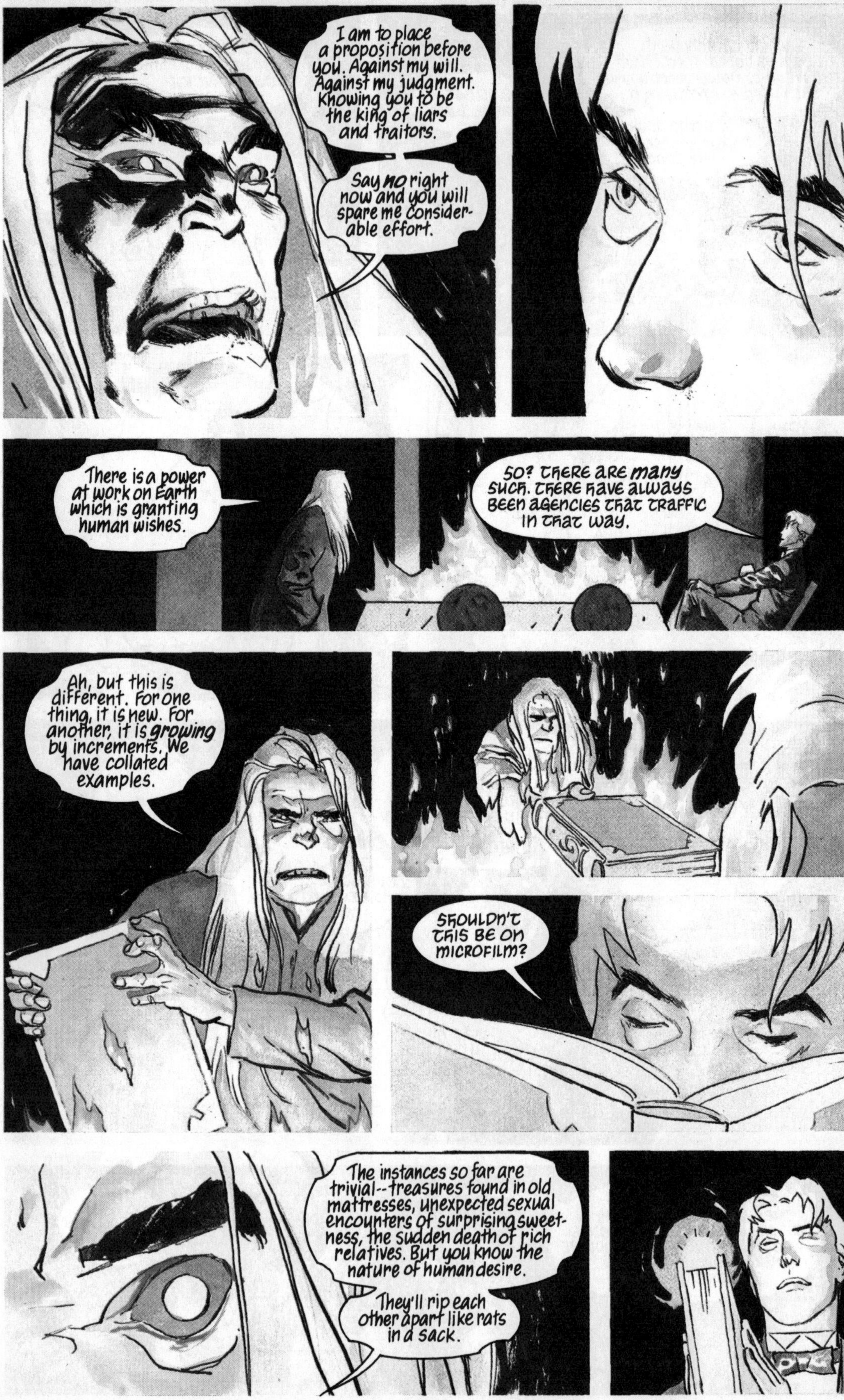
I am to place a proposition before you. Against my will. Against my judgment. Knowing you to be the king of liars and traitors.
Say no right now and you will spare me considerable effort.
There is a power at work on Earth which is granting human wishes.
SO? THERE ARE MANY SUCH. THERE HAVE ALWAYS BEEN AGENCIES THAT TRAFFIC IN THAT WAY.
Ah, but this is different. For one thing, it is new. For another, it is growing by increments. We have collated examples.
SHOULDN'T THIS BE ON MICROFILM?
The instances so far are trivial--treasures found in old mattresses, unexpected sexual encounters of surprising sweetness, the sudden death of rich relatives. But you know the nature of human desire.
They'll rip each other apart like rats in a sack.

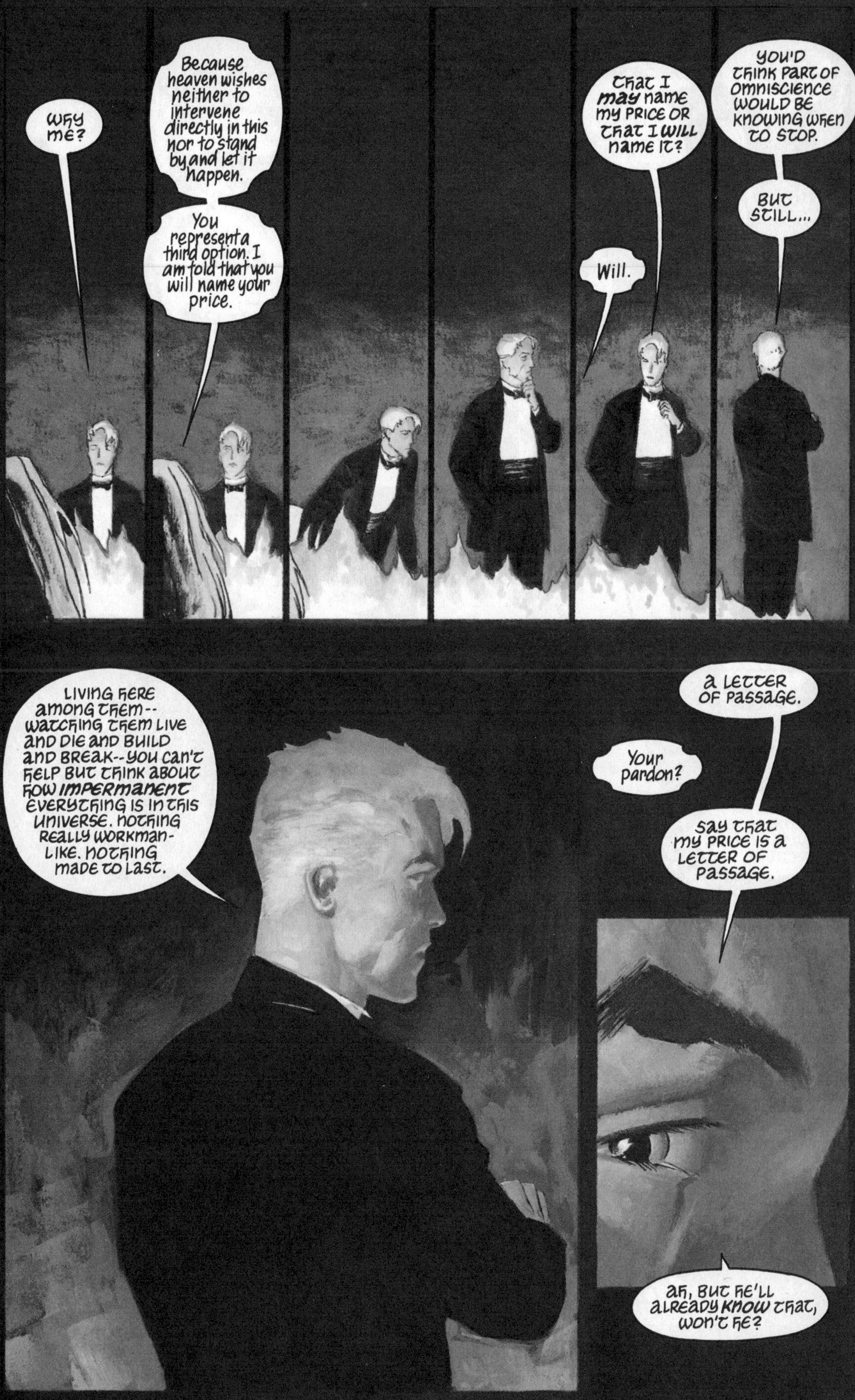
Why me?
Because heaven wishes neither to intervene directly in this nor to stand by and let it happen.
You represent a third option. I am told that you will name your price.
That I may name my price or that I will name it?
Will.
You'd think part of omniscience would be knowing when to stop.
But still...
Living here among them -- watching them live and die and build and break -- you can't help but think about how impermanent everything is in this universe. Nothing really workman-like. Nothing made to last.
A letter of passage.
Your pardon?
Say that my price is a letter of passage.
Ah, but he'll already know that, won't he?

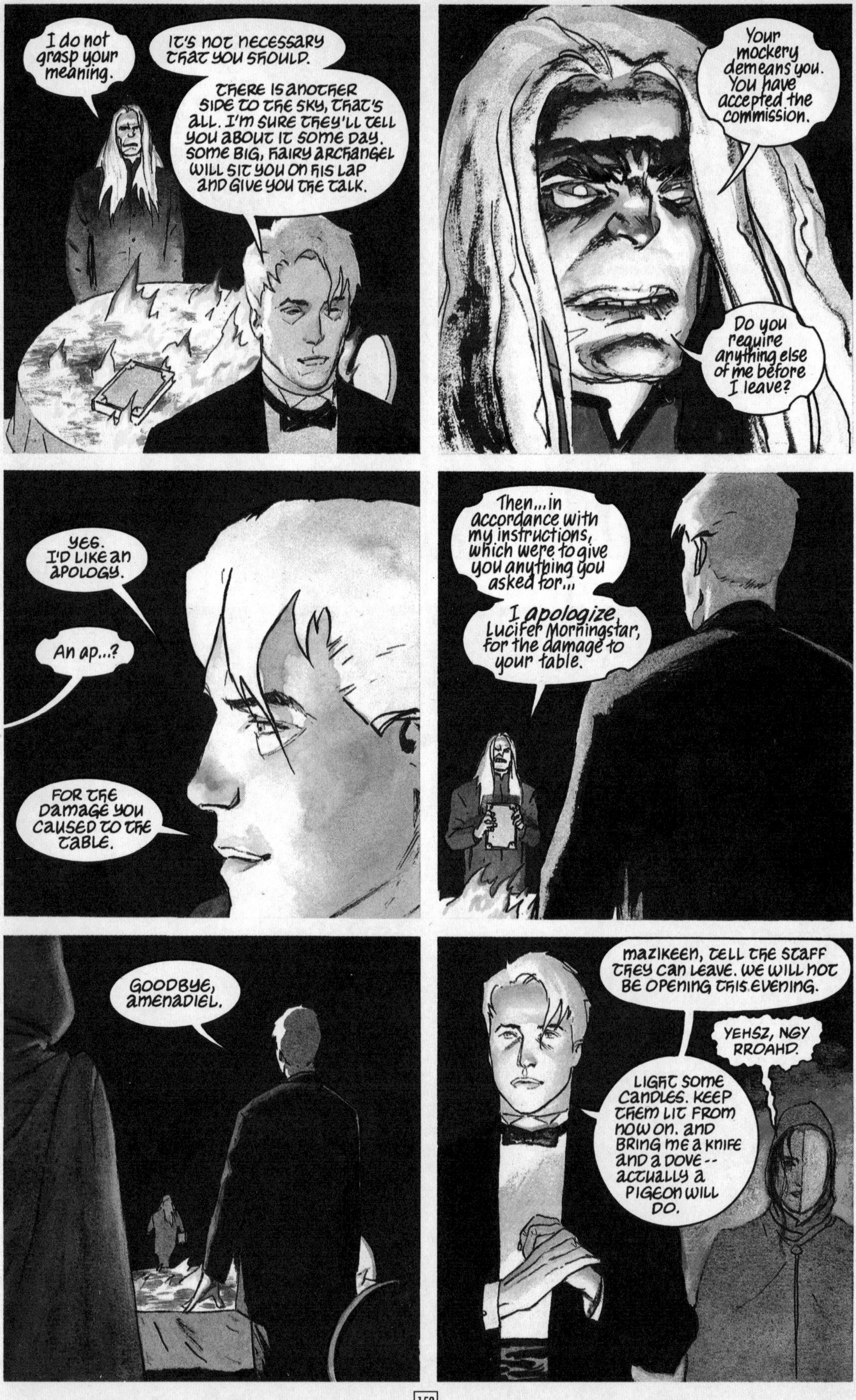
I do not grasp your meaning.
It's not necessary that you should.
There is another side to the sky, that's all. I'm sure they'll tell you about it some day. Some big, hairy archangel will sit you on his lap and give you the talk.
Your mockery demeans you. You have accepted the commission.
Do you require anything else of me before I leave?
Yes. I'd like an apology.
An ap...?
For the damage you caused to the table.
Then... in accordance with my instructions, which were to give you anything you asked for...
I *apologize*, Lucifer Morningstar, for the damage to your table.
Goodbye, Amenadiel.
Mazikeen, tell the staff they can leave. We will not be opening this evening.
YEHSZ, NGY RROAHD.
Light some candles. Keep them lit from now on. And bring me a knife and a dove -- actually a pigeon will do.

OH, WHERE ARE YOU GOING...SAID THE FALSE KNIGHT ON THE ROAD...

NGY RROAHD, HRRALL I NGRING HEOU A BOWL TO CASZSZ GHE VHLOOD?

THANK YOU, MAZIKEEN. NO, THE BIRD'S NOT FOR SACRIFICE. WHO WOULD I SACRIFICE IT TO?

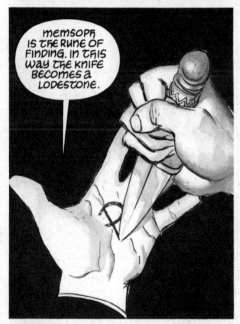

MEMSOPH IS THE RUNE OF FINDING. IN THIS WAY THE KNIFE BECOMES A LODESTONE.

I MAY NOT KNOW WHERE I'M GOING, BUT I SEE NO REASON TO TRAVEL BLIND.

NOW YOU. DON'T BE SO FRIGHTENED. I'M NOT HUNGRY.

I'LL JUST TROUBLE YOU FOR A LOAN OF THESE. I MAY NEED TO FLY BEFORE THIS BUSINESS IS DONE WITH, AND I FORFEITED MY OWN WINGS SOME TIME SINCE.

MAZIKEEN.

YEHSZ, NGY RROAHD.

MY COAT, PLEASE. AND BRING ME MY OTHER BOTTLE. THE ONE ON THE RIGHT.

I'M GOING OUT.

153

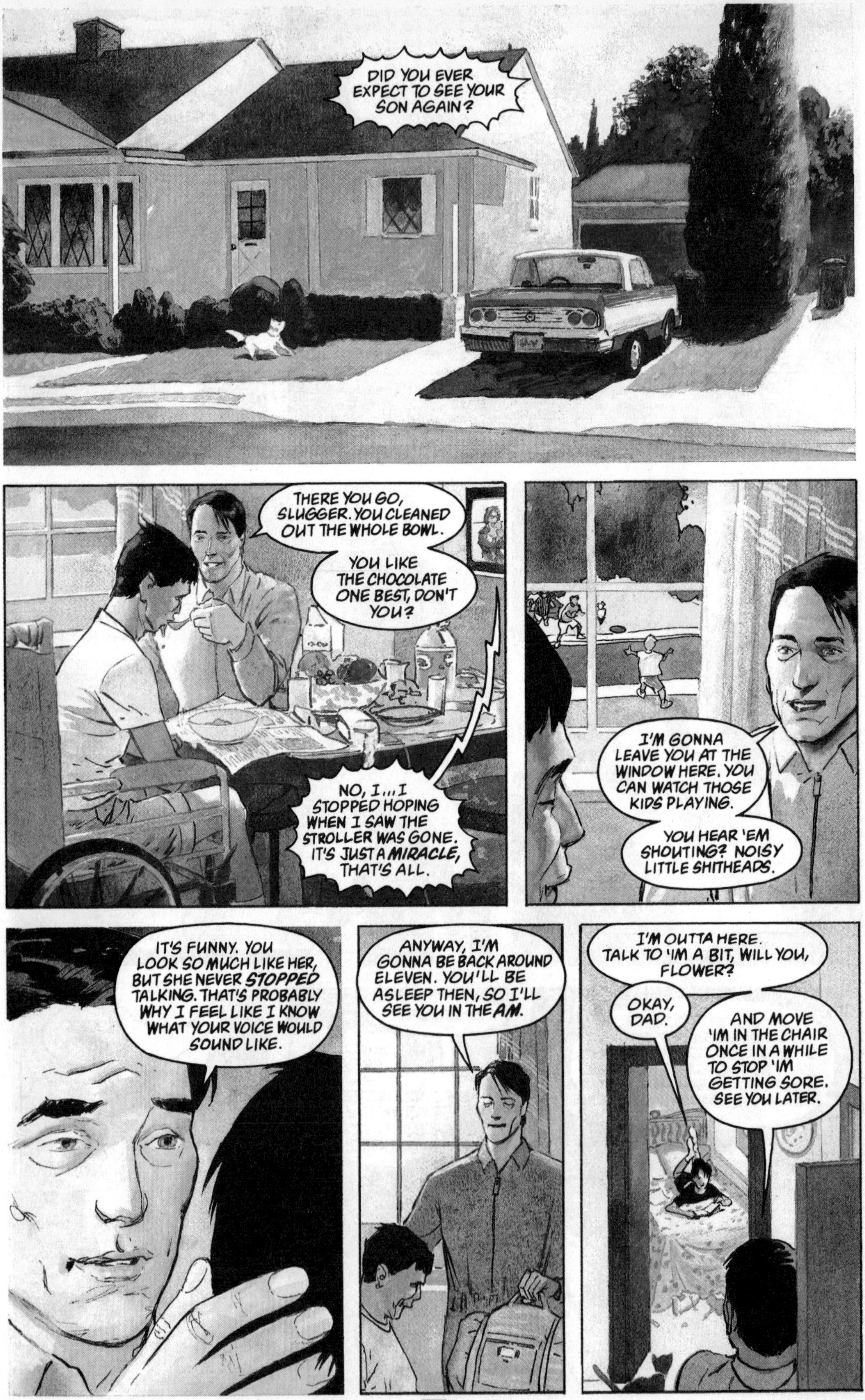
DID YOU EVER EXPECT TO SEE YOUR SON AGAIN?
THERE YOU GO, SLUGGER. YOU CLEANED OUT THE WHOLE BOWL.
YOU LIKE THE CHOCOLATE ONE BEST, DON'T YOU?
NO, I...I STOPPED HOPING WHEN I SAW THE STROLLER WAS GONE. IT'S JUST A MIRACLE, THAT'S ALL.
I'M GONNA LEAVE YOU AT THE WINDOW HERE. YOU CAN WATCH THOSE KIDS PLAYING.
YOU HEAR 'EM SHOUTING? NOISY LITTLE SHITHEADS.
IT'S FUNNY. YOU LOOK SO MUCH LIKE HER, BUT SHE NEVER STOPPED TALKING. THAT'S PROBABLY WHY I FEEL LIKE I KNOW WHAT YOUR VOICE WOULD SOUND LIKE.
ANYWAY, I'M GONNA BE BACK AROUND ELEVEN. YOU'LL BE ASLEEP THEN, SO I'LL SEE YOU IN THE AM.
I'M OUTTA HERE. TALK TO 'IM A BIT, WILL YOU, FLOWER?
OKAY, DAD.
AND MOVE 'IM IN THE CHAIR ONCE IN A WHILE TO STOP 'IM GETTING SORE. SEE YOU LATER.

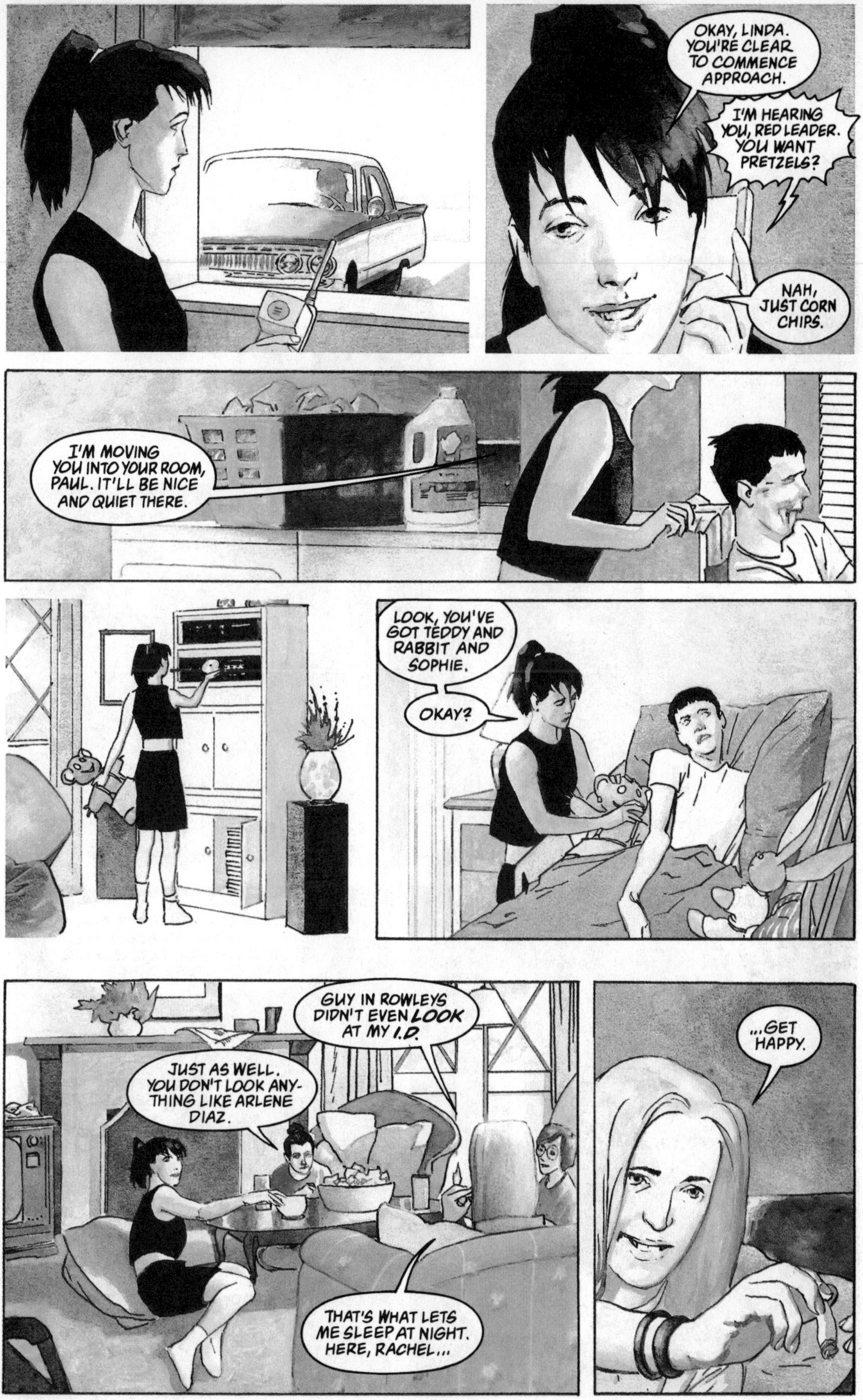
OKAY, LINDA. YOU'RE CLEAR TO COMMENCE APPROACH.
I'M HEARING YOU, RED LEADER. YOU WANT PRETZELS?
NAH, JUST CORN CHIPS.
I'M MOVING YOU INTO YOUR ROOM, PAUL. IT'LL BE NICE AND QUIET THERE.
LOOK, YOU'VE GOT TEDDY AND RABBIT AND SOPHIE.
OKAY?
GUY IN ROWLEYS DIDN'T EVEN LOOK AT MY I.D.
JUST AS WELL. YOU DON'T LOOK ANYTHING LIKE ARLENE DIAZ.
THAT'S WHAT LETS ME SLEEP AT NIGHT. HERE, RACHEL...
...GET HAPPY.

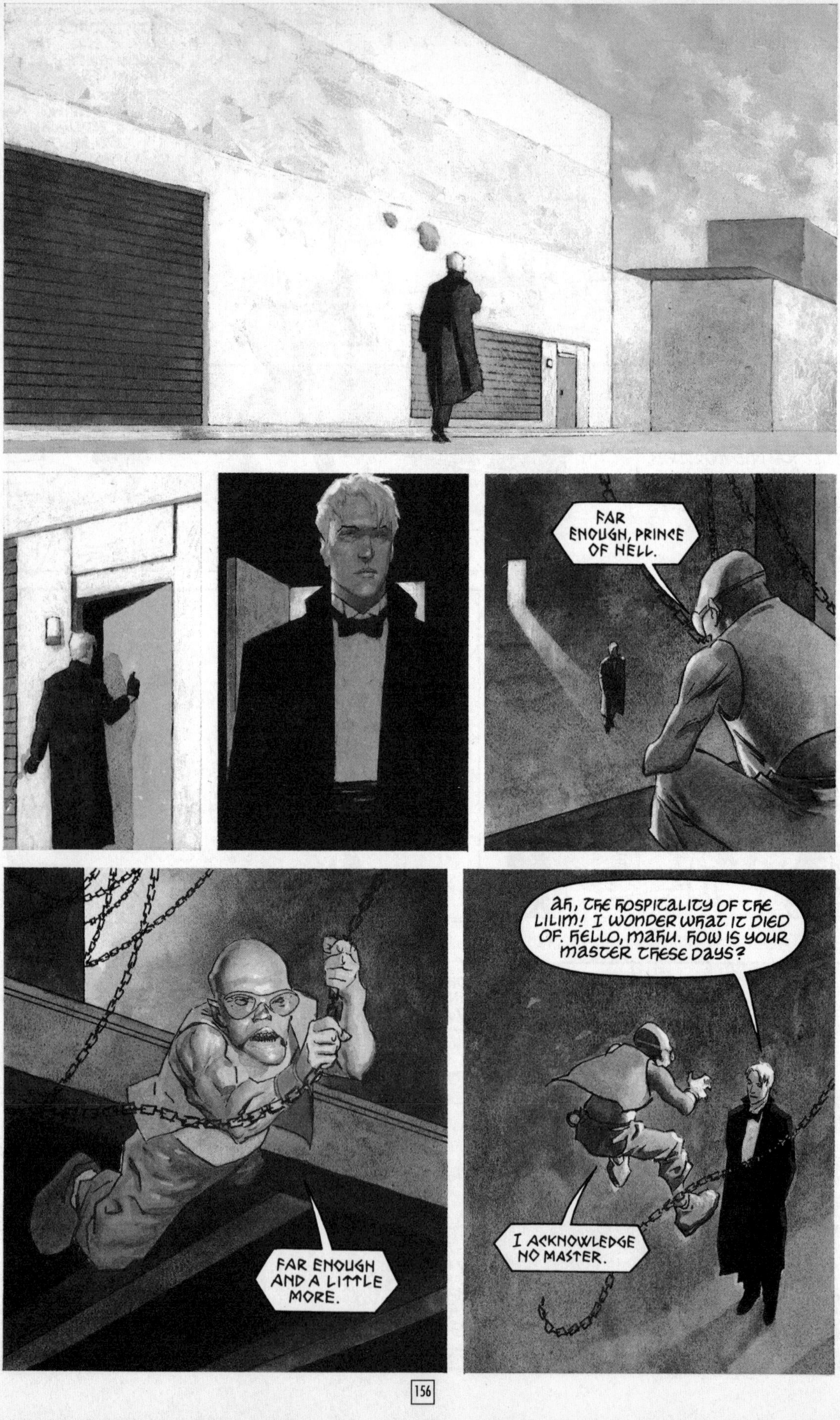
FAR ENOUGH, PRINCE OF HELL.
FAR ENOUGH AND A LITTLE MORE.
AH, THE HOSPITALITY OF THE LILIM! I WONDER WHAT IT DIED OF. HELLO, MAHU. HOW IS YOUR MASTER THESE DAYS?
I ACKNOWLEDGE NO MASTER.

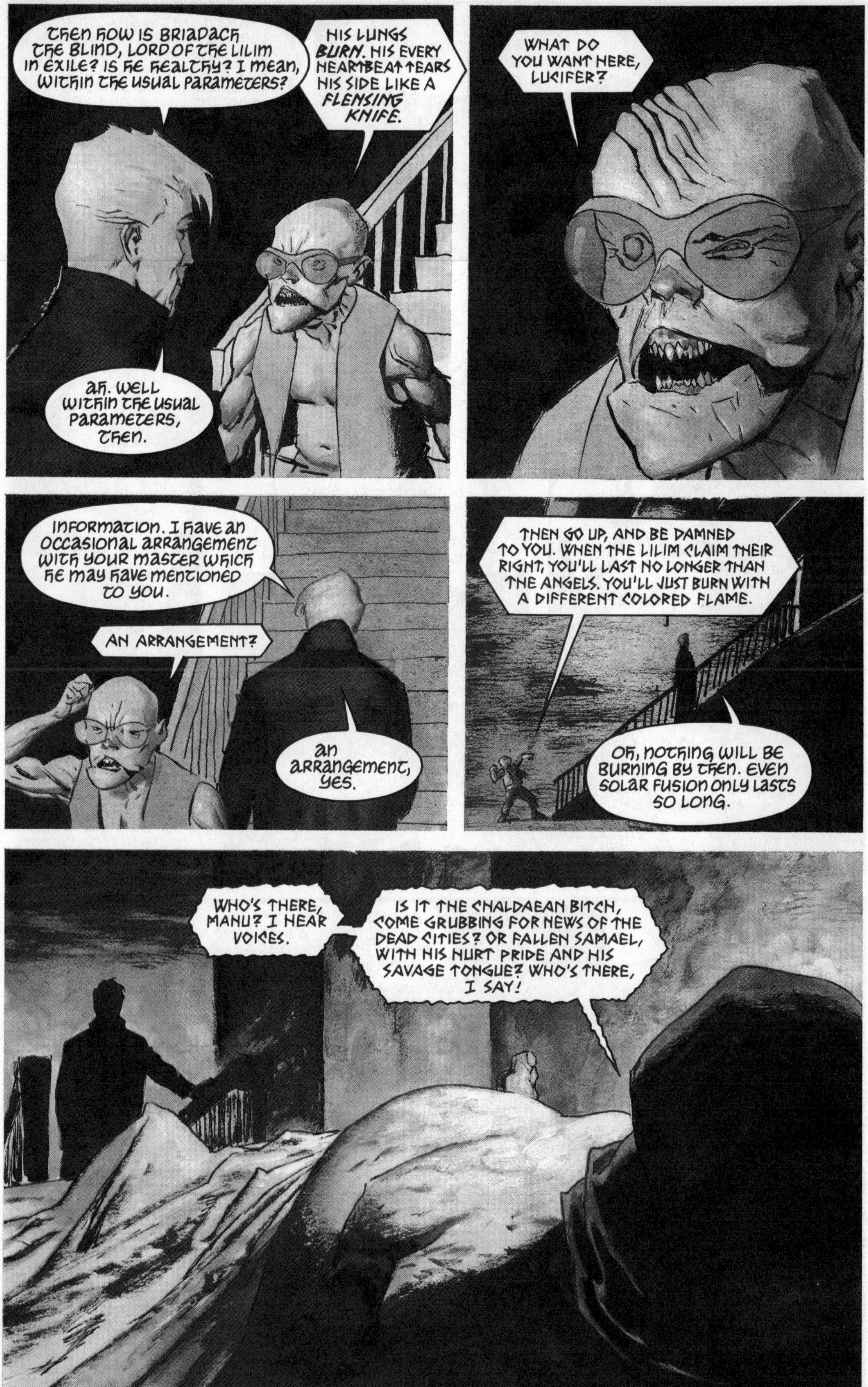
THEN HOW IS BRIADACH THE BLIND, LORD OF THE LILIM IN EXILE? IS HE HEALTHY? I MEAN, WITHIN THE USUAL PARAMETERS?
HIS LUNGS BURN. HIS EVERY HEARTBEAT TEARS HIS SIDE LIKE A FLENSING KNIFE.
AH. WELL WITHIN THE USUAL PARAMETERS, THEN.
WHAT DO YOU WANT HERE, LUCIFER?
INFORMATION. I HAVE AN OCCASIONAL ARRANGEMENT WITH YOUR MASTER WHICH HE MAY HAVE MENTIONED TO YOU.
AN ARRANGEMENT?
AN ARRANGEMENT, YES.
THEN GO UP, AND BE DAMNED TO YOU. WHEN THE LILIM CLAIM THEIR RIGHT, YOU'LL LAST NO LONGER THAN THE ANGELS. YOU'LL JUST BURN WITH A DIFFERENT COLORED FLAME.
OH, NOTHING WILL BE BURNING BY THEN. EVEN SOLAR FUSION ONLY LASTS SO LONG.
WHO'S THERE, MANU? I HEAR VOICES.
IS IT THE CHALDAEAN BITCH, COME GRUBBING FOR NEWS OF THE DEAD CITIES? OR FALLEN SAMAEL, WITH HIS HURT PRIDE AND HIS SAVAGE TONGUE? WHO'S THERE, I SAY!

NOBODY'S CALLED ME SAMAEL FOR SUCH A LONG TIME. IT'S LIKE SOMEONE USING YOUR MAIDEN NAME.

LORD LUCIFER!

BRIADACH. STILL SICK, I SEE.

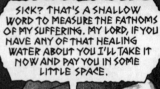

SICK? THAT'S A SHALLOW WORD TO MEASURE THE FATHOMS OF MY SUFFERING. MY LORD, IF YOU HAVE ANY OF THAT HEALING WATER ABOUT YOU I'LL TAKE IT NOW AND PAY YOU IN SOME LITTLE SPACE.

DULLS MY EYES! YOU KNOW *EXACTLY* WHAT I SEE. YOU KNOW EXACTLY HOW MUCH *BLINDNESS* HEAVEN HAS ALLOWED TO ME!

BUT IT *DULLS* YOUR EYES.

"THE SEED AND THE ROT." THERE'S NO NEED TO REMIND ME OF YOUR CURSE. DO YOU THINK THIS IS A *SOCIAL* CALL?

IF YOU WANT THE LETHE WATER, DEMON, YOU'LL HAVE TO *WORK* FOR IT. THE SAME RULES AS ALWAYS.

ASK ME THEN, BUT IN HELL'S NAME BE BRIEF! A BIRTH AND A DEATH. I'LL GIVE YOU TWO MOMENTS FOR TWO SIPS OF OBLIVION.

ONE MOMENT.

IT WILL BE BOTH, YOU SEE.

A BIRTH AND A DEATH.

THE BIRTH AND DEATH OF WHAT? TELL ME WHAT YOU WANT--AND LET ME HEAR YOU POUR, FOR INSPIRATION'S SAKE.

THE BIRTH AND DEATH OF A *DESIRE*. A DESIRE SATISFIED IN THE MOMENT IT'S CONCEIVED. A WISH...

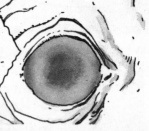

...A WISH BEING GRANTED. YES, YES, I'M NOT SIMPLE. THEY'RE RARE ENOUGH SINCE MAB CLOSED HER BORDERS, BUT TODAY THEY SEEM TO BE AS COMMON AS RAIN.

IN NORTH HOLLYWOOD THERE IS A MAN CALLED PAUL BEGAI. A MAN IN YEARS, I MEAN-- NOT IN ANY OTHER SENSE.

BECAUSE THE POWER *LINGERS* AROUND HIM. IT WINDS OVER AND THROUGH HIM.

WHAT IS IT, LUCIFER? THIS THING THAT OPENS AND OPENS AND SEEMS TO HAVE NO DEATH? HAVE YOU SEEN IT? HAVE YOU TRIED TO TALK TO IT?

WHY FILM?

NO. NOT YET. DRINK SPARINGLY, BRIADACH. I DON'T HAVE A STEADY LINE OF SUPPLY THESE DAYS.

SO KEVIN'S STILL SITTING THERE WITH HIS *DICK* OUT, BUT SUZIE'S CLIMBED OUT OF THE BATHROOM WINDOW. SHE'S HALFWAY DOWN THE STREET. AND THE LAST THING SHE HEARD HIM SAY WAS, "SUUUUZIE! I'VE GOT THE CONDOM ON!"

HEY, SUZIE SAID NO WAY ARE YOU A NAVAJO, COS NAVAJOS ARE BRIGHT RED LIKE TOMATOES. I TOLD HER TO SUCK IT.

UMM, *HALF* NAVAJO. DAD'S THE REAL THING. HE WAS BORN ON A RESERVATION. AND MY GRANDAD'S SOME KIND OF WITCH DOCTOR. SHAMAN. THING.

HAHAHAHAHA!

MMMMMUUUUH!

NNNNNNAAAAH!

KRAASH!

HEY, WHAT WAS THAT? IS THERE SOMEONE ELSE HERE?

SHIT. JUST MY BROTHER. GIVE ME A SECOND, GUYS.

YOU OKAY, PAUL?

AW, NO!

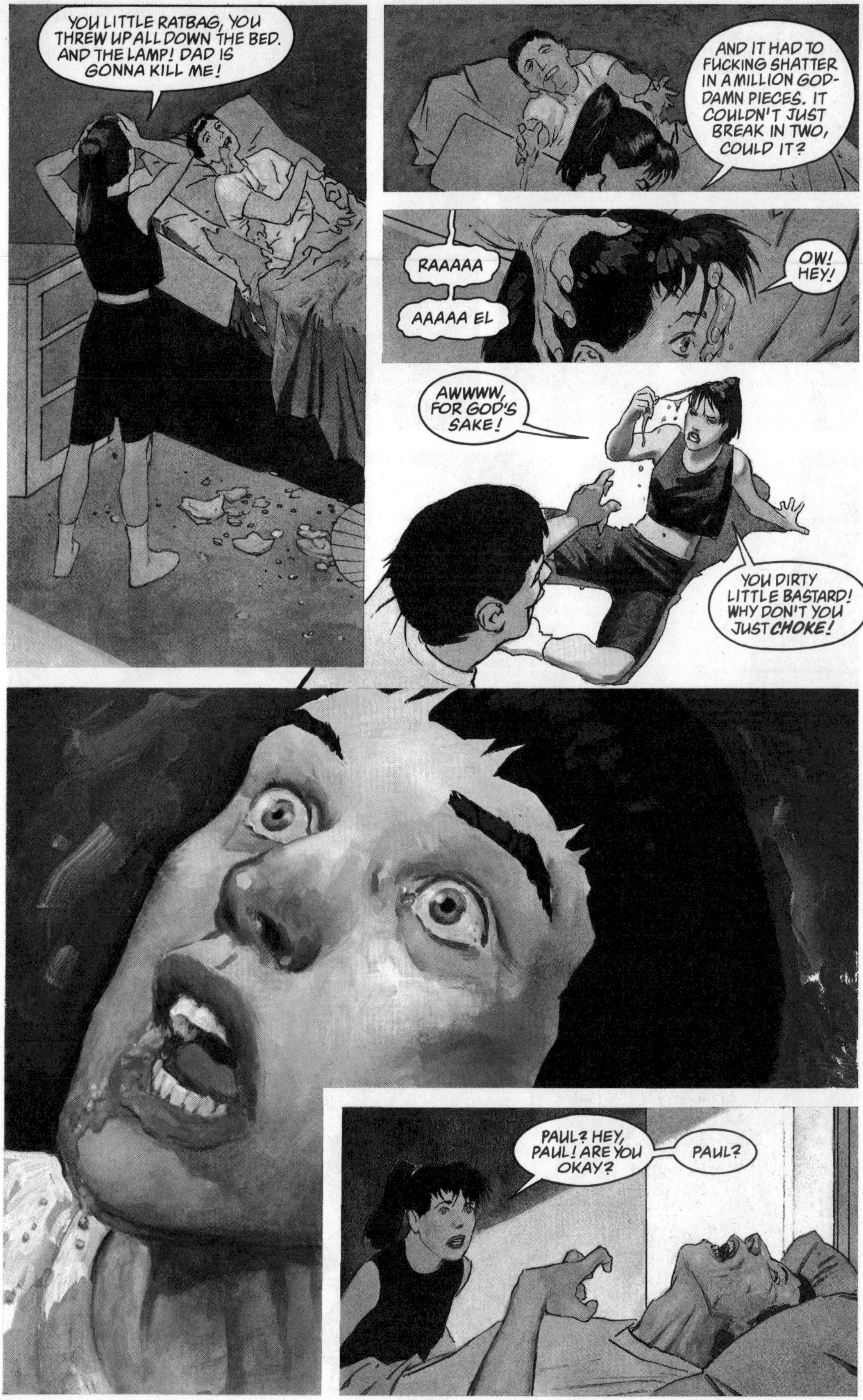
YOU LITTLE RATBAG, YOU THREW UP ALL DOWN THE BED. AND THE LAMP! DAD IS GONNA KILL ME!
AND IT HAD TO FUCKING SHATTER IN A MILLION GOD-DAMN PIECES. IT COULDN'T JUST BREAK IN TWO, COULD IT?
RAAAAA
AAAAA EL
OW! HEY!
AWWWW, FOR GOD'S SAKE!
YOU DIRTY LITTLE BASTARD! WHY DON'T YOU JUST CHOKE!
PAUL? HEY, PAUL! ARE YOU OKAY?
PAUL?

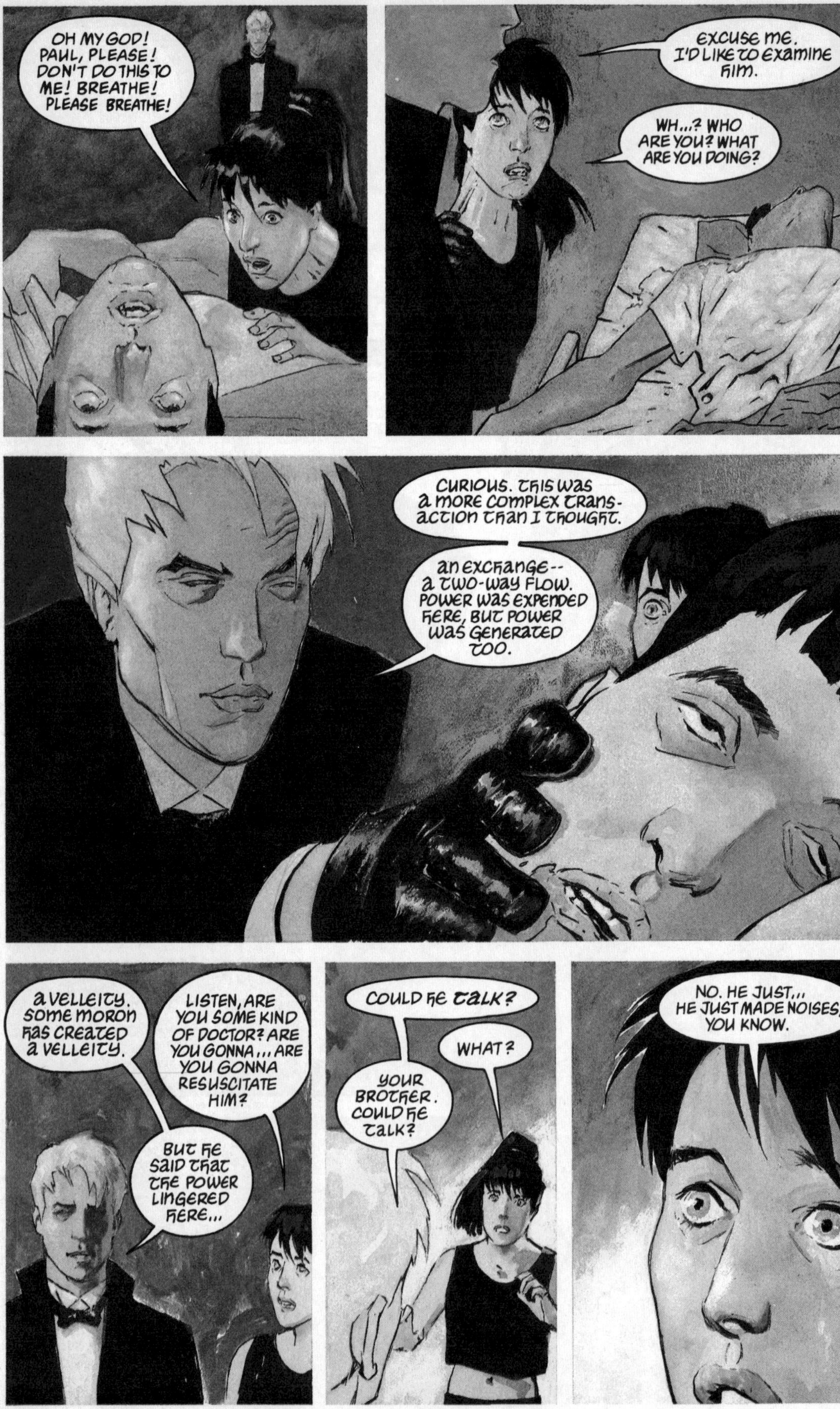
OH MY GOD! PAUL, PLEASE! DON'T DO THIS TO ME! BREATHE! PLEASE BREATHE!
EXCUSE ME. I'D LIKE TO EXAMINE HIM.
WH...? WHO ARE YOU? WHAT ARE YOU DOING?
CURIOUS. THIS WAS A MORE COMPLEX TRANS-ACTION THAN I THOUGHT.
AN EXCHANGE-- A TWO-WAY FLOW. POWER WAS EXPENDED HERE, BUT POWER WAS GENERATED TOO.
A VELLEITY. SOME MORON HAS CREATED A VELLEITY.
LISTEN, ARE YOU SOME KIND OF DOCTOR? ARE YOU GONNA... ARE YOU GONNA RESUSCITATE HIM?
BUT HE SAID THAT THE POWER LINGERED HERE...
COULD HE TALK?
WHAT?
YOUR BROTHER. COULD HE TALK?
NO. HE JUST... HE JUST MADE NOISES, YOU KNOW.

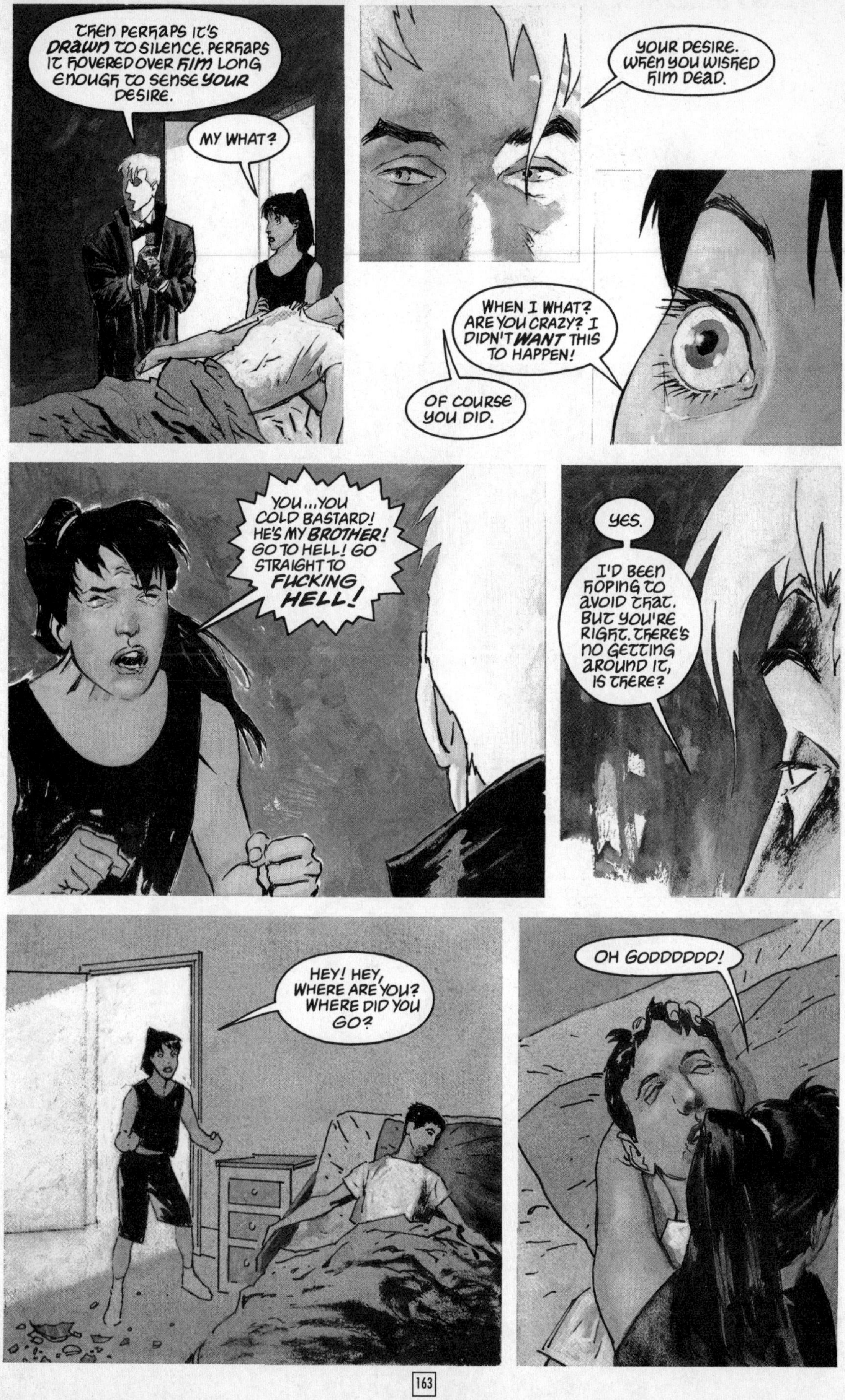
THEN PERHAPS IT'S DRAWN TO SILENCE. PERHAPS IT HOVERED OVER HIM LONG ENOUGH TO SENSE YOUR DESIRE.
MY WHAT?
YOUR DESIRE. WHEN YOU WISHED HIM DEAD.
WHEN I WHAT? ARE YOU CRAZY? I DIDN'T WANT THIS TO HAPPEN!
OF COURSE YOU DID.
YOU...YOU COLD BASTARD! HE'S MY BROTHER! GO TO HELL! GO STRAIGHT TO FUCKING HELL!
YES.
I'D BEEN HOPING TO AVOID THAT. BUT YOU'RE RIGHT. THERE'S NO GETTING AROUND IT, IS THERE?
HEY! HEY, WHERE ARE YOU? WHERE DID YOU GO?
OH GODDDDDD!

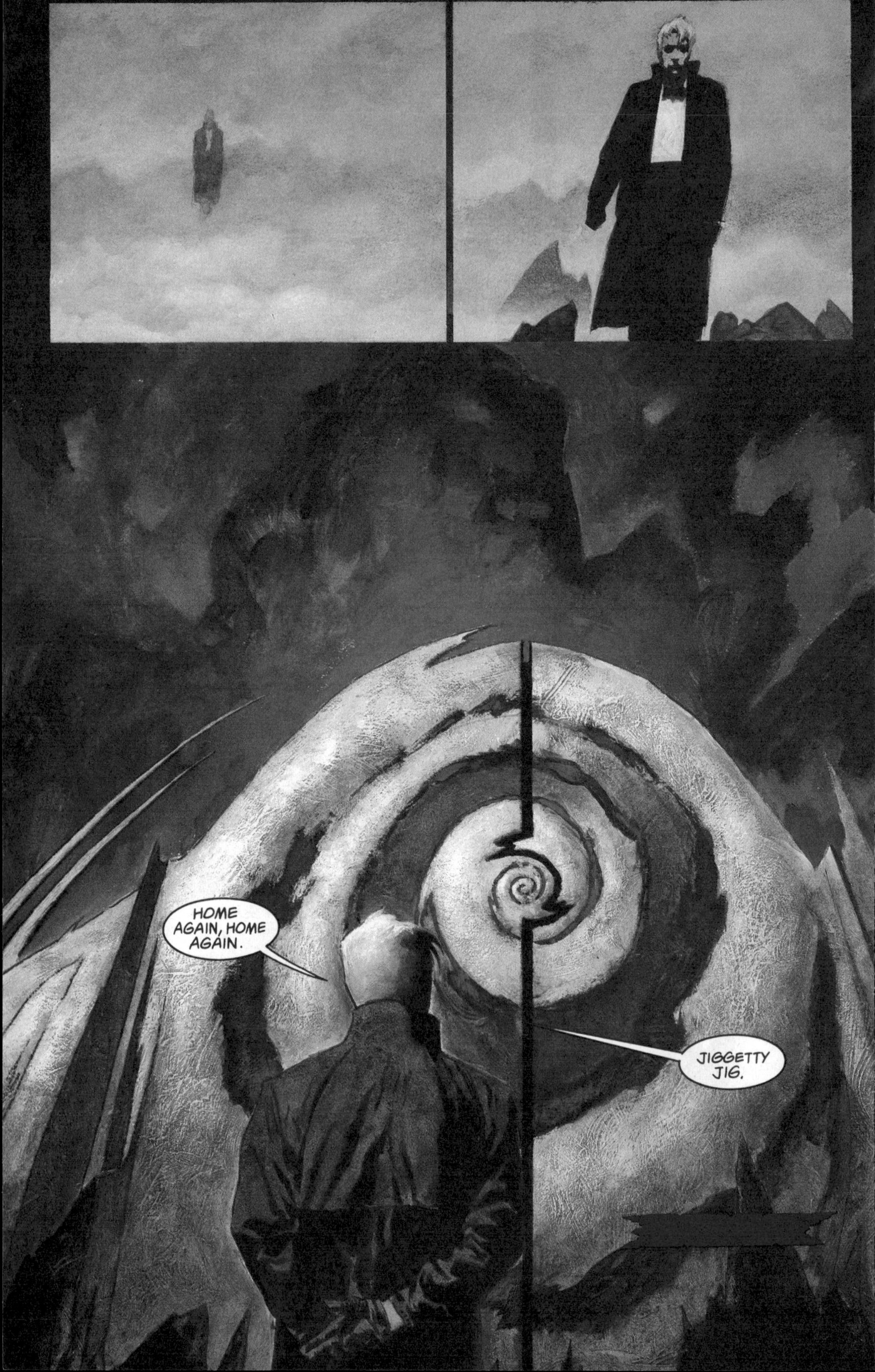
HOME AGAIN, HOME AGAIN.
JIGGETTY JIG.

READ THE REST OF THE STORY IN

LUCIFER VOL 1: DEVIL IN THE GATEWAY

THE FIRST COLLECTION OF WRITER **MIKE CAREY'S** EPIC STORY OF THE LIGHTBRINGER

ILLUSTRATED BY
SCOTT HAMPTON, CHRIS WESTON, JAMES HODGKINS, WARREN PLEECE and DEAN ORMSTON

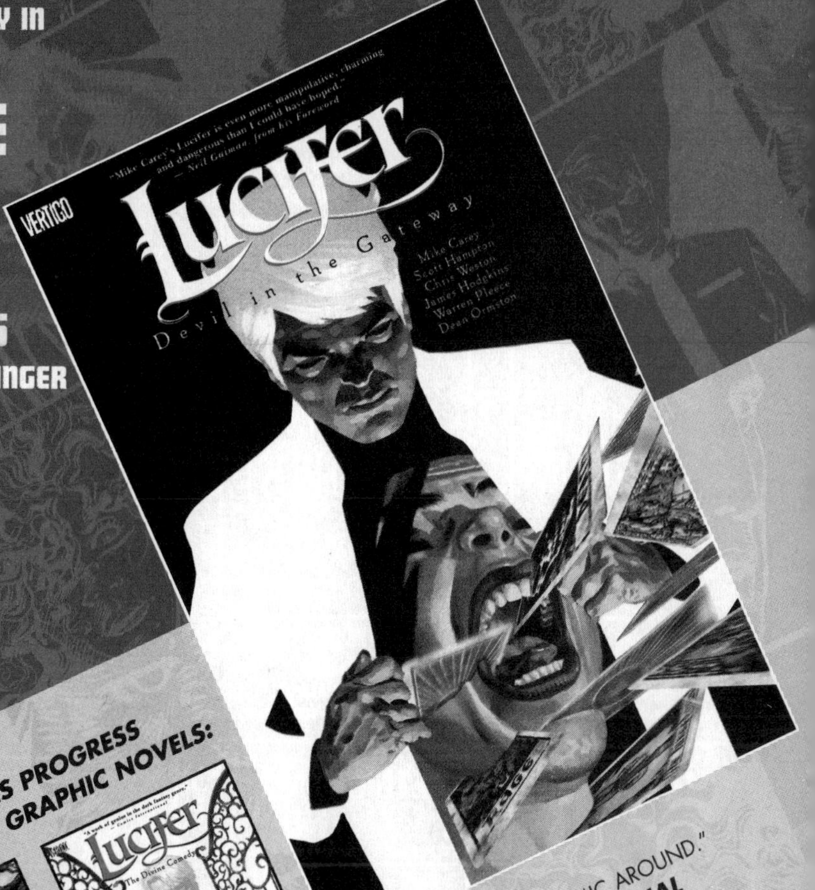
"Mike Carey's Lucifer is even more manipulative, charming and dangerous than I could have hoped."
— Neil Gaiman, from his Foreword
VERTIGO
Lucifer
Devil in the Gateway
Mike Carey
Scott Hampton
Chris Weston
James Hodgkins
Warren Pleece
Dean Ormston

"THE BEST FANTASY COMIC AROUND."
— COMICS INTERNATIONAL

WATCH THE FALLEN ONE'S PLANS PROGRESS BOTH MONTHLY AND IN THESE GRAPHIC NOVELS:

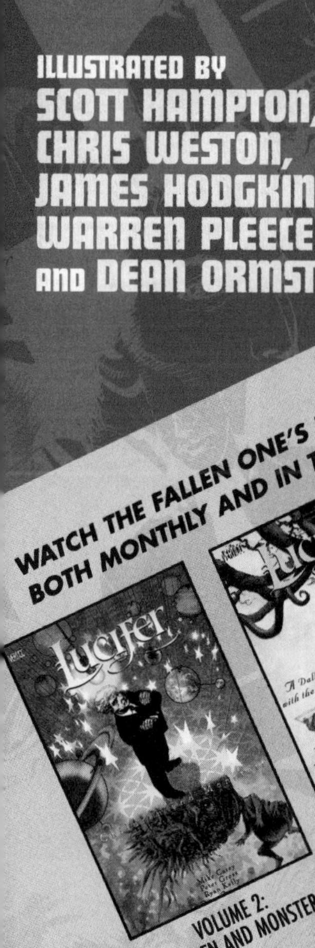
Lucifer

VOLUME 2:
CHILDREN AND MONSTERS

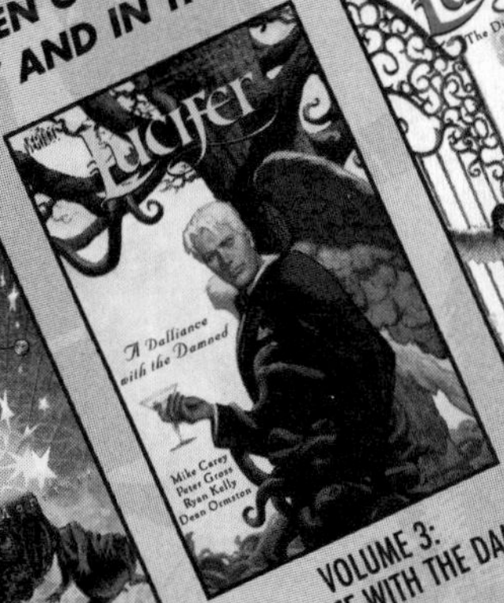
Lucifer
A Dalliance with the Damned
Mike Carey
Peter Gross
Ryan Kelly
Dean Ormston

VOLUME 3:
A DALLIANCE WITH THE DAMNED

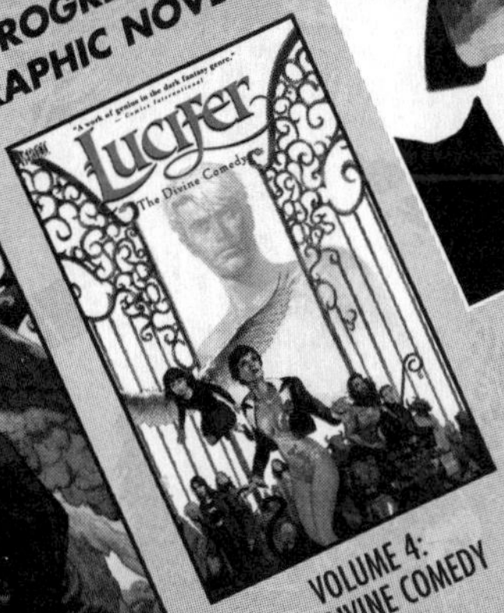
Lucifer
The Divine Comedy

VOLUME 4:
THE DIVINE COMEDY

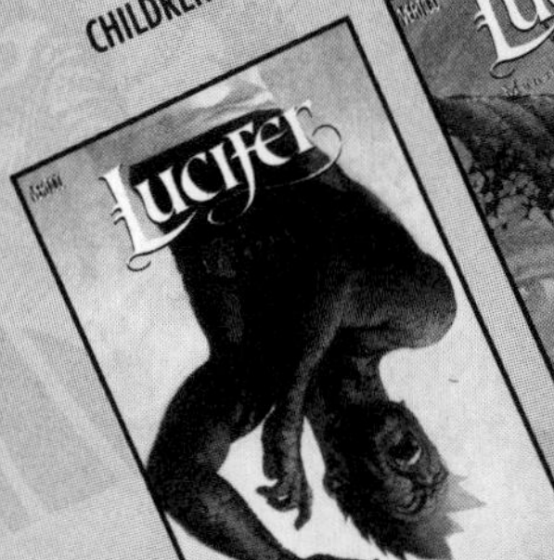
Lucifer

VOLUME 5:
INFERNO

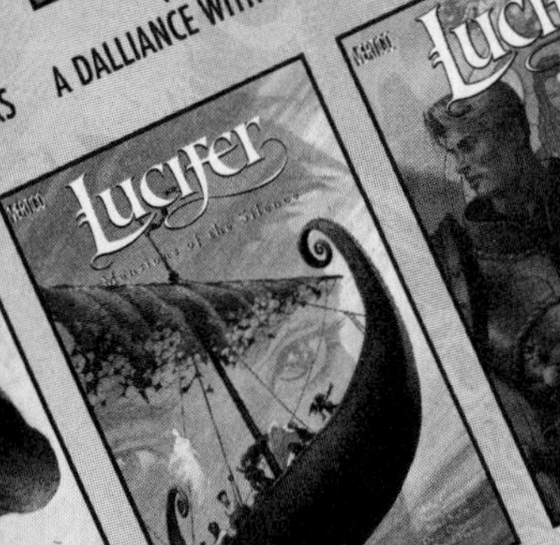
Lucifer

VOLUME 6:
MANSIONS OF THE SILENCE

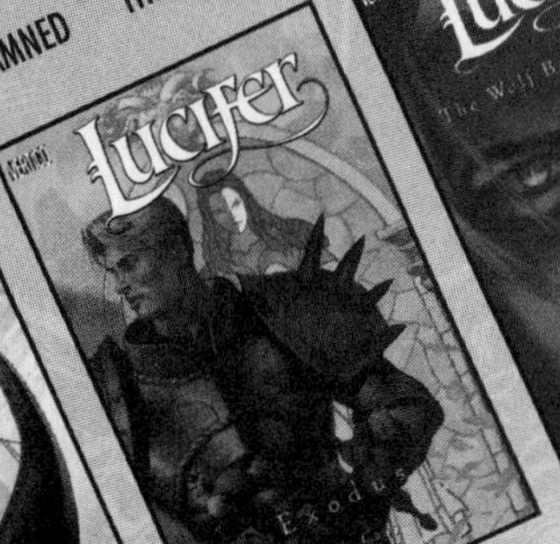
Lucifer
Exodus

VOLUME 7:
EXODUS

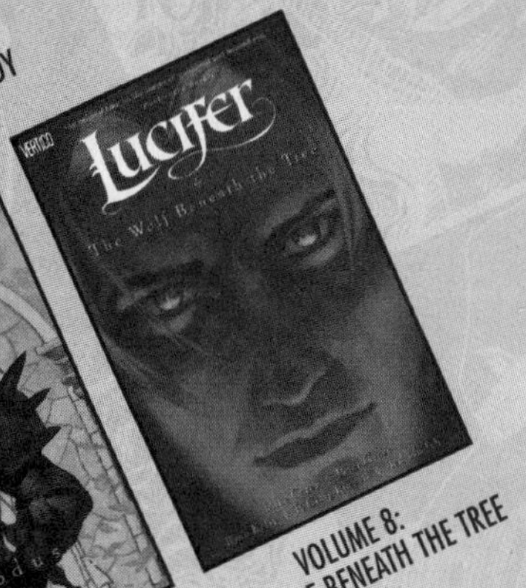
VERTIGO
Lucifer

VOLUME 8:
THE WOLF BENEATH THE TREE

"AN ORIGINAL TAKE ON THE FORCES OF GOOD, EVIL AND BEYOND EVIL."
— PUBLISHERS WEEKLY

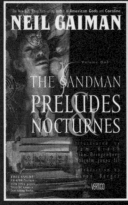

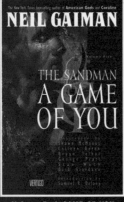

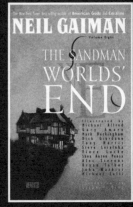